THEODORET OF CYRUS

A Cure for Pagan Maladies

Ancient
Christian
Writers

THE WORKS OF THE FATHERS IN TRANSLATION

No. 67

THEODORET OF CYRUS:
A CURE FOR PAGAN MALADIES

TRANSLATION AND INTRODUCTION

BY

THOMAS HALTON

THE NEWMAN PRESS
New York/Mahwah, NJ

Book design by Lynn Else

Library of Congress Cataloging-in-Publication Data

Theodoret, Bishop of Cyrrhus.
    [Graecarum affectionum curatio. English]
    Theodoret of Cyrus : A cure for pagan maladies / translation and introduction by Thomas Halton.
        pages cm
    Includes bibliographical references and index.
    ISBN 978-0-8091-0606-6 (alk. paper)
    1. Apologetics—Early works to 1800. 2. Philosophy, Ancient—Early works to 1800. I. Halton, Thomas P. (Thomas Patrick) II. Title. III. Title: Cure for pagan maladies.
    BR65.T753G7313 2013
    239'.3—dc23

                                                          2012044042

ISBN: 978-0-8091-0606-6 (hardcover)

Published by The Newman Press
an imprint of Paulist Press
997 Macarthur Boulevard
Mahwah, New Jersey 07430

www.paulistpress.com

PRINTED AND BOUND IN THE UNITED STATES OF AMERICA

CONTENTS

LIST OF ABBREVIATIONS

I. PERIODICALS, SERIES, PARTICULAR WORKS OFTEN CITED

ACW	Ancient Christian Writers (Westminster, Md. London, New York, Mahwah, NJ, 1946–)
Affect.	P. Canivet, ed., *Theodoret de Cyr Curatio affectionum Graecorum*, SC 57 (2 vols., Paris, 1959)
AHC	*Annuarium historiae Conciliorum*
ANF	Ante Nicene Fathers (Buffalo 1885–96; repr. Grand Rapids, Mich., 1951–56)
ANRW	*Aufstieg und Niedergang der römischen Welt*
AJP	*American Journal of Philology*
AugStud	*Augustinian Studies*
Burkert, *Homo*	W. Burkert, Homo necans (Berlin and New York, 1972)
Burkert, *Lore*	W. Burkert, *Lore and Science in Ancient Pythagoreanism* (Cambridge, Mass. 1972)
Burkert, *S & H*	W. Burkert, *Structure and History in Greek Mythology and Ritual* (Berkeley, Calif., 1979)
ByzF	*Byzantinische Forschungen*
ByzSlav	*Byzantinoslavica*
CAH	*Cambridge Ancient History* (London and New York 1923–39; rev. ed. Cambridge,1961–)
Canivet, *Entre*	P. Canivet, *Histoire d'une entrepris apologétique au Ve siècle* (Paris, 1957)
CCL	Corpus Christianorum, Latin series (Turnholt 1953ff.)
ChH	*Church History*
CHLG	*The Cambridge History of Later Greek and Early Medieval Philosophy,* ed. A. H. Armstrong (Cambridge, 1967)

Cic. *ND*	*M. Tulli Ciceronis De natura deorum,* ed. A. S. Pease (2 vols., Cambridge, Mass., 1955–58)
C&M	*Classica et mediaevalia*
CPG	Clavis Patrum Graecorum, ed. M. Geerard (5 vols., Turnhout 1974–87)
CPh	*Classical Philology*
CQ	*Classical Quarterly* (vol. 1, no. 1 [Apr. 1907]– v. 44 [1950]; new ser. v. 1 [1951]– v. 46–)
CrSt	*Cristianesimo e Storia*
CSEL	Corpus scriptorum ecclesiasticorum latinorum (Vienna 1866)
CW	*Classical World*
DACL	*Dictionnaire d'archaeologie chrétienne et de liturgie*
DCB	*Dictionary of Christian Biography, Literature, Sects and Doctrines*
de Vogel, *GP*	C. J. de Vogel, *Greek Philosophy: A Collection of Texts* (Leiden, 1963–67)
DHGE	*Dictionnaire d'histoire et de géographie ecclésiastiques*
Diels, *Dox*	H. Diels, *Doxographi Graeci* (Berlin, 1929, repr. 1965)
Diels-Kranz	H. Diels, W. Kranz, *Die Fragmente der Vorsokratiker* 6th ed. (3 vols., Berlin 1951–52)
DissAbstr	Dissertation Abstracts (Ann Arbor, Mich.)
DOP	*Dumbarton Oaks Papers* (Cambridge, Mass., 1941–)
DPAC	*Dizionario patristico e di antichità cristiane*
DSp	*Dictionnaire de spiritualité*
DTC	*Dictionnaire de théologie catholique*
EThL	*Ephemerides Theologicae Lovaniensis*
FGrH	F. Jacoby, *Die Fragmente der griechischen Historiker* (Berlin, 1923)
FOTC	The Fathers of the Church (Washington, D.C., 1947–)
Frend, *MPEC*	W. H. C. Frend, *Martyrdom and Persecution in the Early Church* (Oxford, 1965)
GCS	Die griechischen christlichen Schriftsteller der ersten drei Jahrhunderte (Leipzig, 1897–)
GOTR	*Greek Orthodox Theological Review*

G & R	*Greece and Rome*
GRBS	*Greek, Roman and Byzantine Studies*
Guthrie, *HGP*	W. K. C. Guthrie, *A History of Greek Philosophy* (London, 1962–81)
HSCP	*Harvard Studies in Classical Philology*
HThR	*Harvard Theological Review*
IThQ	*Irish Theological Quarterly*
JbAC	*Jahrbuch für Antike und Christentum*
JBL	*Journal of Biblical Literature*
JHS	*Journal of Hellenic Studies*
JHPh	*Journal of the History of Philosophy*
JourRoman Arch	*Journal of Roman Archaeology*
JThS	*Journal of Theological Studies*
K.R.S.	G. S. Kirk, J. E. Raven, M. Schofield, *The Presocratic Philosophers* (Cambridge, 1983)
LCC	Library of Christian Classics (Philadelphia, Pa., 1953–66)
LCL	Loeb Classical Library (Cambridge, Mass., 1912–)
LSJ	H. G. Liddell, R. Scott, H. S. Jones, *A Greek-English Lexicon* (Oxford 1968)
LThK	*Lexikon für Theologie und Kirche* 2d ed.
Mikalson	Mikalson, J. D. *The Sacred and Civil Calendar of the Athenian Year* (Princeton, NJ, 1975)
MSR	*Mélanges de science religieuse*
Mus Helv	*Museum Helvetica*
NCE	*New Catholic Encyclopedia*
NPNF	Library of Nicene and Post-Nicene Fathers (2 series of 14 vols. each, New York 1887–94 repr. Grand Rapids 1952–56)
OC	*Oriens Christianus*
OCD	*Oxford Classical Dictionary,* 2d ed.
OCP	*Orientalia christiana periodica*
ODCC²	*Oxford Dictionary of the Christian Church,* 2d ed.
OECT	Oxford Early Christian Texts (Oxford, 1970–)
Parke, *Festivals*	Parke, H. W., *Festivals of the Athenians* (Ithaca, N.Y., 1977)
PG	*Patrologia graeca,* ed. J. P. Migne (Paris, 1857–66)

PL	*Patrologia latina*, ed. J. P. Migne (Paris, 1844–55)
PECS	*Princeton Encyclopedia of Classical Sites*
PGL	*Patristic Greek Lexicon*, ed. G. W. H. Lampe et al. (Oxford, 1961)
Philosoph. Rev.	*Philosophical Review*
RAC	*Reallexikon für Antike und Christentum*
RAL	*Rendiconti della Reale Accademia Nazionale dei Lincei Roma*
RE	A. Pauly–G. Wissowa–W. Kroll, *Real-Encyclopädie der classischen Altertumswissenschaft*
REAnc	*Revue des Etudes Anciennes*
REAug	*Revue des études augustiniennes*
RechScR	*Recherches de science religieuse*
REG	*Revue des études grecques*
Rev. Internat. Philos	*Revue Internationale de Philosophie*
RHE	*Revue d'histoire ecclésiastique*
RHR	*Revue de l'histoire des religions*
RhMus	*Rheinisches Museum*
RPh	*Revue de philologie*
RSLR	*Rivista di storia e letteratura religiosa*
RSPh	*Revue des sciences philosophiques et théologiques*
RSR	*Revue des sciences religieuses*
	RThL Revue théologique de Louvain
RThPh	*Revue de théologie et philosophie*
SC	Sources chrétiennes (Paris 1942–)
SCH	Studies in Church History
SMSR	*Studi e materiali di storia delle religioni*
SP	*Studia patristica*
StC	*Studia catholica*
SVF	H. F. A. von Arnim, *Stoicorum veterum fragmenta* (4 vols., Leipzig, 1921–24; repr. Stuttgart, 1964)
TAPA	*Transactions of the American Philological Society*
ThPh	*Theologie et Philosophie*
Trier ThZ	*Trierer theologische Zeitschrift*
TRE	*Theologische Realenzklopädie*
TU	Texte und Untersuchungen zur Geschichte der altchristliche Literatur (Berlin, 1883–)
VigChr	*Vigiliae Christianae*

ZKG	*Zeitschrift für Kirchengeschichte*
ZNTW	*Zeitschrift für die Neutestamentliche Wissenschaft*
ZNThK	*Zeitschrift für Theologie und Kirche*

II. CLASSICAL AND PATRISTIC ABBREVIATIONS

Aelian, *Nat. an.*	Aelian, *De natura animalium*
Aetius, *Plac.*	Aetius, *Placita* (in *Doxographi Graeci*, ed. H. Diels, [Berlin, 1879])
Aesch, *Agam.*	Aeschylus, *Agamemnon*
Ambrose, *De virg.*	Ambrose, *De virginibus*
Aristides, *Apol.*	Aristides, *Apologia*
Aristophanes, *Acharn.*	Aristophanes, *Acharnians*
Aristotle, *Ath. Pol.*	Aristotle, *Athenaion Politeia*
Aristotle, *Athen. Const.*	Aristotle, *Athenian Constitution*
Aristotle, *De virt. et vitiis*	Aristotle, *De virtutibus et vitiis*
Aristotle, *Eth. Nic.*	Aristotle, *Nichomachean Ethics*
Aristotle, *Metaph.*	Aristotle, *Metaphysica*
Aristotle, *H.A.*	Aristotle, *History of Animals*
Aristotle, *Pol.*	Aristotle, *Politics*
Aristotle, *Probl.*	Aristotle, *Problemata*
Aristotle, *Top.*	Aristotle, *Topica*
Arnobius, *Adv. nat.*	Arnobius, *Adversus Nationes*
Artemidorus, *Oneiroc.*	Artemidorus, *oneirocritica*
Athanasius, *Gent.*	Athanasius, *Contra gentes*
Athenaeus, *Deip.*	Athenaeus, *Deipnosophistai*
Athenagoras, *Leg.*	Athenagoras, *Legatio pro Christianis*
Athenagoras, *Res.*	Athenagoras, *De resurrectione mortuorum*
Augustine, *Civ. Dei*	Augustine, *De Civitate Dei*
Barnabus, *Epist. ad Barn.*	Barnabus, *Epistle of Barnabus*
Basil, *Ep.*	Basil, *Epistulae*
Basil, *Hex.*	Basil, *Homiliae in Hexameron*
Basil, *in hon. S. Mamas,*	Basil, *Homily on St. Mamas*
Basil, *Leg. lib. gent.*	Basil, *Ad adolescentes de legendis libris gentilium*
Chrysostom, *Bapt. hom.*	Chrysostom, *Homily on Baptism*
Chrysostom, *Contra pag.*	Chrysostom, *quod Dem. contra pag. Christus sit Deus*
Chrysostom, *De. sac.*	Chrysostom, *De sacerdocio*
Chrysostom, *Hom. in Gen.*	Chrysostom, *Homiliae in Genesin*

Chrysostom, *Jud. et Gent.*	Chrysostom, *Contra Judaeos et Gentiles*
Chrysostom, *Pan. Bab.*	Chrysostom, *Panegyricum in Babylam martyrem*
Cicero, *Acad.*	Cicero, *Academicae Quaestiones*
Cicero, *ND*	Cicero, *De natura deorum*
Clement, *1 Clem.*	Clement, *Epistula Clementis ad Corinthios*
Clement, *Eclog. prophet.*	Clement, *Eclogae ex scripturis propheticis*
Clement, *Exc. ex Theod.*	Clement. *Excerptac. ex Theodoto*
Clement, *Paed.*	Clement, *Paedagogus*
Clement, *Protr.*	Clement, *Protrepticus sive Cohortatio ad gentes*
Clement, *Str.*	Clement, *Stromateis*
Cyril H. *Catech.*	Cyril of Jerusalem, *Catecheses* 1–18 *illuminandorum*
Cyril, *Juln.*	Cyril of Alexandria, *Contra Julianum*
Diog. *Laert.*	Diogenes Laertius
Empiricus, *Pyrrh. hypotyp.*	Sextus Empiricus, *Pyrrhoneii hypotyposes*
Epist. ad Barn.	*Epistula ad Barnabam*
Euripides, *Andr.*	Euripides, *Andromache*
Euripides, *Bacch.*	Euripides, *Bacchae*
Euripides, *IA*	Euripides, *Iphigenia Aulidensis*
Euripides, *Or.*	Euripides, *Orestes*
Euripides, *Phoen*	Euripides, *Phoenissae*
Eusebius, *He.*	Eusebius of Caesarea, *Historia ecclesiastica*
Eusebius, *P.e.*	Eusebius of Caesarea, *Praeparatio evangelica*
Eusebius, *Vita Const.*	Eusebius, *De Vita Constantini*
Firmicus Maternus, *Err. prof. rel.*	Firmicus Maternus, *De errore profanarum religionum*
Gregory of Nyssa, *C. Eunom.*	Gregory of Nyssa, *Contra Eunomium*
Gregory Nazianzus, 39, *In s. lumina*	Gregory Nazianzus, *Oratio 39, In Orat. sancta lumina*
Gregory Nazianzus, *Orat.*	Gregory Nazianzus, *Orationes*
Gregory Nazianzus, *Contra Jul.*	Gregory Nazianzus, *Orationes Contra Julianum*
Hesiod, *Op.*	Hesiod, *Opera et Dies*
Hesiod, *Theog.*	Hesiod, *Theogonia*

Hippolytus, *Ref.*	Hippolytus, *Refutatio omnium haeresium sive philosophoumena*
Homer, *Il.*	Homer, *Iliad*
Homer, *Od.*	Homer, *Odyssea*
Iamblichus, *VP*	Iamblichus, *De vita Pythagorica*
Irenaeus, *Adv. Haer*	Irenaeus, *Against heresies*
Jerome, *Chron. Euseb.*	Jerome, *Chronicle of Eusebius*
John Chrysostom, *Catech.*	John Chrysostom, *Catechesis*
Justin, *1, 2 Apol.*	Justin, *Apologiae*
Lactantius, *Div. inst.*	Lactantius, *Divinae institutiones*
Lucian, *Apol.*	Lucian, *Apology*
Lucian, *Deorum Conc.*	Lucian, *Deorum concilium*
Lucian, *Dial. D.*	Lucian, *Dialogi Deorum*
Lucian, *De sacr.*	Lucian, *De sacrificiis*
Lucian, *Iup. Trag.*	Lucian, *Jupiter tragoedus*
Lucian, *Sat.*	Lucian, *Saturnalia*
Lucian, *Scyth*	Lucian, *Scytha*
Minucius Felix, *Oct*	Minucius Felix, *Octavius*
Nemesius, *De nat. hom.*	Nemesius, *De natura hominum*
Origen, *C. Cels.*	Origen, Contra Celsum
Origen, *Comm. in Matt.*	Origen, *Commentary on Matthew*
Ovid, *Met.*	Ovid, *Metamorphoses*
Paulinus of Nola, *Carm.*	Paulinus of Nola, *Carmina*
Philo, *Decal.*	Philo, *De Decalogo*
Philo, *Mig.*	Philo, *De migratione Abrahami*
Philo, *Quod deter.*	Philo, *Quod deterius potiori insidiari soleat*
Photius, *Biblioth. cod.*	Photius, *Bibliothecae codices*
Pindar, *Pyth.*	Pindar, *Pythian Odes*
Plato, *Alc.*	Plato, *Alcibiades*
Plato, *Apol.*	Plato, *Apology*
Plato, *Crat.*	Plato, *Cratylus*
Plato, *Epin.*	Plato, *Epinomis*
Plato, *Hipp. maj.*	Plato, *Hippias Major*
Plato, *Leg.*	Plato, *Leges*
Plato, *Menex.*	Plato, *Menexenus*
Plato, *Polit.*	Plato, *Politicus*
Plato, *Protag.*	Plato, *Protagoras*
Plato, *Resp.*	Plato, *Respublica*
Plato, *Symp.*	Plato, *Symposium*

Plato, *Theaet.*	Plato, *Theaetetus*
Plato, *Tim.*	Plato, *Timaeus*
Plotinus, *Enn.*	Plotinus, *Ennead*
Plutarch, *De Is. et Osir.*	Plutarch, *De Iside et Osiride*
Plutarch, *Mor.*	Plutarch, *Moralia*
Plutarch, *Sol.*	Plutarch, *Solon*
Porphyry, *Ad Aneb.*	Porphry, *Ad Anebo*
Porphyry, *De abstin.*	Porphyry, *De abstinentia*
Porphyry, *De philos. ex orac.*	Porphyry, *De philosophia ex oraculis*
Porphyry, *Fr. hist.*	Porphyry, *Fragmenta historica*
Porphyry, *Hist. phil. fr.*	Porphyry, *Historiae philosophiae fragmenta*
Porphyry, *On Philos.*	Porphyry, *On Philosophy from Oracles*
Porphyry, *VP*	Porphyry, *Vita Pythagorae*
ps.-Justin, *Coh. Gr.*	*ps.-Justin, Cohortatio ad Graecos*
ps.-Plut. *De placit. philos.*	ps.-Plutarch, *De placitis philosophorum*
ps.-Xenophon, *Ep. ad Aesch.*	ps.-Xenophon, *Epistula ad Aeschylus*
Salvian, *Gub. Dei*	Salvian, *De Gubernatione Dei*
Seneca, *Quaest. nat.*	Seneca, *Quaestiones naturales*
Sextus Empiricus, *Pyrrh. hypotyp.*	Sextus Empiricus, *Pyrrhoneii hypotyposes*
Stobaeus *Ecl.*	Stobaeus, *Eclogae*
Stobaeus, *Flor.*	Stobaeus, *Florilegium* (also *Anthologion*)
Suetonius, *Vita Aug.*	Suetonius, *Vita Augusti*
Synesius, *De prov.*	Synesius, *De providentia*
Tatian, *Orat.*	Tatian, *Oratio ad Graecos*
Tertullian, *Ad nat.*	Tertullian, *Ad nationes*
Tertullian, *Adv. Marc.*	Tertullian, *Adversus Marcionem*
Tertullian, *Apol.*	Tertullian, *Apologeticum*
Tertullian, *De an.*	Tertullian, *De anima*
Tertullian, *Idol.*	Tertullian, *De idololatria*
Tertullian, *Spect.*	Tertullian, *Spectaculis*
Theodoret, *Affect.*	Theodoret, *Graecarum affectionum curatio*
Theodoret, *Carit.*	Theodoret, *Oratio de divina et sancta caritate*
Theodoret, *Haer.*	Theodoret, *Haereticarum fabularum compendium*
Theordoret, *H.e.*	Theodoret, *Historia ecclesiastica*
Theodoret, *Hist. Rel.*	Theodoret, *Historia religiosa*

Theodoret, *Provid.*	Theodoret, *Or ationes de providentia*
Theodoret, *Quaest.* 3 *in Exod.*	Theodoret, *Quaestio 3 in Exodum*
Theophilus, *Ad Autol.*	Theophilus of Antioch, *Ad Autolycum*
Xenophon, *Mem.*	Xenophon, *Memorabilia*

INTRODUCTION

A Cure for Pagan Maladies (Graecarum affectionum curatio), an early work of Theodoret of Cyrus, is described by J. Quasten as the "last of the Christian apologies," and he considers it as "perhaps the best refutation of paganism which has come down to us."[1] Hereafter in the introduction this work will be referred to as *Curatio.* A previous volume in the Ancient Christian Writers series, *Theodoret of Cyrus on Divine Providence,*[2] contains introductory information.

CONTENTS OF *A CURE FOR PAGAN MALADIES*

This work consists of twelve discourses, which are briefly summarized by the author in his Preface to them (1–7). The paragraphs below pertain to the twelve discourses.

Discourse 1: *On Faith.* Maladies of soul, like physical maladies, have their appropriate remedies, though those who lack faith prove to be poor patients (1–8). Too many are overly impressed by secular literature and smugly skeptical about the literary value of the Scriptures (9–11). The Greeks have their limitations, and most of their achievements are derived from non-Greeks; their chief discoveries have come from outside Greece, especially Egypt, Sicily, and Italy (12–25). That philosophy is not necessarily the product of a formal education is clear from the career of Socrates (26–31). Plato's views on the nature of true philosophy are illustrated from his writings (32–40). The priority and antiquity of Hebrew philosophy are shown (41–53). The notion of faith properly understood is quite reasonable (54–61). The pagan philosophers demand faith from their disciples, and they testify to the wickedness of disbelievers (62–71). Philosophers like Empedocles, Parmenides, and Solon stress the need for faith in approaching intelligibles (72–79). They reproach those who are con-

1

tent with sense knowledge (80–85). Orpheus, Euripides, and Epicharmus are agreed that the higher knowledge is restricted to the initiated (86–89). Various definitions and analogies of faith are presented (90–96). If pagans can accept contradictory and inane teachings, why are Christians criticized for accepting on faith what is true and divinely taught (97–99)? Apprentices to the various crafts take on faith the teaching of their instructors (100–104). We go to the experts when we want a judgment on what is genuine or counterfeit (105–6). Faith is the basis of knowledge (107–9). Only the priest knows the truth about pagan rites and only the initiated can learn Christian truth (110–26). The apologetic method pursued in these discourses is explained (126–28).

Discourse 2: *On the First Principle.* The conflicting views of the Greek philosophers on what the first principle is are exposed (1–11). Plato is quoted to show how great their differences were (12–20). Conjecture admits of too many errors, and the Greeks have been too dependent for their so-called truth on the Egyptians (21–42) and the Hebrews (43–50). The priority of Moses to Homer and his divine inspiration makes him a more reliable guide (50–55). Christian revelation concerning the Trinity (56–94) provides the only certain teaching. There are already intimations of the nature of the triune God in the Old Testament (56–70). This biblical teaching on the Trinity has been pillaged in the writings of Plato (70–80), Plotinus, Plutarch, Numenius, and others (81–89). The scriptural teaching is purer and better (89–94). This is clear from a comparison with writers like Philo of Byblos and Diodorus of Sicily, or the myths described in Eusebius (95–97). Christian teaching about God is positive (98–103). Plato's misconceptions are listed (104–5). God is unengendered Being, which must be accepted on faith, as is clear from Timaeus of Locri and others (106–11). Reading the Old and New Testaments will rescue us from the errors of the atheists and agnostics (111–17).

Discourse 3: *On Angels, So-Called Gods, and Maleficent Demons.* The standard trio of atheists (Diagoras, Theodore, and Euhemeros) is first criticized (1–4), and then the various forms of pagan polytheism are examined: the worship of the sun, moon, and stars (5–23); the deification of human beings like Cronus, Heracles, and the Roman emperors (24–33); the deification of mythical figures, often immoral, like Cronus and Oceanos (34–47); the passions, where sexual desire, anger, drunkenness, and so forth are personified and then made gods (48–58); deification of the most malevolent demons, as is rightly denounced by Porphyry (59–69). The vanity of idols has been denounced by Plato and other philosophers (70–74). Scripture too has proscribed statuary (75–78). The immorality of Greek and Egyptian pagan statuary is described (79–84). The true nature of angels is explained in Scripture (87–90). Ascetic Christians imitate their angelic ways (91–95). The superiority of Christian teaching on angels and demons is superior to the lewdness of the corresponding pagan description (96–99). Scriptural teaching is cited on the origin, nature, and activity of demons (100–102). Plato erred on the demiurge of evil (103–4). It is in fact the Holy Spirit who directs, governs, and sanctifies the good (105–8).

Discourse 4: *On Matter and the Cosmos.* The good effect of Christianity on the corrupt pagan world is noted (1–4). The contradictions of pagan philosophers on the nature, structure, and duration of the universe are next exposed (5–15). Whether the world is one or plural, and the nature of the sun, moon, and stars are examined (16–24). The hopeless contradictions in the views of philosophers on natural phenomena demonstrate the uselessness of scientific research (25). Even Socrates and Plato abandoned cosmology (26–30). Theodoret names his scholarly sources (31). Some of Plato's teachings are valuable (32–44). Some, however, are reprehensible, especially his view that matter is evil (45–49). The teaching of Scripture on cosmogony is far preferable (50–55). The original order of creation was upset by the fallen angels, giving rise to evil (56–59). The order in the world argues for a Creator and divine providence (60–66). The doctrine of Scripture is sounder and more credible than the uncertainties of the pagan cosmologists (67–73).

Discourse 5: *On Human Nature.* Human nature enjoys free will and is in control of its own destiny (1–7). There is a wide variety of philosophical views on the origin, nature, and destiny of the soul and the relationship between soul and body (8–27). The views of Pythagoras and Plato on freedom are examined (28–36). God is not the author of evil (37–38). For Plato the rational soul is a portion of the divine (39–45). Plato and Aristotle differ on the immortality of the soul (46–47). The only unanimity of teaching on human nature is to be found in Scripture (48–57). Difference of sexes and languages do not impede the acquisition of virtue or interfere with the basic unity of the human race (58–64). Scripture has reaffirmed the unity of the human race (65–67) and has extended knowledge of truth to all social classes (68–69). Style and refined language are not essential to truth (70–75). The simple teaching of the evangelists surpasses the drivel of the pagan philosophers (76). Human action is grounded in human nature and free-will, and is liable to reward and punishment (77–80). The wisdom of the Creator and the beauty of creation should call forth a hymn of praise (81–82).

Discourse 6: *On Divine Providence*. Opponents of the doctrine of divine providence are criticized at the outset, especially Diagoras, Protagoras, Epicurus, and Aristotle (1–7). Oenomaos, the Cynic, joins in the criticism (8–10). Such terms as fate, fortune, destiny, and necessity are defined (11–15). Listed is the humorous view of the comic poets on the philosophers (16–21). The "eye of justice" sees and judges everything (22–25). Plato's views are set forth with quotations (26–33). The *Laws* distinguishes divine and human laws and good and evil (34–41). The *Theaetetus* shows that God is not the author of evil (42–43), and the *Laws* demonstrates universal providence from the harmony in nature (44–48). Social and economic inequalities are not necessarily evil (49–55). Divisions into rich and poor can suit both parties (55–56). Plato's views are summarized (57–58). For Plotinus also providence is a major concern and his teachings are borrowed from Scripture (59–73). Christ's Incarnation is a guarantee of continuing providence (74–77). The human and divine natures are united in the Incarnation (78–80). Analogies are provided to illustrate this teaching (82–84). Its timing is shown as well as its efficaciousness (85–87). God's plan as manifested in the Prophets is fulfilled (88–92).

Discourse 7: *On Sacrifices*. The human race has been beguiled by the devil through the agency of the pagan poets, theologians, and philosophers in their lewd accounts of the gods and goddesses (1– 6). Painters and sculptors achieve the same result for the illiterate (7–9). This immorality is carried over into pagan festivals and blood sacrifices (10–16). In the Mosaic law the Egyptians were allowed to do the same by way of concession (17–25). But God does not really need blood sacrifices (26–35). Porphyry's testimony against sacrifices is cited (36–42). Philo, Plutarch, and Sophocles are also quoted against them (43–46). The views are given of Plato and Socrates (47–49).

Discourse 8: *On the Cult of Martyrs*. Simplicity of expression found in the Scriptures is preferable to embellished prose (1–7). Because of its unadorned simplicity the Christian message has reached the widest audience (8–9). Christians are prepared to die for this message (10–11). The pagans deified all too human heroes like Heracles (12–18), Asclepius (19–23), Dionysus (24), the Dioscuri (25), Cleomedes the boxer and Antinous (26–28). The Greeks who have engaged in such worship can hardly afford to criticize the Christian cult of martyrs (29–32). Greek libations and sacrifices for the dead are contrasted with the virtuous martyrs (33–41). Some Greeks, notably Plato, had a belief in survival with rewards and punishments after death (42–50). The Christian departed continue to aid us after death (51–55). Even distinguished pagans like Socrates and Anaxarchus failed to win a personal cult after their deaths (56–58). Neither did the great military generals (59–61). But the martyrs' tombs are world famous and pilgrims flock to them (62–70).

Discourse 9: *On Laws.* This returns to the attack on those who prefer style to substance (1–5). Only Christian laws enshrine truth in simplicity; pagan legislators like Minos, Charondas, and Lycurgus have failed to win continuing acceptance (6–14). The relativity of civil laws is very striking but the laws of the Gospel have outlived them and won permanent acceptance (15–20). The Gospel laws have withstood the persecutions of the Roman emperors (21–31) and the recent persecutions in Persia (32–34). Evangelical laws have replaced the barbarous practices of the Massagetai, the Tibarenians, and others (35–36). Plato erred greatly on much of his proposed legislation on education (37–40), especially in matters pertaining to sex and marriage (41–43), community of wives (44–49), free love, exposure of infants, and abortion (50–52), pederasty (53–54), and homicide (55–56). The evangelical laws are much superior (57), especially on the unity and indissolubility of marriage (58–62), the counsels on celibacy (63), on homicide (64–65), on oaths (66), and on the rewards promised for right conduct (67). These laws reflect credit on law-maker and law-abiding Christians alike (68–73).

Discourse 10: *On True and False Oracles.* The fallen angels tyrannically grabbed power and set up oracular sites where they demanded divine honor (1–3). With the coming of Christ silence now engulfs these workshops of deceit (4). Even Plutarch testifies to their waning influence (5–10). Likewise Porphyry (11–13), who especially condemns the human sacrifices demanded at these oracular sites (14–18). Diogenianus also bears witness against the veracity of the oracles (19–20). Examples of ambiguity and imposture are listed in the responses at Delphi (24–34). Apollo's oracles frequently encouraged immoral behavior (35–42). But Christ's coming has silenced them, as recently dramatized at Daphne, Antioch (43–48). The Scriptures are the only true oracles (49). Isaiah correctly predicted the destruction of pagan oracles (50–55). Idolatrous cults sometimes survive but are totally ridiculous (56–58). Isaiah's messianic prophecies have been triumphantly fulfilled (59–68). The salvation of the Gentiles was prophesied and accomplished (69–72). In Jeremiah also we read that the promises originally made to the Jews were transferred to the Gentiles (73–80). This was foretold and corroborated by other Old Testament prophets (81–92) and in the Historical Books and the Psalms (93–100). These examples should convince us of the emptiness of the false oracles and the accuracy and credibility of the true ones (101–5).

Discourse 11: *On the Last End and Final Judgment.* Aristippus learned philosophy from his mother, but many pagans refuse to accept the truth because they lack the necessary preliminary disposition, faith (1–5). The conflicting views of philosophers on the supreme good and final end of man are presented (6–8). Plato's view on the final end is close to that held by Christians (9–12). Aristotle, the Stoics, and Epicurus have proposed inferior definitions (13–17). Plato has much of value on final judgment and retribution as is shown by liberal quotations from his works (18–26). His sources were the Hebrew prophets (27–32). Plato has some erroneous teaching, notably metempsychosis (33–45). The eschatological views of Plutarch and others are contrasted with those of the Scriptures, especially the Beatitudes (46–51). The joys of heaven after the resurrection of the body and final judgment are detailed in the New Testament (52–65). This teaching is far superior to that of Plato (66–67). Christ will be our judge, as was prophesied in the Old Testament (68–69). Many other prophecies about the beginning of Christianity have also been fulfilled (70–78). Christ remains faithful to his promises (79–83).

Discourse 12: *On Practical Virtue.* Good behavior must be united to knowledge, and a study of the laws of practical virtue helps people to translate theory into practice (1–6). Plato's view that humans should aim at assimilation to the divine has most to recommend it (7–13). Beginning with Moses, God has given us directives on the rewards and punishment that await us and this is further developed in the New Testament (14–18). Greek philosophers, especially Plato, had insights on this subject that were close to Christian (19–25). Plato's source was the Old Testament, and certainly not the lewd example of Socrates (26–32). Pagans are unfairly critical of Christian behavior and quotations from Plato bear this out (33–36). The shortcomings of a few do not warrant wholesale condemnations (37–43). Anecdotal examples of good pagans are listed (44–52). Rules to follow in temptation are culled from Plato (53–56). The immoral proclivities of Socrates are detailed in Porphyry (57–69). Even Plato enjoyed the luxury of Sicily (70–72). Examples are given of pagans who were morally admirable (73). But the Christian moral teaching on chastity and marriage is superior (74-79). Because some transgress the laws is no reason to blame the laws themselves (80–86). Violations of law differ in degree (87–92). Sardanapalos was the supreme sensualist (93–94). Even Porphyry recognizes that Jesus has replaced Asclepius (95–97).

THEODORET'S CLASSICAL LEARNING AND ITS SOURCES

"The *Curatio*," says Quasten, "displays more than any other of his works his classical erudition. The author quotes more than 100 pagan philosophers, poets, and historians in about 340 passages. The great majority of these quotations, however, have not been taken directly from the originals but from secondary sources, especially the *Stromata* of Clement of Alexandria and the *Praeparatio evangelica* of Eusebius of Caesarea."[3]

Quasten may have been too generous, however, when he wrote: "Conversant with classical literature he seems to have read Homer and Plato, Isocrates and Demosthenes, Herodotus and Thucydides, Hesiod, Aristotle, Apollodorus and Plotinus, Plutarch and Porphyry."[4]

To deal with Plato and Plotinus first, Wallace-Hadrill is probably nearer the truth in saying there is little evidence that Theodoret had read any texts from Platonism at first hand (although over 150 passages from Plato are quoted in the *Curatio*) other than Plotinus, *Enneads,* Book 3, Porphyry's *History of Philosophy* and *Life of Pythagoras,* and possibly Plato's *Symposium.*[5]

Plato is, for the most part, saluted as the premier philosopher among the Greeks; he "outdistanced all the others by the eloquence of his language" (1.12), but Theodoret reserves the right to differ from him and on occasion submits him to harsh criticism, especially in Discourses 9, 11, 12.

The Platonist dialogues most frequently quoted are the *Republic* (thirty times), the *Phaedo* (twenty-six times), and the *Laws* (twenty-five times). More than half to almost all are derived from Eusebius, *Praeparatio evangelica*. Eleven of the fifteen quotations from *Timaeus*, all eight from the *Gorgias*, and all five from the *Crito* are from Eusebius. On the other hand, the *Symposium* is mentioned with signs of personal familiarity.

Plotinus, *Enneads*, Book 5 (which is called *On the Three Primary Hypotheses*), appears in two lengthy quotations in Discourse 2, mediated through Eusebius, Book 3, which Theodoret calls *On Providence* and may have known personally.

As for Aristotle, there is little evidence that Theodoret ever read him. Aristotle is blacklisted in the Preface for his shortsighted view on providence and is contrasted unfavorably with Plato for his views on the immortality of the soul and humanity's final end. What few references there are (four) can be traced to Clement, *Stromata* 2 or 8.

Plutarch's anecdotal style has undoubted affinities in Theodoret, but Theodoret himself seems most familiar with ps.-Plutarch, *Placita* (three quotations), and *On the Cessation of Oracles* (five quotations), all mediated through Eusebius, *Praeparatio evangelica*. The quotation from Plutarch's own *On Isis and Osiris* and that from his fragmentary *On the Soul*, as well as that from *Concerning the E at Delphi*, which Theodoret wrongly assigns to *On the Cessation of Oracles*, are all mediated through Eusebius.

Of the historians, Herodotus is three times quoted or referred to; two of these instances are duplicated from Clement of Alexandria, but the other one is unrelated to Clement or Eusebius. Thucydides receives only a brief mention and a standard compliment that may have been derived from Chrysostom's *De Sacerdotio*. Dionysius of Halicarnassus is quoted once only, taken from Eusebius, *Praeparatio evangelica*.

Single quotations from Demosthenes and Isocrates do not derive from either Clement or Eusebius. Apollodorus is quoted once only, as a source on Asclepius; for this Theodoret may have had direct access to the *Library of Apollodorus*, for neither Clement nor Eusebius would oblige here. The single reference to Hellanicus comes from Clement, *Stromata* 1.

Among the poets Homer's *Iliad* is quoted about twenty-five times as against a mere three (or four) citations from the *Odyssey*. Hesiod's

Works and Days is quoted three times and the *Theogony* four times. Theodoret says that Hesiod is known to every schoolboy, just as Homer's *Iliad* is recognized as the basis of the traditional educational system. Pindar is quoted five times, the quotations coming from the *Stromata* of Clement. A solitary quotation from Bacchylides is also from Clement.

Among the tragedians, Aeschylus is quoted twice, once from Prometheus Vinctus and once, in a quotation from Plato, from *Seven against Thebes*; one is derived from Clement and the other from Eusebius. Sophocles is mentioned only once, but the quotation is from ps.-Sophocles, and it is readily available from either Clement or Eusebius. Five citations from Euripides are conveniently present in Clement.

Theodoret shares Clement's antipathy to Epicurus, and all five of his fragments quoted derive from the second book of the *Stromata*. Theodoret betrays a certain predilection for the Cynics. Antisthenes is quoted four times, all traceable to Clement's *Stromata*. The two fragments of Diogenes of Sinope are also from *Stromata*.

Porphyry obviously has a special fascination for Theodoret, who cites him about thirty-five times. Theodoret's use of Porphyry can be seen in six particular areas as evidence:

— for the failure of secular philosophy to attain absolute truth. Three quotations to support this failure are one from the *Letter to Boetus* and two from *Letter to Anebo,* and they are all from Eusebius.
— for the greater antiquity of Hebrew wisdom.[6] In Discourse 1 we read a well-known excerpt from *On the Philosophy from Oracles*. In Discourse 2 he returns to this theme with a long quotation from *Against the Christians*. Theodoret then says: "This is not the place to prove that Porphyry knew nothing about chronology."
— against the pagan gods and the demons masquerading as gods. Besides a telling quotation from *On Abstinence*, misidentified by Theodoret as from the *Letter to Anebo,* the lengthy excerpts from *On Abstinence*, *On the Philosophy from Oracles*, and the *Letter to Anebo* enable Theodoret to conclude triumphantly that the one warring against truth has been forced in spite of himself to war against falsehood also.

— against pagan blood sacrifices. Porphyry's *On Abstinence* proves a useful standby in Discourse 7. Theodoret charges that Porphyry had carefully consulted the Old Testament when he was preparing his *Against the Christians.* Earlier in Discourse 3, he already had skillfully used Porphyry in his indictment of Homer for setting the fashion of believing in gods who love libations and the savor of sacrifices.

— against false oracles. Porphyry's *On the Philosophy from Oracles* is a frequent source of quotations in Discourse 10.

— for the moral bankruptcy of the Greek philosophers. Only three quotations from *Against the Christians* actually appear in the *Curatio,* but they serve to highlight the end of the sway of Asclepius, the healer, and the beginning of the domain of Christus *medicus.* Near the end of Discourse 12, Theodoret presents Porphyry as his star witness: "One is astonished today at the fact that for so many years the city had been the prey of disease when Asclepius and the other gods were sojourning there, but now that Jesus is held in honor it does not experience the least public benefit from any of the gods." The final paragraph shows that Porphyry is the main target: "That is what Porphyry, our worst enemy, has to say. And he recognized clearly that once the true faith appeared, neither Asclepius nor any other of the so-called gods could further play the cheat on human beings."

The highly critical treatment of Socrates seems to be based on Theodoret's personal knowledge of Porphyry, *History of Philosophy.* Socrates is already being cut down to size in Discourse 1; we are reminded of him again in Discourse 4; and in Discourse 12.69 there is a complete rout in which he is mercilessly pummeled as if he were the embodiment of all that is wrong with pagan philosophy. The *History of Philosophy* merits three mentions and three citations. Since there are no counterparts in Eusebius, this may well be one of Theodoret's few primary sources.

J. Sirinelli is doubtless right in rejecting as an excessive simplification the temptation to see Eusebius, *Praeparatio evangelica,* as a *Contra Porphyrium.*[7] But he seems also right to highlight the presence of so many passages of Porphyry in Eusebius and conclude that all the important questions concerning the nature of pagan religion are studied in the *Praeparatio* with reference to Porphyry.[8] This seems equally applicable to Theodoret's *Curatio*.

STYLE AND METHODOLOGY

"The Greek in which he wrote is perfect, and his style clear and simple," says Quasten.[9] Theodoret tells us in his Preface: "I...have given a flowing quality to my style because this method seems most suited to my didactic purposes, especially since, in utilizing arguments from Plato and the other philosophers, it would be appropriate if my style should not be at complete variance with theirs, but should bear some slight resemblance to it." There is no denying that he has succeeded in writing a well-organized, easy-to-read, and respectable treatise in the Platonic manner.

A word should be said about the artistry of the openings of the Discourses, surely more than mere exercises in *captatio benevolentiae*. Particularly good examples are to be found in Discourses 5, 8, 9, 11, and 12. There is some similarity between the beginnings of Discourses 7 and 10, which may indicate lengthy intervals in composition.

There is a pronounced streak of voyeurism in Theodoret's treatment of the immorality of the pagan gods and an almost adolescent, not to say pathological, preoccupation with sexual detail. This is carried to absurd lengths in Discourse 10, where an oracle of Apollo is misread as referring to the phallus of Dionysus (10.39). The extramarital activities of Zeus are relentlessly narrated (3.37, 80–81, 97–98; 7.8), and there are cameo studies of the ithyphallic Priapus (3.84), the nude Aphrodite (3.79–80), the adulterous Ares and Aphrodite (7.5), the feast of Phallagogia (1.113; 7.11), and of Thesmophoria (3.84; 7.10–11), the necrophilic Dionysus (8.24), Pan and the Satyrs (3.81, 7.12), the impotent Sophocles (12.38), the thirteenth Labor of Heracles (8.16), the sleeping but ever vigilant Anacharsis (12.45), the boyfriends of Apollo and of the emperor Hadrian (8.28), Ganymede, the winepourer (3.31), Diogenes of Sinope's public consorting with prostitutes (12.48), the dog-marriage of Crates and Hipparchia (12.49), Aristippus and his mistress (12.50).

At times the style is anecdotal and occasionally humorous, but most of the stories are recycled from Clement or Eusebius: Anaxarchos and Zeno the Eleatic (8.57), the boxer Cleomedes (8.26), the virtuous women like the wife of Kandaules (9.41), Lysidice, Philotera, and Theano (12.73), the theomorphic worship of the Egyptians (3.85), the resemblance between Porphyry using the Scriptures and a monkey (7.36–37), and the sensual Sardanapalos (12.92–94).

Like Clement, his unacknowledged source, Theodoret is a master at name-dropping, at invoking recondite pagan authors to ratify Christian positions, but unquestionably he assembled well and skillfully deployed his quotations. Whenever he saw or heard a happy phrase he obviously catalogued it for future use. Fleeting references to, or lines from, Anacharsis (5.69), Andocides (6.91), Aristippus (12.50), Bion of Borysthenes (6.19), Bacchylides (1.78), Crates (12.49), the comic poets Epicharmus (1.82, 88, 6.22), Menander (6.17), and Philemon (6.16, 23), Empedocles (1.71, 74; 4.14; 8.36), Erathosthenes (8.57), Hellanikos (12.44), Heraclitus (1. 70, 88; 8.39, 41), Hermippus (12.46), Hippodamus (12.77), Hyperides (6.91), Isocrates (6.91), Leander (1.24; 8.30), Neanthes (1.24), Philolaos (5.14), Simonides (11.14, 12.46), Solon (1.73), Theano (12.73), Theopompus (1.24), Timon of Phlius (2.20, 5.16), Zeno of Citium (3.74), all come from the same source.

Likewise one- or two-liners from Amelius (2.88), Antiochus (8.30), Aristocles (8.34, 12.51), Atticos (6.58, 12.52), Diogenianus (10.19–20), Longinus (5.27), Manetho (2.94; 3.44), Numenius (1.14; 2.81, 84-85, 114), Theognis (5.11 and 11.14) come from Clement, while another reading from Theognis (1.69) comes from Eusebius, who set the example by himself frequently borrowing from Clement. Lengthier excerpts, notably from Oenomaos (6.8–10, 8.26–27, 9.10, 10.24, 25–26, 28–32, 33, 38) all come from Eusebius. All references to Diodorus Siculus (1.21, 3.27–28, 8.16–17) are traceable to Eusebius. Sometimes Theodoret draws on both Clement and Eusebius. Of the five fragments from the Orphic Poems (1.86, 115; 2.30, 31; 3.44, 54; 12.35) all but one come from Eusebius, the remaining one from Clement.

DATE AND PLACE OF COMPOSITION

P. Canivet, in arguing for a date for the *Curatio* prior to Theodoret's accession to the see of Cyrus in 423, has clearly summarized earlier views on the date.[10] Mention of it in Epistle 113[11] would place it before 449, but such a reference may not be any more specific than that.

M. Richard from a christological examination placed it earlier than the Council of Ephesus, 431.[12]

The persecutions in Persia, however, are mentioned as "just recent" (9.32), and, as they are described in very similar terms by Theodoret in his *Ecclesiastical History*, the reference may be to the persecution of 426/427. Theodoret wrote his *Ecclesiastical History* sometime between 441 and 449. The present writer would place the date of the *Curatio* in the same time frame, and near the beginning of Theodoret's episcopacy rather than in his monastic period. The view expressed on the interrelations of Hellenism and Christianity sound episcopal, like those of Basil in his *Exhortation to Youths on How They Shall Best Profit from the Writings of Pagan Authors*.[13]

If these Discourses were written for actual delivery, then the logical place of delivery would be Antioch rather than Cyrus, remembering Cardinal Newman's verdict: "He was a great preacher, and his own native place, Antioch, was the natural stage for the exercise of his gift."[14]

THE *CURATIO*—THE LAST OF THE CHRISTIAN APOLOGIES

Many of the themes in the *Curatio* are already well-worn in the second-century apologists.[15] Already in the *Apology of Aristides*, the earliest preserved apology, many of the themes are announced and developed: the priority of Chaldean and Egyptian learning to Greek (c. 2), the folly of deifying the elements (cc. 3–7), the adulterous affairs and parricidal tendencies of the pagan gods (cc. 8–11), the theriomorphic nature of Egyptian religion (c. 12), the contrast of Judaism and Christianity (cc. 14–16).

In Latin apology, in common with Theodoret the *Octavius* of Minucius Felix censures the atheists Theodorus and Diagoras, and also Pan with his hooves, Aesculapius struck by lightning, Plato's bowdlerizing of Homer, and the illicit love of Ares and Aphrodite.

Closer to Theodoret's time John Chrysostom in two apologies touched on many of the points made by Theodoret.[16] The *Demonstration against the Pagans* utilized the Old Testament in a manner very similar to that of Theodoret to prove that Christ's life, death, and resurrection were foretold in great detail by the prophets. "The fisherman, the publican, and the tentmaker" are also mentioned by both writers, and the uneducated apostles are contrasted favorably and in similar terms with the rhetorically trained but ineffectual pagan philosophers. The miraculous spread of the early Church to places like Persia, Sarmatia, and Scythia is dwelt on by both. In his *Discourse on Blessed Babylas and Against the Greeks* Chrysostom blamed demons for introducing the duplicity of blood sacrifices. He criticized sorcerers and magicians and said that the laws of Zoraoaster and Zamolxis were short-lived. The lasting work of the simple apostles is lauded in contrast to the boastings and puerility of the pagan philosophers. As in Theodoret, Diogenes of Sinope is singled out for special attention and the pederasty of Socrates is censured. A particularly close similarity occurs at *Curatio* 1.5, where those suffering from inflammation of the brain kick and bite physicians who wish to minister to them. Pilgrimages to tombs of the martyrs and reverence for their relics are also points of similarity. Babylas is even referred to indirectly by Theodoret, as is the destruction of Apollo's temple, is the escape of the maiden Daphne from the attentions of Apollo, the amours of Ares and Aphrodite, the ambiguous replies of the oracles at Delphi, and the eventual silencing of the oracles by the coming of Christ. Indeed the attempt by the emperor Julian to reinstate paganism, discussed at some length by Chrysostom, lends a new urgency to the apologetic of both Chrysostom and Theodoret. The words of Chrysostom may have been echoing in Theodoret's ears: "Orders were dispatched all over the world to repair the temples of the idols....Whereupon, magicians, sorcerers, soothsayers, augurs, mendicant priests, and the entire workshops of the occult assembled from all quarters of the world." If this could have happened so near at hand in a suburb of Antioch in A.D. 362, it could conceivably happen again a mere seventy years later.

Quasten's verdict—"This last of the Christian Apologies is completely preserved and considered as perhaps the best refutation of paganism which has come down to us,"[17]—is true to the extent that Theodoret shows himself familiar with the major themes of previous Christian apologetic and very adept at synthesizing them.

TEXT AND TRANSLATIONS

The Greek text has been established magisterially by Johannes Raeder in his dissertation, *De Theodoreti Graecarum affectionum curatione*

(Halle, 1900), which provides the background for his Teubner text: *Theodoreti Graecarum affectionum curatio, ad codices optimos denuo collatos recensuit* (Leipzig, 1904; rep. 1969). Raeder uses eight of the known twenty-nine manuscripts, and no new manuscripts have been discovered since his work. These eight are listed as follows by Raeder and Canivet, who follows Raeder with very few departures (p. 69):

1. Vaticanus graecus 2249, saec. X
2. Bodleianus Auct. E. II, 14 saec. XI
3. Laurentianus X 18 saec. XI
4. Marcianus graecus 559 saec. XII
5. Bodleianus Canonicianus 27 saec. XVI
6. Scorialensis X, II, 15 saec. XVI
7. Parisinus Coislinianus 250 saec. XI
8. Vaticanus graecus 626 an. 1307

In conjunction with no. 3 it should be noted that a Latin translation of *Curatio* (as well as *De Providentia*), both dedicated to Pope Leo X, was done prior to the publication of the Greek text by the Florentine humanist Zanobi Acciaioli (1461–1519), who was a Dominican and librarian at the Convento di San Marco, close to the Laurentianum.[18] His translation was published by E. Estienne in Paris in 1519 and is reproduced in Migne, *Patrologia Graeca*, 83, coll. 783–1512. The Greek text in Migne is a reprint of that of Thomas Gaisford (Oxford, 1839). There is a French translation, with critical text, in P. Canivet, *Théodoret de Cyr Thérapeutique des maladies helléniques*, SC 57, 2 vols. (Paris, 1958), which is greatly supplemented by idem, *Histoire d'une enterprise apologétique au Ve siècle* (Paris, 1957). There is also a useful Italian translation: N. Festa, *Teodoreto, Terapia dei morbi pagani*, vol. 1 (Florence, 1930), left incomplete by the translator's death. A Polish translation has also appeared: S. Kalinkowsi (Warsaw, 1981); also P. C. Crego, "A Translation and Commentary on Theodoret of Cyrus' *Graecarum affectionum curatio*, Book Five, On Human Nature," diss., Boston College (1993); see DissAbstr 54 (1993–94), no. 8, 3078–79).

A CURE FOR PAGAN MALADIES
PREFACE

1. I have often encountered those devotees of Greek mythology who are convinced of its truth, and who make fun of our faith[1] under the pretext that the only option we give to those who are being instructed in divine things is to believe. They accuse the apostles of ignorance and regard them as barbarians because they lack the refinement of elegant diction.[2] As for the cult of martyrs, they reduce it to ridicule and regard it as completely absurd that the living would seek aid from the dead. They add other objections of a similar sort, which I will expose in the course of the present work.

2. I, for my part, have provided all the counterarguments necessary to dissipate their charges. But I thought it would be impious and unholy to show a lack of interest in the simple-minded who are their victims in such deceitful attacks if I failed to provide a written refutation of their empty charges.

3. I have divided my work into twelve chapters and have given a flowing quality[3] to my style because this method seems most suited to my didactic purposes, especially since, in utilizing arguments from Plato and the other philosophers, it would be appropriate if my style should not be at complete variance with theirs, but should bear some slight resemblance to it.

4. The first discourse undertakes the defense of our faith and of the apostles' lack of culture by bringing forward proofs taken from the Greek philosophers.

5. The second itemizes the opinions concerning the first principle of the universe advanced by the most distinguished of the Greek sages, and those among their successors who deserved the sobriquet "philosopher." Then, paralleling their opinions with the true philosophy of Moses, who was the doyen of all philosophers, it refutes their error and displays the resplendent truth of Moses' teaching.

6. The third teaches what has been recounted by the Greeks concerning the so-called secondary deities and what, on the other hand, the sacred Scripture teaches us about incorporeal but created natures; we hope by this juxtaposition both to show the admirable nature of our own observances and to refute the evil-looking, foul-smelling aspect of their vile myths.

7. The fourth, which deals with matter and the cosmos, proves that the cosmogony of the Christians is much more consonant with reason than is that of Plato and the others.

8. Discourse five sets forth the debate on anthropology, marshaling the proofs of the Greeks and of the Christians, and reveals a difference between them as great as that between light and darkness.

9. The sixth chapter is allocated to a discourse on divine providence. This chapter is the logical sequel to the preceding ones on God, and on what God created. This treatise, on the one hand, refutes the atheism of Diagoras,[4] the blasphemy of Epicurus,[5] and the short-sighted view of Aristotle on providence.[6] On the other hand, it praises the view of Plato, Plotinus,[7] and all others who hold similar views.

10. It was also necessary to set forth the usefulness of sacrifices. The content of the seventh discourse condemns, with the support of philosophical texts, Greek sacrifices and utilizes texts from the prophets to demonstrate the infantile nature of Jewish legislation.

11. The eighth discourse is concerned with the accusation mounted against those glorifying the martyrs and with the counter-defense. With the assistance of the testimonies of philosophers, historians, and poets, the discourse shows that Greeks honored the dead, not only with libations, but also with sacrifices to their so-called gods, demi-gods, or heroes, the majority of whom passed their lives in debauchery.

12. It also seemed good to me to confront the most renowned of the Greek legislators with ours, I mean the fishermen, the worker in leather, the tax gatherers[8]—and to show again by comparison just how those laws <of the Greeks> have been consigned with their authors to the darkness of oblivion, yet those of the fishermen are flourishing, not only among the Greeks and Romans, but also among the Sarmatians, the Persians, and other barbarians.

The ninth discourse contains this examination.

13. The tenth discourse, on the one hand, teaches what kinds of things the divine oracles predict and how they are fitted to God and

adapted to the good dispositions of the people, and, on the other hand, what the Pythian, the Dodonian, and the other false seers of the Greeks foretold, who were observed to be lying, foretelling nothing of the future, yet prophesying in a manner that no decent person would agree to propose.

14. It was also necessary to make known to those unaware of it our own teaching as well as that of the Greeks on the end of the world and the final judgment. That is the subject matter proposed to the one ready to read the eleventh discourse.

15. In the final chapter I have also attempted to show the differences in practical virtue because I see Greek society turning up its nose at the philosophers of old and trying to raise its life by discourses. The twelfth discourse will show that the life of the ancients did not merit the praise not only of the philosopher but even of runaway slaves, while the life of the apostles and of their followers transcends human nature and is more similar to that of those who have left the body and are already living in heaven.

16. This book has the title *A Cure for Pagan Maladies,* or better, *The Knowledge of Gospel Truth Based on Greek Philosophy.*

17. So, then, I have undertaken this labor to cure those who are ill, and to render beneficial preventive service to those who are in good health. As for those who happen upon the labors of others, I pray that if they find everything that is written acceptable they should glorify the Author of these things and requite with prayers the human authors. But if there are any shortcomings let them not condemn everything forthright but rather derive profit from whatever is well composed.

Discourse 1

ON FAITH

1. If a medical treatment exists for the body, one should also exist for the soul. For while it is true that frequent ailments beset both body and soul, bodily ailments are for the most part involuntary, while spiritual ailments are voluntary.[1]

2. Well aware of this, God, in that He is supremely wise and creator alike of souls, bodies, and the universe, has assigned appropriate remedies to the two parts of our nature, has even instituted specialized medicines of one kind for the body and of another for the soul, and has given them as prescriptions in the war against diseases in order to overcome them.

3. Now those who are physically out of sorts and troubled by their ailment long for a return to good health and put themselves in the hands of their physicians, not just when these administer gentle drugs, but even when they are required to undergo surgery, or cautery, or undertake a strict diet and take potions that are full of bitter, distasteful ingredients.[2]

4. On the other hand, those who have contracted the leprosy of nonbelief not only are unaware of the great seriousness of their malady, but even imagine that they enjoy the height of well-being. And if someone skilled in curing that kind of disease wishes to apply a remedy to it that would overthrow the malady, those who are affected take umbrage at it on the spot, as if they were in the grip of brain fever,[3] and they push aside the remedy proffered to them and run from the remedy in the way they should run from the disease.

5. It is necessary that the specialists come to the aid of those in difficulties, the ones who endure those who offer them insults, even if they box them or kick them.[4] For that is how those act who go to excess. Physicians do not put up with those who become hostile like

20

this, but bring forward restraints and forcibly apply fomentations to their heads, and devise every kind of mechanism as to drive out their malady and restore the former equilibrium of the parts to the whole.

6. That is what we too should do, and we should render the greatest possible attention to those with such dispositions. For even if those who are enslaved to such a disposition are comparatively few, resembling sediment which, because of its density, will not pass through a filter,[5] that is no reason for abandoning them or losing interest in the malady that afflicts them; instead, we should seek all means to dissipate the cloud hanging over them and enable them to see again the splendor of the intelligible light.

7. No industrious farmer cuts away the majority of thorns and leaves a few, but if he finds two, or even one, he hacks them out by the roots and leaves the meadow clean. Much more should we act in a similar fashion. For the law of our husbandry dictates that the thorns should be not eradicated, but transformed.

8. Come now, and just as we apply the hoe in agriculture to the thorns, so with the mattock of the word let us widen the furrow of their ears so that nothing will impede the irrigation of their senses. Similarly, just as in the case of those who are ill, let us apply saving and healing potions.[6]

9. But, before anything else, let us pay careful attention to the malady of smug self-sufficiency.[7] For some of those who have had a share of the expressions of the poets and the rhetoricians and who have had a taste of the elegant diction of Plato, despise the sacred Scriptures under the pretext that these are totally devoid of the ornaments of style, and are reluctant to learn the truth about the One Who Is from men who are mere fishermen.

10. Now when they reap the fruits of the various crafts they are not preoccupied about the language of each of the craftsmen; they do not demand that the workers in leather speak Attic Greek,[8] or the coppersmiths, or the architects, or the painters, or shipbuilders, or pilots. No, even if they happen to be Scythians, Sarmatians, Iberians, or Egyptians, they are pleased to take advantage of their skills, being satisfied to get from them a well-produced article and without concern about what their nationality is.

11. And when they hear a lyre player, they require only that the notes be harmonious, without requiring to know whether the player is a Greek or a non-Greek. But when it comes to the teaching of the

truth they are unwilling to receive it in all simplicity, but are disturbed if they are educated by one who does not speak Greek well. And you will find this conceitedness not among those who have attained the summit of Greek philosophy, but among those who have only tasted it, so to speak, with the tips of their tongues, and got a smattering of a few things here and there.

THE GREEKS LEARN FROM THE BARBARIANS

12. The most illustrious of the Greeks, by contrast, whose memory is recalled to this very day with high regard by the distinguished—I mean people like Pherecydes of Syros,[9] Pythagoras of Samos,[10] Thales of Miletus,[11] Solon of Athens[12] and, most especially, the well-known Plato,[13] son of Aristo, and follower of Socrates, who outdistanced all the others by the eloquence of his language—did not hesitate, in their search for truth, to go to Egypt and Egyptian Thebes,[14] also to Sicily and Italy[15] at a time when these peoples, far from being under the direction of a single empire, each had their own institutions and laws, which differed from city to city.

13. Some were democratic, others oligarchic; some were under the rule of a tyrant, others under a moderate monarchy. But none of these obstacles hindered them from having recourse to the barbarians and learning from them any knowledge in which they thought them superior to themselves.

14. For they say that in Egypt they learned, not just from the Egyptians, but also from the Hebrews,[16] teachings concerning the true God. That is what we learn from Plutarch of Boeotia,[17] and from Porphyry, who warred against the truth,[18] and likewise from Numenius, the Pythagorean,[19] and from many others.

15. It is even recounted that Pythagoras submitted to circumcision,[20] which he learned from the Egyptians. The Egyptians, in turn, adopted this custom from the Hebrews. The patriarch Abraham had, in fact, received the precept about circumcision from the God of the universe, and his race preserved it; they remained a long time in Egypt and the Egyptians imitated the Hebrews.[21]

16. The fact that the circumcision of the newly born was not an old custom in Egypt is sufficiently attested by the Pharaoh's daughter; she found Moses abandoned on the riverbank and immediately rec-

ognized that he was circumcised, knew his gender, and called the child an offspring of the Hebrews.[22]

17. That is to say that those who had come through a superior education acquired such a great love of knowledge as to brave wars and the deepest seas to make their way to the barbarians and learn from every source whatever they thought necessary. The son of Sophroniscus, Socrates, the best of the philosophers, did not think it unworthy of philosophy to learn something useful even from women. He did not blush to name Diotima his teacher,[23] and he also frequented Aspasia.[24]

18. As for our adversaries, most of them do not know what is the *Wrath of Achilles*, which is the basis of the good education traditionally given to the young.[25] Others have collected a few morsels from the poets and orators, but they do not know even the names of the philosophers apart from two or three of the best known. Yet they regard the sacred Scriptures as barbarous and characterize learning truth from that source as dangerous. The cause of their own morbid anger is ignorance.

19. If, in fact, they had read the history of Greece, they would certainly know that the most elevated of the sciences, like most of the arts, were taken by the Greeks from the barbarians. They say that geometry and astronomy were first discovered by the Egyptians. Astrology and the calculation of the horoscope were given to them through the invention of the Chaldeans.[26] It was the Arabs and the Phrygians who were the first to have ideas about taking the auspices.[27]

20. The trumpet is the work of the Tyrennians, and the flute that of the Phrygians[28] after the discovery of drama and then of history. The alphabet is an invention of the Phoenicians, according to the Greeks, and Cadmus introduced it into Greece.[29] Medicine, it is said, owes its origin to the Egyptian Apis and later Asclepius developed its techniques.[30] The first boat was built in Libya.[31]

21. As for the feasts of Dionysus—the Panathenaia, the Thesmophoria, the rites of initiation at Eleusis—all these were introduced at Athens by Orpheus of Odrysae, who after a trip to Egypt transformed the mysteries of Isis and Osiris into those of Demeter and Dionysus just as we learn from Plutarch, who came from Chaeronea, in Boeotia,[32] and Diodorus of Sicily, and as the orator Demosthenes recalls[33] when he says that Orpheus taught them knowledge of the sacred rites.

22. And as for the rites of Rhea[34] and Cybele and Brimo[35] (or whoever you wish to name her; for there is a great abundance of names among you), there is nothing substantial underlying them; nevertheless, the feasts of this goddess, and the rites pertaining to her, were imported from Phrygia in Greece;[36] the authors, whose testimony I have already invoked, teach you in explicit terms.

23. If, then, the arts, the sciences, the rites of the deities, and the letters of the alphabet were learned from the barbarians by the Greeks, who boast elsewhere of their teachers, how come that you, who are even incapable of understanding their works, refuse to accept the truth from men who have received it as a gift of God?

24. And if it is because they are not sprung from Greece that you do not want to give them a hearing, it is time to stop saying that Thales is a wise man and that Pythagoras was a philosopher, and his master, Pherecydes.[37] Because Pherecydes was from Syrus, and not an Athenian, or a Spartan, or a Corinthian; and as for Pythagoras, according to Aristoxenus,[38] Aristarchus, and Theopompus, he was a Tyrennian, although Neanthes says that he was from Tyre. Some say that Thales was born in Miletus, but Leander[39] and Herodotus[40] describe him as a Phoenician. Besides which, Aristotle was from Stagyra,[41] Diogenes from Sinope,[42] and Alcmaeon, son of Peirithos, the first author of a work "On Nature, " was from Croton. Empedocles was from Agrigentum, a city in Sicily.[43]

25. If, however, you assert that even though these men were born and raised outside Greece they were nevertheless users of the Greek language, then first acknowledge that there are wise men born among the non-Greeks. For you hold in esteem for their wisdom Zamolxis, who came from Thrace,[44] and Anacharsis from Scythia,[45] and the Brahmans[46] enjoy great renown with you, although they are Indians, not Greeks.

PHILOSOPHY NOT NECESSARILY THE PRODUCT OF A FORMAL EDUCATION

26. But be convinced by another argument that you are wrong to regard style as more important than truth. You are well aware, I take it, that Socrates, son of Sophroniscus, was the greatest of the Greek philosophers. But his father was a stone-cutter and for a long time he practiced his father's craft.

27. A good number of other writers have reported this fact, including Porphyry, who has related this in the following terms in Book 3 of his *History of Philosophy*. This is what he said:[47]

> Let us mention concerning Socrates what other writers have thought fit to conserve about him. The facts that learned authors many times have presented in his praise or criticism will for the moment command our attention, but we will leave to one side the question whether he collaborated with his father on stone-cutting or whether his father worked on his own: For this did not impede his progress in wisdom if he devoted only a short time to it. And so much the better if he worked in statuary for that is a craft that is pure and irreproachable.

28. What follows is in the same tone. It presents authors who claim that Socrates was a stone-engraver. But possibly he worked in marble in his extreme youth and then, later, being a lover of poetry and rhetoric, undertook a formal education?

29. But of course one cannot say this, because Porphyry has said quite the opposite. This is how he puts it:[48]

> He was not badly endowed but, to tell the truth, he was completely uncultivated. He probably was not very well versed in the alphabet. And he provoked laughter when he tried to read or write because he stammered like an infant.

30. And Plato has given him these lines in the *Apology*:[49]

> Not, I can assure you, gentlemen, in flowery language like theirs, decked out with fine words and phrases. No, what you will hear will be a straightforward speech in the first words that come to my mind.

Then a little later he adds:[50]

> And so in the present case I make this request of you, which I think is only reasonable, to disregard the manner of my speech—it may be better or it may be worse—and to

consider and concentrate your attention upon this one question, whether my claims are fair or not.

31. But however unlearned, ignorant of letters, and uneducated Socrates was, he was more worthy of esteem than, not just anybody else, but even Plato, who surpassed all the Greeks in elegant diction. And this not even the son of Aristo himself would deny. How could he, since he ascribed and adapted all his published *Dialogues* to Socrates, preparing them to be deemed the products of his mind?

PLATO's DEFINITION OF TRUE PHILOSOPHY

32. Further, this Plato who has eclipsed not just the whole world and the other Greeks, but even the Athenians themselves, by his eloquence and the niceties of his style, lays it down that the search should be, not for modes of expression, but for balanced ideas.
33. Hear his own words in the *Statesman*.[51]

If you hold fast to this principle of avoiding contention over names you will be seen to be rich with an ever greater store of wisdom as you come to old age.

Listen to what he says also in Book 5 of the *Republic*.[52]

Are we to designate all these, then, and similar folk and all the practitioners of the minor arts as philosophers?

Not at all, I said, but they do bear a certain likeness to philosophers.

Whom do you mean, then, by the true philosophers?

Those for whom the truth is the spectacle of which they are enamored, said I. For philosophy does not involve geometry, which is based on postulates and hypotheses, nor music which is conjectural, nor astronomy, which is stuffed full of approximations and physical data; no, philosophy is the pursuit of absolute goodness through knowledge and truth.[53]
34. You have heard the philosopher's verdict, my friends: musicians, geometricians, and the others who are competent in the genre,

these he calls, not "philosophers," but "like philosophers," reserving the label "philosopher" for those who are really genuine philosophers of truth.

35. This is what he says also in Book 3 of the *Laws*:[54]

> Then let us take it as definitely settled, and proclaim our conviction that no function of government may be entrusted to citizens who are foolish in this sense. They must be reprehended for their folly, though they are most expert of calculators and laboriously trained in all arcane studies and everything that makes for nimbleness of mind. The people who possess the opposite qualities are to be called wise men, even if, according to the proverb, "they know not how to read or to swim," and authority should be entrusted to them as to sensible people.

36. How could one more truly and more clearly refute the present-day lack of culture and the prevailing malaise of smug self-sufficiency? Because it is a fact that the doyen of philosophers defines wisdom, not in terms of learned lessons, but in terms of knowledge of the truth. And he would name as wise men those who had acquired wisdom, even if they had never mastered the school curriculum.

37. And, indeed, even in the *Theaetetus*, criticizing the star-gazers, he speaks as follows:[56]

> Thales, Theodore, when he was looking up to study the stars and tumbled down a well, a Thracian maidservant, exercising her wit at his expense, is said to have scoffed at him for being so eager to know what was happening in the sky that he could not see what lay at his feet.[57]

38. And again, in the same dialogue,[58]

> A herdsman of this sort, penned up in his castle, is doomed by sheer press of work to be as rude and unculti-vated as the shepherd in his mountain fold. He hears of the marvelous wealth of some landlord who owns ten thou-sand acres or more, but that seems a small matter to one accustomed to think of the earth as a whole.

39. Continuing, he says:[59]

> For to know this is wisdom and excellence of the general
> sort; not to know it is to be manifestly blind and base. All
> other forms of seeming power and intelligence in the
> rulers of society are as mean and vulgar as the mechanic's
> skill in handicraft.

40. That is how even those who had studied every literary genre
acquired knowledge, how truth is more valuable than phrases and
words, and how ignorance of so-called style in no way injures truth.[60]

THE ANTIQUITY OF THE HEBREWS[61]

41. Why, then, my friends, do you not want to investigate the
meaning of the teaching of the apostles, why merely criticize its so-
called "barbarous" style,[62] even though you hear from your own
philosophers that the Greeks strayed far from the truth and that the
barbarians got to it more quickly?
42. In fact, the well-known Porphyry, who has waged a spirited
war against us, in his work *On the Philosophy from Oracles*, has said:[63]

> The road to the gods is paved in bronze; it is hard and
> rough. The barbarians have found many by-paths to it, but
> the Greeks have gone very much astray from it. These have
> prevailed already and have been destroyed. God has borne
> witness to the discovery to the Egyptians, Phoenicians,
> Chaldeans, Lydians, and Hebrews.

43. If the worst of all our enemies has reproached the Greeks
with having been enslaved to error, and if he testifies that the
Hebrews, the Phoenicians, the Egyptians, and the Chaldeans possess
the truth and says that Apollo prophesied as much, why do you not
obey the philosopher, admit the oracle of the tripod of Delphi, and
lend an ear to the Hebrew apostles and prophets? For the Pythian
called them discoverers of truth.
44. And if he united with them the Egyptians, Chaldeans, and
Phoenicians, you must know that, seeing they are neighbors of the

Hebrews, bordering on their country, it was from them that they learned the truth, if indeed they learned it. And indeed the Egyptians derived the greatest benefit; for the Hebrews lived a long time in Egypt.

45. And the Chaldeans reaped the greatest benefit from them likewise. For on one occasion, when deported as prisoners of war to Babylon,[64] and from what happened on the spot concerning the wonders, the furnace and the lions, they assumed the role of worthy teachers of the truth.

46. For his part, Cyrus, son of Cambyses,[65] while he lived with Daniel, learned religious knowledge; and when he conquered and annexed the Lydians,[66] he undoubtedly mingled with these new subjects what he had appropriated from the prophet.

RELATIVITY OF PHILOSOPHICAL SYSTEMS

47. Both the Pythian god, then, has attested that the Hebrews have the truth, and Porphyry has made mention of this oracle. That has been sufficiently proved. But Porphyry has further reproached the Greek philosophers on their total ignorance: listen to what he has written in his *Epistle to Boetus on the Soul.*

48. Besides much else he says the following:[67]

What proposition in philosophical matters is not contestable?

And to Anebo, the Egyptian, he writes in a similar vein:[68]

I will begin from the friendship for you from the gods, and the good demons and the philosophizings that were cognate to them. Concerning these topics very much has been contributed by the Greek philosophers but for the most part what they say derives its credibility merely from conjecture.

And a little later:

Among you there is a great war of words inasmuch as you try to make a construct of the good from human reckon-

ings; but to those for whom association with the prefect
has been contrived on the occasion for investigating continues to present itself.

WHERE THE PHILOSOPHERS DIFFER

49. If, then, the teachings of the philosophers are ambiguous (for
they are the discoveries of human reasonings), there is always ongoing
rivalry between them and an unending war of words, and yet if
Porphyry attested that it was to other people to be together and to be
in communion with God, why, my friend, do you cling to human and
controversial words and do not accept the teachings of God's friends?

CONCLUSION OF THE ARGUMENT

50. But if you exclude them as barbarians, you run the risk of
contradicting yourself. In fact, you lend credence to Pythagoras, who,
according to some, was a Tyrrhenian; according to others was from
Tyre.[69] You take the Stagyrite[70] as your mentor. You admire the one
from Sinope[71] and all the others who are not citizens of Greece but are
non-Greeks. We have also shown that Solon and Plato[72] have used non-
Greeks for almost all their sources.

51. We still hear that word of the Egyptian priest to Solon cited
elsewhere by Plato in the *Timaeus*:[73]

O Solon, Solon,
you Hellenes are never anything but children;
and there is not an old man among you.
For you have no learning which is grown gray with age.

52. But if the teachings of the Greeks are rather recent, those of
the Hebrews are the oldest and most venerable and contain the truth
flowering with time; so they ought clearly to be preferred and judged
obviously superior to those that are new and ambivalent or rather
false and fashioned without any verisimilitude.

53. In any case, unsophisticated language is insufficient excuse
for rejection, since we have shown that Socrates, the doyen of philoso-

phers, was not initiated into Greek culture, and that Plato judged truth preferable to knowledge of any kind or to stylistic considerations.

54. If it is the same notion of "faith" that you now attack (because I have heard you say that we do not produce any proof of our dogmas, but only recommend our disciples to believe), you are directly maligning our teaching, because, in fact, we join to our words the testimony of facts. So, once again, in the words of the proverb, "You have been wounded by your own feathered arrows."

55. In fact, the celebrated Pythagoras, son of Mnesarchus,[74] pupil of Pherecydes, and founder of the Italian school, had laid it down as a rule for his students that they should observe a five-year silence[75] and should only give ear to his words, so that they would accept what was said without question or discussion, believing it to be such and not busying themselves with entertaining doubts.

56. So, Pythagoras's followers had a habit of answering, when anyone demanded proof of what they said: "Himself says it,"[76] considering this to be stronger than any proof and ordering them to obey the word of Pythagoras.

57. If those speaking and those listening thought it was sufficient reason for belief that these were the views of Pythagoras, who, then, would be such a fool, or should I rather say be so stupefied, as to doubt the God of the universe as a teacher and not to believe His words, and not to render as much reverence to the God of the universe as to the members of his school accord to Pythagoras.

THE NOTION OF FAITH: LISTENING TO THE WORD OF GOD

58. Is it not pathetic, my friends, that Plato should order us to obey the poets unquestioningly, and that you are annoyed at us because we advise you to believe in what God teaches?

59. Are not these the words of Plato:[77]

To know or to tell the origin of the other divinities is beyond us, and we must accept the traditions of the men of old time who affirm themselves to be the offspring of the gods—that is what they say—and they must surely have known their own ancestors. How can we doubt the word of the children of the gods? Although they give no probable or certain proofs, still, as they declare that they are speaking of what took place in their own family, we must conform to custom and believe them.

60. That is also what Plato had to say about the poets in the *Timaeus*. He also forbade belief in Homer, Hesiod,[78] and the other poets who composed myths, and he did not hesitate to say that they spoke without probable and rigorous proofs. And that, while at the same time, in another place in his writings, he ridiculed what the poets said, as we will clearly demonstrate by another quotation.

61. Now if Plato encourages belief in these silly inventions of the writers of mythology and those disgraceful stories invented by them, without demanding the slightest proof of their truth, how much more religious and just it is to believe the inspired prophets and apostles when their words contain nothing disgraceful, or mythical, or unconvincing, but rather all their teachings are divine, sacred, and salutary?

THE PHILOSOPHERS INSIST ON FAITH IN THEIR DISCIPLES

62. That those who have followed the opinions of the philosophers, allowing themselves to be guided by faith, attach themselves at one time to this school, at another to that, would be easy to learn from an examination of their doctrinal differences.

63. There are those, for instance, who have stated that the soul is immortal; others that it is mortal; and others still who have defined it as a sort of composite, saying that one part of the soul is mortal, another immortal, and another still a mixture of both, partly mortal, partly immortal.[79]

64. Nonetheless, in spite of the divergences between what they said, each side found some people who were prepared to believe them. Moreover, neither set of followers would admit that this or that view was true if a certain faith did not persuade them to accept what was said.

65. That is why Plato's Socrates, in the *Gorgias*, after speaking at length about those condemned in Hades, has made a special addition about those proclaimed as blessed:[80]

That is what I have heard, Callicles, and I believe it to be true.

66. There is question now of things that are neither evident nor observable, but that for the most part are hidden from the majority of people.

67. Further, in the *Laws*, Book One, Plato has consolidated the bases of faith in these terms:[81]

> If your laws are but reasonably good, as they are, we must reckon among the best of them the enactment that no young man shall raise the question which of them all are what they should be and which not, but that all should agree, without a dissonant voice, that they are all god-given and admirable.

68. Not even in this matter does Plato agree that we should busy ourselves, insisting that we should accept with faith what has been legislated and not raise any questions about which laws are good and which not.

69. And Theognis, the Sicilian poet, publicly proclaims the nursling of faith. He says:[82]

> A man of faith is worthy to be valued equally with gold and
> silver, Kyrnos, in a difficult sedition situation.

If, then, he said, that the one who is faithful in time of revolution is worth more than gold and silver, who could declare the worth of one who believes unquestioningly in the divine utterances?

70. Nevertheless, I think that what Heraclitus the Ephesian[83] said neatly applies likewise to contradictors like you:

> Those that listen without understanding are like the deaf.
> The saying testifies that "they are absent while present."

71. And Empedocles from Agrigentum is in accord with the Ephesian in the following statement of his:[84]

> The wicked are wont to disbelieve. This is what our muse
> invites us to believe.

Unbelievers belong to the wicked, according to the Agrigentian. According to Heraclitus the same are unintelligent and deaf.

72. Elsewhere even Parmenides of Elea, disciple of Xenophanes of Colophon, recommends that faith be utilized in the approach to intellectual matters. He says, for instance:[85]

Contemplate, in spite of its absence, that which is surely present to your spirit. By this he means that the spirit is sufficient of itself to approach intelligibles, but that without faith even the spirit cannot see intellectuals.

73. Solon also makes an allusion to this:[86]

It is most difficult to apprehend the mind's invisible measure which alone holds the boundaries of all things.

If, then, it is very difficult to know, it is absolutely impossible to speak about it.

74. Empedocles, for his part, says concerning invisible things:[87]

It is not possible to bring God near within reach of our eyes, nor to grasp him with our hands. For human beings persuasion is the broadest road that runs into the mind.

75. And Antisthenes, a follower of Socrates and then head of the Cynic school, exclaimed concerning the God of the universe:[88]

From an image he is not known. By the eye he is not seen, He is like to nothing. Wherefore no one can know him from an image.

76. Faith, then, is necessary for those who wish to contemplate the intelligibles, since it is not even possible to find an image that is appropriate for them. The follower of Socrates, Xenophon, the Athenian, the son of Gryllos, in concurring with these views, has written:[89]

77. He who moves all things and is Himself immovable, is manifestly great and powerful. But what He is in form is

not clear. We know that faith is a necessity for those who would probe the depths of what is not clear.

78. One can hear Bacchylides saying also in his *Paeans*:[90]

It is not very easy to find the portals of unutterable words.

We have need, then, of eyes of the spirit to get to know the intelligibles; just as we need bodily eyes to see visible things, likewise we must have recourse to faith to reach initiation[91] into divine things.

79. Faith is to the understanding what the eye is to the body. Or rather, just as the eye needs light to display visible things, so also the intellect needs faith to show divine things and to safeguard firm opinion about these matters.

CONSEQUENCES OF LACK OF FAITH

80. As for those who do not wish to contemplate intelligibles, listen to the reproaches that Plato directs against them:[92]

Then just take a look around and make sure that none of the uninitiate overhears us. By the uninitiate I mean the people who believe that nothing is real except what they can grasp with their hands and do not admit that actions or processes or anything invisible can count as real.

81. Now you too belong to that category. But do not think the worse of the rebuke. For you have confined yourselves only to what is visible; reverencing the statues that you have made with your hands you refuse to accept instruction on what is the nature of the invisible.

82. It is, perhaps, to men who are so disposed that Epicharmus, the comic poet, has applied this iambic verse:[93]

Men's natures…inflated wineskins!

On the other hand, it is characteristic of men who are soberminded not to be enslaved to prejudice nor to be too bound to ancestral customs, but to seek after what is the truth and to collect what is useful from every source.

83. Did not Socrates say as much in the *Crito.*[94]

> You know that this is not a new idea of mine; it has always been my nature never to accept advice from any of my friends unless reflection shows that it is the best course that reason offers.

He makes plain from these words that he desired to find what was beneficial from the use of his reason and he had no law that compelled him to be a slave to prejudice.

84. That is how he also persuades Alcibiades to study after having first divested him of the pretense that he knew. For he first convinced him that he did not know.[95] To Alcibiades' question: "Do you think that I cannot find out?" he replied: "Certainly, if you search." To Alcibiades' further question: "Do you believe that I will not search?" Socrates replied: "I certainly do."

85. The beginning of knowledge, then, is the knowledge of our own ignorance. In addition to this it is necessary to expel false teachings from the soul and so receive divine teachings. That too was a teaching of Plato:[96]

> For one who is impure himself to attain the realm of purity would no doubt be a breach of universal justice.

86. Orpheus says the same thing:[97]

> I will speak to those for whom it is legitimate; let the profane ones close the doors.

Euripides echoes the same sentiment in exclaiming:[98]

> For how would anyone propose divine teachings to the uninitiated? How could one be initiated if he has not reinforced in himself by faith the doctrines which his teachers have proposed? How could one believe if he has not first eradicated from his thought erroneous teachings previously placed there?

87. That statement in Greek tragedy is true which Euripides uttered in the *Phoenissae*:[99]

> But the unjust argument, sick in itself, is in need of wise remedies. But the same tragic poet assures us that God collaborates with those who desire to enjoy his assistance:[100]

> To one who is toiling God lends his help.

88. Faith, then, is a very beneficial thing. In the words of Epicharmus, I mean the one who was a Pythagorean:[101]

> It is the intellect that sees, and the intellect that hears; all else is deaf and blind.

And Heraclitus again commends us to be directed by faith:[102]

> If you do not hope, you will not find what is unhoped for, since it is inaccessible and not to be searched out.

And again:[103]

> Those who excavate the earth for gold dig much but find little.

89. If prospectors, then, for the sake of a little gold dust, endure so much toil, and indeed danger, who is so lacking in love of divine things as to run away from the teaching of the truth which offers infinitely more rewards?

FAITH AND REASON

90. Let none of you, my friends, criticize faith. For Aristotle[104] has called faith the criterion for judging knowledge, and for Epicurus[105] it is a presumption of the intellect, a presumption that joins itself to knowledge to produce comprehension.

91. According to our theory faith is a voluntary assent of the soul, or rather the contemplation of an invisible object, or rather the tak-

ing of a position in relation to reality and the apprehension of the invisible in a way commensurate with our nature or a non-ambivalent disposition rooted in the souls of those who possess it.

92. Now faith has need of knowledge just as knowledge has need of faith, for neither is faith possible without knowledge nor knowledge without faith. Now faith precedes knowledge, and knowledge succeeds faith. The impulse leads to knowledge and action is consequent to it.

93. First we must believe; then we must be instructed. One cannot even comprehend the first elements if one does not believe it on the testimony of the school master that the first letter in the alphabet is "a," the second "b," and so on.

94. For it is obvious that if one immediately contradicted and said that the first letter should not be called "a" but something else, one would never learn the truth.[106] One would inevitably be surrounded by uncertainty and mistake the false for the true. On the other hand, if you believe your teacher and receive teachings according to his rules, knowledge will quickly follow faith.

95. So likewise it is appropriate to believe the teacher of geometry when he teaches us that a point is something totally indivisible and that a line has length without breadth. But this can never be demonstrated rationally by anyone because if one were to take away the breadth of a line the length would disappear with the breadth. Nevertheless geometry imposes such thought processes and the one who desires to study these figures obeys and trusts readily.

96. Astronomers equally enjoy the confidence of their students. They give the number of the stars, calculating the distances that separate them and calculate how many stades the earth is distant from the visible heavens. And what a difference there is in the various distances they give! Some say that it is four million seven hundred thousand stades; others, less than that; others, much more.[107] In spite of everything, their pupils acquiesce with their teachers and have confidence in their teaching.

FAITH AND KNOWLEDGE OF MYSTERIES

97. And again, there is a great war of words between them concerning the sun. Anaximander and Anaximenes[108] asserted that it was

twenty-seven times larger than the earth. For Anaxagoras[109] it was larger than the Peloponnese, and Heraclitus of Ephesus[110] thought it was a foot in diameter.

98. Who would not rightly laugh at such divergences of view? And the differences of opinion are not concerning an insignificant measure, but are concerned with infinity about which mere words cannot give an adequate idea. For who, in fact, could encompass the whole world with a measure and then, having multiplied it by twenty-seven, contract the measure of the counter and compare this to the measurement of a man's foot?

99. In spite of all this, there are those who assume a position, some on one side, some on the other, and because of their faith they accept one view or the other. Why, then, do you find unobjectionable that faith that is most irrational and reserve your criticisms for our faith which is stripped of all such myths and nonsense, and is intelligently open to divine and rational truths?

100. In addition to what has been said, let us add this consideration. Each person, wishing to learn some craft, goes to a knowledgable teacher, and loves what that teacher has to offer. For instance, the tanner[111] shows his pupil how he must hold the knife and cut the skins, and also how to stitch them and fit them to the shoemaker's last. The apprentice believes what he is told, and never questions his teacher. For the teacher is in possession of the facts and the pupil loves faith, and little by little through faith gets knowledge besides.

101. Likewise the shipbuilder[112] educates the apprentice to his skill. The apprentice learns how to stretch out the plumb line, the right way to move the saw, how to use the adze, gimlet, and auger. The apprentice, when he is instructed in all of these details, puts into practice everything he has been ordered, regards the words of his master as mandatory, and believes that through him he will master the craft.

102. Likewise the physician not only learns the skill but also cures those who are ill. For he knows the language of medicine, whereas the one wrestling with disease does not know this but believes he will get rid of his malady by the art of the physician.

103. Furthermore only those who know how to guide a boat know the art of the pilot, while the sailors believe that, thanks to the pilots, they will come to anchor in the harbors of their choice.

104. Therefore, my friends, you see that faith is a sort of com-

mon denominator for those desirous of learning some art, or for those wanting to learn sailing, or agriculture, or for medical patients.

105. Furthermore, if we wish to establish whether gold is genuine and refined, we do not test it ourselves but entrust this task to one who is knowledgeable in such testing. And the expert, by submitting it either to the touchstone[113] or to fire, establishes whether it is fake or genuine. Similarly, when people are buying precious stones, we do not entrust judgment about such things to ourselves, but rather to those who have acquired this expertise by length of time and by practice.

106. And if we want to buy a silk garment, one decorated and gilded,[114] we turn to an expert in the art of weaving to determine what is a reasonable price for such things. Finally, if one wants to know the weight of certain gold or silver objects or coins, one brings them to a weight specialist who evaluates them, and his decision is accepted unquestionably.

107. Knowledge, then, is not for everyone, but for those who have spent study, time, and experience in its acquisition. Faith, by contrast, is for all those who are eager to learn something. Furthermore it is the basis and foundation of all knowledge. As defined by your philosophers, it is a voluntary assent of the soul, and knowledge is a state that reason cannot shake.

108. And so it is a truly inadmissible absurdity that in all other techniques the masters provide the knowledge and the pupils the faith, whereas in this single matter of divine teachings the order is reversed and knowledge is demanded prior to faith, because for the invisible we especially have need of the eyes of faith.

109. That is why the divine apostle exclaims in such precise terms: *whoever would approach him must believe that he exists and that he rewards those who seek him.*[115] That is why we also, before anything else, propose our teaching on faith to those who come to us and want to learn divine things.

110. With you, also, not everybody knows what the hierophant means.[116] The whole congregation looks on at the enactments, the ones who are called the priests carry out the rites of the ceremonies, but only the hierophant knows the meaning of what takes place, and this he reveals to whomsoever he thinks fit.

111. Some of the initiated know that Priapus[117] was the son of Dionysus and Aphrodite. But why he is named their son, and why such a diminutive creature is depicted with a phallus, erect and huge, only

the hierophant in those vile mysteries knows and those who happen upon their wretched writings.

112. For, naming pleasure Aphrodite and intoxication Dionysus,[118] they called the offspring of both Priapus. For pleasure combined with intoxication causes an erection of the sexual organs.

113. It is the same story with the phallus of Dionysus. (Φαλλός is the name given by the comic poets[119] to the male sex organ, and in Greece the feast of the phallus is called the Phallagogie.[120]) All who participate in the rites adore it and shower kisses upon it, but without knowing why. The aforementioned hierophant knows the history of Osiris and Typhon: how the members of Osiris were cut off by Typhon and scattered on all sides,[121] and how Isis, the sister of Osiris, collected the scattered members with great difficulty, but failed to find the phallus. And because of this she caused an image of it to be made and ordered it to be adored by everybody.[122]

114. It was from Egypt, where he had learned these mysteries, that Orpheus of Odrysae imported them to Greece and organized the feast of Dionysus.[123] Consequently, if the impious and scurrilous nature of these rites is not known to all, but only to the so-called hierophants, it is clearly madness to seek knowledge of the divine and sacred mysteries prior to faith.

115. Or are you not persuaded by Pindar, the lyric poet, who clearly defines it:[124]

Do not divulge the traditional words to each and every one;
There are times when the paths of silence bring most
    persuasion.
The word victorious becomes a spur to strife.

Plato gives the same advice:[125]

Take care, however, lest this teaching ever be disclosed among untrained people, for in my opinion there is in general no doctrine more ridiculous in the eyes of the general public than this, nor, on the other hand, any more wonderful or inspiring to those naturally gifted. Often repeated and constantly attended to for many years, it is at last like gold with great effort freed from all alloy.

And you have heard also in earlier pages what Orpheus said:[126]

> I will speak to those who are allowed to hear. You profane
> ones, close the gates.

116. So, then, let faith take the lead and knowledge will follow. For to those who believe with a pure, simple faith, the Lord provides knowledge, and knowledge added to faith makes perfect the knowledge of truth.

117. Yes, happy and thrice happy are those who possess it. This is what Plato set forth in the *Laws*:[127]

> For him who is to know felicity and happiness must be
> endowed with truth from the first, and live all the longer a
> true man.

118. Because for those who have participated in the truth and have spent a life in accordance with truth heaven is prepared and the abode of the angels. By contrast the one who is bereft of truth and has never been initiated into the all holy and sacred mysteries will be deprived of those blessings and will be delivered up to perpetual punishments.

119. In the *Phaedo* Plato returns to this consideration. He recounts that those who have administered the sacred rites have said:[128]

> He who enters the next world uninitiated and unenlightened shall wallow in the mire, but he who arrives there purified and enlightened shall dwell among the gods.

THE GREEK PHILOSOPHERS AND REVELATION

120. Obey, then, my friends, your own philosophers, who have given you preliminary initiation[129] and have instructed you in advance in our teachings. They truly resemble those singing birds[130] who can imitate the human voice without understanding the meaning of what they say. Very similar are your pagan philosophers who dilate on theological subjects without fully appreciating the truth of what they say.

121. I believe that in a certain sense they are excusable because

they had no benefit of the torch carried by the prophets or of the light of the apostles, having nothing to guide them but human nature alone, the impious error of which destroyed the characters already traced by the hand of God. The Creator has nonetheless renewed some of these traits and has not allowed everything to become evanescent, thus showing His own providence for humankind through His creation.

122. This is a point that is well illustrated by the divine apostle in his discourse at Lystra where, among much else, he says:... *"yet he has not left himself without a witness in doing good—giving you rains from heaven and fruitful seasons, and filling you with food and your hearts with joy."* [131]

123. For the race of Abraham both received the law of God and enjoyed the prophetic grace. For the Guide of the universe acted as a guide to religion to other nations through nature[132] and creation.

124. And just as our great Benefactor sends rain principally on cultivated areas in the interest of human beings, but also by way of bonus and out of sheer generosity also rains on desert regions and in the mountains[133] (and as a result the arable lands produce edible fruits while uncultivated areas produce wildfruits, and sometimes we see fig trees growing on tombs and on walls), so also He donated the gift of knowledge especially to the religious, but also to those not so, just like the rain in desert places and in thickets.

125. Whence it happens that often the uncultivated areas produce something edible and imitate the fruits of the cultivated areas, but it is nonetheless evident that they have not had the prophetic culture, for there is a certain admixture of roughness and bitterness. Those who know the difference harvest what is best and leave the rest alone, just as those who cultivate roses leave the thorns but collect the roses.

126. That too is a law of nature for the bees. For they light on bitter flowers as well as on sweet ones. Then they extract the sweet substance and leave behind what is bitter and from different qualities — bitter and sour, piquant and harsh, and they prepare for humanity the sweetest honey.[134]

THE APOLOGIST'S METHODOLOGY

127. And we, imitating the bees, prepare from your bitter meadows the honey whose sweetness will benefit you. And just as physicians pre-

pare effective remedies from poisonous beasts, even from vipers, they first throw away some parts and boil the rest, and with this they expel many maladies, we also, who have taken in hand the works of your poets, your historians, your philosophers, we first lay on one side what is injurious and manipulate the rest for the knowledge of teaching. We apply to you this remedy that acts as an antidote. And even those whom you regard as our enemies we show you that they champion our teachings and we make you see that even they teach you the faith.

128. In this way, with God's help, we will present to you the rest of our teaching. And you, once you have learned how necessary faith is, will love the silence of the Pythagoreans and will listen to the teaching in silence, accepting what is said with faith. And in this way you will in a short time be able to learn the truth.

Discourse 2

ON THE FIRST PRINCIPLE

1. The natural light from above perceived by the eyes and the artificial light produced here below by human ingenuity reveal to one who has eyes the nature of gold, silver, iron, tin, and all such substances. They are equally capable of discerning different colors and different species of plants and animals. But only those with good sight have access to this power of discernment, for the blind do not profit at all from the rays of the sun.[1] Nor do they see the brightness of its rays.

2. Those are in a similar state who refuse to see the splendor of the light of the intellect, and who are complacent about the darkness of ignorance, like those night birds[2] who very properly take from night the names which have been assigned to them. For night bats and hawk owls flee the light as hostile and seek darkness as a protection.

3. It would obviously be a lapse of good sense to be indignant at such birds, since it is nature that has from the beginning assigned them their individual characteristics. As for human beings, who have voluntarily tied themselves to living in darkness, what kind of indulgence could they reasonably expect, especially now that the divine light has filled with its rays every continent and every island, and has extended itself to the very ends of the earth?

4. Those who had fallen into evil before the Lord's epiphany are excusable in some ways; the Sun of justice[3] had not yet risen; they were living, so to speak, in the darkness of night and had only nature as a torch to show them the way. But when He had risen and, to put it poetically,[4] "in his course had reached mid heaven," what kind of excuse remains for those who are today blind at high noon and who shut their eyes so as not to enjoy the light?

5. It is the evil of smug self-conceit[5] that prevents them from dispersing the mist from their eyes. They think they are more knowl-

45

edgeable than the rest of the world about the truth because they have gone to school to the most illustrious teachers. They are reluctant to acknowledge that sea fish, though they are developed in the briniest waters, must nonetheless be cooked in salt.[6]

6. Nor are they aware that it is by no means the eloquent who are masters of truth. What could be more agreeable than the poetry of Homer, or sweeter than his fine sonorities? And yet while the best of the philosophers (you undoubtedly realize that I mean the son of Aristo, I presume), after pouring myrrh down over Homer's head,[7] crowning him as the women do their pudenda, banished him from the city which he had organized, calling him a teacher of immorality and impiety.

7. Plato says (about the poet) that he urges the young to blaspheme, he fills them with evil ideas about the gods, and he introduces into young minds which are still impressionable ideas that are perverse and destructive. And Plato made many other similar serious charges against the leading poet of the Greeks.[8] That is to say, every writer who has mastered style need not necessarily be regarded as a teacher of truth.

DIVERSITY OF VIEWS AMONG PHILOSOPHERS

8. Now if you bring forward for us your philosophers, realize full well that they too have endured all sorts of error. For they all have not followed the same path, nor have they kept in the footsteps of their precursors, but each has carved out his own line of approach, and thousands of pathways have been constructed. For the ways of falsehood are manifold,[9] as will become patently obvious from what follows.

9. Now Thales,[10] the eldest of the so-called seven sages, maintained that water was the first principle of all things, basing his belief, I think, on Homer:[11]

Oceanus is the father of the gods and Thetis, their mother.

But Anaximander, who succeeded Thales, said that infinity was the first principle.[12] His successor, Anaximenes, and Diogenes of Apollonia,[13] both agreed that air should be named the first principle.

10. Hippasos of Metaponte and Heraclitus of Ephesus both assigned to fire the role of first principle.[14] Empedocles of Agrigentum, however, maintained[15] that there were four elements. For Xenophanes

of Colophon[16] the totality is eternal, and all things come from the earth. And Parmenides, his colleague from Elea,[17] similarly held this opinion and demonstrated the unreliability of the senses, maintaining that this least approximated the truth.

11. Democritus of Abdera said[18] that the universe was infinite and uncreated. For Epicurus the Athenian, son of Neocles,[19] the atoms constituted the first principle of the universe, everything being without beginning and eternal. Metrodorus of Chios, Zeno of Elea, and Diogenes of Smyrna[20] supposed that there were different principles of the universe. Likewise Socrates, son of Sophroniscus, ridiculed them incessantly inasmuch as they maintained very strongly that they knew more than is given to men to know while at the same time they were always at war with one another, devising novel and contradictory opinions, as we know from the *Memorabilia* of Xenophon.

12. Plato has depicted Socrates speaking as follows in the *Phaedo:*[21]

When I was young, Cebes, I had an extraordinary passion for that branch of knowledge which is called natural science. I thought it would be marvelous to know the causes for which each thing comes into being, and stops, and continues to be.

13. After a lengthy development of these ideas he adds:[22]

I will give you a sufficient indication of what I mean. I had understood some things plainly before, in my own and other people's estimation, but now I was so befogged by these speculations that I unlearned even what I had thought I had known.

14. Furthermore, Plato, denouncing the rivalry of the philosophers, writes as follows in the *Theaetetus:*[23]

When you put a question, they pluck from their quiver little oracular aphorisms to let fly at you, and if you try to obtain some account of their meaning, you will be instantly transfixed by another, barbed with some newly forged metaphor. You will never get anywhere with any of them; for that matter they cannot get anywhere with one

another, but they take very good care to leave nothing set-
tled either in discourse or in their own minds. I suppose
they think that would be something stationary, a thing they
will fight against to the last.

[Socrates:] Perhaps, Theodorus, you have seen these gentlemen in the fray and never met them in their peaceable
moments; indeed they are no friends of yours. I dare say
that they keep such matters to be explained at leisure to
their pupils whom they want to make like themselves.
Pupils indeed! My good friend, there is no such thing as a
master or a pupil among them. Each gets his own inspiration wherever he can, and not one of them thinks that
another understands anything.

And, a little further on, he says:[24]

15. But I had almost forgotten, Theodorus, another school
that teaches just the opposite, that reality is one,
Immovable being is the name of the all,[25] and much else
that men like Melissus and Parmenides[26] maintain in opposition to all these people.

16. In the *Sophist* the same complaints are also voiced, not by an
apostle, not even by a prophet, but by the first of the philosophers,
whether one wants to call him Plato, the son of Aristo, or Socrates, the
son of Sophroniscus. For the voice is the voice of Socrates, but the
hand, the hand of Plato.
17. Whichever of the two it is, these are his words:[27]

They each and all seem to treat us as children to whom they
are telling a story. According to one there are three real
things, some of which now carry on a sort of warfare with
one another and then make friends and set about marrying
and begetting and bringing up children. Another tells us
that there are two—moist and dry, or hot and cold—whom
he marries off and makes them set up house together. In
our part of the world, the Eleatic sect, who hark back to
Xenophanes or even earlier,[28] unfold their tale on the
assumption that what we call "all things" are only one thing.

Later, certain muses in Ionia and Sicily perceived that
safety lay rather in combining both accounts and saying
that the real is both many and one and is held together by
enmity and friendship.[29]

And after some further remarks of that kind, he adds:[30]

18. [Stranger]: What we shall see is something like a battle of gods
and giants going on between them over their quarrel about reality.

How so?

One party is trying to draw down everything to earth out of
heaven and the unseen, literally grasping rocks and trees in their
hands.

For they lay hands on everything and strenuously affirm that real
existence only belongs to that which can be handled and offers resistance to the touch. They define reality as the same thing as body.

19. It is neither our Peter nor our Paul who brings these accusations against your philosophers, but Plato, who is most eloquent, and
Socrates, whom the Pythian one once described as the wisest of all
mortals. And they said that the philosophers maintained that only
that which could be handled and which offered resistance to touch
was the real reality, that reality and the body could be defined as the
same thing, and they visualized nothing beyond what was visible.

20. How, then, could one use them as guides to truth, if they supported such serious and glaring errors and uttered such contradictory
opinions and waged such an endless war against one another? Timon
of Phlius, the disciple of Pyrrho, in his tragedy, the *Silloi*, has written
about them. I will recall just a few of his lines:[31]

Wretched men, miserable reproaches, mere bellies, of
what wranglings and conjectures have you fashioned men,

Human windbags, stuffed with empty conceit.

THE DEPENDENCE OF GREECE UPON EGYPT

21. We are not the only ones who said that smug self-sufficiency
is the malady that has blinded you, since long, long ago Timon made
the same complaint against your philosophers:[32]

To know is one thing; but to think that you know when you know nothing is another. There is a great difference, my friend, between truth and mere conjecture.

22. For conjecture admits of many errors, but truth does not tolerate any contradictory teaching. That is why the language of the person making conjectures about truth is one thing, while the appearance under which truth is interpreted is something else. For instance, Anaxagoras of Clazomenae, son of Hegesiboulos, when the philosophers who preceded him had no concept of anything beyond what could be perceived by the senses, was the first to say[33] that intellect presided over the cosmos, and that it facilitated the transition of the elements from disorder to order. Pythagoras, son of Mnesarchus, said[34] that the Monad was the principle of everything. Anaxagoras and Pythagoras were contemporaries.[35]

23. The Pythagorean school continued under the leadership of Theano, wife of Pythagoras,[36] and his sons, Teleuges and Mnesarchus. Teleuges had Empedocles of Agrigentum as one of his students. Anaxagoras himself had Archelaos as a student and Archelaus in turn had the Athenian, Socrates.[37] When both Anaxagoras and Pythagoras went to Egypt[38] they had exchanges with Egyptian and Hebrew sages and shared in their knowledge of ontology.

24. Later, Plato undertook the same journey. Plutarch speaks of this in his *Parallel Lives*.[39] Xenophon, son of Gryllus, also mentions it in his letter that he sent to Aeschines, disciple of Socrates. This is what he wrote:[40]

They dearly loved Egypt and the monstrous wisdom of Pythagoras. Their luxury and lack of fidelity to Socrates was proved by their love of tyranny and the preference of their appetites for a Sicilian table to a regime of austerity.

25. It is about Plato that Xenophon has written these lines, because, being suspicious about the teaching of Socrates, he emulated the prodigious, monstrous wisdom of Pythagoras,[41] and he lived at the court of Dionysius, tyrant of Sicily, enjoying Sicilian luxury.[42] But he said Plato was also enthusiastic about the wisdom of the Egyptians.

26. Consequently, Pythagoras, Anaxagoras, and Plato collected from the Egyptians and the Hebrews some obscure notions on being.

Why, then, do you believe in such men who had no exact knowledge of divine things and you yourselves are unwilling to learn from the sources from which they learned?

27. As to their predecessors, the poets and philosophers, they believed that nothing existed except what was visible to the senses. This has been made clear by Plato in the *Cratylus*:[43]

> I suspect that the sun, moon, earth, stars and heaven, which are still the gods of many barbarians, were the only gods known to the aboriginal Hellenes. Seeing that they were always moving and running, from their running nature they were called gods [θεούς] or runners [θεόντας].[44]

28. Homer and Hesiod were completely ignorant of the creator of the universe. Hesiod, in fact, said[45] that Oceanus and Tethys were sprung from Chaos, that Uranus was sprung from Oceanus and Tethys, and from Uranus were born Heaven and Earth. From these last two were sprung Cronus, Rhea and their brothers, and from Cronus and Rhea, Zeus, Hera, Poseidon, and Pluto.

29. Homer, for his part, says that[46]

> from Oceanus are born the gods and Tethys is their mother

and the one he calls "father of gods and men" he also calls Cronides because he is born from Cronus.[47] Truly they were the slaves of a great error. Nonetheless, Plato, who knew better, recommended acceptance of these mythmakers who spoke without probable or certain proofs.

30. He said elsewhere:[48]

> A poet is a light and winged thing, and holy, and never able to compose until he has become inspired, and is beside himself.

Likewise Orpheus of Odrysae, when he arrived in Egypt, learned in some such way about ontology and said:[49]

> The absolute is unique, and all things are fulfilled by him. He is encircled in them, yet none of mortals sees him. Him

see I not, for round about a cloud has enveloped him; for in all mortals the pupils of the eyes are small, and only flesh and bones grow there.

31. And elsewhere:[50]

Moreover he is established in the great heaven on a golden throne, and his feet stride the earth, and he stretches his right hand to the boundaries of ocean. The base of the mountains trembles inwardly at his wrath; nor is it possible to withstand his mighty purpose. He fills the heavens and accomplishes all things on earth because he is the beginning, the middle, and the end.

32. Nevertheless, having learned these things from the Egyptians, who had come by some elements of the truth in the teachings of the Hebrews, he intermingled some of their error in his theology. He also transmitted the accursed orgies of the feasts of Dionysia and Thesmophoria, and coating, so to speak, the rim of the goblet with honey,[51] he offers this poisonous brew to those who have been deceived.[52]

33. Plato also has done the same thing. In his *Timaeus* he has written truly splendid things on the subject of being. How can one fail to marvel when one hears his words:[53]

What is this which always is, and has no becoming, and what is that which is always becoming and never is? That which is apprehended by intelligence and reason is always in the same state, but that which is conceived by opinion with the help of sensation and without reason is always in a process of becoming, and perishing, and never really is.

34. Further on, he says:[54]

They are all parts of time, and the past and future are created species of time which we unconsciously but wrongly transfer to eternal being, for we say that it "was," or "is," or "will be," but the truth is that "is" alone is properly attributed to it, and that "was" and "will be" are only to be spoken of becoming in time, for they are motions, but that which is immovably the same forever cannot become older or younger by time.

35. Who, then, is so given to fault-finding and so querulous as to be angry at what has been said, and not to bear witness in addition to the truth which they contain. For eternal Being in fact is outside of everything, but becoming admits of all sorts of transformations, so Plato rightly says that it never "is." It is evident that a fetus, when it comes to full term, is no longer a fetus.

36. Plato, then, has good reason for not giving the name "being" to what is becoming, or to what is changeable. In his dialogue with Crito Socrates says that the One is the witness of all things. These are his words:[55]

> We are trying to decide about just and unjust, honorable and dishonorable, good and bad? Ought we to be guided and intimidated by the opinion of the many or by that of the one—assuming that there is someone with expert knowledge? Is it true that we ought to respect and fear this person more than all the rest put together, and that if we do not follow his guidance we shall spoil and mutilate that part of us which, as we used to say, is improved by right conduct and destroyed by wrong?

37. And a few lines further on:[56]

> In that case, my dear fellow, what we ought to consider is not so much what people in general will say about us as how we stand with the expert in right and wrong, the one authority who represents the actual truth.

38. You see, friends, how in these lines Plato and Socrates have expelled the band of false gods and have invited us to show respect for none but the Lord of the universe, teaching that if ever there has been mention of a plurality of gods this was provoked by the deceitful crowd of the Athenians.

39. If, then, after such behavior, Socrates has not escaped the

phial of poison, what would he not have suffered if he had openly denied the countless swarm of gods?[57]

40. Plato has illustrated this well in a letter written to Dionysius; after several other remarks he has added:[58]

> Now about the token that distinguishes between the letters that are seriously intended and those that are not, I suppose you remember my instruction, but nevertheless take notice and give me your close attention. There are many who ask me to write, whom it is not easy to put off openly, so at the beginning of letters that are seriously intended I put God; in other cases, the gods.

41. How could one make one's position clearer? For Plato revealed his view concerning the difference between the two terms when he said just now: I employ the plural in speaking of the deity because of the opinion of the multitude, to protect myself against the false prejudices of my fellow citizens. But when I write seriously and when I can trust the letter-carriers and the recipients I refer to the deity in the singular and put it at the beginning of my discourse.

42. And he has written the following about being:[59]

> But the Father and Maker of all the universe is past finding out, and, even if we found him, to tell of him to all would be impossible.

Now he who has theologized so accurately in these words, elsewhere in his writings, either through popular fear, or because he was truly agnostic, has made mention of many gods and has done great harm to those who happened on his writings.

THE SENIORITY AND SUPERIORITY OF THE HEBREWS

43. If this is so, my friends, why do we search the muddy, earthy stream and not seek instead that fountain which is crystal clear and limpid from which Plato took the beginnings of his theology, and then mingled earthy, murky elements with the pure? Or are we not aware that Moses, the legislator of the Hebrews, is older than[60] your poets, his-

torians, and philosophers? If even to this day you still doubt, and if you suspect us of inventing what I am proposing, let Porphyry be a credible witness for you. He became an adversary of impiety and moved his unrestrained tongue against the God of the universe. Listen to his own words in the work he directed against us [Christians]:[61]

44. Sanchuniathon of Berytus gives[62] a narrative of perfectly accurate facts concerning the Jews, for they are in total conformity with both Jewish place-names and surnames. He had taken his Memoirs from Hierombalos, priest of the god Iao, who dedicated the history to Abembalos, king of Berytus. It was accepted by him and by all those in search of truth. But they lived at a time prior to that of the war of Troy and they were practically contemporary with Moses, as the successors of the kings of Phoenicia prove.

45. On the other hand, Sanchuniathon, which in Phoenician means "the friend of truth," lived in the reign of Semiramis, queen of Assyria. He collected and composed the whole of ancient history from the registers of each city and from the writings of the sanctuaries.[63]

46. From those sources it is easy to deduce the number of years by which Moses predated the Trojans. For if, indeed, Sanchuniathon has narrated the history of the Jews, lived in the time of Semiramis (it is clear that the history he composed is of a period that long predated his own), and if Moses was the legislator of the Jews, Moses is thereby automatically considerably older than Sanchuniathon.

47. But Semiramis preceded the Trojan war by more than a thousand years according to the data of certain chronographers.[64] Now this is not the place to prove that Porphyry knew nothing about chronology; it is enough for me to have shown by how many years Moses predates the Trojan war. Homer and Hesiod lived a long time after that war.[65] Orpheus, the first of the poets, preceded by a generation, and he, with Jason, Peleus, Telamon, Heracles, and the Dioscuri, participated in the expedition to Colchis.[66] The Euneus who sent wine to Troy for the Achaeans was Jason's son.[67]

48. Tlepolemus is the son of Heracles and he was pierced with a javelin by Sarpedon at the battle of Troy.[68] Ajax is the son of Telamon and Achilles the son of Peleus. Castor and Pollux were surnamed the

Dioscuri, and Helen wished to see them from the top of the wall because they were her brothers.[69] When she did not get her wish she wept bitterly because she thought that they were dead.

49. It is not just for the pleasure of hearing my own voice that I have set forth these facts, but out of a desire to show clearly that Orpheus lived a generation before the Trojan war. Linos and Musaios lived around the time of the Trojan war, as did Thamyris and Philammon.[70]

50. If, then, according to Porphyry, Moses predated by more than a thousand years those who were the oldest of the poets—Homer and Hesiod, who lived after them, were in fact a good many years senior to Thales and the other philosophers, just as the school of Thales was senior to later philosophers[71]— why, then, not leave all the others on one side and let us cross over to Moses, the profound source of theology, from whom, to put it in poetical terms,[72] are all rivers and every sea.

MOSES, INSPIRED BY GOD

51. Anaxagoras, Pythagoras, and Plato later drew from that source some small scintillas of the truth.[73] And Socrates, who was a contemporary of Anaxagoras and Archelaus, had learned from them what he taught on the subject of being.[74] The divine Moses was not dependent like them on human reasonings when he wrote his theology. His source was the very voice of Being which he heard in a clear fashion. For when he was about to begin the Law, the Maker of the universe told him to reverence the one God: *For I am the Lord, your God*, Scripture says, *who brought you out of the land of Egypt.*[75]

52. And, after recalling this last proof of his benevolence, he urged him to continue in his service without dividing the service due to him, but rendering it to him alone. Scripture said: *You will not have strange gods before me.* Next he taught clearly that no visible thing bore any resemblance to him, and he absolutely forbade them to fashion any image from visible things as an imitation of him or to regard it as a representation or image of the invisible God:

53. *You shall not make for yourself an idol, whether in the form of anything that is in heaven above, or that is on the earth beneath, or that is in the water under the earth. You shall not bow down to them or worship them; for I the Lord your God am a jealous God, punishing children for the iniquity of*

parents, to the third and the fourth generation of those who reject me.[76] You have heard a voice, he means, but you have not seen a form. Do not, then, fashion any representation of one of whose original traits you are ignorant.

54. In another passage where he confutes the false gods and the error of the Egyptians, he tells them: *Hear, O Israel: The Lord is our God, the Lord alone.*[77]

55. Such is the teaching contained in the works of the great Moses; such is the theology with which he has filled his narrative, his laws, and his prophecies. In the Pentateuch, which he composed, he forbade giving honor to countless beings who passed for gods and who were named gods without really being gods. He laid it down that worship should be offered only to the Creator of the universe. Those too are the lessons that Joshua, the successor of Moses as head of the people and the army, and with him the whole choir of the prophets, inculcated incessantly in their exhortations and their laws.

INTIMATIONS OF THE TRINITY IN THE OLD TESTAMENT

56. But perhaps you will say to me: But neither have you kept unbroken this law. You adore a trinity and not just one god; the Jews, who are nourished on the word of Moses and the prophets, honor one god and reject your trinity.

57. For my part, my dear friends, I feel that you are quite excusable for not knowing the sacred text. As for the Jews I deplore their profound ignorance because, as the prophet says, *who formed you in the womb*[78] and formed in the divine Scripture since their early childhood up until their old age, they remain ignorant of the truth of theology.

58. It is true that they spent a long time in Egypt where they had learned the polytheistic cult of the Egyptians. And so the Lord in His great wisdom did not too clearly reveal to them the teachings concerning the Trinity so as to avoid giving them a pretext for polytheism and falling into the same error as the Egyptians. He did not completely reveal the dogmas of the Trinity to future generations, when he sowed the beginnings of a more perfect theology.

59. That is why, in formulating the Law in the name of a sole being, Scripture indicates the Trinity in an enigmatic fashion. The statement: *Hear, O Israel, the Lord your God is one Lord*[79] both teaches

God's unity and hints at the Trinity, for by using the word "God" once, and the word "Lord" twice it has revealed the number of the Trinity. In adding "is one" it brought forward a helpful teaching to the Jews and indicated the unity of the divine substance.

60. For the substance, and the power, and the will of the holy Trinity is one. Wherefore, when the choirs of the invisible powers chant their hymn to God they repeat three times "Holy, holy, holy is the Lord of hosts"[80] and "Lord" once. Thus, on the one hand, they express the number of persons, and, on the other hand, it is indicated that they hold sovereignty in common.

61. But in these texts the mysteries of the Trinity have been manifested enigmatically whereas other inspired writers give the teaching in more unambiguous terms. The most inspired of them, Moses, in his cosmogony, which he has inserted after the account of human creation, gives these words to the Creator of the universe: *So God created humankind in his image.*[81]

62. Then he added: *Let us make humankind in our image, according to our likeness.*[82] Not that the reality of one differed from that of the other; the nature of the Trinity is one. And that is precisely why Moses reports God as saying: *Let us make the human in our image and likeness.*

63. By adding, *So God created humankind in his image,*[83] he marked the distinction of persons. Likewise, when he gave his instructions to Noah on the use of food and forbade him to consume blood, the God of the universe, according to Moses, expressed Himself in these terms: *Every moving thing that lives shall be food for you; and just as I gave you the green plants, I give you everything. Only, you shall not eat flesh with its life, that is, its blood. For your own lifeblood I will surely require a reckoning: from every animal I will require it and from human beings, each one for the blood of another, I will require a reckoning for human life. Whoever sheds the blood of a human, by a human shall that person's blood be shed; for in his own image God made humankind.*[84]

64. And he did not say, "in my own image," but "*in God's image*" showing once again the difference in persons. And when, according to the same author, men got together in their war against their Maker and built that very great tower, which bore the name of the confusion of tongues, the lawmaker reported that God said: "*Come, let us go down, and confuse their language there, so that they will not understand one another's speech.*"[85]

65. And the phrase *let us go down and confuse* indicates the equal-

ity of peers. He did not in fact say "descend" or "let him descend," expressions that suggest a relation of inferiors to superiors, but rather let us descend and confuse, words which focus properly on the equality of peers. The term *Come* (in the plural) signifies the Son and the Spirit, collaborators in the work of creation.

66. Since, in making humanity, He said: *let us make man in our image and likeness,* it is likely that in using the plural "us" instead of the singular "me" He included as collaborators the Son and the Holy Spirit.

67. Later, when He decided to destroy by lightning and thunderbolt Sodom and the neighboring towns, which were its accomplices in its impious and disorderly conduct, he showed us a duality of Lords; that is what Moses says in reporting the event: *Then the Lord rained on Sodom and Gomorrah sulphur and fire from the Lord out of heaven.*[86]

68. And lest you think that this was the only prophet to speak of the divine Trinity, listen, beloved friends, to the inspired David exclaim: *Therefore let all who are faithful offer prayer to you; at a time of distress, the rush of mighty waters shall not reach them.*[87] And again: *They say, "Appoint a wicked man against him; let an accuser stand on his right."*[88] A little further on, the Lord's Father said to the same Lord: *They beset me with words of hate, and attack me without cause.*[89] And in another Psalm: *But you have saved us from our foes, and have put to confusion those who hate us.*[90]

69. It is the same teaching that is presented to us by Isaiah, the prophet, and also by Jeremiah, Ezekiel, Daniel, Zachary, Micheas, and the whole choir of the prophets. But I feel that it is superfluous to quote them to you since you have not yet made the profession of faith.

70. So I will have recourse to another method of instructing you. I will demonstrate to you that Plato and his successors pillaged certain elements of the theology of these men of God in order to insert them in their own works.

THE TRINITY IN GREEK PHILOSOPHY

71. In his *Letter to Coriscus,* Plato writes among other things as follows:[91]

In your oath, combine a not unenlightened seriousness with the jesting that is kin to earnest, invoking the god who is ruler of all things present and to come, who is rightful

Father of the ruling active principle, whom you shall certainly come to know if you genuinely practice philosophy.

These are Plato's own views, my friends.

72. Among his statements some are praiseworthy and approximate closely to the teachings of the apostles and the prophets, while others are the products of Greek mythology.

73. For when Plato affirms that the beginning and cause of everything is one being, while the father of the cause is a separate being, he has shown quite simply the source of the truth from which he draws to adorn his own discourses. For to call one the chief of the gods, and of things present and to come, he hints at one of two things, either that the philosopher has fallen in with the weakness of ignorance or that he is assuming the role of those who have this disease and is mingling truth with falsehood.

74. Besides, he shows that the so-called gods are not gods by nature. For what person who is not completely demented would call someone a god who is not a god for all time? But Plato has said that these gods were born in time. For he spoke of gods in the present and in the time to come.

75. Now how would one be god if he is not yet born? How would he have a right to this name that is most venerable if he has not yet received being? The divine oracles do not call any of these beings who had a beginning God by nature.

76. In fact, the name "god" is indeterminately applied by them to those to whom the function of judging has been confided and, of course, to those in whom the image of divinity has been preserved as intact as possible; as for the term "God by nature" the practice was to reserve that exclusively for beings who always are and who maintain their identity absolutely. But we will postpone a treatment of this until later. For the present, it will suffice to note that philosophy knows the chief and cause of all things, as well as the father of the cause.

77. Hear further what Plato says in the *Epinomis*:[92]

When we render them their honors, we are not to give the year to one and the month to another, and a part of a month to a third, but leave the rest no time in which each completes his circuit and so does his part to perfect the order which law, divinest of things that are, has set before

our eyes. In the happy man this order first awakens wonder and then the passion to learn all of it that nature possibly can.

Plato says in this passage that it is the Logos who has organized
the universe; he does not say that it is the Father of the Logos.
78. In his *Letter to Dionysius* he puts it like this:[93]

I must state it to you in riddles so that, in case something
happens to the tablet "by land or by sea" he who reads may
not understand. It is like this. It is in relation to the king of
all and on his account that everything exists; and that fact
is the cause of everything that is beautiful. In relation to a
second, the second class of things exist, and in relation to
a third, the third class.

79. You see, then, with what misgivings and fears the philosophers presented the dogmas of truth, and how they announce the
truth in riddles and not in clear terms, viewing with suspicion the error
of the many. It is this fear that Plato has manifested in the *Timaeus*. For
he puts it thus:[94]

80. And let me say this much. I will not now speak of the
first principle of the universe, or principles of all things, or
by whatever terms they are to be called for this reason,
because it is difficult to set forth my opinion according to
the method of discussion that we are at present employing.

81. But Numenius, the Pythagorean, in his work *On the Good*,
expressed this teaching in clearer terms. For he says:[95]

It neither pertains of necessity to the First to fill the role of
the Demiurge but the First God must be regarded as the
Father of the Demiurge.

THE TRINITY IN NEOPLATONISM

82. Plotinus also, who warmly espoused the philosophy of Plato, has composed a book, *On the Three Primary Hypotheses*, in which he speaks as follows:[96]

> What then ought we to say about the Most Perfect? That nothing comes from It except the Greatest after It. But that the greatest intelligence after it is the second, for intelligence sees this.

83. And he continues:[97]

> All being loves and desires what it has engendered, especially when that which engenders and engendered being are alone. But whenever that which is engendered is the best being, it is necessary for it to be united to it so that it be not separated except by altereity. For we say that Intelligence is the image of Being, for it is necessary to speak more clearly.

84. Numerous other statements have been made by Plotinus and by Plutarch, Numenius, and the others who belonged to their school. It is evident that these philosophers who postdate the Incarnation of our Savior have mingled in their own writings many elements borrowed from Christian theology.[98]

85. For instance, Plotinus and Numenius, wishing to explain Plato's thought, said that he had posited three supratemporal and eternal principles, the Good, Intelligence, and the Soul of the Universe, whom we call the Father, and naming Intelligence the one whom we designate under the name of Son and Logos; and naming as Soul that which animates and vivifies the whole, and which the sacred Scriptures call the Holy Spirit.[99]

86. But, as I have said, these teachings have been stolen from the philosophy and theology of the Hebrews. For David, the psalmist, when he struck up the divine melody, being echoed by divine grace, exclaimed, saying: *Therefore let all who are faithful offer prayer to you; at a time of distress, the rush of mighty waters shall not reach them.*[100]

87. What is more, Plutarch and Plotinus both have listened to

the voice of the divine gospels; that is what is clearly shown by Amelius, who had a leading role in the school of Porphyry.[101] This is how he expresses the high regard in which he held the prologue of John's theology:[102]

> 88. It was, then, the Logos, the eternal Logos in whose image everything made has come into existence, as Heraclitus himself thought. And yes, by Zeus, this barbarian thought that the Logos constituted at the rank and dignity of a Principle was with God and was indeed God, through whom all things simply came into being, and who living came into the world and is by nature life and being, and who put himself into a body and, having put on flesh, appeared as man and showed at the same time the grandeur of his nature and that it is certain that, once dead, he becomes god again and that he is god just as he was before coming down in the flesh, and in the flesh of man.

89. That is how one nourished on the elegant diction of Plato and of the other philosophers has expressed his admiration for the theology of the barbarian. He has clearly recognized that the Logos was in the beginning, and that He is God, that He is with God, that He has created all things, that He is the cause and dispenser of life to all things, that for the sake of universal salvation He veiled in flesh the magnificence of His divinity and under a small, dense cloud the nobility that pertained to him from His Father was concealed by Him.

90. In fact, the divinely inspired evangelist, after saying that the Word was made flesh and having shown the immutability of the His divine nature goes on to say: *and the Word was with God,* [103] since, as he explains, however enveloped He was by the flesh he allowed the ineffable and incorruptible brightness of divinity to show through. *And the Word became flesh and lived among us, and we have seen his glory, the glory as of a father's only son, full of grace and truth.*[104] The envelope of the flesh did not completely obscure the rays of his divinity but it was clear, once He donned flesh, that who He was and from whom He shone forth.

91. And if the adversaries of truth so love the truth as to embellish their own writings with short extracts stolen from the truth, and these pieces of truth do not dull their own beauty by being mingled with much falsehood but, like pearls lying in a ditch, continue to be

resplendent, and, as the Gospel teaches, *the light shines in the darkness, and the darkness did not overcome it*,[105] it is easy to see how lovable and desirable the divine teachings are when they are separated from falsehood.

92. For assuredly there is a difference between a pearl lying in the mud and one shining in a diadem. Again, take, for example, the joints of our fingers. When they are not joined together and are independent of one another, they have not the same beauty, nor the same grace, nor the same usefulness as when they are joined together and interdependent, as we see them now.

93. We see, then, that the beauty of truth should be contemplated in its entirety and in its purest state, because, if it continues to shine with varying hues, a mélange of contradictory colors, it is evident that it appears more brilliant when it is separated from the elements that militate against it.

94. One can learn this very clearly if one compares the Greek mythology with the teaching of the apostles and prophets and if one studies the resultant difference.

THE THEOGONIES COMPARED WITH THE GOSPEL TRUTH

Sanchoniathon of Berytus has committed to writing the theology of the Phoenicians, a work that Philo—not the Jewish writer, but Philo of Byblos[106]—has translated into Greek. It is precisely of this Sanchoniathon that Porphyry has produced a great eulogy. Manetho, for his part, has composed[107] in a mythological work the events concerning Isis, Osiris, Apis, Sarapis, and the rest of the Egyptian deities.

95. As to Diodorus of Sicily, he has composed a cosmogony.[108] The *Theogony* of the poet from Ascra is known even to youngsters,[109] whereas Orpheus from Odrysae has educated the Greeks on the rites of initiation of the Egyptians.[110] Cadmus has done the same thing for the Phoenicians.[111] Cornutus, the philosopher, has composed a theology of the Hellenes.[112] Plutarch and Aetios have compiled the opinions of the philosophers.[113] Porphyry has undertaken the same task, adding individual biographies to the opinions of each of the philosophers.[114]

96. My friends, I ask you to compare our teachings with theirs and you will learn, not merely that they are as far apart as the heavens

are from the earth, as the poet says,[115] but as far as so-called Tartarus is from the heavens. I refuse to give an exposition to you of the myths themselves lest I be called garrulous and a babbler. But I will recall some slight few examples in the next discourse which, with God's help, I am going to write after this one so that I may show that what the myths composed about the so-called gods have to say is not only incredible but also stupid and impious.

97. If anyone wants to check out this comparison he will find it in the work of Eusebius of Palestine, entitled *The Preparation for the Gospel.*[116] I for my part will say in brief that the Phoenicians as well as the Greek poets and philosophers have taken the visible elements for gods, or have attributed the name "god" to men who had been public benefactors and who won distinction for their public activities. They had sanctuaries erected to them after their death.[117]

98. We, on the other hand, do not divinize visible things. As for those men who are noteworthy for their virtue, we honor them like superior types while at the same time reserving the honor of adoration for the God of the universe, for His Logos, and for the Holy Spirit.

99. It is the same one whom we call Only Son, Logos, Life, Light, Truth. We have elsewhere had recourse to other expressions to celebrate the divine nature; we are not content to name it in positive terms; we also name it by that which it is not.[118]

100. Not having a beginning, not corruptible, not destructible, not mortal, not finite, not visible, not having form, not having a figure, not having limits or boundaries, not accessible—these descriptions are all of qualities it does not have.

101. Since, then, the divine nature cannot be seen, it is called invisible, unseen. Insofar as it transcends representations by our intelligence it is called inaccessible. It is called infinite because it has no beginning and no end. Because it triumphs over corruption and death it is called incorruptible and immortal.

102. The other expressions similar to these happen to be indicative of qualities not possessed by the divine nature. On the contrary, the words "just," "light," "life," "demiurge," "sovereign," "governor of the universe" and other similar terms are indicative of qualities that the divine nature has and operates, directing creation and being beneficent to human nature.

PLATONIC DEFINITION OF MATTER

103. Likewise He is called "Son" because He was begotten by the Father and He is called Logos because He proceeds from all eternity, without suffering, without dividing the One who engendered Him. We further call Him "the splendor of his glory" because He is coeternal with the One who engendered Him.

104. But do not be disturbed because you have heard it said that the Logos is from the Father and that He is "with the Father." For it is among the strangest paradoxes to put up with Plato, on the one hand, when he says that God is the cause of matter and yet matter is coeternal with God, and that the "ideas" are from God and with God, and, on the other hand, not to believe that the Logos of God and the all-holy Spirit both come from God and are with God.

105. If the philosopher said that matter was of a different nature and of a different kind and of another breed, and yet that it was of God and from God, doubtless you would accept our doctrine as much more sensible and more credible. For we do not say that the Son is of a different nature from the Father, or from the Holy Spirit either, but we proclaim that the Trinity is one in essence.[119]

UNENGENDERED BEING

106. But if anyone is curious about the mode of existence of the Son and of the Holy Spirit, let him begin to tell what is the mode of unengendered Being, that is to say, how it exists without having a cause; for that is a problem that is completely without a solution and that is approachable only by faith, pure and unadulterated.

107. Human nature could readily admit that a thing can come into existence from a cause, either by being born or by being created; but no reason could accept the possibility of a being existing without a cause, unless somehow faith guaranteed it. But if we believe that some being exists that is unengendered, without beginning and without cause, we assuredly believe that the Logos was begotten from this being, and that the Holy Spirit came forth from it.

108. That some among the ancients call the God of the universe unengendered is clear from Timaeus of Locri, who says:[120]

There is one ungenerate Beginning of all things because if he were engendered He would not be the principle, but rather the one who engendered him would be the principle.

For his part, Parmenides of Elea, wishing to say that the world is not engendered, exclaims:[121]

Alone, only born, imperturbable, and unoriginated.

And Plutarch of Chaeronea, in his *Concerning the E at Delphi*, spoke as follows:[122]

What is it, then, which is eternal, unengendered, incorruptible, to which no time brings any change?

109. If, then, we affirm that there exists a being that is not engendered and is without cause—the world, according to Parmenides,[123] the Demiurge of the universe according to Plato, Timaeus of Locri, Plutarch,[124] and ourselves—we can assert with a good measure of probability that from the unengendered being come the Logos and the Holy Spirit, the one as the Word who is engendered from Intelligence, the other as a Spirit that proceeds.

110. But we do not maintain that the Spirit is an exhalation of the breath (for the divine reality is simple, and without form), nor that the Logos is a word that circulates in the air, but we intend to designate the essential Logos and the substantial Spirit. They are contemplated in the Father, and we believe that they are persons; they are at once one and many, one, because of identity of nature, and distinct, because of their different properties and in themselves they are objects of distinct thought.

111. Now all this is impossible to understand exactly if one has not frequent recourse to the divine oracles and if one has not received with the help of divine grace the light of knowledge.

CONCLUSION

112. We must read, then, not only the teachings of the holy apostles but also the oracles of the divine prophets, because in seeing the

harmonious accord between the old and new theologies one will be filled with admiration for the truth and will flee from the atheism of Diagoras of Miletus, Theodore of Cyrene, and Euhemerus of Tegea, those men who, Plutarch tells us, have believed there was no god.[125]

113. One must also avoid the unbecoming idea the Stoics have of the divinity when they say that God is corporeal.[126] We should also repudiate the ambivalent views that Protagoras had about the deity and his words of incredulity. For these are his actual words:[127]

> Concerning the gods I do not know whether they exist or do not exist, or what idea can be formed of them.

114. One will likewise avoid the errors of the other mythmakers. As to Plato and those like him, one will be amazed at discovering how many borrowings they have made from the sacred Scriptures and how many falsehoods they have intermingled with Scriptures. But all the false accretions one will scrape off and throw away like so much rubbish, and drive out from the regions of the soul. And, seeing the damning evidence of plagiarism, one will believe Numenius the Pythagorean saying:[128]

> Who is Plato except a Moses speaking Attic?

115. By these words Numenius has shown us clearly that whatever Plato has expressed in religious terms he has plagiarized from the theology of Moses.

116. But now is the time, my friends, to get on the tracks of truth in our investigations. And like those searching for metals or digging for gold or silver in the earth, whenever they find small seams they follow them and investigate their every vein and never stop their excavations until they find an abundance of gold from which the seams consist. So too, after hearing the words of Anaxagoras, Pythagoras, Plato, yes, and Numenius, Plutarch, Plotinus, and the others, you should seek the source from which these have taken, even drawn off whatever small quantities of the divine streams and embellished with them their own writings.

117. You should leave aside their paltry contributions and proceed rather to the depths of divine wisdom.[129] Recognize who is the Creator and what is creation, and what is the dignity of invisible crea-

tures and what the worth of visible creatures. Once you have come to that recognition, you will no longer divide the homage due to God among a crowd of deities. You will rather adore Him who is always Being, truly Being, and who, out of sheer generosity, has granted being to beings. Then you will be transformed from enemies and adversaries into members of our household and our friends and, like intimate friends, you will enjoy great freedom of speech. And you who today are in need of guides will become yourselves guides for those wandering and direct them to the goal of truth.

Discourse 3

ON ANGELS, SO-CALLED GODS, AND MALEFICENT DEMONS

The Origin of Polytheism

1. We are in the habit of admiring well-constituted bodies that are free from defects and that preserve intact and unblemished the total harmony which they have received from nature. Those that are different either by defect or excess, however, we are accustomed to call deformed.

2. And, while condemning anarchy and polyarchy as pernicious, we admire monarchy,[1] and we approve the sentiment of Homer who introduces this law:[2]

> It is not good that many govern;
> let there be one chief, one king.

3. I do not say this for the sake of idle chatter but in an attempt to enunciate divine matters in human terms, and to beg you, my friends, to preserve on this point this rule: regard as "sound" those bodies which have embraced the true theology—what was given by nature at the beginning of time and confirmed later by the divine oracles—but label as "deformed," on the other hand, not merely those that deny the existence of God but also those that have promoted a multiplicity of gods and that have placed the Creator and His creation on the same footing.

4. The only atheists are not just Diagoras of Miletus,[3] Theodore of Cyrene,[4] Euhemeros of Tegea,[5] and their devotees, who absolutely deny the existence of gods, as we learn from Plutarch,[6] but also Homer, Hesiod,[7] and the schools of philosophers who in their fables

70

have invented hosts of gods and presented them as totally enslaved to human passions.

5. There are those too who shamelessly deify the most disgraceful passions, and those very passions that they themselves condemn and warn their children to be closely on guard against, to these have they assigned honor as gods.

PAGAN FORMS OF DIVINATION

1. Worshiping Sun, Moon, and Stars as Gods

6. Diodorus of Sicily tells us that the Egyptians were the first to assign the name of gods to the sun and moon.[8] They called the sun Osiris and the moon Isis.[9] He states further that the Phoenicians, having learned this from them, rival the Egyptians in the manufacture of statues.[10]

7. Plato also, in the *Cratylus*, similarly recognized that the Greeks were the first to introduce this error concerning the so-called gods. He states it thus:[11]

> I suspect that the sun, moon, earth, stars, and heaven, which are still the gods of many barbarians, were the only gods known to the aboriginal Hellenes. Seeing that they were always moving and running, from their running nature they were called gods or runners (θεούς, θεόντας).[12]

8. In fact, the all-wise Demiurge of the universe, lacking nothing at all in any way and having absolutely no need of anything,[13] visible or invisible, has created the heavens, earth, sun, moon, and other sensible, visible things for man's benefit; but even in the display of His munificence, He did not stop at mere necessities but made available to humans through these things all sorts of blessings for their greater enjoyment.

9. For instance, the sun, when it rises and starts the day[14] wakens humankind to labor, while the moon, when the great luminary goes to rest, tempers the depths of darkness without interfering by excess of light with those who wish to sleep, while at the same time affording sufficient brightness for those who wish to go on a trip, or do some other task.[15] And when it vanishes, the stars take its place.

10. That is how the Demiurge, as I have said, exercises His care for mortals. But those who have received the greatest gifts and who should be guided by these things to hymn as the great Benefactor the One who has created and orchestrated these things, have in fact left Him without honor and, in the words of the apostle, *because they exchanged the truth about God for a lie and worshipped and served the creature rather than the Creator*,[16] and the grandeur and splendor of His gifts afford them an occasion for ingratitude, since they have failed to recognize the Author of these gifts and have given to the gifts the adoration that belongs to God.

11. In spite of this, the Demiurge who, in His great wisdom, foresaw this error of human beings, has allocated certain weaknesses to the elements[17] in order that their beauty and grandeur would prepare people to admire the Creator, and their attendant defects would prevent them from eliciting divine adoration.

12. For instance, small clouds conceal the sun in all its brightness and the moon. Mist and fog tend to blunt the rays of both, and sometimes even at high noon, when there is no cloud or mist or shade, the light of the sun disappears. The same phenomenon occurs with the moon during the night.

13. But there is yet another thing that the Creator has imagined in His wisdom. Since the heat of the sun in moderation is beneficial to bodies, to seeds and to plants, inasmuch as it develops and nourishes bodies and brings fruits to maturity, sometimes the Lord makes the sun intensify its rays, oppress the bodies of humans and animals, and destroy the offshoots of plants and seeds, to keep us from thinking that the sun is the cause of life, but to lead us instead to believe that it is an instrument of the divine will.[18]

14. He has shown us also that air is an auxiliary of life. Not just every human being, but every animal, lives by breathing and tempers its native heat by the air that it absorbs. Sometimes, however, the air is also a conductor of pestilential maladies that destroy bodies that are customarily nourished by air when it is evenly balanced.[19]

15. Likewise the earth, "source of life," "benefactor of wealth," and "common fountain of all," is the work of the Demiurge; but so that, despite seeing all these things, we be not led astray like cattle and deify the earth as the source of blessings, He has assigned to the earth certain shortcomings and defects.[20] For instance, too much heat or cold is damaging to the earth and when rainfall exceeds what is nec-

essary it dissolves and destroys plants and seeds; again, if the clouds at the appropriate time do not discharge their burden the earth becomes parched and sterile. But often when showers come at the wrong time they cause a rot, and in this way the earth is forced to produce insects and wild beasts for the destruction of humankind.

16. Accordingly, when people perceive this defect, those of sound mind are reluctant to adore the earth as god, but rather are guided by the earth and what grows in it toward its Creator and its products and are conducted to the invisible by what is visible. That is why one of our writers has said wisely and fittingly: *For from the greatness and beauty of created things comes a corresponding perception of their Creator.*[21] Created objects are not the same as the Creator, nor is their grandeur the same as His. They can be seen and touched and the senses can perceive certain deficiencies. But the Creator cannot be touched, or seen, or affected in any way, or altered, and He does not admit of circumscription like His creations.

17. So it is with justice that the expression "by analogy" is added to this text. When we view the coverings of the heavens and the extent of the earth and the vastness of the seas and the brightness of the sun and the sheen of the moon and everything else that is visible, we do not equate them with the Creator, but we say that He is greater than His creations in His infinite greatness and beauty.

18. Rightly, then, did that wise man say: *For from the greatness and beauty of created things comes a corresponding perception of their Creator.* This sentiment is corroborated by the divine apostle when He says: For since the creation of the world his invisible attributes are clearly seen—His everlasting power also and His divinity—being understood through the things that are made.

19. It is, then, through visible phenomena that we are able to visualize their invisible Creator. And, just as when we see a coffer or a chair, we do not call these creations by the name of creator, but rather we call them the products of their creator, and when we see a boat very skillfully constructed, we not only marvel at it, but we also praise its shipwright, especially in his absence; likewise if we see a gold chain or any other necklace that has been well crafted, we bring forth the praises of the goldsmith.[22] In the same way when we set eyes on the creation we indeed rejoice at its size and its beauty and its gushing utility, but leaving these considerations behind, our mind runs forward to the One who has fashioned this so wisely.

20. It has been well said by the divine apostle: *Ever since the creation of the world his eternal power and divine nature, invisible though they are, have been understood and seen through the things he has made.*[23] He goes on to say that those people are unpardonable who contemplate His creation and who, instead of admiring the Creator, attribute instead divine majesty to His creation.

21. And so he rightly adds: *Ever since the creation of the world his eternal power and divine nature, invisible though they are, have been understood and seen through the things he has made. So they are without excuse; for though they knew God, they did not honour him as God or give thanks to him, but they became futile in their thinking, and their senseless minds were darkened.*[24] And magnifying the charge, he introduced their smug self-sufficiency: *Claiming to be wise, they became fools; and they exchanged the glory of the immortal God for images resembling a mortal human being or birds or four-footed animals or reptiles.*[25]

22. In fact, all the while they declared God incorruptible, they have been fabricating perishable images, for they have no real knowledge of an immortal soul and have rendered to it the worship due to God. And the silliness of this folly was not enough impiety for them, but they also prepared representations of winged creatures, four-footed beasts, and reptiles, and called these gods. And those creatures which, if alive, they would kill as poisonous and destructive, they named as savior gods in the form of images.

23. But let us return to the point from which we made our digression, namely, that as their first deities the Phoenicians, the Egyptians, and even the Greeks believed in the sun, moon, the earth, the stars, and the other elements. That is what we learn from the teaching of Plato, Diodorus of Sicily, and Plutarch of Chaeronea.[26]

2. Public Figures as Gods

24. Somewhat later those who had done some famous deed, either a successful campaign in war, some innovation in agriculture, or a breakthrough in the medical cure of bodily complaints, were deified and had temples erected in their honor.

25. So it is that, according to Sanchuniathon,[27] Cronus was a man, Rhea, his wife, was a woman, and their children were Zeus and Hera. After they had completed some successful undertaking and had come to the end of their human lives the Phoenicians judged them

worthy of divine honors. They were proclaimed gods and honored with altars, sacrifices, and annual banquets.

26. As for Heracles,[28] it was on account of his nobility and valor that the Greeks deified him, and Asclepius,[29] as an inventor in medical science, was named a god after his death. For the same reason, too, the Egyptians deemed Apis[30] worthy of the title of divinity.

27. Now the Greeks say that Heracles burned himself to death because of a plot devised by Deianira and so ended his life,[31] and as for Asclepius, they say that he was a man and that through his knowledge of medicine he cured many mortals from various diseases, but then he was put to death, smitten by the thunderbolt of Zeus.[32]

28. These are the facts that, among other things, Diodorus of Sicily[33] has recounted in Book 4 of his *Libraries.* Nevertheless the Greeks, who knew all this, gave the name gods to Heracles and Asclepius, and with them the children of Tyndareus, Castor and Pollux, whom they called the Dioscuri, even though they were not very old and had sailed with the Argonauts.[34]

29. In fact, the Dioscuri, Heracles, and with them Orpheus, who played his lyre and charmed with its strains the fish, forcing them to follow its harmonious echo,[35] constituted the crew of the Argonauts. That they were senior by one generation to the Trojans we have shown in our previous discourse.

30. And, in that Dionysus was the first to grow the vine and to draw off its fruit and show the utility of wine, they joined him to the ranks of the other gods.[36] And Aphrodite they named a goddess although she did not initiate any benefaction, but was a teacher of immorality, for they say that she was a very low-down type and was the mistress and lover of Cinyrus.[37]

31. And this is not to be wondered at. For some assigned the name of deity to poisonous reptiles and in a leisurely way deprived women of their honor. And Ganymede, as the poets relate,

the gods snatched up to be a winepourer.[38]

And they led off Helen to heaven, after her much-publicized and egregious adultery, when she separated from Menelaos, as Euripides relates the story.[39]

32. Therefore the Greeks deified, not just those who did some good, but also the most immoral men and women. And the Romans,

when they learned these things from them, thought fit to make their emperors gods after they reached the end of life, and not only those emperors who had ruled lawfully and shown some concern for justice, but even those who had directed the empire tyrannically, unjustly, and unlawfully.

33. Nero, having gone unnoticed as he insatiably performed every kind of immorality and illegality, and Domitian and Commodus, and other assassins and most lustful characters were inscribed in the list of their gods.[40] That is the second form of divinization that men have conjured up.

3. The Apotheosis of Mythical Figures

34. There is a third type that is based on their faith in the narratives of the poets. Plato also, in the *Timaeus*, elicits belief in these narratives:[41]

> To know or to tell the origin of the other divinities is beyond us, and we must accept the traditions of the men of old time who affirm themselves to be the offspring of the gods—that is what they say and they must have known their own ancestors. How can we doubt the word of the children of the gods? Although they give no probable or certain proofs, still, as they declare they are speaking of what took place in their own family, we must conform to custom and believe them.

35. Next, he brings Hesiod on the scene, naming Chaos, Oceanus, Tethys, and Uranus and Earth, with their children Cronus, Rhea, Iapetos, and others. Next, there are the descendants of Cronus and Rhea: Zeus, Hera, Poseidon, and Pluto.[42]

36. And, without blushing, the philosopher wants to make us believe in these quacks of history who present to us as gods roués, murderers of fathers and of infants. Cronus, for instance, cut off the testicles of his father, Uranus, and devoured the sons who were born to him.[43] Zeus dethroned his father, Cronus, bound him in Tartarus, and proved himself to be a tyrant given to debauchery and excess.

37. Not satisfied with marrying his sister, he also married his mother and daughter, and had illicit unions with countless others, goddesses and mortals.[44] Plato knew all this well,[45] yet he wanted us to

believe the poets, even if they did not have probable or certain proofs, but simply because of conformity to usage.

38. It is quite clear, then, that he also accepted this error out of deference to the mass of the Athenians. And the proof that this is so is given in his own words in the *Republic*:[46]

> There is first of all, said I, the greatest lie about the things of greatest concern, which was no pretty invention of him who told how Uranus did what Hesiod says he did to Cronus, and how Cronus in turn took his revenge, and then there are the doings and sufferings of Cronus at the hands of his son. Even if they were true I should not think they ought to be thus told lightly to thoughtless young persons. But the best way would be to bury them in silence, and if there were some necessity for relating them, then only to an audience admitted under pledge of secrecy.

39. A little later he goes on to say:[47]

> Yes, and they are not to be told, Adimantus, in our city, nor is it to be said in the hearing of a young man that in doing the utmost wrong he would do nothing to surprise anyone, nor again in punishing his father's wrongdoings to the limit, but he would only be following the example of the first and greatest of the gods.

> 40. Neither must we admit at all, said I, that gods war with gods and plot against one another and contend—for it is not true either—if we wish our future guardians to deem nothing more shameful than lightly to fall out with one another. Still less must we make battles of gods and giants the subject for them of stories and embroideries and other enmities many and manifold of gods and heroes toward their kith and kin.

41. Then, after prescribing by law the kind of teaching that should be given to the young, Plato makes this further observation:[48]

But Hera's fetters installed by her son, and the hurling out
of heaven of Hephaestus by his father when he was trying to
save his mother from a beating, and the battles of the gods
in Homer's verse are things that we must not admit into our
city either wrought in allegory or not wrought in allegory.

42. I know that, even for those who are completely uninitiated
into these matters, all this is completely at variance with what Plato
wrote in the Timaeus. For in that work, without the slightest ambivalence or ambiguity, he insisted that the poets must be believed even
when they speak without probable or certain proofs; here, by contrast,
he unrestrainedly lambastes them as fabricators of falsehoods and
blasphemies.

43. Surely that is why he has given an allegorical meaning to the
names of the gods, attempting to cast a shadow over the disgraceful
aspect of the myths. The Cratylus is full of this kind of argument. In
this dialogue, in fact, he named Cronus at one time Koros because he
considered him as the product of Intelligence; at another time,
Chronos (Time); he called the fluid element, Rhea, and air, Hera,
because, according to him, when the nominative of Rhea is used constantly, it comes to be pronounced "air" instead of "Hera."

44. He calls the liquid element Poseidon because, according to
him, he bound and chained the feet of voyagers to stop them in their
tracks. With Orpheus and other writers he called the earth Demeter
because, according to him, the earth is the mother and nourisher of
everything living on the earth.[49] The Egyptians, for their part, say Isis
and Osiris are the sun and moon, Zeus the spirit that penetrates
through everything, Hephaestus is fire, Demeter the earth, and
Ocean the liquid element. That is what Manetho and Diodorus say.[50]

45. They have given the name Hestia to the power that rules
over the nether regions, and they have named the goddess of the
rocks and mountains Rhea. Demeter is the one who rules the plains,
Dionysus is the god of vegetation. As for the moon, deriving it from
σέλας light, they call it Artemis, like Air-temis, which means going
through, and clearing, the air.

46. That is why the Egyptians cultivated Apis, by which I mean the
cow, and Mnevis as the sun.[51] Likewise it is through a sense of delicacy
that some of the philosophers have transformed into allegories the legends of the poets. But the Romans have never accepted this mythology.

A Credible Witness

47. Dionysius of Halicarnassus, who has written of the Romans in his *Roman Antiquities*, says:[52]

> Among the Romans there is no tradition of Uranus muti-lated by his children, nor of Cronus suspected an attack against him on their part, nor of Zeus, who ended the dominion of his father, Cronus, and locked his own father up in the prison of Tartarus.

As for the other mythologies and initiations into the mysteries, Dionysius adds that these too have been likewise rejected by the Romans.

4. Deification of the Passions and Allegorical Meaning

48. We have treated of the third form of deification imagined by the Greeks. In fact there is even a fourth form, which is the lowest type of folly. It is, in fact, that part of the soul that they call "sensible" and "irrational" that they deify—that very part which they tell people should be submitted to reason.

49. They call sexual desire Aphrodite and Eros, and they name anger Ares, and drunkenness Dionysus. Theft is called Hermes, and reason, Athena. The crafts are called Hephaestus because they employ fire as their collaborator.[53] And they are not ashamed, while repudiating intemperance and punishing those who practice it, to honor sex as a god.

50. They invoke law to punish adulterers and adulteresses and even put to death those who plunder the marriage beds of others; they go as far as impaling and crucifying assassins, yet they assign the title of heavenly gods to sexual desire, anger, and intoxication, which are the causes of these crimes, yet are treated with divine worship. They enact all these laws to curb the passions but the passions them-selves are prescribed by law to be honored, and in other statements they show deference to virtue, but in these religious injunctions they expel such considerations as superfluous.

51. But if, according to their description, concupiscence is truly a god, then the one who does not succumb to it is truly an atheist.

Similarly, if drunkenness and anger are likewise gods, then those who are abstemious and mild-mannered are complete atheists. Virtue, then, must be avoided as being opposed to the gods, and intemperance should be espoused in that it is named as deity.

52. But this is more preposterous and pernicious than the myths of the poets. For in fleeing the smoke, as the proverb has it, they have fallen into the fire itself. Such is the error of falsehood. And if one escapes by that route he will fall into one more dangerous. Such, then, is the fourth type of deification.[54]

53. In any case, Antisthenes, the disciple of Socrates and teacher of Diogenes, in giving the highest rating to temperance and in discounting pleasure, is said to have made the following pronouncement about Aphrodite:[55]

> I would pierce Aphrodite with an arrow if I captured her,
> because she has corrupted so many of our fine good women
>
> And he called love a natural vice, while the poor devils who
> are its victims call their disease a god! In this fashion he
> preferred to be demented than to be delighted.

54. As for their disagreement on the allegorical meaning, one can discern this accurately in reading the philosophers. Plato, for example, has named air "Hera,"[56] but Plutarch of Chaeronea called earth "Hera," and forgetfulness "Leto," or rather night, in the course of which the spirit is delivered, so to speak, from a form of forgetfulness.[57] Orpheus, in turn, says:[58]

> Earth, universal mother, Demeter, who dispenses wealth.

55. And that they mutually overthrow the theology of their rivals, Plato makes clear in the *Epinomis* in these terms:[59]

> Since my predecessors have given such a bad account of
> the generation of gods and living beings, my first task, I
> presume, is to sketch out a better account in accordance
> with my previous discourse and to embody the points
> which I tried to make against unbelievers when I argued
> that there are gods, that their care extends to all things

great and small, and that no entreaties can win them to depart from the path of justice.

56. With regard to men who have been deified, Plutarch has this to say in his work *On the Disappearance of Oracles*:[60]

> The exploits of the Giants and Titans celebrated among the Greeks, the many lawless deeds, the stubborn resistance of Python against Apollo, the flights of Dionysus, and the wanderings of Demeter do not fall at all short of the exploits of Osiris and Typhon, and other exploits which anyone may hear freely repeated in traditional story.

57. The same author has this further to say:[61]

> In fact, I learn that the Solymi, who live next to the Lycians, paid especial honor to Cronus. But when he had slain their rulers, Arsalus, Aryus, and Tosobius, he fled away from that place to some place or other, where they cannot say; and then he ceases to be regarded, but Arsalus and those connected with him are called the "stern gods," and the Lycians employ their names in invoking curses both in public and in private.

58. The Egyptians, however, as Porphyry tells us in his *Letter to Anebo the Egyptian*,[62] adored a man who lived in the town of Annabis; they offered sacrifices to him on the altars, and finally, at the appropriate times, they brought him his own food.

5. The Cult of Maleficent Demons

59. But, as if this fourth aberration of theirs were not enough for them, they devised a fifth one. They have made gods out of the most malevolent demons and, trained by them in the art of magical incantations,[63] have honored them by rites of initiation and sacrifices. Porphyry has given a clear exposition of this in his work, *On the Philosophy from Oracles*.

60. I will cite his actual words:[64]

> Through the intervention of these hostile demons all the practices of sorcery are accomplished. They are in fact and

this is true especially of the power that presides over them, venerated by the criminal practitioners of sorcery. They are resourceful at striking the imagination of all and adept at deception through their wonder-working. Thanks to their intervention, unfortunate victims prepare malicious brews and love-potions. All forms of intemperance and all hope of possessing wealth and glory come from these, especially mystification. They wish to be gods and the power that rules them is ambitious to be the Supreme Deity. These are they who take pleasure in libations and the odor of meat sacrifices[65] on which both the pneumatic and somatic parts of their being are nourished.

61. It seems opportune to me to compare these words of Porphyry with the descriptions of the Homeric gods: these latter also consider the libations and savor of sacrifices as the natural portion of the gods. Accordingly it is obvious that the so-called gods of the poet [Homer] are named by Porphyry wicked demons. For Homer maintains about his gods, on the one hand, and Porphyry about his demons, on the other, that they love the libations and savor of sacrifices.

62. Now we must investigate the nature of this power that reigns over the maleficent demons and of which Porphyry treats when he says it falsely attributed to itself the title of Supreme Deity. But I do not have to go to the trouble of investigating since, in the same work, Porphyry continues:[66]

We suspect it is not by accident that the maleficent demons are subject to Serapis; we do not let ourselves be guided merely by pointers, but by the fact that expiatory and pro-pitiatory sacrifices are offered to Pluto, as we have pointed out in our first chapter. But Serapis is identified with Pluto, and that is the chief reason why he is chief of the demons.

63. He adds elsewhere:[67]

It is these probably that Serapis rules over; they have a dog with three heads as their symbol, that is the maleficent demon that resides in the three elements, water, earth, and air, whom god keeps in check, keeping them under thumb. And Hecate rules over them, as containing them in threefold elements.

64. It is neither Moses, the legislator, nor Peter, Paul, and John, the heralds of virtue, who have written thus against the demons, but Porphyry, the adversary of truth. He has named Pluto and Hecate as the leaders of the evil demons and has said that Pluto falsely arrogated to himself the title of god.

65. This prodigy is strangely similar to the problem of the valorous Samson: "*Out of the eater came something to eat. Out of the strong came something sweet.*"[68] These words against lying have been delivered by the advocate of lying. In spite of himself, the accuser of truth has been seen as the defender of truth. He who has forced the tongue of Balaam[69] the prophet to bring forth a blessing when it wished to utter a curse, he has also forced the tongue of this one (i.e., Porphyry) warring against truth to war unwillingly also against falsehood.

66. And that is not the only place in his works in which he has so expressed himself. In his *Letter to Anebo the Egyptian*, he has recorded similar sentiments. This is how he speaks of the so-called gods who in fact are really wicked demons:[70]

It is very disquieting how those who are invoked as better give orders as worse: They advocate that it is right to inflict punishment on a slave who does wrong; but they themselves when ordered to do unjust acts perform them. They do not listen to the appeal of one who is unclean because of sexual excesses, yet they themselves do not shrink from leading anyone they meet into unlawful sexual activity. They give orders that the priest interpreters must abstain from eating flesh meat lest they be defiled by the vapors of the bodies, but they themselves are especially ensnared by the vapors of sacrifices. Finally, the initiate is forbidden to touch a carcass, but it is through the corpses of living creatures that the gods are invoked in the evocations of the gods.

67. And much more unreasonable than the above is the fact that one should be at the mercy of any chance passer-by, hurling threats, not against a demon (if that indeed were possible), nor against the

soul of one dead, but against King Sun himself, or the moon, or some other heavenly body, lying so that they may tell the truth. For to say that he will storm heaven, and reveal the secrets of Isis, and show what is forbidden in Abydos, and bring the Egyptian boat to a halt, and scatter the limbs of Osiris for Typho,[71] what an excess of stupidity does not this show in the one threatening what he neither knows nor is able to accomplish, and what cowardice in those who fear such an empty threat and such figments of utterly childish folly.

68. Yet Chaeremon, the sacred scribe, writes that in Egypt these things are frequently respected and he says that these formulae and others of the same kind have a powerful coercive force. After several other remarks he says the following:[72]

> Concerning happiness they have nothing reliable or guaranteed. Consequently it was not about the gods nor about good demons, but about that aberration, of which we spoke.

69. Who, then, of those who have been educated in divine matters and who despise this error could refute more clearly the error concerning the so-called deities? For this adversary of the truth explicitly says that these are not gods nor good demons but rather masters of falsehood and fathers of immorality.

70. In the *Timaeus* Plato denies them an immortal nature since the creator says to them, in his words:[73]

> Athenians, you are not altogether immortal and indissoluble, but you shall certainly not be dissolved in my will.

Nevertheless, it seems to be quite the opposite for Homer, because he constantly gives them the name of immortals:[74]

> ...who eat no food, who drink no tawny wine, and thereby being bloodless have the name of being immortal.

Vanity of Idols Denounced by the Philosophers

71. Such was the controversy among the poets and philosophers concerning those so-called gods who are not really gods. For them

they have built temples, and set up altars, and honored them with sacrifices, and fashioning some shapes and likenesses from wood, stone, and other materials, they have called these handmade idols gods and have dignified with the name of deities these creations of the workshops of Pheidias, Polycleitus, and Praxiteles.[75]

72. In refutation of this error Xenophanes of Colophon speaks as follows:[76]

> But mortals consider that the gods are born
> and that they have equal perception and voice and form.

And again:[77]

> But if cattle and lions [and horses] had hands to inscribe
> with hands and perform works like men, horses would
> have fashioned their ideas like horses, and oxen like oxen,
> and they would have designed the bodies of the gods like
> their own.

73. Then,[78] more clearly satirizing the deceit, he refutes the falsehood from the color of the idols. For he said that Ethiopians made the images of their own gods black and snub-nosed, similar to their own nature, and that the Thracians made them tawny and red, and that the Medes and Persians likewise made their gods in their own likeness, and the Egyptians formed them like themselves.

74. Reviewing such considerations, Zeno of Citium in his book On the Republic[79] says not to build temples or sculpt statues because, in his view, none of these art objects is worthy of the gods. Plato, for his part, has not absolutely forbidden their construction because he apparently dreaded the friendship cup of the Athenians, suspecting the hemlock offered to Socrates.[80]

SCRIPTURE PROSCRIBES STATUARY

75. He jokes nevertheless at most aspects of the craft of image-making, saying:[81]

> No man shall reconsecrate what is dedicated already. In
> other societies you will find gold and silver in temples as

well as in private houses, but they are possessions which breed ill will against their owner. Ivory, a body that soul has forsaken, is no clean offering; bronze and iron are tools of battle. But any man at his pleasure may dedicate in our public temples an image of wood.

76. It was because he feared the Athenian people that he did not prohibit the making of images outright. He said bronze and iron were tools of battle, not matter for images of the gods. He ordered that only wood and stone should be used in fashioning them, realizing, I presume, that the material was cheap and sufficient to persuade the viewers not to regard it as divine, and not to worship what was cheap and inexpensive.

77. Elsewhere the god of the universe, through the mouth of the prophet, brings the same accusation against those who craft these statues as well as those who worship them. Scripture says: *As a gift one chooses mulberry wood—wood that will not rot—then seeks out a skilled artisan to set up an image that will not topple.*[82] He not only takes away the superfluous parts of the wood, reproduces the image of the human form, and sculpts with great care each individual member, but he also takes the greatest care with its sitting or standing position, and he busies himself about its stability with underprops and nails, and this product that is the joint contribution of timber and craftsmanship gets the name of god.

78. The half of this material, says the prophet, he has burned in the fire. And on its embers he has boiled his meat. He has eaten his meat and said: "What a pleasure it is for me to be warm and to have seen the light of the fire." Of what remained he made a god, his idol, he adored it, and he prayed to it as follows: "*Save me, for you are my god!*"[83] After that he clearly made fun of their folly in adding: *He feeds on ashes; a deluded mind has led him astray, and he cannot save himself or say, "Is not this thing in my right hand a fraud?"*[84]

79. For my part, I am amazed at the stupidity of the Hellenizers[85] of today. For, resenting the fact that the world is healthy and rid of the ancient error, they say what the poets have told us about the gods is false, but they do not blush to be accused for their own conduct; for they worship the idols that are fashioned in accordance with the myths. The posture of Aphrodite, for instance, is more disgraceful than that of any call girl standing in a brothel.[86]

80. Who has ever seen a prostitute nude in the agora, without tunic or girdle? Yet the teacher of these women, the sculptors and the makers of statues, represent them completely nude, without even the cover of an undershirt. Likewise Europa[87] sits on the bull, and she is depicted by the artists completely nude, and similarly by the sculptors. And Dionysus also, lithesome and effeminate, is depicted by the artists as completely nude.[88]

81. Both Pan and the Satyrs they construct in a pose outstretched and mounting, very similar to horses and donkeys.[89] Zeus[90] also they represent in the form of an eagle making an attack on Ganymede, or having intercourse in the form of a swan with Leda,[91] or, like a shower of rain, being carried into the bosom of Danae.[92] And for all the rest likewise, the makers of statues take their shapes from the indications of the poets.

82. If, then, you say that the poets have compiled false mythologies why do you allow the makers of statues, the sculptors and the painters, to reinforce the falsehood with their artistic creations? And why do you pay such reverence to the statues they fashion?

83. For if your accusations against the poets were really well founded, then their poems should be burned and a law should forbid the artists, under pain of death, ever to construct images of this kind in any way; anybody violating the law in the slightest detail should be put to death.

84. But none of these things have been done by any of you up to now. In fact, you have done quite the opposite as can be seen: your admiration for the poets and their compositions, your excessive adulation of the sculptors, the makers of statues, and painters, and of their creations; your genuflections before the idols who are condemned in words but are held in deeds in honor by the celebration of sacrifices and mysteries. And this diminutive creature, I mean Priapus,[93] with his huge phallus erect, is held in honor and the phallus of Dionysus is adored by the participants in the feast of the Phallagogia,[94] and the feminine "comb"—that is, the name of the female organ—has been judged worthy of honor by those female initiates who participate in the Thesmophoria.[95]

85. The Egyptians have been so enslaved to shameful pleasures that they give the name of god to the he-goat because of his copulation-mania. The race of the Mendes hold this animal in special veneration.[96] Other cities have organized special cults for other animals: at Memphis,

for instance, the bull is honored; at Lycopolis, the wolf; at Leontopolis, the lion; at Cynopolis, the dog; at Latos the inhabitants adore a type of fish called the "latos," or perch; for others, it is the ibis; and for others still, the crocodile.[97] Each of these animals has been consecrated in the temples and has been assigned an appropriate nourishment. And in that they are regarded as gods they are offered sacrifices and at their deaths are given a costly funeral. Such, then, at that time was the error that occupied the entire inhabited earth.

86. But this error has now entirely vanished and has been completely expelled by the One whom we adore and whom you do not know. And human nature, which had been intoxicated and delirious, has been rendered sober by Him and returned to its senses.

The Nature of Angels according to Scripture[98]

87. But I know well that you are going to say to me: "You also speak of certain invisible powers whom you call angels and archangels and whom you salute with the title of Principalities and Powers, Dominations and Thrones. You know others who in the Hebrew language are called Cherubim and Seraphim.[99] How, then, can you be angry at us if, next to Him who is eternal and absolutely identical with Himself, we admit and venerate secondary gods who are certainly inferior to Him?"

88. I know the sacred Scripture teaches us there certainly exist invisible powers who chant the praises of the creator and who are at the service of His divine will. But we assuredly do not style them "gods" anymore than we assign them divine honor; we do not divide divine honor between the true God and them. But we say, on the one hand, they are more worthy of honor than humans, and, on the other, they are also our fellow slaves.

89. We do not distinguish between them as male and female since their nature is incorporeal. In fact, such a distinction is appropriate only to beings who are subject to death; when death enslaves this nature, marriage for the production of children substitutes for the expenditure of life. The Maker has contrived the production of children as a sort of preparatory stage to immortality. In this the use of the female sex is necessary for those who have a mortal nature, but for those who are immortal the female is completely superfluous. For

they neither needed increase since they did not suffer diminution, nor did they need copulation since they were without bodies.[100]

90. The manner in which they were respectively created bears witness to what I say. On the one hand, as regards humans, it is certain at the beginning God did not create them in large numbers but initially He fashioned only one man and one woman, and through their physical union He has peopled every land and sea with the human race. On the other hand, God has not made incorporeal beings from an original pair, but God created them collectively,[101] by which I mean that all the myriads whose existence He had decided on, He created at the beginning of time.

91. Because of this the use of sex is superfluous in their case, because immortals have no need to increase and multiply, and as incorporeal they have no mechanism for copulation. And so we call them "saints,"[102] because they have nothing of earth and are exempt from carnal passions, and their function is to dance in the heavens and sing the glory of the Creator; furthermore they fulfill all the services that they are ordered to by the divine will, sent as they are by the God of the universe for the salvation of humankind.

92. This is undoubtedly what the divine apostle said concerning them: *Are not all angels spirits in the divine service, sent to serve for the sake of those who are to inherit salvation?*[103] Imitating their way of life, so many humans embrace the service of God. For they flee even legitimate carnal intercourse as drawing them away from divine things; they leave fatherland and family behind, so they may devote all their cares to divine things and so no bond may restrain their spirit, eager to fly upward to the heavens to contemplate the invisible and ineffable beauty of God.[104]

93. They fill the towns and villages, the mountaintops and ravines. Some dwell in communities and carve on their souls the images of wisdom; others live in twos or threes, or even as complete solitaries,[105] withholding their eyes from the enjoyment of visible things and providing leisure to their mind for the enjoyment of the contemplation of intellectual things.

94. Now if those who are attached to a body and are troubled with a host of every kind of passions can embrace with joy a way of life that is incorporeal, elevated, and close to the life of the heavens, how could one describe the life of incorporeal natures, exempt from passions and free from all disturbance?

95. Such is our view of natures that are invisible but created, as we have been taught by the teaching of the divine oracles. You, on the other hand, accuse them of such turpitude and intemperance of base conduct of every kind, and even of rivalry and wars and tyranny, such as are not assigned to even the most corrupt of mortals by those who give an account of such doings.

96. No, not even the most hardened criminals have ever committed the crimes of which you accuse the father of the gods, the loftiest and greatest of them all. Those, in fact, who were enslaved to pederasty did not undermine the marriages of others, but those who were victims of this passion spared their own domestics. If anyone was smitten with love of his sister at least he did not attack his mother, or become infatuated with his daughter, but he was respectful of human nature and did not rival the folly of irrational animals.

97. The Persians are the only ones to commit actions of this kind,[106] obeying an ancient and abominable custom and without a thought that they are acting against the law. But even Homer has married the one who is called the father of the gods and men to his sister, Hera, and in his folly he has also married him to Rhea, who is also called Deo and Demeter, and who actually was his mother. He also had as his concubine Pherrephatta, whom he had sired by his own mother and he became the husband of her daughter.[107]

98. As for the stories of Ganymede, Leda, Danae, Semele, Alcmene,[108] and the multitude of others who are featured in the myths, I am ashamed to speak. In any case I think it is superfluous to dilate on those mythological themes with which you are already familiar. This would only stir up the foul odor of the poets whose mythology you repudiate and reject as false, but whose theology, by contrast, you embrace as true.

99. Compare, then, the accounts in your histories of immaterial but created beings with what we say on our side about celestial powers and carefully note the difference. And judge with reason and sobriety which of the two fits in better with invisible beings. Then you will find, if you are willing to present a fair verdict, that the offerings in your worship are more appropriate to utterly corrupt demons than to holy angels.

100. And since I mentioned demons,[109] I presume it is appropriate that I explain what my views are concerning them. They are regarded by us as demons and their chief, whom the sacred Scriptures call Satan, a word which in Hebrew means "adversary,"[110] is also called

the devil because he slanders God before men and sows the seeds of discord and war among them.

101. We do not say that they have been evil from the beginning, and were so created by the God of the universe, nor do we maintain that they participate in such a nature, but rather that through their own perversity of spirit they have fallen from a higher to a lower state.[111] They were dissatisfied with all that they had received from their Maker and longed for more. So they exposed themselves to the passion of pride and were deprived of the honor which had been assigned to them at creation. They were enraged at the human race because it had been honored with the divine image, and went to war against them.[112] We further believe our Maker protects the human race with the help of guardian angels,[113] in this way preventing the invisible enemy from resorting to force and tyranny and so destroying with impunity those whom out of envy he had hated. But God has allowed the struggle to be contested so that the best side would win and become models of virtue for humankind.

102. That is why, having intervened in the violent assault of the devil with the help of the guardian angels, God has allowed the struggle between the passions and reason so that those deserving of victory could prove themselves worthy of crowns. Not that God has assigned Satan to the role of adversary, but rather He uses his malice when necessary, much as physicians use serpents for the alleviation of certain maladies.

ERRORS OF PLATO

103. These are the views which we have been taught to hold about the power of the enemy. But what Plato's views on these matters were, one can easily deduce from reading the tenth book of his Laws, where he has expressed himself as follows:[114]

Well, then, if indwelling soul thus controls all things universally that move anywhere, are we not bound to say that it controls heaven itself?

Yes, of course.

And is this done by one single soul or by more than one?

I will give the answer for both of you. By more than one.

At least we must assume not fewer than two, one beneficent, the other capable of the contrary effect.

104. Those are Plato's words. It is easy to see how totally out of
place these words are. He has graced with the name of soul the power
that directs all things, visible and even invisible. And he maintains that
this is the governing force, not just of earth, but of the heavens. And
then he asks if we ought to say that there is only one, or more than one,
and replies that we must speak at least of two; to one he gives the name
of the beneficent, and to the other, that capable of contrary effect. And
he has assigned to them an equal power for good and for evil; he has
even affirmed that the demiurge of evil governs, the heavens.[115]

CONCLUSION

105. But we, on the other hand, maintain that it is the Holy
Spirit, called in the sacred Scriptures the Paraclete,[116] who directs, governs and sanctifies, not just the angels, the archangels, and the other
heavenly hosts, but also those human beings who choose a life of piety
and who place a high regard on divine things. As for the demons and
their leader, we believe, not merely that they have been expelled from
the vault of the heavens but that they cower in fear before the athletes
of virtue and turn to flight. They exercise power only over renegades
and those who freely accept enslavement to them. For the sacred
Scripture says: *following the ruler of the power of the air, the spirit that is now
at work among those who are disobedient.*[117]

106. Concerning this, Plato has also said the following in the
Phaedrus:[118]

There are, to be sure, other evils in life, but with most of
them heaven has mixed some momentary pleasure. Having
used this pleasure as a lure and concealing in it the destructive hook,[119] he leads astray like cattle those of us who are

easy to deceive and destroys them, but those who have their wits about them foresee the traps and avoid them.

107. Now that we have presented in parallel form the Christian and pagan views on these beings, consider which side is more in accordance with the divine nature. Is it more correct to speak of a good creator of an evil nature to which he entrusts and turns over, not only the earth, but also the heavens to direct in whatever way he wishes? Or to say the opposite, that God is completely blameless for evils, but that demons became wicked by the free act of their own will, like the majority of men?

108. But I happen to think you will agree that the Christian teachings are superior to the pagan ones. So, if you happen upon the divine teachings themselves and carefully master their contents, you will know more accurately how greatly superior the divinely inspired sayings are to human reasonings, and what kind the dogmas of the Holy Spirit are, and by contrast what kind the teachings of the wretched demons are.

Discourse 4

ON MATTER AND THE COSMOS

1. They say Democritus of Abdera, son of Damasippus, remarked[1] that the best teaching is that which is close to nature, for this transforms and improves the soul and renews pristine traits that nature has engraved on it at its origin.

2. For my part, I think that this is a very reasonable idea. In fact, Socrates, the son of Sophroniscus, was, if we believe the testimony of Porphyry,[2] too inclined in his youth to intemperance but eradicated by his own efforts these inclinations and reshaped them with images of philosophy. The divine Scriptures have taught us many such models. Our Savior has taken publicans, abandoned to avarice and injustice, and a low-down prostitute, full of lewdness, and a thief, full of transgressions, and other such types;[3] these, by his counsels and exhortations, he has taken from the pit of sinfulness and transformed into lovers of virtue.

3. And why do I mention three, or four, or ten, or fifteen instances? Because, in a way, it was the whole world that was in this sad situation, and it was thanks to the example of this relatively small number that He completely transformed the world and made those temperate who earlier gave the impression of resembling people out of their senses and demented. And because we clearly know this, we offer you this teaching which will give you salvation. And when we see you in rebellious mood, contradicting us and resisting our ministration, we do not grow exhausted; rather with the sponge of our discourse we apply fomentations to the fever of your disbelief.[4]

4. We have already made three presentations. We have demonstrated the necessity and utility of the remedy of faith. We have shown what opinion it is necessary to hold concerning the divine substance, and what views to hold concerning invisible things and natures that are

generated. We have laid bare the shamefulness of the mythology of the poets and refuted the shameless allegorizing of the philosophers.

WEAKNESSES AND CONTRADICTIONS IN HUMAN SCIENCES

But since their views on the visible creation are neither true nor inherently congruous but they are fragmented as in a night battle into many divisions shamelessly engaging one another as enemy, I assuredly think it would be useful both to bring to the front their opinions and lay alongside them the teachings of holy Scripture and to show unmistakenly that "the reasonings of mortals are unsure and their intentions unstable," as our wise men have said.[5]

THE STRUCTURE AND ETERNITY OF THE UNIVERSE

5. Now Xenophanes of Colophon, son of Orthomenes and head of the Eleatic school, has asserted[6] that the universe is one, spherical in shape, and limited, uncreated, but eternal and absolutely immobile. But then again, forgetful of these words, he has said that everything was produced from the earth. These are his own words:[7]

All these things come from the earth
And into earth all things find their end.

6. These two statements are absolutely contradictory. If the world is eternal it is also without beginning. And if it is without beginning, it is also without cause. And if it is without cause, then surely it has not the earth for its mother. But if the earth is its mother, if it has the earth as cause, then assuredly it is not without cause, nor without beginning. And if it is not without beginning then it is not eternal.[8]

7. Besides, Parmenides of Elea, the son of Pyrrhus, who was a disciple of Xenophanes, is in perfect accord with his master in his publications as regards the first part of his theory. In fact the following verse is attributed to him:[9]

Intact, unique, immobile, and unengendered.

But the cause of the universe is not only earth, as Xenophanes thought; it is also fire, as Parmenides said.[10]

8. Melissus of Miletus, son of Ithagenes,[11] was a follower of Parmenides, but he did not preserve uncontaminated the doctrine which had been transmitted to him. He claimed that the world is infinite, although his masters had said that it was finite.[12]

MATTER AND THE PRIMORDIAL ELEMENTS

9. Democritus of Abdera, son of Damasippus, was the first to introduce the notion of "void" and "solids,"[13] principles that Metrodorus of Chios called "indivisibles" and "void."[14] Likewise Epicurus of Athens, son of Neocles, born in the fifth generation after Democritus,[15] called "atoms" what his predecessor had called "solids" and "indivisible."

10. "Indivisible," "atom," and "solid" are terms which for some have the meaning "impassible," for others, because they are extremely minuscule, their meaning is incapable of admitting division or sectioning.

11. Ekphantus of Syracuse, the Pythagorean,[16] is also a follower of this school. As for Plato, the son of Ariston, he says[17] the universal principles are God, matter, and the ideas. Aristotle the Stagyrite, son of Nichomachus, says[18] it is form, matter, and privation, and the number of elements is five, not four; the fifth[19] he named the ethereal, being immobile and unchangeable.

12. Xenocrates, the Chalcedonian,[20] has called matter, from which all things originate, everlasting. Zeno of Citium, son of Mnaseus, follower of Crates, founder of the Stoic school,[21] has said God and matter are the (first) principles. Hippasos of Metapontus and Heraclitus of Ephesus, son of Bloson, assert[22] the All is one, immobile and finite, and it took its origin from fire. Diogenes of Apollonia, on the other hand, said the All is composed of air.[23]

13. Matter, however, according to Thales, Pythagoras, Anaxagoras, Heraclitus, and the whole band of the Stoics, is mutable, alterable, and fluid.[24] On the other hand, Democritus, Metrodorus, and Epicurus have called the atoms and the void "impassible."[25] For his part, Plato maintained that matter is corporeal and completely formless, without space, figure, or quality because, according to him, it received all these things

later from the Creator.[26] Aristotle, for his part, has called matter corporeal,[27] and the Stoics have called it a body.[28]

14. The followers of Democritus have called the location of atoms the void,[29] but all the others simply laugh at such a theory. For instance, Empedocles has this to say:[30]

In the All there is neither void nor anything superfluous.

15. The Stoics do not admit any void within the All, but outside the void is absolute and limitless.[31] At the other extreme, Strato says that outside the All there is no void, but that inside there could be.[32]

THE WORLD, ONE OR MULTIPLE?

Not only in these details but in others they show the greatest disagreement. Furthermore, Thales, Pythagoras, Anaxagoras, Parmenides, Melissos, Heraclitus, Plato, Aristotle, and Zeno are all agreed that the world is one.[33] But Anaximander, Anaximenes, Archelaos, Xenophanes, Diogenes, Leucippus, Democritus, and Epicurus held the view that there are many, unlimited worlds.[34]

16. Some said that the world is spherical in shape; others, that it is of some other shape.[35] Some said that it is whirled around like a millstone; others, like a wheel.[36] Some said that it is animated and breathing;[37] others, that it is completely inanimate.[38] Some said that it is generated in the order of thought but not in the order of time;[39] others maintained that it is absolutely unbegotten and uncaused. For some it is corruptible; for others, incorruptible and uncaused. For the former it is corruptible, for the latter, incorruptible.[40]

THE NATURE AND NUMBER OF THE STARS

17. As for the stars, Thales has defined that they are made of earth and fire.[41] On the other hand, Anaxagoras said that they are made of stones that are detached in the rotation of the universe, that these burned up and were fixed on high, and were called stars.[42] And Democritus corroborated this theory.[43] Diogenes said that the stars were made of pumice stone, and had vents for breathing through.[44] For

Anaximander, they were of a substance composed of air, compressed in the form of discs, which are full of fire, and which allow the flames to escape through certain openings.[45]

18. Diogenes has said also that some of them fell on the earth and that, having been extinguished, they have been perceived to have the nature of stones. He took as proof of this the fiery mass that once fell at Aegispotami.[46] Plato asserted that the stars are composed chiefly of fire, but that other elements are intermingled.[47] Aristotle, for his part, considered them as of the same family as the fifth body.[48]

19. Xenophanes said the stars, are composed of incandescent clouds. Extinguished during the day, they come to life again by night like burning coals.[49]

20. Heraclides and some others among the Pythagoreans maintained that each star forms a world composed of earth and air.[50] Some have attributed a spherical shape to the stars,[51] but Cleanthes, the Stoic, says they are conical.[52]

21. As for the sun and moon, Xenophanes says they are fiery clouds;[53] Anaxagoras, Democritus, and Metrodorus, a mass of iron, or a fiery stone.[54] Thales says they are made of earth;[55] Diogenes, of pumice stone.[56] Aristotle says they are spherical and composed from the fifth element.[57] Plato says they are composed chiefly of fire,[58] but other elements enter into their composition. Philolaos, the Pythagorean, says that they are vitrescent bodies that are mirrorlike receivers of the reflection of the fire in the universe and direct light and warmth toward us.[59] Others still have held different opinions on this matter, which I find superfluous to mention, lest I run the risk of sharing in the same claptrap.

22. And what great discussion there has been among them also on the size and shape of the sun and moon! Some say that the sun is spherical; others, that it is boat-shaped; others, that it is like a chariot wheel.[60] Anaxagoras says it is twenty-seven times the size of the earth;[61] Empedocles says it is the same size as the earth,[62] Anaximander, it is twenty-seven times larger than the Peloponnese;[63] Heraclitus, it is a foot wide.[64]

23. And their talk about the moon is similar nonsense. Thales says that it is made of earth;[65] Anaximenes, Parmenides, and Heraclitus, that it is made only of fire.[66] Anaxagoras and Democritus, for their part, thought it was a fiery, solid body, containing plains, mountains, and valleys.[67] For Pythagoras it is a rocky body;[68] for Heraclides, it is earth

encompassed in mist.[69] Some maintain that it is larger than the earth; others, that it is similar in size; others, smaller; while still others maintain it is a finger span in diameter.[70]

24. What need is there to relate how many mythologies they have composed about the phases, shapes, and eclipses and distances of the moon?[71] Not content with giving the distance between the sun and moon, they even give the distance from the earth to the moon; they reckon it is more than four hundred thousand stades from the earth to the moon, and further still from the moon to the sun.[72] And they are not ashamed to be ignorant of the depth of the sea, into which they can drop a fishing line, or a rope as for a draw well, but they boast they know accurately the measurement of the air or the ether, without any consciousness of the uselessness of this information, and with no regard for the advice of Aeschylus:[73]

Do not vainly seek after things that are not beneficial.

The Uselessness of Scientific Research

25. For each of these projects, even if attainable, would be completely unprofitable. For when the discovery is unattainable to persons, they resemble people who write in the water or draw water in a sieve.[74] The fact is that both operations entail useless toil and scholarly research is wasted to no purpose.

26. That is what Socrates realized when he bade farewell to the astronomers and the natural philosophers and dedicated himself to ethical teaching, as Xenophon informs us in his *Memorabilia*, where he writes as follows:[75]

He deprecated curiosity to learn how the deity contrives the phenomena of the heavens; he held that their secrets could not be discovered by men, and believed that any attempt to search out what the gods had not chosen to reveal must be displeasing to them. He said that he who meddles with these matters runs the risk of losing his sanity as completely as Anaxagoras, who took an insane pride in his explanation of the divine machinery.[76]

27. This is what the same author wrote on the same subject:[77]

No one ever knew Socrates to offend against piety and religion in deed and word. He did not even discuss that topic so favored by other talkers, "the Nature of the Universe"; and he avoided speculation on the so-called "Cosmos" of the professors, how it works, and on the laws that govern the phenomena of the heavens: indeed he would argue that to trouble one's mind with such problems is sheer folly.

28. In the first place, he would inquire, did these thinkers suppose that their knowledge of human affairs was so complete they must seek these new fields for the exercise of their brains or that it was their duty to neglect human affairs and consider only things divine? Moreover he marveled at their blindness in not seeing that man cannot solve these riddles, since even the most conceited talkers on these problems did not agree in their theories, but behaved toward one another like madmen.

29. As some madmen have no fear of danger and others are afraid where there is nothing to be afraid of, as some will do or say anything in a crowd with no sense of shame, while others shrink even from going abroad among men, some respect neither temple nor altar, nor any other sacred site. Some hold that what is is one; others, that it is infinite in number; some, that all things are in perpetual motion; others, that nothing can ever be moved at any time; some, that all life is birth and decay, and others that nothing can ever be born or ever die.

30. And he continues at length in similar style, refuting their copious verbiage. It is not one of our Christian authors who has made the case against this stargazing but Xenophon and Socrates, the leaders of the Greeks. And it is very easy for anyone who wishes to check in the *Memorabilia* of Xenophon to see that he is the author of such views concerning the much-vaunted philosophers.

31. And if one supposes that I calumniate these fine gentlemen when I denounce the extreme contradictions in their teachings, let him read the collection of the *Placita* of Aetius,[78] or the work of Plutarch, *On the Opinions of the Philosophers.*[79] *The History of Philosophy* by Porphyry also provides many similar examples.[80]

32. But the citations from Xenophon that I have just provided

are sufficient proof of the truth of what I have said, because he especially has exposed the total ignorance of the philosophers and the internal wrangling among them. And so I will leave them completely on one side. Some of Plato's teachings are valuable.

THE VALUE OF SOME TEACHINGS OF PLATO

However, I will approve of some of Plato's ideas, while others of them I will refute as being not well founded. Ideas of his which are especially praiseworthy are those he has set forth in his *Timaeus*.[81]

33. Let me tell you, then, why the creator made this world of generation. Then he introduced that best of answers which is praiseworthy. He was good, and the good can never have any jealousy of anything. And being free from jealousy, he desired that all things should be as like himself as they could be.

> He does not speak of a natural resemblance but only of a resemblance of being, because he wished that non-beings should come into existence and be like him. But he simply is and receives being from nobody, but he himself has bestowed being on creatures coming into existence.

34. And what follows is similar to what we have just quoted:[82]

> It was not out of necessity that God created the world in order that he might reap the fruits in relation to men, and other gods and demons, earning an income, so to speak, on creation, namely, on our part, smoke, and, on the part of the gods and demons, the services of their own liturgies.

35. He reiterates in this passage that God has no need of anything and that he has made all things because of his sheer goodness. Furthermore, he has given the name "gods" and "demons" to what we call "angels," and those are precisely the beings who, according to him, are "the ministers" of the God of the universe.

36. That which he has written also in the *Republic* likewise merits our praise:[83]

In like manner, then, you are to say that the objects of knowledge not only receive from the presence of the good their being known, but their very existence and essence is derived to them from it, though the good itself is not essence, but still transcends essence in dignity and surpassing power.

Not merely, Plato says, is the form common to them that he has imposed upon them, as a worker in bronze or gold might, but also the very being he has created and given to them, although he has not the same nature as his creatures. God is, in fact, above and beyond all, being superior, not merely by his eternity alone, but also by the majesty of his works.

37. Thus Plato has shown in the clearest terms that it is not in virtue of some substrate of matter that God has made the universe, but that he has created from nothing as he wished. The following from Plato is worthy of admiration and praise:[84]

I am asking a question which has to be asked at the beginning of an inquiry about anything. Was the world, I say, always in existence and without beginning, or created, and did it have a beginning?

And then he replies in answer:

Created, being visible and tangible, and having a body, and therefore sensible, and all sensible things are apprehended by opinion and sense, and are in a process of becoming and of being created. Now that which is created must, as we affirm, of necessity be created by a cause.

38. Having said such things about created beings, he very wisely gave instructions about what should be thought about the Creator. For he said:[85]

But the father and maker of all this universe is past finding out, and even if we found him, to tell of him to all would be impossible. For it is in no way expressible in words like other objects of teaching.

39. Now he shows us also the Word of God creating all things. For he had learned this from the Scripture of the Hebrews, and he exclaims as follows:[86]

Such was the mind and thought of God in the creation of time. The sun and moon and five other stars, which are called the planets, were created by him in order to distinguish and preserve the numbers of time, and when he had made their several bodies, he placed them in the orbits.

40. In these words he has taught us that not only has God made creation through the Logos, but that the sun, moon, and stars are created and have derived their being from God. But none of these things, in the words of Plato, is God. But they have been created for the benefit of human beings. And this Euripides has shown in the *Phoenissae*, saying:[87]

Sun and night are the slaves of mortals,
And you, will you not endure to have an equal in your house?

41. Now Euripides said that sun and moon were slaves to mortals. But you endure to be slaves to your slaves in assigning divine worship to them. But I will resort once more to Plato. For he speaks in terms almost identical with ours about the creation of the universe. 42. These are his words:[88]

If this world be indeed fair and the artificer good, it is manifest that he must have looked to that which is eternal.

And concerning the heavens he added:[89]

for the world is the fairest of creations and he is the best of causes.

And he goes on to say:

He has formed the heavens visible and tangible.

And he further adds:[90]

Time, then, and the heaven came into being at the same instant in order that, having been created together, if ever there was to be a dissolution of them, they might be dissolved together.

43. And in the *Statesman* he says similar things:[91]

Ever to be the same, steadfast and abiding, is the prerogative of the divinest of things only. The nature of the bodily does not entitle it to this rank. Now the heaven, or the universe as we have chosen to call it, has received many blessed gifts from him who brought it into being, but it has also been made to partake of bodily form. Hence it is impossible that it should abide forever free from every change.

44. Another passage from him reads as follows:[92]

And now the pilot of the ship of the universe, for so we speak of it, let go the handle of its rudder and be retired to his conning tower in a place apart. Then destiny and its own inborn urge took control of the world again and reversed the revolution of it. Then the gods of the provinces, who had ruled under the greatest god, knew at once what was happening and relinquished the oversight of their regions. A shudder passed through the world at the reversing of its rotation, checked as it was between the old control and the new impulse that had turned end into beginning for it and beginning into end. This shock set up a great quaking which caused, in this crisis of the world just as in the former one, destruction of living creatures of all kinds.

45. Plato is in accord with our views in these words of his when he asserts that the universe changes, and that once God has abandoned the rudders these invisible powers charged with the rule of certain provinces of the universe retire, and visible things are henceforth submitted to change. But for the rest, Plato remains firmly committed to the prevailing error, which sees the innate desire of matter as upsetting the universe according to the fate that has been allocated to it in virtue of its origin.

46. This is precisely the reproach that we level at the philosopher in his theories on creation. He has said that matter coexisted with God, just as Pythagoras, Aristotle, and the philosophers named from the Stoa had done.[93] And he sometimes designated matter as evil. For we can hear his own words about the cosmos:[94]

It is from God's act when he set it in its order that it has received all the virtues it possesses, while it is from its primal chaotic condition that all the wrongs and evils arise in it—evils that it engenders in turn in the living creatures within it.

47. And he has made this further remark:[95]

The corporeal element in its constitution was responsible for its failure. This bodily factor belonged to it in its most primeval condition, for before it came into its present order as a universe it was an utter chaos of disorder.

I think anybody of sound mind would be indignant at these words. For Plato completely misrepresents the nature of matter. He maintains that it is so strongly and invincibly evil that even the creator has not the power to make it better, because it has remained innately evil and, even after receiving its form from God, it has not expelled its initial wickedness. For this reason, not only on earth but even in heaven it is the cause of disorders and injustices that it transmits to living beings.

48. These ideas of Plato are not on a par with those that were quoted previously and are at variance with his elevated language and his theology. They are the products of down-to-earth, pedestrian reasoning. For in saying that even in heaven disorder persists inclines one to presume that matter is very powerful and that the creator is weak. And yet Plato says that he created the heaven itself according to an intellectual model.

49. This is how he puts it in the *Timaeus*:[96]

Are we right in saying that there is one world, or is it more correct to say that there are many and infinite worlds?

There must be one only if the created copy is to accord with the original model.

By "model" I take it that Plato meant either God, insofar as He is one, or the Idea, which in his view is the thought of God, or the intelligible universe, which, according to the sacred Scripture, is outside of this. But a model that is any one of those things does not accord in the least with the accomplishment of evil and injustice.

SCRIPTURE TEACHES *CREATIO EX NIHILO*

50. Such, then, are the conflicting views of the so-called philosophers. But it is now time to show the excellence of the sacred Scripture and the veracity of its cosmogony. On the one hand, the myths concerning matter in the Chaos of Hesiod[97] have been completely rejected in Scripture, which affirms, on the other hand, that God has absolutely created everything, not just acting like architects, shipbuilders, workers in bronze, goldsmiths, nor, for that matter, weavers, tentmakers, and other craftsmen who collect the raw materials, endow them with form, and fashion them thoroughly, borrowing tools from one another, but that God has both willed and brought into existence things that have never existed in any place at any time.

51. The God of the universe has no need of any help. The human crafts, by contrast, have need of one another.[98] The naval pilot, for instance, has need of the shipbuilder, the shipbuilder has need of the carpenter, of the blacksmith, of the maker of pitch, and of the towmaker. Again, the woodcutter has need of the gardener and likewise the gardener has need of the earth and irrigation and plants and seeds and of a blacksmith to make a hoe and a two-pronged fork. The blacksmith needs the construction worker to build his forge, adjust the anvil on the block, and insert the ax in the hammer. And all equally have need of the shoemaker, the weaver, and the laborer to provide nourishment and bodily covering. And all of these in turn have need of the blacksmith's craft so that he may provide the appropriate tools for each.

52. The maker of the universe, on the other hand, has no need of either tools or of material. In God, will takes the place of material, and tools, time, and work are replaced by competence and attention.

The Word has made everything that He wished in heaven and earth, in the seas and in abysses, as the sacred Scripture says.[99]

53. He has wished, not everything that he could, but everything that seemed sufficient for us. It would have been very easy for him to create ten thousand, or twenty thousand, worlds, in that to will is the easiest of all things to be done. Even for us, to will is the easiest of all things, but our ability does not keep in step with our will. But to the God of the universe everything He wills is possible. For there is no distinction in his case between potency and act. Nevertheless He has not measured the creation in accordance with his potency, but He has created everything that He wished.

54. And since, among creatures, some are sensible and some spiritual, some terrestrial and others celestial, He has of necessity made some living creatures sensible and others spiritual. To the spiritual he has assigned the ether, that is, the clear upper air, and the heavens, while to the creatures of sense he has assigned as their dwelling place the earth and the sun.[100]

55. Certain ones of those spiritual beings, having been allowed to turn to evil, were rightly banished from the celestial regions,[101] and God assigned to them as their destiny to frequent the air and the earth, not so that they could accomplish everything that they would undertake against us mortals (for you are well aware that the guardian angels would prevent them), but in order that they might learn from this change in location what great evils perversity sponsors.

THE ORDER OF NATURE AND ITS DISTURBANCE

56. After He had divided sensible creatures into two species, making one class rational, and the other irrational, He made the irrational creatures submissive to the rational. Now among the irrational creatures, some conducted themselves like tyrants, and revolted against their masters and sought to do evil, since their masters acted in the same manner and after receiving the honor of reason they had violently revolted from their Creator. That is assuredly why the irrational creatures rose in revolt, in order that men might understand the consequences of their conduct, how abominable and perverse a thing it is to transgress order and to go beyond the fixed boundaries without the least concern.

57. Now these limits, it can be said, are observed by the irrational elements. For example the sea, when it is whipped up by squalls and becomes embroiled and is dashed against the coastline, respects the sand[102] and is reluctant to transgress its established limits. But, just as a horse at full gallop is restrained by the bit, so the sea recoils, when it sees the unwritten law of God on the shore just as if the support of the reins choked off its breath.

58. It is in this way that the rivers follow their course as they had been laid out from the beginning, and the fountains gush forth and the reservoirs bestow their abundance on people, and the seasons of the year succeed one another harmoniously, respecting equality and not demanding more than their due.

59. This law is continuously observed by days and nights. When they are lengthened they do not become boastful, nor are they irritated when they are shortened, but whatever time they borrow from one another they continue to pay back punctually and with no hostilities, giving and receiving without strife.[103]

THE ORDER OF DIVINE PROVIDENCE

60. Here likewise are some other examples that further show us the wisdom and power of the Creator. The earth, which during so many thousands of years has been tilled, sown, and planted, which nourishes its fruits, which is trod upon, channeled, moistened by rain and by snow, scorched by sun, nevertheless does not endure any diminution or give less good fruits to the farmers. And the sea is never observed shrinking, while the clouds unceasingly produce the liquid element that they give in the form of rain to the earth. The sea level never gets lower nor does it overflow its brim despite the fact of it receives the incoming flow of rivers from all sides.

61. I have not said where the currents of the river are flowing from because that for me continues to be a very mysterious question. But it is very easy to give an account, if you so wish, of how the sun has the property of making humidity disappear. In fact, it dries up the marshes and causes the accumulations of water to disappear and it completely dries our bodies. Furthermore one can see the rivers reducing in size when the sun, having abandoned the southern regions, has recourse to northern parts and produces summer.

62. That is why the Nile, it is said, does not overflow at the same time as other rivers.[104] Rather, it is at the height of summer that it inundates Egypt because it is precisely the sun that covers the northern region and overwhelms the other rivers whereas it increases the Nile in length. Other explanations of the inundation are available. My own opinion is that this question is not at the moment particularly relevant. Indeed my advice to others is that they should not indiscriminately pry into the causes of the divine economy but should admire whatever comes their way and celebrate the Creator.

63. Furthermore, I, for my part, marvel at the fact that the air does not grow scarcer in spite of the number of people and animals who inhale it, and although so many rays and such intense heat traverse it. And the moon and the stars do the same thing as the sun.

64. But it is a miracle that is more than a miracle; I would even venture to say that the miracle is not even a miracle. For in the presence of God the Creator it is appropriate to use the word "miracle" as little as possible and to glorify as much as possible. It is, in fact, very easy for God to do everything pleasing to Him. So He has infused into each thing that He has made a force that suffices to make it endure for as long a period as He wishes. That is why the earth has lasted exactly as it was made at creation, and the sea has neither increased nor diminished, and the air has preserved intact the nature that it acquired at the beginning, and the sun can neither liquefy nor dissolve the firmament that surrounds it, any more than can the firmament that is humid extinguish the natural heat of the sun. In fact each element has preserved the role assigned to it at creation, because the warring elements of wet and dry, heat and cold have been united in harmony by the Creator.

65. Whenever, then, we see each of these phenomena, the sun, now extending over the north, now the south, and again traversing the middle of the heavens, and the moon waxing and waning, and the stars, which rise and set at the appropriate moments, indicating the season for harvesting and planting and informing sailors about tempests and periods of calm, let us not, my friends, deify these phenomena, but rather let us hymn the praises of their Maker, their Creator and their Pilot, and let us make the transition from the visible to the invisible.

66. But we need the transition of faith for this, not a physical transition. Only by faith will we be able to see the invisible. When we

see the seasons duly replace one another at the proper time, and rain beating down bountifully on the earth, and the earth coming to life, covered with grass, and the meadows flowering, and the groves sprouting and brimming with fruit, let us move our lips to hymn the praises of the One who has bestowed these favors on us, and let us not make gods out of the mountain nymphs, or the nymphs of fountains or rivers;[105] let us not sing the song of the corn-sheaf in honor of Demeter, or the reaper's song named after lityerses, or the dithyramb to Dionysus, or the paean to Pythian Apollo, or the oupingos to Artemis,[106] but rather let us address the chant of David to the Creator of the universe and with him let us exclaim: *Bless the Lord, all his works, in all places of his dominion.*[107]

67. When we hear the tuneful birds singing such a variety of songs and the cicadas noise-making, let us bid farewell to the Sirens and Muses[108] and worship instead the omniscient and omnipotent God who has given such harmonious melody to such tiny, winged creatures and who by every means nourishes, rejoices, and enchants the human race.

68. Compare all this, my dear friends, with the opinions of the philosophers and examine with right and just judgment which of their statements that pertain to the gods is opportune and harmonious, that the All is ingenerate, or comes about by chance, or that it is a harmony of atoms and the void, or that it has been created by God, or from matter, or that it is impious to say any of these things concerning God, and rather that to say this is just and proper, namely, that God is the maker of the universe and that He has made things, not like other artisans, from matter, but that He Himself has introduced all existing things from nonexistence and has willed to provide existence to the nonexistent.

69. It is, in fact, easy for Him to create either from nothing or from something. And that is clearly what He has done of old and what He does, so to speak, on a daily basis. For from underlying bodies He fashions the bodies of living creatures and He creates the souls from nothing, not for all living beings, but for humans only. He creates winged creatures from winged creatures and fish from fish, and each species from that particular species.

70. Likewise it is through seeds and plants that He provides mortals with the fruits of the earth. Of old the earth was untilled and unplowed and it sprouted forth every kind of shoots and seeds and

the various kinds of creeping things and four-footed beasts. And the nature of the waters produced, as it was commanded, both the creatures living in the waters and those whose nature allowed them to traverse the air.

71. In any case, as to the earth, the heavens, the air, the waters, the fire, and the light, God has not changed matter with producing them, but He has introduced them from the nonexistent and He Himself is the gardener. And, having become the shipbuilder of the huge vessel of creation, He Himself also pilots and directs the vessel that He has constructed with consummate wisdom.[109]

72. We have been taught these things, not just by the evangelists and the apostles, but also by the prophets and by Moses, the chief of the prophets, the author of the cosmogony, and before these by Abraham and Melchisedech and the whole chorus of the patriarchs. Each of these taught, not a multiplicity of gods, but one Creator of the universe. And this you will know if you have encountered the sacred Scriptures.

73. Instructed by this comparison of the enormous distance between human reasonings and the teachings of the sacred Scriptures, flee from error, my dear friends, and cling to the truth which is more luminous than the sun, so that you may be illumined by it and may perceive the meaning of the divine oracles and admire the teachers so that, *falling on your face*, to quote the apostle,[110] *that person will bow down before God and worship him, declaring, "God is really among you."*

Discourse 5

ON HUMAN NATURE

Humans Are Free and Masters of Their Own Destiny

1. There is a type of stone called a magnet that leaves every other substance unmoved and attracts only iron. And this it sometimes displays in a raised position, neither propped up by anything from below, nor tied to anything visible from above, but suspended without either visible tie from above or prop from below.[1]

2. One can observe a similar phenomenon in the case of the divine oracles. It is a fact that the majority of humans, indeed all of them, so to speak, rush to them. But only the nurslings of the faith hunt them out, neither attracted by any good fortune from below, nor fastened to anything visible from above, but only by fastening the mind to invisible hopes. Likewise the divine apostle has spoken of *for the message about the cross is foolishness to those who are perishing, but to us who are being saved it is the power of God.*[2]

3. Now this magnet, then, in virtue of its natural property, forces iron to run toward it, whereas the grace of the divine oracles does not of itself attract some and repel others (for it pours forth its streams to all who wish to take their fill), but the free will of the hearers leads on those who are thirsty and, on the other hand, puts far away those who are least inclined to have this yearning.

4. In any case, the Physician of souls does not force the conscience of those who do not wish to take advantage of His treatment. For He created rational nature free and autonomous; by His exhortations and His laws He has diverted us from what is lower and directed

us toward the higher, but He does not force us lest He violate the boundaries of nature.

5. That is why He exclaims through the prophets: *If you are willing and obedient, you shall eat the good of the land.*[3] And again: *Come, O children, listen to me; I will teach you the fear of the Lord. Which of you desires life, and covets many days to enjoy good?*[4] Then, turning us away from what is evil, He indicates what must be done: *Keep your tongue from evil, and your lips from speaking deceit. Depart from evil, and do good; seek peace, and pursue it.*[5] And to those who obey Him He shows the rewards of their efforts: *The face of the Lord is against evildoers, to cut off the remembrance of them from the earth.*

6. And since fear pertains to those under instruction it is still necessary that He scare with his threats those who lead an easygoing life, and He says: *The face of the Lord is against those who do evil, to cause their memory to disappear from the face of the earth.*[6] And the one who has proffered this advice by the prophet in the holy Gospels does not use any intermediary but expresses himself by means of the flesh which He has assumed: *Let anyone who is thirsty come to me, and let the one who believes in me drink. If anyone is thirsty, let him come to Me and drink.*[7] And again: *Come to me, all you that are weary and are carrying heavy burdens, and I will give you rest.*[8]

7. And you could find countless other examples in the holy Gospels and in the writings of the apostles that would clearly show that human nature enjoys free will. It is for this reason, dearly beloved, that I am publishing this fifth exhortation. I do not merely ask you, I earnestly beg and implore you, not to let this occasion pass but to take care and not to put off your salvation until tomorrow, for we do not know if we will live that long, but we should recall the advice of the poet from Ascra, saying:

Do not put it off until tomorrow or the day after.

And we should pay careful attention to the advice of the same poet when he says:[9]

Always the man who is dilatory wrestles with unhappiness.

8. Now that we have learned what we should believe about the universe and about matter, and what a great distance separates the

sacred and secular teachings, let us pass on to an examination of what the sacred Scriptures have taught us to believe about human nature and what those say who beautify their speeches with euphemism and with a florid vocabulary in their presentation of falsehood.

PHILOSOPHICAL VIEWS ON THE ORIGIN OF THE SOUL

9. So we must now for the moment leave to one side all the narratives that the poets have invented on this subject, not anointing them with perfume, as Plato says,[10] but protecting our senses against the foul odor that they exude. For they not only say that men are earthborn but they say they are sprung from the teeth of dragons.[11] But it is only the most commonly discussed topics of the philosophers and the historians that we must compare with the teaching of truth.

10. Before everything else we should state the extent of the quarrel that divided them on the question of the formation of human nature. One side has said that human nature is eternal and that the earth has always been full of the human species. Others have said that it originated in Attica; others, in Arcadia; and others, by contrast, in Egypt;[12] while others still have contended for the honor of place of origin.

11. In addition to these views some have called the living being happy, others have called it cowardly and thrice wretched; Homer called it "feeble" and "wretched,"[13] and Theognis, the Sicilian from Megara, exclaimed:[14]

> Best of all for mortals is not to be born or to look upon the
> rays of the bitter sun,

Or, once born, to pass as quickly as possible through the portals of Hades.

12. This is re-echoed in some iambs from a tragedy of Euripides:[15]

> You had to form an assembly and lament the mortal who
> has come to such evils.

> But he who in dying has ceased from toils, him we should
> accompany from his home with cries of joy and good
> omen.

And concerning Solon, the Athenian legislator, Herodotus said he told Croesus:[16]

Croesus, every man is a disaster.

On the Relations of Soul and Body

13. Pythagoras and Plato introduced a people of souls without bodies and said they were sent into bodies as a form of punishment for some fault committed.[17] For this reason Plato in the *Cratylus* has called the body a prison because, according to him, the soul is somehow buried in the body.[18]

14. Philolaus, the Pythagorean, speaks in the same vein. This is what he says:[19]

Theologians of old and prophets testify that the soul has been yoked to the body for some punishment, and that it is buried in it, as in a tomb.

But Plato is unmindful of this. In the third book of the *Republic* he propounds quite a different view:

It is necessary, he says,[20] to take care of the body for the sake of harmony of soul; it is thanks to this that it can live and live well in announcing the message of truth.

On the Nature of the Soul

15. If, then, the soul enjoys life and the good life through the body, it assuredly did not exist prior to the body. But if it existed prior to the body, then assuredly it lived a real life, for it had an immortal and reasonable nature. But if it existed of old it did not live rightly, separated from the body; but, once in the body and properly nurtured, then thanks to the body it gets possession of those blessings that it lacked before it existed in the body. Why, then, does Plato say that the soul was buried in the body as in a tomb?

OPINIONS ON THE NATURE OF THE SOUL

16. In all this we see that the philosophers have been at odds, not merely with one another, but even with themselves. And, to grasp the extent of their discord, let us set forth what the most celebrated of them have thought about the soul, and how vainglory, in the words of Timaeus:[21] "By their disaccord he has trained them to fight." All that I am going to say I will borrow, with God's help, from the writings of Plutarch, Porphyry, and Aetius.[22]

17. Thales, then, has called the soul an immovable nature.[23] Alcmaeon has said it was endowed with spontaneous movement.[24] Pythagoras called it a self-moving number.[25] That, too, was the view of Xenocrates.[26] For Plato the soul was an intelligible, self-moving substance.[27] For the Stagirite it was the first entelechy of the physical, organic body that possesses life in potency. He has called the energy entelechy.[28]

18. For Clearchus, it was a harmony of four elements.[29] Anaximenes, Anaximander, Anaxagoras, and Archelaos have said that the nature of the soul is airy.[30] For the Stoics, on the other hand, it is spiritual, endowed with considerable heat.[31] Parmenides, Hippasos, and Heraclitus have called it a fire;[32] Heraclides, a lamp;[33] and finally Epicurus, son of Neocles, makes it an amalgam of four qualities, fire, air, spirit, and the fourth, an indeterminate quality.[34] Empedocles made it a mixture of ethereal and aerial being.[35] Critias said it was a mixture of blood and moisture.[36] And others have said contradictory and nonsensical things.

19. But when it comes to analyzing the parts of the soul the greatest battle has ensued. Pythagoras and Plato maintain that it is divided into two parts, the first, rational, the second, irrational, and the second further subdivided into irascible and concupiscible.[37] But Xenocrates, while he was the second successor of Plato, since he was the disciple of Speusippus, the nephew of Plato, divided the soul into the sensible and the rational.[38]

20. [Aristotle,] the son of Nicomachus, says that the soul has five activities: the appetitive, nutritive, sentient, discursive, and cognitive.[39] The Stoics, however, do not agree with this enumeration. According to them the soul is made up of eight parts: the five senses, sight, hearing, smell, taste and touch. To these they add a sixth, the faculty of speech; a seventh, the organ of generation; and an eighth, the direct-

ing faculty that gives to each of the others its activity. They also compare the soul to the tentacles of a polyp.[40]

21. The successors of Pythagoras, for whom the body is composed of five elements (they add ether to the regular four) attribute to it an equal number of faculties, which they call spirit, intelligence, knowledge, opinion, and sensation.[41]

22. It is easy to see the many differences that separate them when they come to localize reason. In fact, Hippocrates, Democritus, and Plato say that it resides in the brain.[42] Strato locates it between the eyebrows,[43] Erasistratus, the physician, around the membrane of the cerebellum, which he calls the ἐπικρανίς,[44] Herophilus, in the cerebral cavity;[45] Parmenides and Epicurus, in the thorax.[46] Empedocles, Aristotle, and the Stoic school have assigned it to the heart.[47] And among the last-named, some place it in the cavity of the heart; others, in the blood; others, in the pericardium; and others still, in the diaphragm.[48]

On the Origin and Destiny of the Soul

23. Pythagoras, Anaxagoras, Diogenes, Plato, Empedocles, and Xenocrates have stated that the soul is indestructible,[49] although Heraclitus has maintained that souls separated from bodies return to the soul of the universe, which is connatural and consubstantial with them.[50] On the other hand, the Stoics maintain that the souls separated from bodies subsist by themselves, but the weakest survive only for a time whereas the strongest persevere until the universal conflagration.[51]

24. Democritus, Epicurus, and Aristotle quite simply say that the soul is corruptible.[52] But for Plato and Pythagoras the rational part of the soul is incorruptible while the irrational part is corruptible.[53] Plato has given to plants the nomenclature of animals even though they participate only in the third part of the soul, the concupiscible.[54] Aristotle, on the other hand, has refused to give the name "animals," to plants because, according to him, it is what participates in the sensitive soul that deserves to be called "animals." His view is that in plants there is a vegetative and nutritive soul.[55]

25. The philosophers of the Stoa, however, have not accepted this theory since they do not agree to assign the name "soul" to the vegetative faculty.[56] Zeno of Citium, the founder of this sect, has

taught his immediate followers the following views on the soul. The human semen, at once humid and endowed with spirit, is, in his view, a separable part of the soul, a fusion and collection of the sperm of the parents. It is a mingling of all the parts of the soul. And for this reason it is rightly considered corruptible.[57]

26. Numenius, the Pythagorean, however, in opposition to the Stoics, says:[58]

> They say that the soul is born and dies, not that it dies as soon as it leaves the body, but that it subsists on its own for a time, the soul of the wise lasting until the universe is dissolved in conflagration, the soul of the foolish for a shorter period.

27. Longinus rebukes them categorically when he writes:[59]

> One would be rightly indignant at Zeno and Cleanthes for speaking in such a supercilious fashion about the soul. Both of them maintained that the soul was an exhalation of the solid body.

FREEDOM OR NECESSITY?

28. Their opinions are in complete contradiction with those of Pythagoras and Plato. These latter maintained that the mind is a portion of the divine.[60] The son of Nicomachus is in agreement with them in this view, and yet he says that the soul is mortal, for he maintained that the mind is something distinct from the soul.[61]

Those in the circle of Pythagoras and Plato say that the spirit enters the body from the outside. But some of them say that the mind is in full control and can direct the passions in any way it wishes, while others regard it as a slave of necessity and fate, directed by the threads of the Fates, depending in its actions and activities on the heavenly revolutions and the conjunctions of the stars.[62]

29. Plato as a matter of fact has advanced a view of the soul totally opposed to these. He maintained that the soul is free, that it is in control of the passions that disturb it, that it conducts itself freely from one

side to the other, and that of its own volition it overcomes or is overcome. And this he has clearly set forth in the *Laws*, where he says:[63]

> Why here, stranger, is the place to win the first and fairest
> victory, victory over self, and where defeat, defeat by self, is
> the worst and most serious. This signifies that in each of us
> there is a war against ourselves.

30. And again a little later:[64]

> We know that these interior states are, so to say, the cords
> or strings by which we are drawn; they are opposed to one
> another and draw us to contrary deeds, and therein lies
> the distinction between virtue and vice. In fact, reason tells
> us that we must always yield to one of these tensions with-
> out resistance, and never abandon it, but we must resist the
> other, such is the force of reason that serves as our guide.

31. In these excerpts Plato has well shown that we have not been
allocated an immoral nature, that we, humans, do not sin by necessity
and compulsion, that we are directed toward action neither by the
strings of Clotho nor by the conjunction of the stars. But the soul is in
conflict with itself and has the power of success, if it wills to incline
toward virtue. The concupiscible appetite drags it toward itself, the
irascible appetite draws it in the opposite direction; but reason has
the power to obey or disobey, because it is assigned the role of holding
the reins and being the guide, and not to be led and to be drawn.

32. Plato has corroborated this teaching in Book 10 of the *Laws*
in the following words:[65]

> But the causes of the formation of either type he left free
> to our individual volitions. For as a man's desires tend, and
> as is the soul that conceives them, so and such, as a general
> rule, does every one of us come to be.

And, a few lines further on, he adds:[66]

> If a soul has drunk still deeper of vice and virtue, by reason
> of its own volition and the potent influence of past con-

verse with others, when near contact with divine goodness has made it itself especially godlike, so surely is it removed to a special place of utter holiness and translated to another and a better world or, in the contrary case, transported to live in the opposite realm.

PLATO'S VIEW ON FREE WILL AND RESPONSIBILITY

33. Then, further, Plato teaches in somewhat similar terms that the Creator has attributed with the will to the soul the choice between good and evil; then free will disposes it in one direction or the other, and that practice and habit fortify its dispositions. Therefore when, in love with virtue, it takes on its impression, it passes on into another place that is holy and much better than its present abode; but if it has chosen vice and has welcomed a lifestyle that is dishonorable, it will have for its lot the contrary destination.

34. In Book 2 of the *Republic* Plato has expressed sentiments in agreement with the above. This is what it says there:[67]

And is not God of course good in reality and always to be spoken of as such?

Certainly.

But further, no good thing is harmful, is it?

I think not.

Can that which does not harm do any evil?

Not that either.

But that which does no evil would not be the cause of any evil either?

How could it?

Once more, is the good beneficent?

Yes.

It is the cause, then, of welfare?

Yes.

Then the good is not the cause of all things, but of things that are well it is the cause; of things that are ill it is blameless.

Entirely so, he said.

35. Neither, then, could God, said I, since He is good; be, as He is, the cause of few things, but for many things not the cause. For good things are far fewer with us than evil, and for the good we must assume no other cause than God, but the cause of evil we must look for in other things and not in God.

What you say seems to me most true, he replied.

Then, said he, we must not accept from Homer or any other poet the folly of such error as this about the gods, when he says:[68]

Two urns stand on the floor of the palace of Zeus and are filled with dooms he allots, one of blessings, the other of gifts that are evil. And to whomsoever Zeus gives of both commingled: Now upon evil he chances, and now again good is his portion.

36. Plato adds further:[69]

But as to saying that God, who is good, becomes the cause of evil to anyone, we must contend in every way that neither should anyone assert this in his own city if it is to be well governed, nor anyone hear it, neither younger nor older, neither telling a story in meter or without meter for neither would the telling of such things, if they are told, be holy, nor would they be profitable to us or concordant with themselves. I cast my vote with yours for this law, he said, and am well pleased with it.

This, then, said I, will be one of the laws and patterns concerning the gods to which speakers and poets will be required to conform, that God is not the cause of all things but only of the good.

37. These are the views that Plato has taught us to hold and to believe concerning the God who created us and concerning ourselves, and he has ordered us to expel those who maintain that God is the cause of evils because, in his view, such views are impious, disgusting to us, and self-contradictory. But if God is good, as indeed He is (on that we are all agreed), He cannot be the cause of evil, He who is good.

38. If, then, God is not the cause of the evils that occur (as evils, properly so called, we do not so define such commonly accepted things as hunger, disease, and all such similar phenomena that some love to call disasters), we are the ones who have the audacity to commit such, and so it is we who are responsible, not God, who has ordered us to do the opposite. Such, then, are the points that Socrates and Plato have given us for our reflection.

FOR PLATO THE SOUL IS A PORTION OF THE DIVINE

39. There are those too who have called the reasonable part of the soul divine, and it is possible to hear Socrates saying in the *Alcibiades*, which Plato wrote:[70]

Can we therefore say that there is any part of the soul more divine than that part with which we know and think?

No! This part of the soul, then, is like God. And whoever looks to that and knowing everything divine, namely, God and wisdom, would thus especially know himself.

40. Plato says practically the same thing also in the *Phaedo*:[71]

So you think that we should assume two classes of things, one visible and the other invisible?

Yes, we should.

The invisible being invariable, and the visible never being the same?

Yes, we should assume that too.

Well now, said Socrates, are we not part body, part soul?

Certainly.

Then to which class do we say that the body would have the closer resemblance and relation?

Quite obviously to the visible.

41. And the soul, is it visible or invisible?

Invisible to men, at any rate, Socrates, he said.

But surely we have been speaking of things visible or invisible to our human nature. Do you think that we had some other nature n view?

No, human nature.

What do we say about the soul, then? Is it visible or invisible?

Not visible.

Invisible, then?

Yes.

So the soul is more like the invisible, and the body like the visible?

That follows inevitably, Socrates.

42. Then, having discussed many other questions at length, he continued:[72]

Then which does the soul resemble?

Obviously, Socrates, soul resembles the divine, and body, the mortal.

And again, a little further on:[73]

Very well, in that case is it not natural for a body to disintegrate rapidly but for a soul to be quite or very nearly indissoluble?

Certainly.

43. Then, having discussed the nature of the dissolution of the body, he added:[74]

The soul which goes away to a place that is, like itself, glorious, pure, and invisible—the true Hades or unseen world—into the presence of the good and wise God where, if God so wills, my soul must shortly go—will it, if its very nature is such as I have described, be dispersed and destroyed at the moment of its release from the body as is the popular view?

Far from it, my dear Simmias and Cebes. The truth is much more like this.

And in what follows there is contained the same view, clearly proving the immortality of the soul.

44. Such is the squabbling and conflict of the historians, philosophers, and poets concerning the soul and body, and the composition itself of the human being, some championing one view, others another, each side elaborating opinions the opposite of their opponents. For they had no desire to learn truth but, being slaves of empty fame and renown, desired instead to be hailed as inventors of new opinions.

45. And, for this very reason, they have endured great error, as successors overthrew the opinions of their elders. After the death of Thales, Anaximander espoused different principles, and after the death of Anaximander, Anaximenes did the same thing. Likewise Anaxagoras.[75]

46. And Aristotle openly broke with Plato during the latter's lifetime, set himself in opposition to the Academy, showing no respect

for the school from which he had so eagerly benefited, showing no regard for the renown of his distinguished teacher, with no deference toward his intellectual rigor, but impudently setting himself up as his adversary, and espousing principles that, far from being better, were much inferior to his.[76]

47. Plato, for instance, had asserted that the soul was immortal; Aristotle called it mortal. Plato had maintained that God exercised providence over the universe; Aristotle, to judge by his words, excluded the world from divine government, for he said that God's rule over the universe extended as far as the moon and that the rest came under the sway of destiny.[77] Aristotle has introduced other novelties of which it seems to me superfluous to talk at the moment.

Human Nature according to the Scriptures. Creation.

48. It is only to be expected that the philosophers would have destroyed one another's systems, since falsehood is not merely the enemy of truth but its own enemy as well, while truth is consistent with itself and has only falsehood as an enemy.

49. And so it is, for instance, concerning human nature that we find unanimity in the teaching of Moses the legislator, David the prophet, the great Job, Isaiah, Jeremiah, and the whole choir of the prophets, Matthew, John, Luke, Mark, Peter, Paul, and the whole crowd of the apostles.

50. For it is impossible to hear some of them say that such and such a people is autochthonous, and others, such and such. Some of them do not say the soul is mortal, and others, immortal; some do not assert that the reason is absolutely sovereign over the passions, while others say that it is totally enslaved to them. All unanimously teach that the body was fashioned from earth, water, and the other elements, and that the soul that had no pre-existence before being sent into the body was created after the body's formation: God fashioned man from the clay of the earth. He breathed on his countenance a breath of air, and man became a living being.[78]

51. We must see in this breathing, not an emission of air (because divine being is incorporeal, simple, and without parts), but

the nature of the soul itself, which is a spirit, endowed with intelligence and reason.

52. See, then, that which the legislator has written in his cosmogony. Virtually the same teaching is to be found in His laws.

PROCREATION

Speaking of a pregnant woman who has a miscarriage as a result of blows, Scripture says that the fetus begins by taking form in the maternal womb, then that it is animated, not that the soul comes from anywhere outside or that it originates from the semen, but it has its own beginnings from a divine prescription, in conformity with a law established from the beginning in nature.[79]

53. That is also the gist of what mighty Job says when in his famous trials he discusses with his Creator the cause of his trials: *Remember that you fashioned me like clay; and will you turn me to dust again? Did you not pour me out like milk and curdle me like cheese? You clothed me with skin and flesh, and knit me together with bones and sinews. You have granted me life and steadfast love, and your care has preserved my spirit.*[80]

54. He designated by these words conjugal relations and also has described the origins of procreation, this little semen, which is transformed into an infinity of forms, and then the soul, which is created and united to the body, and after the delivery the divine assistance that protects and governs.

55. And the inspired David exclaimed: *Your hands have made and fashioned me; give me understanding that I may learn your commandments.*[81] And at the same time, always recalling to the Creator that he is His creature, he prays that he may receive discernment from Him. And all the prophets propound a teaching that is in conformity with that.

UNITY OF THE HUMAN RACE

So that nobody would presume that the Greeks were made one way, the Romans another, the Egyptians another way still, and that the Persians, Massagetes, Scythians, and Sarmatians have all been endowed with different essences, the author of our cosmogony has taught that the Creator made from the earth only one man, and that from one of his ribs he made a woman, and that then from the union of this one couple he filled the whole earth with people, and their children and grandchildren for their part increased the race.[82]

56. It would have been very easy for God to have given the order and then to have filled the whole earth and sea with inhabitants; but, so that people would not suppose that the natures of peoples were different, He ordered the countless tribes of people to be descended from this one couple. It is for this same reason that He did not fashion woman differently, but took the beginnings of her origin from man lest woman, thinking that she came from a different source, would take a different path from men.

57. And so, for this reason He established the same laws for men and women, seeing that they differ, not in their soul, but only in the shape of their bodies. Just like man, woman is endowed with reason, being capable of knowing what must be done, what avoided, and what sought; it happens sometimes that woman judges better than man about what is useful and that she is a good counselor. And so it is not just men but also women who should have access to religious temples, and the law that allows men to participate in divine mysteries does not forbid women to enter; each are equally entitled to be initiated and participate in the mysteries. The law proposes to men and women alike the recompenses of virtue since they participate in common in the struggle for virtue.[83]

In Spite of Differences of Languages

58. The diversity of languages does not inflict any damage on human nature. In fact among Greeks and non-Greeks alike it is possible to see both practitioners of virtue and devotees of vice. Even the Greeks themselves are in accord with this view. They admire Anacharsis, a Scythian, who was not from Athens, Argos, Corinth, Tegea, or Sparta,[84] and they are ardent admirers of the Brahmans who are Indians,[85] not Dorians, nor Aeolians, nor Ionians. They praise the Egyptians as very wise people; in fact, they have learned from them many of their sciences.

59. Differences in languages, then, have not caused any injury to the human condition. Indeed Homer has called the Hippomalgoi the justest of peoples,[86] and they are a Thracian race. And Xenophon, son of Gryllos, has admired Cyrus, son of Cambyses, who was Persian on

his father's side and Mede on his mother's, because of his prudence, his temperance, his justice, and his fortitude.[87]

60. Consequently, the Greeks also share the view that among the non-Greeks there is a concern for virtue and that language differences do not impede its acquisition. And indeed all the heralds of virtue—I mean the prophets and apostles—did not share in a knowledge of Greek eloquence but, being full of divine wisdom, they carried the divine teaching to all nations, Greek and non-Greek, and they filled every land and every sea with their writings on virtue and religion.

61. And now all the philosophers, abandoning their own trivialities, luxuriate in the teachings of the fishermen, the tax-gatherers, and they pay great heed to the writings of the tent-maker. They did not even know the names of the philosophical schools of Italy, Ionia, or Elea, because time has eradicated their memory, but they all have on their lips the names of the prophets who predate the philosophers by more than fifteen hundred years.

62. Not to mention those who are older still—I mean Abraham and his children, and those older than these—Abel, Enoch, Noah, and those others who became illustrious because of their praiseworthy life. By contrast, even devotees of the Greek language do not know even the names of the Seven Sages and their successors who were born later than the prophets.

63. But why speak of our contemporaries? Even in antiquity there has been considerable ambivalence about these matters. Some reckoned among the sages[88] Periander of Corinth, others, Epimenides of Crete, or Acousilaos of Argos, or Anacharsis of Scythia, or Pherecydes of Syros. Plato himself counted Myson of Chenea among them.[89]

64. These men, then, are no longer known by our contemporaries. By contrast, the names of Matthew, Bartholomew, James, and even Moses, David, Isaac, and the other prophets and apostles are as well known to them as the names of their own children. Now the Hellenists poke fun at these names as being somewhat barbarian. But we only pity their folly because we recognize that those men unversed in the Greek language have vanquished Greek eloquence, that the elegant myths have all been expelled, and that the solecisms of the fishermen have destroyed the syllogisms of the Greeks.[90] Our critics do not blush at this, or cover their faces, but they stubbornly persist in their defense of error. And for all that, they are not so numerous that they cannot be easily counted; nor are they well endowed with Hellenic elo-

quence but they are guilty of as many barbarisms, so to speak, as words properly pronounced, and they think it is the height of culture and linguistic distinction if they say when swearing, "Yes, by God" and "No, by the sun," plastering their conversation with such swearwords.[91]

SCRIPTURE REHABILITATES THE UNITY OF HUMAN NATURE

65. If what I say is untrue, then tell me, my friends, who succeeded Xenophanes of Colophon as head of his school? Who succeeded Parmenides of Elea? Who Protagoras and Melissos? Who succeeded Pythagoras or Anaxagoras? Who Speussipus or Xenocrates? Who succeeded Anaximander or Anaximenes? Who Archesilas or Philolaos? Who were the heads of the Stoic school?[92] Who follow the teachings of the Stagirite? Who are those whose way of life is in accordance with the *Laws* of Plato? Who are those who have adopted the way of life described in the *Republic*?

66. Now you will be unable to show us one devotee of these teachings whereas we, for our part, can clearly demonstrate the cogency of the teachings of the apostles and prophets. Every country under the sun is filled with their words. And the Hebrew has been translated, not only into Greek, but also into Latin, Egyptian, Persian, Indian, Armenian, Scythian, Sarmatian, in a word into all the languages that all peoples have continued to use.[93]

67. The all-wise Plato went on at length on the immortality of the soul, but he did not persuade his successor, Aristotle, to adopt his definition. Our fishermen, however, our tax-gatherers, and the tent-maker have persuaded the Greeks, the Romans, the Egyptians, indeed, once and for all, every race on the earth that the soul is immortal, that it has been endowed with reason and is capable of controlling the passions, and that it transgresses the laws because of its own neglect and not from external pressure. And again, if it turns itself again toward the good, it separates itself from the former evil and impresses on it the divine characters.

68. And it is possible to see that those who know these teachings are not merely the leaders of the church, but also workers in leather, coppersmiths, weavers, and other manual workers. And women also, not just those who are educated, but those also who are mere weavers, seamstresses, and daily laborers. This knowledge is possessed not just by

city dwellers but also by country folk. And it is possible to find agricultural workers, drovers, and gardeners engaged in discussions on the blessed Trinity, and knowing much more than Aristotle or Plato about the Creator of the universe and the composition of human nature.[94]

69. These people are concerned about virtue and avoidance of vice; they fear future punishments and await without the least skepticism the final judgment; they philosophize about eternity and immortality, and they freely accept all sorts of difficulties for the sake of the kingdom of heaven and these things they have learned, not from somebody else, but from those whom you call barbarians because of their speech. And you do not heed Anacharsis when he says:[95]

To me all Greeks speak Scythian.

70. These words closely resemble those of our tent-maker: *If then I do not know the meaning of a sound, I will be a foreigner to the speaker and the speaker a foreigner to me.*[96] In fact, just as for the Greeks, the Illyrians, the Paeonians, the Taulantians, the Atintanes, sound like they are speaking a foreign language, so for different peoples who do not understand Greek, Attic, Dorian, Aeolian, and Doric, have the sound of foreign dialects.[97]

71. All languages have the same meaning since human nature is one; that is a fact of experience. And so one can find among foreigners arts, sciences, and military accomplishments. Others have often invented more sophisticated weapons than those of the Greeks, better military stratagems, cleverer ambuscades.

72. Some of the foreigners outdo the Greeks in the conciseness of their eloquence. That is a fact noted by the ancient historians in favor of the Persians and known even today by those who have diplomatic, military, or commercial dealings with them.[98] These report that the Persians are very adept at the subterfuges of language and can in debate dispose of their rivals in a very few words, being exceedingly agile in their use of syllogisms, having resort to proverbs and enigmatic statements full of wisdom and without needing research in the labyrinths of Chrysippus and Aristotle,[99] and without benefit of instruction from Socrates and Plato in this type of argument. In fact, they have been nourished not on the discourses of the orators or the philosophers, but have only had nature as their teacher.

73. And they say that the Indians are even much wiser still than

the Persians. And the Nomads, our neighbors—I mean the Ishmaelites[100] who live in the desert and have had no exposure whatever to Greek culture—are adorned with a lively and profound intelligence and their judgment is capable of discerning truth and refuting falsehood.

74. Concerning the Egyptians, I think it is superfluous to speak, since the foremost among our philosophers have agreed that they surpassed even the most outstanding of the Greeks. The Romans, for their part, have had their poets, historians, and orators; those who are bilingual even say that the Romans are more profound than the Greeks in thought and more concise in expression.[101]

75. I do not say this to detract from the Greek language, in which I, in a manner of speaking, participate myself, or to be remiss in paying the price of my nurture for the culture I have got, but simply to close the mouths of those who brag about it,[102] and to expose their superciliousness and teach them not to ridicule a tongue that is resplendent with truth or to bear themselves haughtily at discourses adorned with the art of embellishment but devoid of truth, but rather to marvel at those who expound the truth without any training in embellishing and prettifying their discourses with eloquence, but rather revealing the truth in all its naked grandeur without the least recourse to extraneous and imported flourishes.

DOCTRINAL SYNTHESIS: THE HUMAN ACT

76. Compare, then, my dear friends, the simple teaching of the fishermen with the drivel of the philosophers, and realize the difference. Count up the thousands of volumes that you possess and comprehend the weakness of their contents. For nobody has followed either the myths of the poets or the opinions of the philosophers. But marvel instead at the conciseness of the divine sayings; hymn the cogency of its message and learn the truth of the divine dogmas: the body's formation by God, the immortal nature of the soul, the reasonable part of which controls the passions, which also have a necessary and useful function to play in human nature.

77. The concupiscible part, for instance, has a most important role, as has the irascible, its sparring partner. Thanks to the first we desire eternal things and look down on visible things; thus we imag-

ine the intelligibles and, while still walking this earth, we long to see our Master in the heavens and aspire after virtue. And during our mortal life we have our share of food and drink, and besides these the human race is multiplied by the legitimate procreation.

78. The irascible part is a collaborator with reason, helping it to avoid the excesses of the concupiscible appetite. In fact, since the concupiscible tends to go beyond the appointed limits, the Creator has reined it in, so to speak, with the irascible part, as He would a young pony, jerking it in the opposite direction when it is forcibly going too far in one direction.[103] And just as heat is contrary to cold but the mixture of the two provides a nice balance, so the concupiscible and irascible appetites, when properly blended together, act as a mutual corrective force and achieve the best mixture.

79. Reason maintains control over acts so that it can restrain the concupiscible and incite the irascible, or rather throttle the latter and urge on the former. For the concupiscible checks the excesses of the irascible, and the irascible chastises the greediness of the concupiscible. All this is done perfectly if reason skillfully holds on to the reins. But if reason, either through being enchanted by the slack and smooth or if it is urged on in an untimely fashion by the goading of the irascible, allowing the reins to be slacker than is fitting, the passions, like horses, gallop in a disorderly fashion, champing the bit, and reason, the rider, is dragged along and becomes an object of ridicule and censure to the spectators. For this it is punished because it voluntarily endured the passion.

80. In fact that is why human laws punish those who commit offenses and why God has threatened wrongdoers with unquenchable fire. For neither would God, good and just as He is, inflict punishment on those who cultivate a lawless life if their sins were a result of compulsion, nor would the wisest of mortals have laid down such laws if they realized that human misdeeds were not done deliberately, nor would those who govern inflict cruel punishments on malefactors if they had known that those who transgressed their laws acted, not out of a free choice of the will but by necessity, or by destiny, or naturally. But if they refuse pardon to malefactors they show clearly that wicked behavior is a product of deliberate choice.

Conclusion

81. Such are the considerations we have been taught to have, and which we in turn teach, on human nature. We are full of admiration in viewing the wisdom of the Creator that is manifested in us: the diverse activities of the five senses brought forth from one center, the brain, bringing to it one or other perception, that of sight, or hearing, or smell, or taste, or touch; then again the various uses of all the organs, external and internal; the memory, which is the receptacle of so many and such varied elements that it does not confuse but keeps intact and can recall long afterwards exactly as they were received; and all these items of knowledge are not injurious to one another but each is brought to the surface at the appropriate moment.

82. Each time that we examine these things and others of a similar type, let us exclaim with the prophet: *For though the Lord is high, he regards the lowly; but the haughty he perceives from far away.*[104] For what expression could ever describe the harmony that is displayed in the human body, or the wisdom that we contemplate in our soul? Certainly much has been written on this subject by Hippocrates and Galen, not to mention Plato, Xenophon, Aristotle, Theophrastus,[105] and countless other authors. And what has been said is only a small fraction of what remains to be said because the human spirit cannot attain to what has been brought about by the divine wisdom. That is the reason that the prophet has sung a hymn for what he has been able to grasp, but being unable to take in everything he saw in us, he freely admits defeat, thinking that such a view was sufficient to make a worthy hymn of praise.

Discourse 6

ON DIVINE PROVIDENCE

1. Of those engaged in seafaring activities, some act as rowers of merchantmen, others direct the ships with the helm; and indeed every fisherman borne out on the briny water lowers his net and fishes for the products of the sea, while another sits propped up on a rock, casts his line, and tries to lure the fish with bait. But there are those who suffer shipwreck and become submerged, either because in their folly they put out to sea when it was still not the season to sail, or because they rashly decided to confront the surge of the billows.[1]

2. I make these observations, not just to indulge in idle clichés, but in an attempt to utilize an image to show up the folly of those who put themselves in opposition to creation and unrestrainedly criticize the providence governing it. In fact some see creation and praise the Creator; but others admire creation more than is appropriate and foolishly deify it. Some hold in the highest regard whatever happens and see the pilot of the universe directing with great precision and so they exalt the wisdom manifested in the steering of affairs. But others, in contrast, are indignant at everything that occurs, and nothing at all that happens to them meets their approval; they condemn riches and make fun of poverty; they find fault with illness and cannot stand those who have their health. In a word, nothing that happens pleases them: neither good fortune nor misfortune; likewise they are equally dissatisfied with a good harvest or a bad one, and they find fault alike with childlessness and having too many children, with peace and war.[2]

3. That is why they find fault with the controls of providence, or rather why they completely exclude it insofar as they can. They invoke Fate, Destiny, Fortune, and the three Sisters,[3] and impose on everything compulsive necessity, which, they allege, turns men, even against their will, into assassins, thieves, and adulterers.[4]

134

4. And so we will examine once more the opinions of the Greeks and compare them with the teachings of the apostles and prophets. As for the poets, let us leave them out of consideration, with their impious fables. For the leading poet shows us the leader of the gods bewailing the fact that he is unable to defend his child but is overcome by the threads of Clotho, and although he wants to unravel he is prevented by Atropos and Lachesis, and for this reason is bewailing and shrieking, and mingling much complaint with his utterances.[5]

5. This poet further has shown Poseidon wanting to punish the chief of the Cephallenians for making his son Polyphemus blind, but unable to vanquish Fate since it had made a precise decree that the son of Laertes would return to Ithaca.[6] So let us leave these aside and grant entrance to the swarm of the philosophers.

PHILOSOPHERS OPPOSED TO PROVIDENCE

6. They say that the followers of Diagoras were labeled atheists because they denied outright the divinity.[7] Protagoras held an ambivalent opinion on this matter, for he asserted, as the account goes, that he did not know whether the gods exist or whether they were completely nonexistent.[8] As for Epicurus, son of Neocles, and his circle, they affirmed on the one hand that the gods exist, but on the other that God became introverted, having no care for anything else and having no desire to give to others.[9]

7. The son of Nicomachus maintained[10] that God extended his government as far as the moon, but that he had no care for sublunar beings, that he abandoned control of them to Necessity and Fate and assigned to the fate the distribution to humans, not just of riches and poverty, health and sickness, slavery and freedom, war and peace, but also the allocation of virtue and vice.

8. Oenomaos, the Cynic[11] has openly broken with these philosophers and has jointly criticized with them the Pythian priestess whose oracles are similar. He has entitled his work *The Charlatans Exposed*, in which he says:[12]

> There has disappeared, as far at least as the wise men are concerned, there has disappeared from human life, whether you want to call it a rudder or a support or a foundation,

that is, a power of life that we maintain is in absolute control over the most pressing necessities. But Democritus, if I am not mistaken, and Chrysippus are desirous of showing, the first that it is a most beautiful slave, the second, a half slave, of human affairs. But this thesis has only as much credibility as a man can entrust to men. But if the divinity makes war upon us, alas, what sufferings may we expect.

9. And, after many other observations, he has this further comment:[13]

Come now, let us also protest. But why? For if a thing seems good to us, we will find it most credible and respect it. But when it does not appear good to us, are we not under the influence of some unknown Fatality or Destiny, which is variously disposed toward each one of us. For one it is God who is at the origin, for another it is those tiny corpuscles borne aloft into the air, rebounding, separating, and coming together from necessity.

10. And again, a little further on:[14]

If I have added this to my discourse, it is because you, divine one, are ignorant of that of which we are masters, you who know all things and yet who do not know those things whose strings are tied to our will.

11. Such were the reproaches that the Cynic addressed to the Pythian oracle and at the same time to Democritus and Chrysippus, rightly indignant at the fact that after reducing to slavery the natural freedom of our soul, they had then delivered it to the exigencies of Fate and of Destiny. Destiny, according to Chrysippus,[15] is the organization of a design perfectly completed and achieved. Fatality[16] is a sort of woven design made by the will of God or some other cause; the Moirai are named from their task of apportioning and assigning a portion to each one;[17] Obligation is so-called from its association with indebtedness, that is to say, that which is imposed on us and makes us be obliged to Destiny.[18]

12. The number of the Fates signifies the three stages of time in

which all things proceed in a circular motion and through which they are accomplished.[19] The name "Lachesis" is derived from the allocation to each one of what is destined. "Atropos" expresses the fixity and immutability of what is apportioned; the name "Clotho recalls that all things are connected by spinning and are strung together, and that they constitute one sole preordained thought.[20] They call all this "providence" because it governs everything for a useful end. They also name it "Adrastea," because nothing runs away from it.[21]

13. Not merely the followers of Democritus, Chrysippus and Epicurus have asserted that everything comes by Necessity, by that meaning Fate, but the celebrated philosopher Pythagoras has also said[22] that the world is entirely enveloped by Necessity. Parmenides assigns to Necessity the names of Demon, Dike, and Providence.[23] Heraclitus maintains that everything comes in virtue of Fatality, and he has said that Fatality is Necessity.[24]

14. Chrysippus, the Stoic, for his part, says[25] that there is no difference between what is fated and what is imposed by necessity, and that Fatality is a movement that is eternal, continuous, and regulated. Zeno of Citium defines Fatality as a dynamic force of matter, and he names it also Providence and Nature.[26] His successors, however, claim that Fatality is the reason of things governed by Providence in the world, but again, in other writings, they have called Fate a series of causes.[27]

15. The same goes for Fortune. There are those who have deified it and have worshiped it as such. Plato has said that it is a cause produced by a certain coincidence and elsewhere has called it an accident of nature or of will.[28] Aristotle likewise has said that it is a fortuitous cause that is obscure and inconstant in beings which are directed by impulse toward some end.[29] Anaxagoras, Democritus, and the Stoic philosophers call it a cause that escapes human reason.[30]

16. But Philemon, the comic poet, consummate artist of the farcical that he is, completely contradicts those who regard Fortune as a deity and exclaims in the clearest terms:[31]

No, we have no goddess called Fortune.

There is no such being, but whatever happens by chance,
what happens for each is called Chance.

Philemon is also the one who mocks those who have recourse to auguries and omens. He says:[32]

> When I behold a slave on the watch to see who sneezes, or who speaks, or who comes out of the house, I at once offer him to the first bidder. It is to himself that each of us walks and speaks and sneezes, and not to all the city. Things happen as it is their nature.

17. Menander, likewise, in his *Superstitious Man*, laughs at those who have recourse to practices of this sort and says:[33]

> Now may some blessing be mine, O highly honored gods.
>
> For as I was fastening on my sandals,
>
> I broke the strap on the right-hand one.
>
> Naturally, you babbling fool! For it was rotten and you were too stingy to buy a new pair.

18. So, those who had devoted their lives to the theater and to comedy knew well that such fears and observances are ridiculous. And Antiphon, when someone was disturbed and regarded it as an omen signifying trouble when a sow ate her own offspring, said:[34]

> Be of good cheer at the sign. In her hunger the sow might well have eaten your own children.

19. Very similar is Bion's remark. He said with a smile:[35]

> "What is so wonderful about a mouse eating a sack when he is hungry! It would be astonishing if, as Archesilaus said in jest, the sack had devoured the mouse."

20. Diogenes, when someone saw a serpent wrapped around a pestle and was astonished, thinking it was a bad omen, said:[36]

Don't be astonished; because it would have been stranger
still if you saw the serpent upright and the pestle wrapped
around it.

On another occasion this same Diogenes, having read on the
house of a man of bad character the inscription:[37]

Here dwells Hercules the victor, son of Zeus, let nothing
evil enter here.

And how, he said, will the master of the house enter?

21. That is how even those who were enslaved to the error of superstition made fun of omens and auguries and of everything that people
even to the present day regard as prodigies. They say that when people
who sneeze, sneeze, they do not foretell anything to others except that
they suffer from the common cold. And that those who converse do not
foretell anything to others but merely make conversations about their
present circumstances. And that when the mouse, under the pressure of
hunger, ate the sack he did not foretell any prophecy to the owner of the
sack. And that when shoelaces break because of their age, it is not to
make some difficult prophecy, like the makers of oracles.

22. Keenly aware of all this, the Pythagorean Epicharmus urges
us to make light of all these things, and asks us to fear the all-seeing
One. This is how he expresses it:[38]

Nothing escapes the divinity. This you must know.

He is our overseer, and nothing is impossible to God.

23. And Diphilus, the comic poet, mingling a little true philosophy with his comedy, puts it this way: [39]

Do you think, Nicaretus, that the dead who have had their
share of pleasure in this life have escaped the divinity as if
they were forgotten?

There is an Eye of Justice that sees everything.

And so we believe that two ways lead to Hades,

One for the just and the other for the impious.

And a little later:[40]

Make no mistake. There is a judgment in Hades, which God will render, the Lord of the universe.

24. Since, then, all who commit sin do not pay their debt here below, and again the athletes of virtue deserving of victory do not all get their awards here, Diphilus has very appropriately shown the all-seeing eye and has proclaimed the future judgment, so that both fearing these punishments and believing that one day they will see Him, they will all devote themselves to the contests of virtue and not be despondent about not receiving the recompense for their efforts.

25. The Theban poet, Pindar, after bidding farewell to Fatality, Fortune, and Destiny, teaches those who do not know it the infinite power of God:[41]

God can make chaste light rise from black night and can conceal the pure light of day in cloud-wrapped darkness.

26. In his turn, the son of Aristo shows us still more clearly that He who presides over the universe takes in his hands the reins of government of the entire universe. This is what he says in the *Laws*:[42]

God, who, as the old saying has it, holds in his hands beginning, end, and middle of all that is, moves through the cycle of nature, straight to his end, and ever at his side walks right, he who administers justice for those who forsake God's law. He who would be happy follows close in her train with lowly and chastened mien, but whosoever is lifted up with vanity—with pride of riches or rank or foolish conceit of youthful comeliness—and all on fire within with wantonness, as one that needs neither governor nor guide, but is fitted rather to be himself a guide to others— such a one is left alone, forsaken by God. In his abandonment he takes to himself others like himself, and works general confusion by his frantic career. Now to some he seems some great one, but after no long while he makes no stinted amend to right by the sheer ruin of himself, his house, and his state.

27. That is how the philosopher represents the protector of the universe, the patience he sometimes exercises toward some, the injury that results from this in the case of the empty-headed, and the total destruction ensuing for them later.

28. In the *Gorgias* he also presents the reasons for punishment:[43]

> And it is proper for everyone who suffers a punishment rightly inflicted by another that he should either be improved and benefited thereby, or become a warning to the rest, in order that they may be afraid when they see him suffering what he does and may become better men. Now, those who are benefited through suffering punishment by gods and men are beings whose evil deeds are curable; nevertheless it is from pain and agony that they derive their benefit both here and in the other world, for it is impossible to get rid of evil otherwise. But those who have been guilty of the most heinous crimes and whose misdeeds are past cure—of these warnings are made, and they are no longer capable themselves of receiving any benefit, because they are incurable—but others are benefited who behold them suffering throughout eternity the greatest and most excruciating and terrifying tortures because of their misdeeds, literally suspended there as examples.

29. These sentiments the philosopher likely plagiarized from the divine oracles. For he certainly heard what divine words Moses was inspired to write to Pharaoh: *But this is why I have let you live: to show you my power, and to make my name resound through all the earth.*[44] For God inflicted all kinds of punishments on this man who had become totally depraved. It was not to make him better, for he knew that his mind was perverse and that his malady was incurable, but so that the events related concerning him might become examples beneficial for all.

30. Just as cities employ public executioners[45] in order to serve as correctors of assassins, thieves, and other delinquents, but without holding them in high esteem, for they greatly despise their chosen

avocation. But rather putting up with their services because it serves the public good, so likewise the One who presides over the universe allows tyrants to act like executioners, so that through their agency He may punish delinquents and wrongdoers. But later on He delivers the tyrants themselves to the most extreme punishments since they have performed their cruel deeds, not as ministers of the deity, but as slaves of their own iniquity.

31. It was thus that God delivered Israel, who had sinned, to the cruelty of the Assyrians; but as they did not comprehend the reason for this chastisement, God then destroyed their empire and forced them into subjection to others.[46] That is what Isaiah and Ezekiel and all the prophets clearly teach. They are the source, I think, of the pillagings of Plato when he says that those who are incurably disposed are punished as a lesson for others.

32. And in the *Philebus* he confirmed anew his view on providence:[47]

> For all the wise agree, thereby glorifying themselves in earnest, that in reason we have the king of heaven and earth. And I fancy they are right. But I should like us, if you don't mind, to make a fuller investigation of the kind in question itself.

Then, after using several reasonings, he continued thus:[48]

> Then are you willing that we should assent to what earlier thinkers agreed upon, that this is the truth? And ought we not only to think fit to record the opinions of other people without any risk to ourselves, but to participate in the risk and take our share of censure when some clever person asserts that the world is not as we describe it, but devoid of order?

33. And after several further developments he adds the following:[49]

> Discarding that, then, we should do better to follow the other view and say, as we have said many times already, there exist in the universe much "unlimited" and abundance of "limit," and a presiding cause of no mean power, which

orders and regulates the years, the seasons, and the months, and has every claim to the names of wisdom and reason.

And he has taken these remarks from the streams of the Hebrews. For there Scripture clearly teaches: *The Lord by wisdom founded the earth; by understanding he established the heavens,* and so on.[50]

34. In the *Laws* this same philosopher distinguished between the natures of blessings, showing that some are human and some divine. This is what he says:[51]

> But there are two different kinds of blessings, the merely human and the divine; the former are consequential on the latter. Hence a city that accepts the greater goods acquires the lesser along with them, but one that refuses them misses both. The lesser are those among which health holds the first place, comeliness the second, strength for the race and all other bodily exercises the third, while the fourth place belongs to a wealth that is not "blind," but clear-sighted, because it is attendant on wisdom. Of divine blessings, the first and foremost is this same wisdom, and next after it, sobriety of spirit; a third, resultant from the blending of both these with valor, is righteousness, and valor itself is fourth. All of these naturally rank before the former class and, of course, a lawgiver must observe that order. Next, he should impress it on his citizens that all his other injunctions have a view to these ends, and that among the ends, the human look to the divine, and all the divine to their leader, wisdom.

35. Then Plato teaches at greater length that only virtue is a natural blessing and that all other blessings have the same definition in an equivocal manner, but only in name:[52]

> For the things popularly called blessings do not really deserve the name. The saying, you know, is that health is the greatest of all blessings; beauty ranks second; and wealth, third; and there are innumerable other blessings, such as keen sight and hearing, and acute sensibility generally. It is good also to be an autocrat and gratify all one's

passions, and the very crown of felicity would be that the possessor of all these advantages should forthwith become immune from death. But what you and I maintain is that though all these endowments are great blessings to men of justice and religion, one and all of them, from health down, are great evils to the unjust. To be more specific, sight, hearing, sensation, life itself, are superlatively evil if one could persist forever without dying in the enjoyment of all these so-called blessings unaccompanied by justice and virtue at large, though less evil if he who is in such case survive only for a short while.

36. And a little later he adds:[53]

I affirm with confidence that so-called evils are good for the just, though evil for the unjust, and so-called blessings, though really good for good persons, evil for bad ones.

And I am totally in agreement with this distinction. The greatest blessing is in knowing what is properly a blessing and why it is called a blessing, and how a thing becomes a blessing, or, on the other hand, how it becomes the opposite.

37. Now health and beauty and bodily strength and, for that matter, wealth have been an advantage to some, and have shown them worthy of possessions, but for others they have been instruments of wickedness and intemperance. Temperance and justice and all such similar qualities are spiritual possessions; they are beneficial to all who possess them and are no inconvenience to them.

38. That is why, my dear friends, you should not confound the natures of things, but rather make the proper distinctions between what is truly good and evil, and what holds an intermediary position between the two. And let us not give the title "happy" to the wealthy, the physically strong, and those who are invested with a certain amount of power. For it is more appropriate to call such people truly unfortunate and thrice wretched, in that they make such possessions the basis for wickedness and immorality.

39. Now, when we see a person who is superabounding in riches leading a very immoral life, let us not call him thrice blessed simply because he has abundant opportunities for wrongdoing. Likewise

when we see someone else who appears a person of moderation and yet is tied to some misfortune or to poverty let us not define him as wretched or blame providence for being unjust.

40. For, in the first place, the one who seems to be just is not really just. The all-seeing eye sees and judges these things quite differently. This is the teaching that the one who oversees the universe gave to the prophet Samuel, saying: *"for the Lord does not see as mortals see; they look on the outward appearance, but the Lord looks on the heart."*[54]

41. And in order that we may define as truly just the one who is in the grip of some mischance this is a proof to everyone that the one educated as an athlete of virtue will not introduce any injury from a period of bad luck to bear his misfortunes. For just as they who live in wickedness make so-called blessings the instruments of viciousness, so they who love virtue succeed in translating so-called evils into the materials of a true philosophy.

42. Thus, then, if we make all of these distinctions we will never call God unjust, but rather will recognize that Plato was right in what he wrote in the *Theaetetus*:[55]

> The deity is never in any way unrighteous and nothing is more like the divine than any one of us who becomes as righteous as possible.

43. Again, elsewhere in Book 10 of the *Laws,* he tries to cure those who do not accept the idea of divine providence. This is what he says:[56]

> We are now to admonish him who confesses that gods exist but denies that they take any heed of the affairs of men. Fair sir, we will say, as to your belief in gods, it is perhaps some kinship with the divine that draws you to your native stock in worship and acknowledgment. On the other side there are private and public fortunes of ill and wicked men, fortunes truly unblessed, but passionately, though tastelessly, extolled as blessed by the voice of public repute, and these draw you toward irreligion.

44. After having described the so-called success of the wicked, see what Plato adds:[57]

Well, perhaps it would not be hard to establish as much as this, that the gods are more, not less, careful for small things than for the great. The man was present, you know, at our recent discussion and was told that the gods, who are good with perfect goodness, have the universal charge of all things as their special and proper function.

45. He corroborates this idea with certain proofs and proceeds:[58]

We are never, then, to fancy God the inferior of human workmen. The better they are at their work, the more exactly and perfectly do they accomplish their proper tasks, small or great, in virtue of one and the same skill and we must never suppose that God, who is at once supremely wise and both willing and able to provide, makes no provision for the small matters, which we have found it easier to care for, but only for the great, like some idle fellow or faintheart who shirks his work from fear of exertion.

46. Then he adds:[59]

No, sir, let us never entertain such a belief about gods; the thought would be wholly impious and utterly false.

Athenian. And now, I take it, we have had quite enough of controversy with him who is prone to charge the gods with negligence.

47. After numerous digressions he continues:[60]

For any physician or craftsman in any profession does all his work for the sake of some whole, to contribute to the general good, not the whole for the part's sake. And yet you murmur because you see not how in your own case what is best for the whole proves best also for yourself.

48. With all these reasons Plato has shown the justice of providence and has established that everything that happens is useful for the universe. For the universe has not been made for its most minute

part, but the parts produce the harmony of the whole. And the body has not been constituted for a single joint of a single finger, but the fingers and their joints have been constituted for the body.

49. Since, then, human nature is mortal and, being mortal, is in need of many things: agriculture, horticulture, navigation, the art of house building, working in bronze, weaving, tanning, and all the other crafts that contribute to serve the necessities of the body, it was exceedingly appropriate that the One who cares for the universe should allocate poverty to some and wealth to others, so that some would provide the raw materials and the others, the hands trained for the crafts.

50. He who presides over the universe has so allocated things that need makes those who pride themselves on their riches dependent on poverty through service.[61] For they need, not just bakers and pastry-makers and wine-servers, but also housebuilders, farmers, wool spinners, shoemakers, and those noted for painting, modeling, and the other crafts which beautify the homes of the wealthy. Manual workers, for their part, are in need of the wealthy few to pay cash for the work they do.

51. As for those who deplore and are embittered at the difference, in that all do not have an equal share in everything, let them also blame painters because they do not paint a single portrait but embellish their paintings differently. Let them also censure lyre-makers, and indeed the lyre players themselves, because the strings do not all emit the same sound, but the low has one sound, the high another, and the sharp, base, and medium, others still.[62]

52. It is fitting also that they be indignant at the geometers who, instead of showing their pupils that there is only one figure, also demonstrate the triangle, rectangle, crescent-shaped, circles, trapeziums, and many other such shapes too numerous to mention. And let them also criticize those who teach arithmetic, because some numbers are even, some odd, some even-odd, others odd-even, some cube numbers, others the product of two cube numbers.[63]

53. But if different numbers are a necessity, as well as a variety of shapes, differences of sounds, and a multiplicity of colors, why do you assail yourselves because you are not all like Croesus, Midas, and Darius?[64] In fact, with such a desire for equality you do not want anything else except the complete destruction of the human race caused by hunger and a shortage of the basic necessities.

54. If all were on the same level of equality who would find it acceptable to give of himself, to render service to another, the trouble, for instance, of laboring, tilling the earth, sowing the seeds, reaping, planting, pressing grapes and olives? Since equality of rank would not countenance one person serving another, how would each person be self-sufficient, being all at once a cowherd, goatherd, shepherd, swineherd, and also weaver, shoemaker, housebuilder, coppersmith, baker, pastry-maker, farmer, gardener, shipbuilder, sailor, and sea pilot?[65] For each has need of all these services and many besides.

55. Since this is so, why don't you praise so fine a distribution as the present, you who have servants and slaves, and farmers as many as you please? For the farmer loves the rank allotted to him, the servant likewise;[66] the manual worker loves his craft and the tasks assigned to him, while you who have a life of luxury and are overindulged and enjoy every kind of delicacy, thanks to the services of others, you counterattack with blasphemies the One who has orchestrated these blessings.

56. You bring forth these arguments, choosing to enslave yourselves to intemperance and hoping to find a pretext to justify the idea that there is no divine providence directing the rudders of the universe, and that, not just the body and its ambit are submitted to the necessity of fate, but even the very freewill of the soul.

57. But Plato teaches quite the opposite, saying:[67]

But virtue has no master over her, and each shall have more or less of her as he honors her or does her despite.

And further:[68]

The blame is his who chooses. God is blameless.

And Plato further shows Socrates in the midst of the worst dangers meditating on providence and on not fearing death. These are his words in the *Apology*:[69]

You too, gentlemen of the jury, must look forward to death with confidence and fix your minds on this one belief which is certain that nothing can harm a good man either in life or after death, and fortunes are not a matter of indifference to the gods.

58. So, then, poverty, disease, slavery, and death are not real evils; they are called evil by the ignorant, but they become blessings for those who use them wisely and well. That disbelieving in the fact that the universe is directed by providence will serve to increase the wretchedness of human beings, Atticus, the Platonist, exclaims:[70]

How provocative of wickedness is the failure to recognize providence!

PLOTINUS ON PROVIDENCE

59. And Plotinus too, famous also for his philosophical works, has placed this Preface at the beginning of his treatise *On Providence*:[71]

To attribute the being and structure of this All to accident and chance is unreasonable and belongs to a man without intelligence or perception; this is obvious, even before demonstration, and many adequate demonstrations have been set down that show it.

Then, after developing many similar ideas, he continues:[72]

So from Intellect which is one, and the formative principle that proceeds from it, this All has arisen and separated into parts.

60. These ideas also he has stolen from the sacred oracles. For he had certainly heard the theology of the divine Gospels which teaches that *all things came into being through him, and without him not one thing came into being.*[73] Plotinus lived some years after the Apostles, who were sent to preach salvation under Tiberius Caesar; Tiberius was succeeded by Gaius, Gaius by Nero, Vespasian, Titus, Domitian, Nerva, Trajan, Hadrian, Antoninus the first, Verus, and Commodus.[74] It was under Commodus that Ammonius, surnamed Saccas, abandoned the sacks in which he carried the wheat and undertook the philosophical life. It is said that he had the Christian Origen as a student, and that Plotinus in turn was his student.[75] Porphyry was a student of Plotinus.
61. It is not just for the pleasure of empty chatter that I have pro-

vided these chronological signposts but to show that Plotinus had not merely like Plato studied the doctrine of the Hebrews, but also the doctrine of the fishermen and of the tanner, and had derived from this source the fact that it was from Intelligence and his Logos that the universe derives its beginnings and its dimensions and has been able to find the harmony that belongs to it.[76]

62. Then he refutes the folly of those who try to slander certain parts of creation, speaking as follows:[77]

> For it produced a whole, all-beautiful and self-sufficient friends with itself and with its parts, both the more important and the lesser, which are all equally well adapted to it. So he who blamed the whole because of the parts would be quite unreasonable in his blame; one must consider the parts in relation to the whole to see if they are harmonious and in concord with it; and when one considers the whole one must not look at a few little parts.

> This is not blaming the universe but asking some of its parts separately, as if one were to take a single hair of a whole living being, or a toe, and neglect the whole man, a wonderful sight to see; or, really, to ignore the rest of living beings and pick out the meanest; or to pass over the whole race, say, of men and bring forward Thersites. Since, then, what has come into being is the whole universe, if you contemplate this, you might hear it say, "A god made me, and I came from him perfect above all living things and complete in myself and self-sufficient, lacking nothing, because all things are in me, plants and animals and the nature of all things that have come into being."

63. In this text Plotinus has manifested yet another plagiarism from his borrowings, for he seems to me to have heard the inspired David say: *The heavens are telling the glory of God; and the firmament proclaims his handiwork.*[78] A little further on, Plotinus shows the difference between things that have come into being:[79]

> And some things appear to participate only in being others in life; others more fully in life in that they have sense-

perception; others at the next stage have reason; and others, the fullness of life. One must not demand equal gifts in things which are not equal. It is not the finger's business to see, but this is the eyes' function, and the finger is something else, to be essentially finger and to have its function.

64. For Plotinus, stones and things of that sort participate only in existence, but he says that plants participate also in life, that animals, along with life, have also sense-perception, that humankind participates in reason, and that beings that are immaterial by nature have the perfect life. He then adds the following:[80]

> That water extinguishes fire and fire consumes other things should not astonish us. The thing destroyed derives its being from outside itself.

65. In the same treatise Plotinus has some observations about virtue and vice:[81]

> Many things are affected by other things bent on some other object and unintentionally. But living beings which have of themselves a movement under their own control might incline sometimes to what is better, sometimes to what is worse. It is probably not worth inquiring into the reason for this self-caused turning towards the worse; for a deviation that is slight to begin with, as it goes on in this way continually makes the fault wider and graver; and the body is there too, and, necessarily, its lust. And the first beginning, the sudden impulse, if it is overlooked and not immediately corrected even produces a settled choice of that into which one has fallen. Punishment certainly follows; and it is not unjust that someone who has come to be this sort of person should suffer the consequences of his condition. People must not demand to be well-off who have not done what deserves well-being. Only the good are well-off; that, too, is what gives the gods their well-being. If, then, it is possible for souls to be well-off in this All, we must not blame the place if some are not well-off, but their own incapacity, in that they have not been able to take a

noble part in the contest for which the prizes of virtue are offered. Why is it disconcerting if men who have not become godlike do not have a godlike life?

66. Then he enumerates the adversities and says that they are necessary for sinners:[82]

And poverty, too, and sickness, are nothing to the good, but advantageous to the bad; and men must fall sick if they have bodies. And even these troubles are not altogether without usefulness for the coordination and completion of the whole.

67. He then explains how these examples profit the majority of other persons:[83]

Vice works something useful to the whole by becoming an example of just punishment; and also of itself it offers much that is of use. For it makes men awake and wakes up the intelligence and understanding of those who are opposed to the ways of wickedness, and makes us learn what a good virtue is by comparison with the evils of which the wicked have a share. And evils did not come into existence for these reasons, but we have explained that, when they have come into existence, the formative principle uses even them to meet a need. This belongs to the greatest power, to be able to use even the evil nobly and to be strong enough to use things that have become shapeless for making other shapes. In general, we must define evil as a falling short of good.

68. After further reflections of this kind, Plotinus advises that we must not require perfection completely and unalloyed in the mingled, saying:[84]

A preliminary observation: in looking for excellence in this thing of mixture, we cannot require all that is implied in the excellence of the unmingled; it is folly to ask for Firsts in the Secondary but since (this Universe) contains body, we must allow for some bodily influence upon the total and be thankful if the mingled existent lack nothing of what its nature allowed it to receive from the Logos.

69. He is indignant at those who are unwilling to fight for virtue but who demand salvation from God. These are his words:[85]

One set are unarmed, and those who are armed get the mastery. Here it would not be right for a god to fight in person for the unwarlike; the law says that those who fight bravely, not those who pray, are to come safe out of wars; for, in just the same way, it is not those who pray but those who look after their land who are to get in a harvest, and those who do not look after their health are not to be healthy; and we are not to be vexed if the bad get larger harvests, or if their farming generally goes better. Then again it is ridiculous for people to do everything else in life according to their own ideas, even if they are not doing it in the way which the gods like, and then be merely saved by the gods without even doing the things by means of which the gods command them to be saved themselves. And certainly death is better for them than to stay living in a way in which the universal laws do not want them to live; so that if the opposite happened, and peace was preserved in every sort of folly and vice, providence would be neglecting its duty in allowing the worse really to get the upper hand. But the wicked rule by the cowardice of the ruled; for this is just, and the opposite is not. Providence ought not to exist in such a way as to make us nothing. If everything was providence and nothing but providence, then providence would not exist; for what would it have to provide for? There would be nothing but the divine.

70. A little further on he indicates the rewards of the good:[86]

Those who have become good, he says, shall have a good life now and laid up for them hereafter as well. But for the wicked, the opposite. But it is not lawful for those who have become wicked to demand others to be their saviors and to sacrifice themselves in answer to their prayers.

71. This is what he goes on to say about other living beings:[87]

And besides, no one of any intelligence complains of all the other creatures, lower than himself, which ornament the earth. It would be ridiculous if someone complained of their biting men, as if men ought to pass their lives asleep. No, it is necessary these too should exist; and some of the benefits that come from them are obvious, and those that are not evident many of them time discovers; so that none of them exists without good purpose, even for men. But it is absurd, too, to complain that many of them are savage, when there are savage men as well.

72. And after some other considerations he adds this:[88]

But we are like people who know nothing about the art of painting and criticize the painter because the colors are not beautiful everywhere, though the artist has really distributed the appropriate tint to every spot. Or we are like someone who censures a drama because all the characters in it are not all heroes, but include a servant and a rustic and one who speaks in a scurrilous way. The drama is not a good one, however, if one takes away the low characters because they too help to complete it.

73. The whole work of Plotinus, Books Two and Three, is filled with such considerations. But I, for my part, will not draw it out too much and will dispense with further quotations. I could, however, use the witness of Xenophon, student of Socrates, also that of the Stoic Epictetus,[89] and some others, and with arguments from nature would be in a position to respond to the stupidity of those who do not believe in the teaching that I have presented. But I believe the texts I have assembled are sufficient to confirm the truth of what I have said.

74. There is one observation that I think might be good to add to what I have said. Granted that the Creator exercises His providence over the universe, the principle of the economy of the Savior seems impervious to attack and unambiguous. For it would be inappropriate for the Architect of the universe who had conferred being on the non-

existent to overlook humanity destroying itself seeing that He had created for it the entire visible world.

75. The earth, in fact, is the abode of humans and the heavens are their roof. Air, sea, rivers, fountains, gatherings of clouds, dew and winds, fruit trees and non-fruit trees, living creatures, terrestrial, aquatic and amphibian, the many species of flowers, and the varied metals are all placed at the disposal of humankind.[90]

76. And so it is that sun and moon and the multitude of stars, in dividing time in two, divided it equally. The sun illuminates the day and summons us to work, while the moon and stars have provided light for night.[91]

77. And so the Lord of the universe did not think it right that He should disregard the one besieged by sin and about to be handed over as a prisoner to death for whose sake He had already done all these good things. For this reason he took on human form and veiled His invisible nature under a visible one. He preserved His visible nature free from sin and maintained His hidden nature in its state of integrity.

78. The divine nature did not partake of the passions of the flesh, nor did the flesh share in the defilements of sin. For it would have been easy for the Lord to effect the salvation of humankind without this veil of the flesh and by a mere act of will to destroy the empire of death, to cause sin, the mother of death, to disappear utterly, and to drive from the face of the earth the all-wicked devil, who was in travail to produce sin, and to commit him to the darkness of hell to which he would shortly deliver him. But He preferred to manifest the justice of His providence rather than His power.

79. Likewise He could have addressed humanity from the heavens to warn them about living the life of ease, but He did not pursue that course of action for He knew they could not endure that course of action. Apart from manifesting Himself occasionally, adapting his appearances to the capacities of his audience, it is always through mortals that He has continued to legislate for mortals and exhort them, utilizing the prophets as intermediaries and ministers of his words. So when, later on, He wished to bring to all humanity the remedies of salvation He had recourse not to the ministry of angels or of archangels, nor did He cause to shine a voice from the heights of heaven that everybody would be able to understand, but He constructed his human body in a virgin's womb, from which He emerged, a man in appearance but God as adored, the same who before all the

ages was engendered from the Father's substance, and has taken what is visible of Him from the virgin, which is at once new and eternal.[92]

80. The union is, in fact, not a blending of natures, nor has it subjected to time the Maker of time, not to mention that He who was born in time was anterior to time. On the contrary, each of the two natures has remained intact; the human nature endures the weaknesses of nature, namely, hunger, thirst, tiredness, fatigue, the cross, death. The divine nature enacts divine actions, performing miracles quite naturally, enabling human feet to walk on the surface of the sea, causing five loaves to more than satisfy many thousands, donating wine at the wedding feast, curing withered bodies, fashioning with mud eyes that nature had neglected to form in the maternal womb, with a mere word binding fast infirm limbs, opening tombs and calling forth the interred, causing them to run, and doing other things taught in the writings of the divine Gospels.[93]

81. If you marvel at all this and say it is an offering of God, but insist on calling this organization disharmonious, it is total recklessness and madness to present oneself as wiser than the wisdom that has ordained the universe, to be discontented with that which happens thanks to His care, and to feel that a better mode of operation can be found than the present system.

82. But since you are so callow as to think you can come up with plans that surpass the abyss of wisdom, then let you show a plan that is better than ours to procure salvation. But you will fail hopelessly to do so. God has given proof of such excess of love for humans that you and those like you are incapable of believing that the only-begotten Son of God, God the Word, anterior to all ages, the Demiurge of the universe, has taken on human nature, become incarnate, and accomplished our salvation.[94]

83. And yet you greatly admire those medical practitioners who do not just prescribe a remedy for others but actually take off their coats and belt their loins, then take the lance in hand and perform the surgery, while enduring the stench, allowing the drops of puss to overflow, fomenting the wounds with a sponge, administering medications, and performing all the prescriptions of medical science.

84. And furthermore, it is your good pleasure to admire and speak highly of those kings who do not just confine themselves to their regal quarters and revel in luxury of all kinds, but who join their

subjects in running risks, put on their battle array, and take a leadership role in their army divisions.

85. But if you say why, then, did not the Creator of the universe take these measures long ago,[95] then again you should think of the medical practitioners who keep the most extreme measures as a last recourse; they use greater remedies at first, and apply the most potent ones at the end.

PROVIDENCE ACCORDING TO PLATO

86. That too is what the all-wise Physician of our souls has done. For, having applied many different remedies, using creation and human nature to convince all, and the law and the prophets for the Hebrews, at last He has applied this sovereign and salvific remedy, and has banished the disease.

87. Facts bear out my words. Earth and sea are freed from their ancient ignorance; the error of idols is no longer to be seen; the darkness of ignorance has been dispersed, and the light of knowledge fills with its rays the whole inhabited world. Greeks, Romans, and barbarians recognize the divinity of the crucified and venerate the sign of the cross. The Trinity is worshiped in place of a multitude of false gods. The temples of the demons have been leveled to the ground. The altars of idols have been wrenched from their bases. Splendid churches have grown up on all sides; in towns, cities, in the countryside, and in the remotest areas beautiful monuments to the martyrs have been erected. The abodes of the ascetics sanctify the mountaintops and populate deserts that had previously been uninhabited.

88. These and similar events show that the Incarnation of the Savior has a divine stamp.[96] And in turn the divine prophecies carry to the Gospels the witness of truth. They contain, in fact, the prediction of the Gospels, and the Gospels show their fulfillment. The Gospels have announced the virginal birth; the prophecies teach the truth of the prophecy. The prophecies have predicted the crucifixion. The Gospels have brought it before our eyes. The prophecies predict wonders; the Gospels narrate them.[97]

89. The prophecies foretold the salvation of the world. We have seen the fulfillment of these prophecies. They have foretold in advance both the incredulity of the Jews and their mass destruction. We have witnessed their incredulity, and their Diaspora and enslavement.[98]

90. Had I not been reluctant, because of the length of my discourse, to alienate both you and those who happen on them at a later time, I would have brought forward the actual words of the blessed prophecies, so that you might with greater accuracy have learned the truth of the narrative from the actual events. But since the actual quantity of the words did not allow me to do this, I demand, my friends, that you believe in the prophecies, and hear the actual events crying out, and obey the tragic poet Euripides in the *Oenomaos*:[99]

We have indications of the unseen in the visible.

And again, in the *Phoenix*:

The unseen can reasonably be inferred from the seen.

91. And if the tragic poet is not a credible witness for you, then give ear to the orator, Hyperides, who says:[100]

For whatever is not evident, it is necessary that those who teach should seek with proofs and comparisons that have probability.

And Isocrates, in the same vein, says:[101]

The future must be borne witness to by the past.

Furthermore, Andocides, one of the ten great Greek orators, also said:[102]

For the future one must have recourse to the pointers from the past.

92. For since, in fact, you hold to excessive elegance of expression, from there we have the demonstrations come to you, so that, led step by step through them to the truth and seeing the epiphany of our God and Savior proclaimed through deeds, you will gladly accept the account of his economy and may not fail to attain salvation so desirable and so thrice desired.

Discourse 7

ON SACRIFICES

THE DEVIL STIFLES THE MORAL SENSE OF IDOLATERS

1. For the most part the majority of people like to be amused and love to laugh; they find their pleasure, not in a serious, disciplined life but in a relaxed, easygoing one. That is why the all-evil demon so easily wins sway over them. For he does not order them to take that straight and narrow path, the one which is hard to walk on and goes uphill, but rather the one which goes down and is steep, smooth, and easy to travel.[1]

2. In fact, far from prescribing that they should show concern for temperance and chastity, the demon by contrast has taught them to deliver themselves unrestrainedly to license and debauchery and every kind of immorality. That is why it has been so easy for him to reduce to slavery the greater part of the human race.[2] In fact, people flee from attempting to live virtuously and tend to run away from the hardship of virtue and the ardors of the divine laws. Instead, they transfer without difficulty to the one who has legalized what is easiest and most pleasant.

3. Having enslaved them in this way, the devil then proceeds to eradicate the ideas that the God of the universe has engraved on them from the beginning. Next he has taught them the perverse doctrines of the false gods and has schooled them to adore this crowd of non-beings instead of the One who is. Such is the basis and foundation which he has prearranged for the dissolute life.

4. For men, when they commit a fault, feel some kind of remorse. Reason gnaws at them from within and does not allow the pleasure of the sin to remain unmixed, but mingles with it the bitterest pain. One can see a person experiencing this who has dared to rob a tomb, or

159

commit fornication, or do a burglary, or a betrayal, or any other kind of misdeed. But the charlatan of wickedness has invented a drug to immunize the housebreaker, the footpad, the traitor, and other malefactors.

5. For he has taught them perverse beliefs concerning the so-called gods. He has displayed them as unbridled, extremely sexual and pederastic wreckers of marriages, parricides, matricides, ones who sleep with their mothers, sisters, even daughters.[3] He has depicted them as plundering one another's marriage beds, being caught in the act, and then, chained by the wronged party, being shamelessly laughed at by the other deities,[4] and that all these things are dared by the heavenly beings in the heavens and on earth, as they themselves admit, and by amphibian creatures in the sea and on land, and by the so-called nymphs in mountains, valleys, and ravines.

6. Not only did he (the devil) re-echo those scurrilous and shameful myths in the poets, but also in the theologians and philosophers, preparing such errors in such a variety of ways and using so many teachers for deceit. But since not everybody is knowledgable in literature, nor adequately equipped to utilize poetical and philosophical tracts, he prepared other traps for those who could not study the matter in writing.

7. He taught the painters, the bronze-workers, the gem-cutters, the makers of stone and wooden statues to design, sculpt, and shape images of the so-called gods just as the mythmakers have described in their works, so that those who cannot benefit from the written works may have archetypes of vice and might not be deprived of this pornographic teaching.[5] And with such monuments he has filled not only their sanctuaries but even their public squares, the highways, and indeed the homes of the well-to-do.[6]

8. On every side it is possible to find the so-called gods in poses of lovemaking, and warring, and mounting, and the father of the gods is depicted as an eagle, a bull, or a swan, and in this way having sex with his loved one,[7] and Hermes, the eloquent one, becoming transformed into a goat,[8] and Pan, with the shanks of a goat and the horns of a goat, having sex.[9]

9. And why is it necessary to speak of the love of the Pythian one,[10] and the chastity of the virgin,[11] and the frantic intertwining of the laurel tree,[12] and the rape of Demeter by Pluto,[13] and the wandering of Deo?[14] All these things the poets have narrated in their myths

and the theologians have maintained and have striven to inject a certain measure of solemnity into them, thereby making the allegory more laughable than the myths.

10. The avenging demon of humanity has decreed festivals to be solemnized for these, and feasts, and public holy days—the Pandia and Diasia for Zeus,[15] the Heraia for Hera,[16] the Panathenaia for Athena,[17] the Dionysia for Dionysus,[18] the Eleusinia and Thesmophoria for Demeter,[19] the Delia and the Pythia for Apollo.[20] And for each of the other gods, for there is a great crowd of them, he has allocated festivals, naming the feast after the name of each of the daimons, the Hermaia,[21] and Kronia,[22] and Poseidonia,[23] and Heracleia,[24] and Asclepia,[25] and Anakia.[26] For they have assigned this reverence not just to the so-called gods but even to mortals.

11. For the rest, in these assemblies people are delivered up to every kind of debauchery. Their mysteries and their orgies have their appropriate symbols: the feast at Eleusis, the female sex organ;[27] the Phallagogia, the phallus.[28] But, independently of the symbols, the deeds and gestures of the celebrants excite the audience to every kind of gross behavior.

12. So, in fact, what the inveterate roué does in the secret of his bedroom, the choir of Satyrs do quite openly in the course of the public processions with Silenus and Pan, the one in the upsurge of his passion rushing on the Bacchants,[29] and the other, who was, it is said, the pedagogue of this young effeminate creature, being dead drunk.[30]

13. For them, they sacrificed hundreds, indeed thousands, of victims; they butchered flocks of sheep and droves of cattle; they offered incense and poured out wine profusely in libation and everything the priests prescribed.

14. The poets say in fact that the gods greatly appreciate libations and the smoke of fat and that they themselves have prescribed it as a mark of honor. It is precisely for this reason that they went to seek sacrifices in Ethiopia and that they found Hector worthy of every attention because he never left their altars without sacrifices.[31] As for Chryses, it was not about justice or chastity that he conversed with Apollo, but of fat thighs, and goats, and bulls, and the garlands with which he decorated his temple.[32]

15. They also loved the smoke and the bad odor of a burnt sacrifice, and they truly had the air of chefs. Still it would not be quite accurate to compare them with cooks![33] For cooks smell and taste the dishes

which are prepared with such care, while the others gather the putrid odor of burnt bones. As for us, if any offscourings of that kind fall in the fire we become very upset and hold our nose and try to expel the offensive odor, but those who can feast on nectar and ambrosia are apparently overpowered by the infectious odor of burning bone.

16. Perhaps they will dare to say similar things also about the true and eternal God since they have heard the Scriptures speak of sacrificial laws, and they are completely ignorant of the import of such laws. In fact during their entire stay in Egypt the people of Israel had contracted the evil habits of the natives, and had taken to their practice of sacrificing to idols and to demons, to playing and dancing and becoming distracted with musical instruments. Wishing to free them from this kind of activity, God allowed them to offer sacrifices, not indeed every kind of sacrifice, and certainly not sacrifice to the false gods of Egypt, but only to offer to the real Egyptian gods. It is known that the Egyptians sometimes deified the cow, the sheep, the goat, the dove, the turtle, and certain other animals which are not edible but are regarded as unclean.[34]

17. So as to avoid irritating them by completely forbidding them involvement in such practices, God forbade them to sacrifice to false gods, but He prescribed for them in the law that they should sacrifice to that which they had lately adored: earthly animals like the goat, the cow, and the sheep; and birds like the turtle and the dove. Notice that all of these are domestic creatures, the friends of human beings.

18. Such is the remedy that this skilled Physician has applied to the Egyptian malady. He allowed them to offer sacrifices as a concession to their weakness, but with the understanding that they should consecrate the ancient objects of their worship, so that by this act of sacrifice they would learn not to mistake for gods what was sacrificed as a sacred object.

19. It was also for this reason that He forbade them to eat pork. The Egyptians eat only pork and they abstain from the other animals because they regard the other animals as gods. So, having decreed they should consider these animals as unclean, He ordered them to eat the deified animals, so that what was eaten by them might appear despicable and might be alienated from divine worship.[35]

20. Knowing, in fact, that they were superstitious and very gluttonous, he opposed disease to disease and juxtaposed gluttony and superstition. He ordered them to abstain from pork because it was

impure, prescribed the enjoyment of other foods by declaring them pure, and forced them to replace the imaginary gods with the desire of eating meat.

21. It was not, then, because He had need of sacrificial victims, or that He wished for the odor of fat, that God has prescribed the offering of sacrifices, but because He wished to cure the maladies of their weaknesses. Similarly He tolerated musical instruments, not that He was sensible to their harmony but to put an end bit by bit to the error of idol worship. In fact, if God had given them the laws in their perfect state when they were coming close to being liberated from permanent contact with the Egyptians, they would surely have become capricious; they would have rejected the bridle and would have hastened to return to their first misery. If in such an order of things they tried to do this often, what would they not have dared if he had given them the evangelical legislation right from the beginning?

22. To realize that God had no need for sacrifices or musical instruments, listen to what He himself says through the prophets: *I will not accept a bull from your house, or goats from your folds. For every wild animal of the forest is mine, the cattle on a thousand hills.*[36] In these words God has rejected all that the Law prescribed in offerings, not just animals of the earth but also the wine from the winepress, and the olive oil which was offered with the finest flour and sacrificial cakes.

23. He calls all these things "the beauty of the field" and shows that all those creations, the one and the others, belong to Him, teaching thereby that the divine nature is in need of nothing. Then with charming irony that is very instructive he proves to them that they are ignorant and demonstrates his power.

24. *If I were hungry, I would not tell you, for the world and all that is in it is mine.*[37] Thus, having clearly shown his creativity and absolute power through these things, he has resorted to ironic statement in the words: *Do I eat the flesh of bulls, or drink the blood of goats?*[38] And through all these statements he has shown that sacrifices are perfectly superfluous and unworthy of the divine nature and He has substituted a new kind of sacrifice which does not pour blood upon the altar but is accomplished by the tongue and the lips: *Offer to God a sacrifice of thanksgiving, and pay your vows to the Most High. Call on me in the day of trouble; I will deliver you, and you shall glorify me.*[39]

25. Because God is content with a word of blessing and of offering over and above all the flocks of sheep, and of goats, and of cattle.

And when He receives that much He requites those who offer it to him, proffering assistance, coming to one's defense at the appropriate time, and offering deliverance from attempts at corruption. It is the same consideration he repeats at the end of the psalm: *Those who bring thanksgiving as their sacrifice honour me; to those who go the right way I will show the salvation of God.*[40]

26. Because it is not enough to chant the praises of the Benefactor; it is necessary to continue on that road which leads to true salvation. This is what, in another psalm, the prophet says to God: *Not for your sacrifices do I rebuke you; your burnt-offerings are continually before me.*[41] And in another psalm he has said this to us: *I will praise the name of God with a song; I will magnify him with thanksgiving. This will please the Lord more than an ox or a bull with horns and hoofs.*[42]

27. But, lest anyone suppose that David is the only one to have written like this, listen, my friends, to what God Himself has again said through the mouth of Isaiah. These are his words: *What to me is the multitude of your sacrifices? says the Lord; I have had enough of burnt-offerings of rams and the fat of fed beasts; I do not delight in the blood of bulls, or of lambs, or of goats. When you come to appear before me, who asked this from your hand?*[43]

28. He has shown precisely by these words that it is not out of necessity that He has established these laws but out of condescension to our weakness. That is the significance of the final phrase—*who asked this from your hands?* And he continued: *Trample my courts no more; bringing offerings is futile; incense is an abomination to me. New moon and sabbath and calling of convocation—I cannot endure solemn assemblies with iniquity. Your new moons and your appointed festivals my soul hates; they have become a burden to me, I am weary of bearing them.*[44]

PREFIGURATION OF BAPTISM

29. These words are very similar to those of the canticle of David. Because here God has equally rejected not merely bulls, rams, and sheep, but also flour, aromatic perfume, and the list of festivals. And just as by the mouth of David he had proscribed such ceremonies and ordered them to offer a sacrifice of praise, so here, rejecting each of these things, he indicated to them the baptism of immortality and regeneration, saying: *Wash yourselves; make yourselves clean.*[45]

30. And, lest they think that He was ordering them to have recourse to the usual ablutions, he was forced to add: *Remove the evil of your doings from before my eyes.*[46] By this he clearly hints at the gift of the all-holy baptism. In the midst of the prophecy the God of prophecy says through the prophet:

31. *Yet you did not call upon me, O Jacob; but you have been weary of me, O Israel! You have not brought me your sheep for burnt-offerings, or honoured me with your sacrifices. I have not burdened you with offerings, or wearied you with frankincense. You have not bought me sweet cane with money, or satisfied me with the fat of your sacrifices. But you have burdened me with your sins; you have wearied me with your iniquities.*[47]

32. Thus again, having shown them the folly of their forms of worship under the law, He promised them remission of sins which He bestowed upon them through the all-holy baptism. *I, I am He who blots out your transgressions for my own sake, and I will not remember your sins.*[48] For clearly it is not through praiseworthy actions but by faith alone that we obtain mystical blessings.

33. It is for this reason that the divine apostle has also proclaimed: *For by grace you have been saved through faith, and this is not your own doing; it is the gift of God—not the result of works, so that no one may boast.*[49] Wishing to show that here, the prophet has inserted the words "for my sake."

34. For it is clear that what He prescribed in the law concerning these things sprang, not from God's own need or will, but from mankind's imperceptiveness. This is also attested through the mouth of Jeremiah when he says: *Thus says the Lord of hosts, the God of Israel: Add your burnt-offerings to your sacrifices, and eat the flesh. For on the day that I brought your ancestors out of the land of Egypt, I did not speak to them or command them concerning burnt-offerings and sacrifices.*[50] Elsewhere He has also said: *Your burnt-offerings are not acceptable, nor are your sacrifices pleasing to me.*[51] And again He has exclaimed: *Take away from me the noise of your songs; I will not listen to the melody of your harps..*[52]

35. It is easy to find elsewhere other texts of the same kind which show clearly that God prescribed these things, not because he was in need of sacrifices and delighted in smoke and smell of fat and musical instruments, but because He was preoccupied with their cure.

PORPHYRY'S TESTIMONY AGAINST SACRIFICES

36. Do not think, then, that this counteraccusation exonerates you from the charge brought against your sacrifices, because the Legislator has shown in no uncertain terms through the prophets the scope of the law. Porphyry had carefully consulted them—for he spent much time involved with them when he was churning up his work, *Against the Christians*[53]—and he himself demonstrates that the offering of sacrifices is alien to true piety. Acting a little like monkeys he arrives at the same conclusions.

37. For just as monkeys imitate what humans do without turning into human beings, but while still remaining monkeys, so Porphyry in the same way plundered the sacred oracles and introduced the thought of some of them into his own writings without being willing to exchange his own ideas for the truth; he has remained a monkey, or rather a jackdaw dressed up in borrowed plumes.[54]

38. After having written at length on the obligation of abstaining from live animals Porphyry cites Theophrastus to the effect that men of old did not offer incense or other sacrifice, but that they raised a little green grass in their hands and burned it up like fine efflorescence of a fecund nature wishing to honor by that kind of sacrifice those who seemed to be heavenly gods.

39. After dilating some more on that subject he adds:[55]

In due course the firstfruits produced disorders for men; the usage of the worst kind of sacrifices was accompanied with savagery so that the curse formerly pronounced against us now received its fulfillment in consequence of men slaughtering and bloodying the altars.

40. After a lengthy development of this theme he adds that he cannot imagine that those who take pleasure in sacrifices made from living beings can be real gods, because there is a great element of injustice in the act of making a live sacrifice; it is impious, abominable, and execrable, and so it could not possibly be pleasing to the gods. He adds the following remark:[56]

Rightly has Theophrastus forbidden the sacrifice of living

beings to those who wish to perform true worship, employing other similar arguments.

41. He then shows what kind of sacrifice is appropriate, adding:[57]

Those kinds of sacrifices should be offered which cause no injury in the course of the sacrifice, for nothing should cause less injury to anyone than a sacrifice.

And he says elsewhere:[58]

We must abstain from offering living beings in sacrifice.

And he recalls to memory the human sacrifices that were attempted in former times. He says:[59]

There was a sacrifice in Rhodes at the beginning of the month of Metageitnion on the sixth day when a man was sacrificed to Cronus. This practice was maintained for a long time and became converted into an established custom. They used to keep one of those condemned to death for the feast of Cronus.

42. He goes on to say that in the island of Cyprus at Salamis a man is sacrificed also to Agraulos, the son of Cecrops, and that at Heliopolis in Egypt three men are slaughtered daily. And he says that a man is sacrificed by the Spartans to Ares, and that similar sacrifices are performed in Laodicea in Syria and in Carthage in Libya; also that the Greeks offer a human sacrifice at the outset of war, and he relates other facts of the same nature.[60]

43. Philo, the historian, for his part relates[61] that Aristomenus, the Messenian, sacrificed three hundred men to Zeus Ithomete. And Plutarch relates[62] other things similar to these, and other writers have made many similar contributions. The tragedians have related similar distressful matters in their tragedies, that of Menoecus at Thebes,[63] and of Codros and the daughters of Leo at Athens.[64]

44. And it is easy for anyone who wishes to consult the ancient historians and to learn that the so-called gods ordered this kind of sacrifice. As for our Creator and Master He denounces outright this dis-

order and He exclaimed through the mouth of David: *They sacrificed their sons and their daughters to the demons; they poured out innocent blood, the blood of their sons and daughters, whom they sacrificed to the idols of Canaan.*[65] And through the prophet Ezekiel he formulated the reproach anew, saying: *You took your sons and your daughters, whom you had borne to me, and these you sacrificed to them to be devoured. As if your whorings were not enough!* [66]

SOPHOCLES AND SOCRATES CORROBORATE THE SCRIPTURES

45. Such, then, were the outrageous practices of old of the Greeks, Romans, and Egyptians, and indeed of the Hebrews and the other non-Greek speakers. But after the epiphany of our God and Lord, all that was snuffed out and the divine laws of the Gospel became publicized.

46. When Sophocles, the Athenian, composed those tragedies full of bloodshed he included some excellent theology in them and wisely parodied the statues of the demons and the unlawful sacrifices. He speaks as follows:[67]

> There is in truth one god, who has fashioned
> the heavens and the broad earth,
> and the blue depths of the sea and the gusts of the winds;
> But many of us mortals, erring in our hearts,
> have constructed as consolation for our pains
> statues of the gods made of stone and bronze,
> or images of chiseled gold or of ivory
> crowning them with sacrifices and fair festivals
> thus thinking that we are acting with piety.

47. That is why it is not just us, but also your own poets, historians, and philosophers, who laugh at your concepts of the gods. As for me, I believe that when Socrates, son of Sophroniscus, ordered a cock to be sacrificed, it was in order to refute the case that was made against him (for Anytus and Meletus had prosecuted him on a charge of not believing in the gods);[68] I further feel he knew the divinity was in need of nothing as he has clearly shown elsewhere in his writings.

48. And this was the view of Socrates himself, for Plato has simply recorded the views of Socrates.[69] For it was not out of any need that God created the universe or that He might enjoy honors from men and from other gods and demons. He has clearly shown through these remarks that the deity is in need of nothing and that such sacrifices are so much smoke, and indeed they are full of rank-smelling fumes.

49. Having learned all these things from your teachers and from the divine Scriptures, from which these writers have plundered those teachings to reinforce their own, reject those sacrifices which are appropriate to chefs and butchers, and offer instead the sacrifice of praise to the Lord. Be persuaded to follow this line of action, not by civil laws[70] nor by fear of chastisement, but by the power of truth which has become known everywhere.

Discourse 8

ON THE CULT OF MARTYRS

Truth in Simplicity

1. The illustrious Pythagoras, whose fame is widespread among you, has stated, according to his biographers, that the Muses are to be preferred to the Sirens.[1] In my opinion, if Pythagoras were in the habit of using a simple, clear style, similar to that employed by other philosophers, I would have said that he preferred the voice of the Muses because he found it more agreeable. But since his style is enigmatic and abstruse—indeed he has offered his views in the form of allegorical expressions such as "Do not poke a fire with a sword," "Do not sit on a peck measure," "Do not taste of black tails," "Do not step over the beam of a balance," and other injunctions of that kind[2]—I imagine that he is associating elegant, recondite discourses with the Sirens, and discourses that have nothing superadded but reveal the truth in all its naked beauty with the Muses.[3] For the more natural beauty surpasses the artificial beauty derived from cosmetics, so much superior is the simple decorum of truth to contrived cleverness of diction.

2. We must then, my friends, place credence, if in nobody else, at least in the celebrated philosopher who has laid down such precepts, and we should not think that the divine oracles should be disdained because they have not employed any extraordinary type of discourse but, on the contrary, present us with the truth in unvarnished splendor. For it would have been easy and relatively simple for the source of Wisdom, who has given even to the impious that which is called the Good News, to make the heralds of the truth more eloquent than Plato, more vigorous than Demosthenes, and to cause them to eclipse

the son of Olorus in amplitude,[4] and Chrysippus and the son of Nicomachus in the insoluble knots of their syllogisms.[5]

3. But Wisdom did not wish for merely five, ten, fifteen, a hundred, or two hundred, to benefit from the streams of salvation, but rather everybody, Greeks and non-Greeks, and those nourished in rhetoric as well as those with no taste for speeches: shoemakers, weavers, coppersmiths, and all craftsmen, and besides these, maids and mendicants, tillers of fields and tenders of groves, and besides women, both those swimming in riches and those yoked to toil and forced to make a living by manual labor.[6]

4. That is why, with the fishermen, the publicans, and the tentmaker for collaborators, Wisdom has brought to humanity its saving and divine teachings, not in exchanges with them in their maternal tongue, which they always had, but by pouring on them the limpid, translucent streams of wisdom. He acted rather like a host who serves his dinner guests a wine with a fine bouquet that is fragrant and excellent, having poured it in glasses and goblets that have no pretensions to beauty. His thirsty guests, however, take their fill of the drink, enjoying the wine and not paying attention to what is in them.

THE APOSTLES' HUMILITY AND GREATNESS

5. That is what everybody does in practice. Profiting from the divine fountains, far from ridiculing the language of the apostles, they greatly appreciate it because they are not initiated into the niceties of language; some who have been trained in fishing from childhood, others who have been engaged full time in customs and excise, others still who have worked as tanners, have suddenly appeared as ministers of the divine word, dispensers of the heavenly gifts, saviors who avert disasters, most illustrious beacons of light, enlightening not just one nation but everywhere the sun shines.

6. The world was uncommonly delighted and amazed that after their death they continued their earthly pursuits or, to put it more correctly, that which is done after their departure from this life is even more distinguished and illustrious.

7. Clearly their writings, which are simple and devoid of Hellenic brilliance,[7] and furthermore are neither voluminous nor numerous, are taken to heart by all men except you and those like you who are

engulfed in the mist of incredulity and refuse to see the truth in all its brilliance. And not only are they bereft of Hellenic adornment, but even the topics which are treated are often in themselves not particularly imposing or brilliant or remarkable.

8. Indeed it is not a visible kingdom which they present to their initiates, one adorned in purple and gleaming with crowns, imposing in the number and size of its spear-carriers and shield-bearers, and having such a host with generals taught to be victorious in battles and all the other qualities which make their possessors much talked about. No, all they had were a cave, a manger, a poor virgin, an infant wrapped in swaddling clothes and laid in a bare manger, and a small, undistinguished place in which these events took place. And it is the poverty of this Infant which increases, His hunger, thirst, fatigue from journeys, and His passion, which is celebrated by all; the blows on His forehead, the lashes on His back, the nails, the vinegar, the gall, and finally His death.

9. Nonetheless, the Scriptures of the apostles which recount these things and others like them have persuaded everyone that He is the Son of God, the God who predates time, the Creator and Demiurge of the universe who has donned human nature and who, thanks to that, has accomplished the salvation of humanity. And they have not simply persuaded, but have instilled such faith in most people that they have gladly accepted death on behalf of these beliefs, and to those who have ordered them to deny their faith they have not uttered a word but have bared their backs to those who wished to flog them and submitted their limbs to burning torches and iron hooks and their heads to the sword.

THE POWER OF THE RELICS OF THE MARTYRS

10. That is why the One who presides at these contests has conferred immortal glory on them and a memory that outlasts time. For time knows how to make all things wither, but it has preserved their glory unfading. And the souls of those valiant heroes inhabit the heavens and join in chorus with the choirs of the immortals. Their bodies are not concealed in the grave of a single individual, but cities and towns hail them and name them as saviors and physicians of both bodies and souls, honoring them as protectors and guardians.

11. Although the body has been severed, grace has remained undivided, and this tiny piece of a relic[8] has a power equal to that which the martyr would have had if he had never been carved up. For grace when it blooms extends its gifts proportionate to the faith of those who pray.

AN OBJECTION TO THE CULT OF MARTYRS

But as for you, not even all this persuades you to sing the praises of the God of martyrs; on the contrary, you laugh and scoff at the honor accorded the martyrs by the whole world and consider it an abomination to approach their tombs.[9]

A RESPONSE TO THIS OBJECTION: GODS AND HEROES ARE ONLY DEIFIED MEN

12. But if all people objected to these, the Greeks alone would not have the right to object to such practices. For the Greeks are the ones who have the libations, the offerings to the dead, the heroes, the demigods, and the mortals who are deified. Heracles, for instance, came to the world as a man, the son of Alcmene and Amphitryon,[10] but they made him a god in accordance with their views, and they numbered him among their other gods.

13. That Plato was aware that he was the son of Amphitryon, and not of Zeus, is obvious from these words of his in the *Theaetetus*:[11]

To pride himself on a catalogue of twenty-five progenitors going back to Heracles, son of Amphitryon, strikes him as showing a strange pettiness of outlook. He laughs at a man who cannot rid his mind of foolish vanity by reckoning that before Amphitryon there was a twenty-fifth ancestor and before him a fiftieth, whose fortunes were as luck would have it.

14. And Isocrates the orator also speaks as follows:[12]

Zeus, having begotten Heracles and Tantalus, as the legends have it and all the world believes.

That is how those who were capable of a well-rounded view scoffed at what the makers of myths had to say. And yet, although Heracles was a mere man, forced to be a slave to Eurystheus,[13] they constructed temples to him and built altars to him, offered sacrifices in his honor, and dedicated feast days to him, and not just the Athenians and Spartans but the whole of Greece and the greater part of Europe.[14]

15. The disease of this error has reached even to Asia; for instance, in Tyre and in other cities they have constructed for him enormous and countless sanctuaries. And not satisfied with offering annual celebrations, they have special games every four years in his honor.[15] They are aware that he was a mere man, one who had esteemed neither temperance nor philosophy, but who had spent all his life in debauchery and dissolute conduct.

16. And, to pass over his other heinous actions, they say that in one night he slept with fifty virgins. That perhaps was labor number thirteen![16] This should suffice to show what was the driving force of his life. And indeed it was such immoral conduct that led to his premature death. For Deianeira was his wife, but he burned with love for another woman and, unintentionally, he became the victim of his wife's plots.[17]

17. She prepared an aphrodisiac and anointed her husband's cloak. Then she sent it to him when he asked for it, thinking that it would lure him to herself. But she was disappointed in her hopes. For the drug burned Heracles' body and made him dreadfully ill. As he suffered and was unable to endure the pain he piled up a funeral pyre, placed himself upon it, and found an end worthy of his life.[18] For the habits of this man whom you thought worthy of deification were not worthy of apotheosis.

18. But in spite of knowing all this, for the writings of antiquity teach all this, they nonetheless hailed him as their savior and gave him the title of protector from evil, and added to their accounts the invocation "Lord Heracles." And you likewise reverence him with such expressions, thinking that it is a sufficient display of culture to invoke such little aphorisms.[19]

19. And as for Asclepius, he is, according to Apollodorus,[20] the son of Arsinoe according to some authorities, but, according to oth-

ers, the son of Coronis.[21] She was secretly violated by Apollo, became pregnant, and after labor exposed her newly born son. The foundling was discovered by hunters, nourished by a dog, and transferred to Chiron, the Centaur—still quoting Apollodorus—and practiced the art of medicine, first in Trikke, and then at Epidauros.[22]

20. Asclepius, according to Apollodorus, received such a well-rounded and serious education that he not only cured the sick but even called the dead back to life. Accordingly Zeus of the thunderbolt was disturbed and smote him with his bolt and took him out of this life.[23] He was, then, a mere man and was not even raised by other men, but got his first nurture from a dog and was rescued because hunters took pity on him. He had the gift of healing, not from some divine wisdom and education, but from Chiron.

21. Now this Chiron was also the teacher of Achilles, a fact that proves that they were contemporaries, or rather that Chiron was slightly older than Achilles since he took part in the voyage of the Argonauts and his son, Machaon, campaigned in battle with Achilles.[24] At any rate the thunderbolt and ensuing combustion revealed the mortality of his nature.

22. For, after being born in such circumstances as I have described, and being rescued, brought up, and then killed by lightning, they have enlisted him with the other gods to whom they have dedicated temples and consecrated altars. With libations and the smoke of sacrifice, formerly quite openly, even today perhaps in some remote corner, you honor him and deem his statues worthy of divine worship. You marvel at the serpent coiled around him and call it a symbol of medicine, because, just as the serpent put off old age, so the art of medicine frees from disease.

23. This person in the time of Homer had not yet received deification. That poet gives us such assurance since he cures the wounds of Ares, not by Asclepius but by Paion,[25] since the gods of that sort had to have wounds and physicians. And as for Machaon, Homer makes him, not the son of a god or even of a demigod, but of a physician. For he says:[26]

a mortal, son of Asclepius, a blameless physician.

24. As for Dionysus, Homer, Euripides, and numerous others say that he was the son of Semele.[27] But Semele was the son of Cadmus.

And yet he was also judged worthy of a divine cult although he was effeminate, womanish, and androgynous. For he promised to give a reward to his helpers, not gold or silver, but sexual perversion. And he was so faithful to this base promise that if one of his helpers should die before he received this much-desired reward, then Dionysus devised another method for fulfilling it.[28] And I pass over in silence the phallus made of a fig tree and the rites accomplished in honor of this. For I am ashamed to speak of the reasons why the Greeks hold festivals.

25. Furthermore the Greeks called the sons of Tyndareus gods and gave them the names of Dioscouri, Ephestioi, and Necessities.[29] And they judged them worthy to have temples not only at Sparta but at Athens. Demosthenes, the orator, mentions them when he says:[30]

in the inn which is near the temple of the Dioscouri.

26. And the Leocorion is a temple of the daughters of Leo.[31] And how many more unfortunates, and very unfortunates, have the Greeks made into gods and honored with public festivals. The Pythian oracle, for instance, decreed that Cleomedes, the boxer, son of Astypaleus, should enjoy divine prerogatives. This is the oracle which the Pythian uttered:[32]

Cleomedes of Astypalea is the last of the heroes;

honor him with sacrifices, for he is no more a mortal.

27. But, so that you may know why Cleomedes was arrayed with Zeus and the other gods, I will tell you the exploits that are narrated about him. He once knocked out his opponent with one blow, opened his side, put in his hand and took out his innards. The judges, angered at the excess of his brutality, imposed a fine on him. But he went away in a rage, and as he passed by the agora he dragged down one of the pillars supporting the roof and showered it down on a band of youths who regularly attended school there with their teacher.

28. It was for exploits of that sort that the Pythian joined him to the ranks of the gods. And they say that Hadrian, the Roman emperor, proclaimed his boyfriend Antinous one of the gods. He erected a tem-

ple in his honor and decreed that his subjects should confer divine honor on him.[33] For their part, the Spartans celebrated a great feast for Hyacinthus, making the day a public holiday.[34]

THE PAGANS VENERATE THE TOMBS OF HEROES

29. Why, then, do you, who have given the name of gods to so many of the dead, express such indignation at us who, without deifying them, honor our martyrs in that they are witnesses to God and faithful servants? And why do you think that anyone who approaches the tomb of a martyr incurs some sort of taint?

30. For in Athens, as Antiochus has recorded in Book 9 of his History,[35] the tomb of Cecrops is found at the top of the Acropolis at the side of the Protector Goddess of the city. At Larissa in Thessaly, in the temple of Athena, Acrisios is said to be interred.[36] In Miletus, according to Leander, Cleomachus reposes in Didyma.[37] Lycophrone was buried in the sanctuary of Artemis in Magnesia, according to Zeno of Myndos.[38] As for the altar of Apollo which is at Telmissos, it is said that this is the tomb of the prophet Telmisseus.[39] Yet those who bury in such places do not think they pollute the altars nor do those who offer sacrifices subsequently suspect they incur a curse as a result.

31. You are the only ones who imagine any such thing. The ancients had no such suspicion. The proof of this is in Homer: in his epic he depicts Achilles, son of Peleus, grandson of Aeacus, and son of Thetis, and son of Zeus according to you, enfolding in his arms the corpse of Patroclus, and carrying the head when the Myrmidons brought the body to the pyre for burial, and then he extinguished the pyre, collected the bones, placed them in a golden phial, and kept them in his own tent.[40]

32. And Thucydides narrates[41] the honor given to those who died in the Peloponnesian war and how each thought fit to bury the bodies of neighbors as they were taken up from the battlefield, and the kinds of honors that were devised for bodies which were not found, providing coffins made of cypress wood for them, surrounded by mourners, in front, at the rear, and around the sides. They constructed a huge tomb for those who had been the prey of birds, dogs, and jackals. That is how they honored those who had fallen on the field of battle at Marathon.

LIBATIONS AND SACRIFICES FOR THE DEAD

33. You are well aware that they offered libations to the dead, you who dare to do these things by night in transgression of the laws. Homer is our witness, who shows us the son of Laertes, against the suggestions of Circe digging a pit, pouring libations, and giving this account to Alcinous:[42]

> I drew my sharp sword from along my thigh,
> Dug a pit the size of a cubit on all sides,
> And poured a libation about it for all the dead.
> First of honey mixture, and then of sweet wine,
> and the third one of water; I sprinkled white barley on it.
> I besought the feeble heads of the gods for many things,
> Saying that when I went to Ithaca I would sacrifice
> My best barren cow in my halls, heap a pyre with goods,
> And consecrate apart for Teiresias alone
> a sheep all of black that stands out among my flocks,
> And when I had besought the tribes of the dead with prayers
>   and vows,
> Then I took the sheep and cut their throats into the pit.
> And the black-clouded blood poured out. And out of Erebos
> the souls gathered up the corpses of those who had died.

34. Then Homer explains how the souls run in a crowd and are eager to partake of the libations. And why do I quote the poet? For Aristocles, the Peripatetic, reports,[43] quoting Lycon, the Pythagorean, that Aristotle, son of Nichomachus, was in the habit of offering in honor of his dead wife a sacrifice of the same kind as the Athenians offered to Demeter. As for us, my friends, it is not sacrifices or libations we offer to our martyrs; we honor them like men of God and friends of God, because they have loved their Creator and Savior to the point of believing nothing is so desirable as to lay down their lives for Him.

35. And if you think that they are insensible to what happened to them and that they do not enjoy some divine and truly thrice-blest lot, let Pindar, the lyric poet, expel this false opinion of yours when he says:[44]

> The souls of the pious dwell in the heavens,
> celebrating their great happiness with songs and hymns.

36. And if heaven is the abode of those who have lived a good life the martyrs have this as their portion as well. For nothing surpasses their piety. Empedocles of Agrigentum puts it like this:[45]

To the end there are seers, and lyric poets, and physicians,
and leading men among mortals on earth; and from here
they blossom forth like gods with the fairest honors.

37. Now if this author says that seers and physicians deserve such great honor, what should be said of those who have given proof of such great fortitude in defense of their religion and whose deeds give testimony not just to their fortitude but their justice also, and to their temperance, wisdom, and prudence? What is more prudent than that those people should stand up for those principles which they had maintained were correct from the start? What is more just than that those should requite the divine blessings by their own lives and should deliver up their bodies for Him who delivered His for them on the cross?

38. What could be more prudent or more wise than that those who have made similar decisions, both despising the things here below as insubstantial and having no solidity and at the same time loving those things which are inexpressible in words? And what betrays more fortitude than that those who have warred against sufferings of every sort should overcome their persecutors by the strength of their character?

39. That is why they are truly first in the ranks of humanity, their champions and protectors, averters of evils and diverting the injuries brought forward by the demons. Heraclitus feels that those who have been elevated in wars should merit all kinds of honors when he says, for instance:[46]

The gods and men honor the victims of Ares.

Or again:[47]

Only the greater get as their lot a greater fate.

40. I do not accept that judgment because it is a fact that very many who have lived a life of depravity have endured a violent death.

If, then, it is appropriate to recompense all the victims of Ares it is time for you also to assign this mark of honor to the sons of Oedipus,[48] who abandoned their father and who confronted one another in a power struggle and stained their hands with their own blood.

41. And honor, I take it, must also be paid to the sons of Peisistratus, who were justly put to death by Harmodius and Aristogeiton.[49] That, however, is not how the Athenians acted, for they erected statues of bronze in honor of those who had eliminated the tyrants and they granted exemption from taxes to their descendants. Therefore we should not follow Heraclitus' dictum and honor all the victims of Ares, but only those who have joyfully accepted to die on behalf of religion since they are the only ones who are "greater," to use the word in its proper sense. It was for this reason that they enjoyed a better fate and now they obtain honor from all and await immortal crowns. Another saying of Heraclitus that greatly delights me is this:[50]

> What awaits men at their death they neither imagine nor visualize.

42. Plato has shown in the *Phaedo* that the souls of the saints enjoy a divine lot. This is how he puts it:[51]

> But those who are judged to have lived a life of surpassing holiness—these are they who are released and set free from confinement in these regions of the earth, passing upward to their true abode.

And a little later he continues:[52]

> They reach habitations even more beautiful, which it is not easy to portray; and there is no time to do so now.

43. And lest anyone on hearing this and becoming so enamored of that heavenly abode that he would think it pious to undertake some way of self-release from here by force or necessity, he adds of necessity:[53]

> One must not release oneself or run away and, in a word, reckon this earthly existence evil.

44. Plato further says that the soul, when it has become isolated and on its own, is able to participate in true wisdom and power that is superhuman, whenever love takes wing from here to the heavens when it has arrived through the conduct of philosophy to the hoped-for end, receiving the beginning of another everlasting life.

45. Again he says in the same dialogue:[54] "With good hope" the good souls will depart from here, but evil souls, he says, will live "with a bad hope." He it is who has called philosophy a practice for dying. For he says:[55]

Ordinary people seem not to realize that those who really apply themselves in the right way to philosophy are directly and of their own accord preparing themselves for dying and death.

All this he has written in the *Phaedo*.
46. And in the tenth book of the *Republic* he speaks as follows:[56]

And of those who die on campaign, if anyone's death has been especially glorious, shall we not, to begin with, affirm that he belongs to the golden race?

By all means.

And a little further on:[57]

What then? And ever after we will bestow on their graves the watchful care and worship paid to spirits divine. And we will practice the same observance when any who have been judged exceptionally good in the ordinary course of life die of old age or otherwise?

47. In the *Cratylus* also he has developed this idea. He praises Hesiod and the other poets for having said that[58]

when a good man dies he has honor and a mighty portion among the dead, and becomes a demon, which is a name given to him to signify wisdom.

And I say too that every man-demon is defined by this.
Here is what Hesiod says elsewhere about the golden race:[59]

But now that Fate has closed over this race, there are holy demons upon the earth beneficent, averters of evil, guardians of mortal men.

48. If the poet, then, gives the names of "beneficent," "averters of evil," and "guardians of mortals" to those who died after leading the good life, and if the best of the philosophers has reinforced the poet's definition and said it is necessary to attend to them and venerate their tombs, why, then, my good friends, do you take exception to what is done by us? For we have named those who were illustrious in piety and accepted death on its behalf, as averters of evil and healers, not calling them demons—we would not be so foolish—but regarding them as friends of God and well-disposed servants who use their influence and intercede for a supply of blessings for us.

49. The doyen of the philosophers has shown this well in the *Epinomis*:[60]

I declare that it is impossible for humankind, with the exception of a select few, to find bliss and felicity in this life. I would limit the statement to the span of life on earth, for there is a good hope that after death all blessings are attainable.

This is truly similar to the words of sacred Scripture: *Call no one happy before his death by how he ends, a person becomes known.*[61] And *the light of dawn which shines brighter and brighter until full day,*[62] and *the souls of the righteous are in the hand of God,*[63] and other passages of this kind.

50. The outrages, insults, and mistreatments which the Guide of the universe has allocated to the just during the present life are also described by Plato in the *Republic*:[64]

The just man will have to endure the lash, the rack, chains, gouging out of eyes, and finally, after every extremity of suffering, he will be crucified. Are not those who do such things thrice wretched, and those who suffer them thrice blessed?

51. That the souls of the just, even after they leave the body, can be concerned with human affairs is taught by Plato also in the eleventh book of the *Laws*. This is what he says:[65]

> I believe, in fact, there was something really opportune in all we said before of a power of taking an interest in human life retained by the souls of the departed after death. The tales which convey this moral may be lengthy, but they are true, and we ought to give our credence to general tradition on the subject.

52. Now clearly the philosopher orders belief in traditions. As for you, not only do you not believe this and refuse to listen to facts which proclaim the truth, but you do not wish even to believe your own philosopher, who tells you without ambiguity that the souls of the saints, when they have been separated from their bodies, are concerned with human affairs. And for this reason, is it not appropriate that they obtain this honor, those who have stayed attached with all their heart to divine things, who remain faithful to the end to principles which they have adopted from the beginning, and have refused to abandon the principles which they have originally taken.

53. Plato confirms this view in the *Apology*. These are his words:[66]

> The truth of the matter is this, men of Athens. Where a man has once taken up his stand, either because it seems best to him or in obedience to his orders, there, I believe, he is bound to remain and face the danger, taking no account of death or anything else before dishonor.

54. And a little further on:[67]

> For let me tell you, gentlemen, that to be afraid of death is only another form of thinking that one is wise when one is not.

And immediately afterwards:[68]

> I shall never feel more fear or aversion for something for which, for all I know, may really be a blessing than for those evils which I know to be evils.

And in another place:[69]

Apart from the other happiness in which their world surpasses ours, they are now immortal.

55. And this, my friends, is a further citation from him:[70]

Neither Meletus nor Anytus[71] can do me any harm at all; they would not have the power, because I do not think that the law of god permits a better man to be harmed by a worse. No doubt my accuser might put me to death, or have me banished, or have me deprived of civic rights. And he perhaps, or someone else, might think that these are great calamities, I do not think so. I think that it is far worse to do what he is doing now, trying to put an innocent man to death.

56. Such, then, were the philosophizings of Socrates even during the course of his trial as Plato has testified, but he failed nonetheless to attain the honor accorded to the martyrs. Those who were present at his discourse erected no sanctuary to him, nor did they dedicate a sacred enclosure to him, nor assign him any festival. However wise and courageous he had become, they left him unrewarded and inflicted on him an unjust death. But his religious life was far from perfect and unblemished. For he had blended it with many elements of the error prevalent at that time.[72]

57. That was evidently the reason why he was not judged worthy of honor after his death. Neither was the well-known Anaxarchos honored. They say that when he was being crushed in an iron pestle he exclaimed:

Pound, pound the pouch of Anaxarchos, but you don't pound Anaxarchos.[73]

Zeno, the Eleatic, was not honored either. When he was being pressed to reveal something from the secret plans, he resisted under tortures, refusing to confess. As Erathosthenes relates in his book *Concerning Goods and Evils*,[74] Zeno was afraid that the excess of his sufferings would compel him to reveal some of the agreements and give information on some of the partisans, so he cut off his tongue with his teeth and spat it at the tyrant.

58. They say that the Pythagorean, Theodotus, and Paulus, the well-known son of Lacyddos, did the same thing, as Timotheus of Pergamum records in his book *Concerning the Courage of Philosophers*.[75] Achaicos corroborates this in his work *The Moralia*.[76]

59. Nonetheless not one of these has been judged worthy of the same honor as that given to the martyrs. Nor has anyone of those who have had glorious and far-famed trophies erected to them—Miltiades, Cimon, Pericles, Themistocles, or Aristides, the son of Lysimachus.[77] Yet the last-named was not only brave but also was regarded as just. Yet he did not rank with the martyrs, no, nor did Brasidas, the Spartan,[78] nor Argesilaos, nor Lysander,[79] who abolished the might of Athens, nor Pelopidas of Boeotia, nor Epaminondas,[80] who dared to lead his army against Sparta, nor the most illustrious Roman generals, Scipio the Elder and his namesake, Scipio the Younger, nor Cato, Sulla, Marius, even Caesar.[81]

60. Each of these distinguished himself for bravery at the head of his armies and on the battlefield, but he received no share of the glory of the martyrs. And why speak of generals? Not even those who have ruled the world have enjoyed this honor, neither Cyrus, nor Darius, nor Xerxes, nor Alexander, son of Philip[82] (I am merely counting the most illustrious), nor Augustus, nor Vespasian, nor Trajan, nor Hadrian, nor Antoninus.[83] All of them during their lifetimes were the center of everybody's attention. They vanquished the barbarians and after their victories celebrated triumphs and feasts. But once dead nothing distinguished them from anybody else.

61. Their tombs were undistinguished and no public annual festivals were instituted in their honor. Who knows the tomb of Xerxes or of Darius? Who knows the tomb of Alexander, who vanquished in the briefest span so many nations?[84] But why speak of the ancients, since not even a trace of Augustus's tomb[85] is to be seen, or that of the others who succeeded him as emperor of Rome and failed to recognize the One who had given them rule and sustained them in power. Only the tombs of religious emperors are manifest and well-known, and the tombs of those in the interval who ruled impiously can be seen indeed, but they do not enjoy the least mark of respect. For not only are they deprived of imperial honors, but they do not even get the share of honor that belongs to the tombs of simple individuals.

THE CULT OF MARTYRS: PILGRIMAGES AND CURES

62. And yet some of those foolish ones both proclaimed themselves gods and erected temples to themselves. Antiochus,[86] for instance, has been called a god; Gaius, the successor of Tiberius, Vespasian, and Hadrian[87] built enormous temples to themselves. But this impious cult expired with their own decease. On the other hand, the sanctuaries of our triumphant martyrs are resplendent and admired, imposing in size, of different colors, and luminous in beauty.[88]

63. And we make pilgrimage[89] to them, not once or twice or five times a year, but frequently, and celebrate holy days, often spending whole days in singing hymns to the Lord of martyrs. And those in good health petition continued health, while those struggling with some ailment ask for relief from their maladies. Those who are childless pray for offspring, and the barren pray to become child-bearing, while those who already possess this gift pray for continued fertility. Pilgrims from afar invoke the martyrs to be their fellow travelers and guides on their journey home, and those who have a chance to return bring expressions of their gratitude. They do not treat the martyrs as gods but invoke them as men of God and pray to them to be divine ambassadors for them.

64. The *ex-voto* offerings of those who are cured testify to the success of the intercession of those who plead with faith. Some leave as offerings statues of eyes, others of feet, others of hands. Some of the replicas are made of gold, others of wood.[90] Their Master, in fact, accepts offerings that are small and have no monetary value, assessing the gift in accordance with the means of the donor. These offerings proclaim the cure of ailments, placed there as souvenirs by those who have been recently cured.

65. They proclaim the power of the martyrs who repose there, and this power guarantees that their God is the true God. Let us inquire, therefore, who these were who merited such a grace and where they originated. Were they well-known and illustrious who could boast a distinguished pedigree or an ocean of wealth? Did they acquire fame because of some power and influence?

66. Not at all, my friends. None of the above. They were lay people and soldiers; some of them were female domestics and servants who contended nobly with very weak constitutions. Of these some bore chastely the yoke of marriage; others were unaware of what mar-

riage was. And I hear that some of the men who had long been in the military camp suddenly enrolled in the ranks of the combatants and, once victorious and in possession of their crowns, after the public proclamation they became an enormous menace to the very demons to whom they had previously been subject. Many priests and sacristans of temples erected trophies gained in their fight against impiety.[91]

67. It is from the ranks of these poor men and women that the choirs of martyrs are composed. The philosophers and orators are buried in obscurity. The man in the street does not know even the names of emperors and generals, but everybody knows the names of the martyrs even better than they know the names of their closest friends. And they are eager to give the names of the martyrs to their children as a guaranteed source for them of safety and protection.[92]

68. But why speak of philosophers, emperors, and generals, since the martyrs have eradicated from human perception even the memory of the so-called gods. In fact their temples have been so completely destroyed that one cannot even conjure up an image of their outline, and those of the present time have no idea of the shape of their altars, and their remains have been used as building materials for the sanctuaries of the martyrs.

69. In fact the Master has replaced your gods with the remains of his martyrs, declaring your gods banished and reassigning the honor formerly given to them to the martyrs.[93] Instead of the festivals of Pandia, Diasia, Dionysia, and all the others are the public holy days of Peter, Paul, Thomas, Sergius, Marcellus, Leontius, Pantelemon, Antoninus, Mauricius, and the other martyrs.[94] And instead of the pagan processions with their rites and appropriate obscenities are the chaste festivals which are not characterized by drunkenness, revelry, or laughter, but by sacred chant, listening to sacred eloquence, a prayer adorned with laudable tears.[95]

70. Seeing, then, the advantage of the cult of the martyrs, my friends, you should flee the error of the demons. And, with the martyrs as your trailblazers and guides, take the path that leads to God so that you may join their choir for eternity.

Discourse 9

ON LAWS

1. My friends, you long to hear well-embellished speeches and seek to be enchanted by them. And if, by chance, you do not get them, then you jeer and mock and stop up your ears, and you refuse to listen to what is said.

2. You should have considered how most of the very highly prized products come concealed in cheap containers. For instance, the precious pearl, so highly prized by the wealthy, originates and gets its nourishment from the totally forgettable oyster which serves as its place of concealment. Those who buy the pearl and pay a top price in gold for it soon bid farewell to the outside oyster.[1]

3. And those gleaming gems which adorn the heads of royalty come wrapped on the outside in totally useless stone settings. Cutters of gems, by cutting around and discarding this odd, useless exterior, reveal the beauty of those delicate jewels.[2]

4. Gold, which so many find delectable, just like silver, bronze, and iron, is concealed in sand and earth. The workers who excavate the veins of gold and silver dig up the metals and collect the shavings. But once the gold or silver has been struck with an imprint and given the emperor's image, it is kept, not in a gold container, but in coffers of leather or wood.

5. It is, then, perfectly normal also that true beliefs about God and humanity should be heralded, not in majestic, brilliant discourses, but rather in simple, down-to-earth, easily understood terms, and that this noble, ineffable treasure should be contained within very modest covers.[3]

Relativity of Civil Laws

6. It is easy to form an idea of the force and cogency of these discourses by producing the legislators of Greece and Rome and comparing them with our fishermen and publicans. It is only then that you will discover that the former failed to persuade even their neighbors to be governed according to their laws, whereas the Galileans have persuaded, not only the Romans and Greeks, but even the non-Greeks of all nations, to embrace the legislation of the Gospel.

7. Minos, according to the legend, boasted that Zeus was his father and he took the occasion, on his visits to his father's cave, to make the laws.[4] He became the legislator for Crete, but he failed to persuade the Sicilians, or the Carthaginians, or even the Greeks to govern themselves according to these laws. There was not an island over which he ruled that he did not compel the occupants to embrace his legislation, but this did not last for long, for on the day when Rome conquered the world, the Cretans were also ruled by Roman law.

8. Charondas is said to have been the first to legislate for Italy and Sicily.[5] But neither did he succeed in persuading the Tyrrhenians, the Celts, Iberians, or Celteberi, even though they were neighbors bordering him, to accept the laws which he had drafted. And why speak of neighbors, since even those who admired and supported those laws do not live according to them at the present day. In fact, they too have passed under the Roman yoke.

9. Zaleucos passed on to the Locrians the laws which he had learned from Athena, according to those whose pleasure it is to fashion the myths.[6] But neither the Acharnians nor the Phocians, nor even the rest of the Locrians, admired his legislation, and yet they did not live far away, but they were neighboring his city.

10. As for Lycurgus, those who reverence his laws say he hastened to Delphi and, upon arrival at the Pythian, was inspired by Apollo and made laws for the people of Sparta.[7] They even quote the oracle that the Pythian issued on that occasion. Here is the text:[8]

> Have you come, Lycurgus, to my richly endowed sanctuary,
> a friend of Zeus and of all those who dwell in Olympus?
> I hesitate whether to call you a god or a mortal,
> but I rather hope, Lycurgus, that you are a god.

You have come in search of sound legislation.
This I will give you.

11. Such is the oracle concerning this affair. But neither the legislator's great repute, nor the splendor of Sparta, nor the oracle of the Pythian Apollo could constrain the inhabitants of Argos, or Tegea, or Mantinea, or Corinth, all nearby dwellers, to adopt the constitution of Sparta. But why cite the others? Even the residents of Phlius in Argos, who lived in a small town and always accepted the hegemony of Sparta, and had special treaty arrangements with it, taking their marching orders from them and always fighting side by side with them, even they refused to adopt their legislation.[9]

12. And I will not speak of other legislators, Apis of Argos, Mnason of Phocis, Demonax of Cyrene, Pagondas of Achaia, Archias of Cnidos, Eudoxus of Miletus, Philolaus of Thebes, Pittacus of Mytelene,[10] and finally Nestor of Pylos, of whom Homer said his words were sweeter than honey.[11] Nor will I speak of the legislators of other nations, the famous Solon,[12] and Draco,[13] and Cleisthenes,[14] who were legislators at Athens. But the Athenians never persuaded the Euboeans or the Thebans, who shared a common border with them and were their next-door neighbors, to adopt the laws of Solon, Draco, or Cleisthenes.

13. And the Athenians themselves, after bidding farewell to these laws, and likewise the Spartans, the Locrians, the Thebans, and the rest of the Greeks governed themselves according to Roman law. And the Romans, having collected the laws which were in force among the Greeks and barbarians, and having taken from each legislator that which seemed best to them, forced all the peoples who had come under their yoke to observe these laws, but never succeeded either by persuasion or by violence to direct the recalcitrant to adopt their legislation.

14. There are many peoples who have been enslaved to the Roman yoke who did not endure to live under their laws. In fact, neither the Ethiopians, whose country shares a border with the Egyptian Thebaid, nor the countless tribes of Ishmael, nor the Lazoi, nor the Samnoi, nor the Abasges, nor the other barbarians who submitted to Roman power, based themselves on Roman law when they made accords with one another.[15]

15. On the other hand, our fishermen, our publicans, and our tent-maker have brought the laws of the Gospel to all peoples. And it is not only to the Romans and their subjects, but also to the peoples

of Scythia, Sarmatia, to the Indians, Ethiopians, Persians, Chinese, Hyrcanians, Bactrians, Britons, Cimbrians, Germans,[16] in short to the people of every nation and every race who have been persuaded to accept the laws of the Crucified, using, not the weapons of war and the countless hordes of soldiers, and not using now the force of the savage Persians, but rather by persuasion and by showing the laws were beneficial.

16. And they accomplished all this, not without undergoing some hazards, but by enduring many injuries throughout their cities, receiving many lashes, enduring the rack, and being imprisoned and receiving every kind of tortures. Some drove out their benefactors, saviors, and physicians as plotters and enemy; others disbanded them; others bound them with fetters and stocks; some they cudgeled to death, others they impaled, and others still they threw to wild beasts. They shot down the legislators, yes, but they failed to dissolve the binding force of their laws. The laws lasted with even greater force after the death of the legislators.

THE PERMANENCE OF THE LAWS OF THE GOSPEL

17. Because it was after the death of the legislators that their laws penetrated the territories of the Persians, the Scythians, and the other barbarian peoples. And despite the combined efforts of the barbarians and even of the Romans, they kept their strength intact. The Romans pulled every string to eliminate the memory of our fishermen and our tanner, but that only made them more illustrious and widely known. They sought to annul the laws of Lycurgus, Solon, Zaleuchos, Charondas, Minos, and the other legislators. And nobody resisted the legislations set up by them but their word became law. The memory of the much heralded legislators was extinguished, and the laws of the Romans now govern the Greek cities.

18. At Athens everything has disappeared: the Areopagus, the Eliaea, the tribunal near the Delphinium, the council of the Five Hundred, the Eleven, the thesmothet, the polemarch, the annual archonship,[17] whose names are now known to the mere few who are prepared to read the writings of the ancients.

At Sparta the expulsion of the foreigners is no longer seen, nor the naturalizations of new citizens, nor the impunity associated with the laws of Lycurgus on pederasty, nor the illegalities which the laws recognized in regard to marriage.[18]

19. But you should know that this Lycurgus, the best of legislators according to the wise men of the Greeks, established in his laws, as we are told by the historians of the Spartan constitution, permission for men and women already joined in matrimonial union to have relations with the husbands and wives of others and to procreate children in total sexual freedom.[19] These laws were much admired by Plato and he wished that the city of his imagining would be governed by them.[20]

20. But let us reserve for the end this philosopher who, being a philosopher, boasts of being the best of legislators. For the present we are going to show the weakness of the Pythian laws (they are variously called Pythian and Lycurgan). It is a fact that, as soon as Rome decreed to abolish those laws and substitute their own, the laws of Lycurgus lost their binding force.

THE LAWS OF THE GOSPEL
STRENGTHENED BY PERSECUTION

21. On the other hand, the laws of our fishermen, and publicans, and tent-maker withstood destruction at the hands of Gaius or Claudius.

Nero, their successor, put to death the two best of our legislators; he destroyed Peter and Paul, yes, but he did not destroy their laws.[21] No more successful at this were Vespasian, Titus, and Domitian.[22] Domitian employed all sorts of stratagems against the laws; you know how he condemned to death surrounded by all kinds of sufferings a crowd of people who obeyed those laws. Trajan and Hadrian waged a violent war against our laws.[23] But Trajan, who succeeded in destroying the Persian empire and in forcing the peoples of Scythia to submit to his rule,[24] did not succeed in destroying the legislation of our fisherman and our tent-maker.

22. Hadrian reduced to ruins the city of those who had crucified Jesus, but did not succeed in persuading those who believed in Jesus to abandon His service.[25] Antoninus, his successor, and his son, Verus, erected many illustrious trophies won against the barbarians.[26] They imposed the yoke of their power on those who had enjoyed autonomous rule. But they failed to persuade those who loved to bear the yoke of the Savior's cross or compel them to abandon the One

they loved, despite the fact that they had recourse to all kinds of threats and used all kinds of punishments.

23. And, not to mention Commodus, Maximian, and all those who were emperors down to Aurelian, Carus, and Carinus, [27] who does not know of the antireligious furor of a Diocletian, a Maxentius, or a Licinius?[28] For it was not in ones, or twos, or threes that they killed the Christians but in herds, and they destroyed them in thousands and tens of thousands.

24. In some cities they have set fire to churches filled with men, women, and children. And, what is more, it was on the very day of our Savior's passion, when we assemble to celebrate the memory of the passion and resurrection of our Lord, that they demolished all the churches of the Roman empire.[29]

25. And even if they have demolished the material buildings of stone, they have not demolished the spiritual religion. Older people still know the atrocities they perpetrated against the Christians in the reign of Julian; we ourselves have heard eyewitness accounts of this tragedy.[30] But all these enemies, however numerous, however large the empire which they governed, however great the courage of the barbarians whom they annihilated, however brilliantly they campaigned in wars and despite the use of countless devices of war, failed to vanquish manual workers and rustics eking out a living in poverty and women who made a living from manual labor.

26. And why speak of men and women? They could not even persuade the youngsters, who only knew the first rudiments, to reject their beliefs in our Lord and Savior. And Corybants in all their fury utilizing all the stratagems of deceit and perfidy did not succeed in destroying the laws of the fishermen, but rather by this hostility only rendered them all the more secure; they were like those who want to extinguish a fire, but actually they pour oil on it and increase its ferocity.

27. But it is very obvious that in combating religion they have only reinforced the strength of the truth. And just as of old they did not succeed in burning down that famous bush,[31] so now the persecuted were not destroyed by the acts of their persecutors. On the contrary, just as when foresters cut down trees and more offshoots blossom from the roots than those cut down, so likewise at the same time as the pious were being suppressed, even greater numbers were coming to the schools of the evangelists, and the blood of the sacrificed Christians became a nourishing stream for the new converts.[32]

28. What we see with our own eyes bears testimony to this. Those who now pride themselves in the name of the faithful are far more numerous than believers of old. The descendants of the persecutors, in a sense of loathing the fury of their fathers, have transferred into the ranks of those who were warred against. Hellenism has disappeared, buried in complete oblivion,[33] but the teachings of the fishermen have spread, and the God whom they preach is believed in as the God of the universe.

29. The cities are filled with people who share the Christian faith; the rural areas are likewise filled, and the mountainsides are freed from error because, in place of the pagan altars and the imposture of old, choirs of ascetics have taken their stand who chant the praise of the Crucified, and of His Father, and of the Holy Spirit.[34]

30. And if one supposed that it is the piety of the emperors that has confirmed the teaching of the fishermen, that only goes to show the strength of this same teaching. In fact, they would not have turned their backs on the ancient laws, the writings of the past, the customs established at an early date, and their ancestral traditions if they had not admired the truth of the Christians and hated pagan mythology.

31. Why, then, do you not recall the wars waged of old against the church? Thereby you would very easily destroy the reputation achieved through them. For if emperors were so great and so numerous, and were arrayed in such strength against their religion, and with such varied war machines, and yet did not make the slightest crack in the walls, one would be a fool and completely stupid to believe that the power of the fishermen is not divine but that its spread was merely due to the imperial power.[35]

RECENT PERSECUTIONS IN PERSIA

32. To make this clearer to you, learn of the enormities attempted just now by the Persians.[36] What extremes of slaughter have they not devised against the faithful? Have they not resorted to flaying, cutting off of hands and feet, mutilation of ears and noses? They have devised chains of most exquisite cruelty and trenches carefully greased and filled with huge rats to feast on those who were chained.[37] And yet, in devising such punishments and others like them against the Christians they may have mutilated and maltreated their bodies

and sometimes even destroyed them totally, but they have not robbed the treasure of their faith.

33. However, while compelling their subjects to be submissive to their other laws, they did not persuade the faithful to abjure the laws of the fishermen. The Persians who were once ruled by the laws of Zoroaster[38] had no scruple about marrying their mothers, their sisters, and even their daughters,[39] thinking that such immoral conduct was perfectly legitimate. But when they heard of the legislation of the fishermen they trampled on the laws of Zoroaster as immoral and embraced evangelical moderation. They had also learned from Zoroaster to expose their dead to dogs and birds of prey;[40] today those who have been converted to the true faith do not put up with such conduct, but inter their dead in the ground and ignore those laws which prohibit this practice and in no way fear the savagery of those who would punish them. They are much more in fear of the court of justice of Christ. They laugh at visible things and are haunted by fear of what is not visible. And these laws they received from the Galileans.

34. They did not fear the power of the Romans but submitted to the kingdom of the Crucified. Neither did Augustus compel them to regulate their lives according to Roman laws, nor Trajan, who destroyed their independent state. Instead they reverence the Scriptures of Peter and Paul, John, Matthew, Luke, and Mark as heaven-sent, and the native people submit to the laws of strangers and foreigners.

35. The Massagetai,[41] for their part, thought in times past that any death except one by slaughter was thrice miserable, and for this reason made a law to sacrifice their elderly and eat their corpses.[42] But when they heard of the laws of the fishermen and the tanners they found such disgraceful slaughter and cannibalism revolting.[43]

36. The Tibarenians, who were accustomed to hurl their elders from the tops of the highest crags, abolished this abominable custom when they heard the evangelical laws. The Hyrcanians and the Caspians[44] no longer feed their dogs with the corpses of their dead. The Scythians[45] do not inter with their dead the living whom they loved while alive. Such is the great transformation effected by the laws of the fishermen.

Plato's Errors in Civil Legislation

37. And these the latter have persuaded even the barbarians to be governed according to their laws, yet Plato, the best of the philosophers, wrote his Laws but failed to persuade the Athenians, his own compatriots, to regulate their lives in accordance with them. And that was altogether proper. For Plato's prescriptions are completely ridiculous.

Formation of the Young

38. And, so that nobody will think that I am jeering at the philosopher, listen, my friends, to what kind of laws he has enacted. Having decided that women, not just young women but old ones as well, should do their gymnastic exercises in the nude, and noticing that his interlocutors were disposed to laugh at this, he interjected, saying:[46]

> But the man who ridicules unclad women exercising because it is best that they should "plucks the unripe fruit" of laughter and does not know, it appears, the end of his laughter.

39. And elsewhere:[47]

> And, mind you, my law will apply in all respects to girls as much as to boys; the girls must be trained exactly like the boys. And in stating my doctrine I intend no reservation on any point of horsemanship or physical training, as appropriate for men but not for women.

Who would not rightly laugh at hearing such things? For nature has assigned to each sex its proper functions, to women to do their spinning, and to men to farm and to show skill in war.

40. Homer has also made this same distinction. For instance, in those verses which he makes Hector address to Andromache:[48]

> But go into the house and take care of your work;
> the loom and the distaff, and give orders to your servants

to get on with their work.
For war will be the care of the menfolk.

The philosopher does not make the same distinction as the poets; for instance, he prescribes that women should do their physical exercises in the nude and should ride on horseback. And what follows is in harmony with what goes before. For he says:[49]

41. The suitability or unsuitability of the marriage in point of years shall be determined by inspection, and the judge shall view the males stripped and the females stripped to the navel.

The one who made such a law surely did not recall the words of the wife of Candaules. For when she was ordered by her husband to show him her body nude, with great self-control she replied,

The woman who takes off her clothes takes off her sense of shame at the same time.[50]

42. Such, then, is the philosopher who takes the veil of modesty off of wives and who teaches them shamelessness. He has written in similar terms in Book Ten of the *Laws*:[51]

To ensure that grave result, even the sports of our lads and lasses should take the form of dances of both sexes, which will incidentally give them the opportunity, within reason and at an age which affords a colorable justification, of inspecting and being inspected in undress so far as sober modesty in all the parties will permit.

43. As for me, I see the harm that eventuates from that, and I also see no concomitant good result. For not only were naked women being educated in shamelessness, viewing naked men, but they were also providing many incentives to one another to sexual license. For the sight of naked bodies excites both men and women to erotic licentiousness.

PLATO'S COMMUNITY OF WIVES

44. But, so as not to give the impression, in exposing fully the harm that comes from these laws, of merely jeering at the philosopher instead of refuting him, let us pass on to those very fine laws of his on marriage and give them a reasonable critique. Let us hear him speaking in the *Republic*:[52]

> that these women shall all be common to all these men, and that none shall cohabit with any privately; and that the children shall be common, and that no parent shall know its own offspring nor any child its parent.

45. And then he goes on:[53]

> One lawgiver, then, I said, has picked these men and similarly will select to give over to them women as nearly as possible of the same nature. And they, having houses and meals in common, and no private possessions of any kind, will dwell together, and being commingled in gymnastics and in all the rest of their life, will be conducted by innate necessity to sexual union.

> Is not what I say a necessary consequence?

> Not by the necessities of geometry, he replied, but by the constraints of love, which are perhaps keener and more potent than the other to persuade and constrain the multitude.

46. There is no need, then, of long speeches to prove that the philosopher has formally approved of the community of wives and has countenanced the necessity of sexual permissiveness. Since they live in community and take their exercises in common, he said they will be driven by natural desire to sexual intercourse. And this is why he declares that children will be in common since each can have casual sex and regard all offspring as part of the community.

47. And when his interlocutor reflected on Socrates' question, he added:[54] assuredly it is not by the mathematical necessities of geom-

etry but by the constraints of love, which are perhaps keener and more potent than the other to persuade and constrain the multitude.

48. For my part, I am astonished at the impudence of today's people who want to interpret the words of Plato, or rather try to misinterpret his meaning. They maintain that Plato did not establish by law a community of wives but merely a friendly community. They turn a deaf ear to his own words: having in common a dwelling, board, the gymnasia, they will be led by necessity and natural desire to having sex.

49. But perhaps it is in their embarrassment at the manifestly ridiculous laws of the philosopher that they try to pretend that there is no error in their teacher. But they should still follow his words:[55]

> Man is a friend; truth also is a friend. And if both are friends, truth is the greater friend.

50. But we must also take into account the other laws of the philosopher. The following is a sample:[56]

> The women, I said, beginning at the age of twenty, shall bear for the state to the age of forty, and the man shall beget for the state from the time he passes his prime in swiftness of running to the age of fifty-five.

All this apparently contains nothing reprehensible but the consequences invite, not laughter, but tears, and a bonfire to burn those infamous laws to ashes.

51. Plato continues as follows:[57]

> But when the men and the women have passed the age of prescribed procreation we shall leave the men free to form such relations with whomsoever they please, admonishing them preferably not even to bring to light anything whatever thus conceived but if they are unable to prevent a birth to dispose of it on the understanding that we cannot rear such an offspring.

52. What Echetus or Phalaris[58] has ever established such laws? Who has ever dared such nefarious actions under the guise of acting lawfully? For in ordering not to bring the child into the light he guar-

anteed, of course, that the infants would be slaughtered by abortive drugs;[59] in any case if they survived the drugs and were brought to full term they were so treated as to receive no care but were either killed by hunger or exposure to frost or given as fodder to animals. What excesses of cruelty he has left behind.

PEDERASTY

53. Such, then, are the laws which Plato decreed on marriage and procreation. The other forms of incontinence which he taught are easy to learn for anyone who wants to find out. In fact, those who love unnatural lewdness he classifies as happy, says that after departing this life they will be happy.[60] They carry off for themselves no small prize for their lovers' madness. For it is ordained that all such as have taken the first steps on the celestial highway shall no more return to the dark pathways beneath the earth, but shall walk together in a life of shining bliss and be furnished in due time with like plumage, the one to the other, because of their love.

54. To these remarks he makes the following addition:[61]

These, then, my boy, are the blessings great and glorious which will come to you from the friendship of a lover.

And he does not say this about those who love in a chaste fashion but about those whose love is not bound by the regular laws. And these things can easily be learned from his dialogues. Now neither Nero, the basest of the Roman emperors, nor the Assyrian Sardanapalus,[62] notorious for his pleasures and his luxury, ever wrote or extolled such a law. But I think that those who are excessively enslaved to pleasures do not praise the disease but in the course of time their predilection becomes a permanent condition.

HOMICIDE

55. And why is it necessary to speak of the enormities that he has legislated illegally concerning murder?[63] For he enjoined that anyone who killed his own domestic servant should in effect be let off free. If

one killed another person's slave in anger the penalty was only a fine. If in anger one killed a freeman he was merely condemned to two years in exile. If the killing was premeditated the penalty was three years in exile, and if one murdered a second time after returning from exile he would then be merely exiled permanently. His legislation is much the same concerning fathers who kill their children, or children their fathers, or wives who kill their husbands or husbands who kill their wives.

56. And so, the philosopher has composed such laws and has persuaded no one, native or stranger, city dweller or rustic, Greek or barbarian, man or woman, young or old, educated or uneducated, to direct his life in accordance with his principles.

57. As for me, it remains to explain to you the laws which the fishermen, the publicans, and the tent-maker have offered to the human race. On your side, when you have compared the two sets of laws, you will admire the divine rays of our laws. The philosopher, as we said, admired unrestrained pederasty and has pointed out its threefold rewards. Our Savior, on the other hand, has repudiated not only acts of debauchery but even a glance of that type: *But I say to you that everyone who looks at a woman with lust has already committed adultery with her in his heart.*[64]

The Unity and Indissolubility of Marriage

58. The philosopher has unrestrainedly made a law that one can have sexual intercourse with other people's wives. But the maker of human nature, when fashioning our nature in the beginning, fashioned only one man and one woman, and he forbade marriage to be dissolved, only allowing one mode of dissolution which would truly end the conjugal union. Scripture says: *But I say to you that anyone who divorces his wife, except on the ground of unchastity, causes her to commit adultery; and whoever marries a divorced woman commits adultery.*[65]

59. In these words He orders the husband to put up with the shortcomings of his spouse even if she is loquacious, even if she is alcoholic, even if she is prone to abuse others. But if she breaks the marriage laws and looks to another, then such conduct calls out for the marriage contract to be dissolved.

60. Again he has enacted similar prescriptions by the mouth of

the tanner. Writing to the Corinthians, Paul has promulgated these laws for all: *Now concerning the matters about which you wrote: "It is well for a man not to touch a woman." But because of cases of sexual immorality, each man should have his own wife and each woman her own husband.*

[66] You see how great is the difference between the laws of the philosopher and those of the worker in leather? Paul has ordered every man to have his own wife and every woman to have her own husband.

61. He has also laid down laws concerning continence; he does not allow a wife to abstain from conjugal relations unless her husband agrees to this, nor does he allow the husband likewise, if she does not agree. For Scripture says: *For the wife does not have authority over her own body, but the husband does; likewise the husband does not have authority over his own body, but the wife does. Do not deprive one another except perhaps by agreement.*[67] In fact the one who without the other's consent practices continence he supposes to be deprived of his authority.

62. Then, shortly passing on imperceptibly to what is perfection, Paul adds: *for a set time, to devote yourselves to prayer, and then come together again.*[68] In modifying the laws to our nature, he states the reason: *So that Satan may not tempt you.*[69] And teaching that Satan launches his attacks on us from our own selves because of our lack of self-control, he adds: *Because of your lack of self-control.*[70]

63. Concerning celibacy there exist, not laws, but counsels[71] which propose the advantage of non-marriage. Scripture says: *The unmarried man is anxious about the affairs of the Lord, how to please the Lord; but the married man is anxious about the affairs of the world, how to please his wife.*[72] Scripture says the same thing about women, teaching that virginity provides a life free from care.

EVANGELICAL COMMANDS AND COUNSELS

64. Admire, my friends, the language of Paul the tanner and adore the one who is expressed in his words. If you wish, notice further the laws on murder. For, while the philosopher has not even legislated that parricide should be requited by capital punishment, our Savior himself punishes even abusive words spoken unseasonably or by one unjustly moved to anger. *But I say to you that if you are angry with a brother or sister, you will be liable to judgement; and if you insult a brother*

or sister, you will be liable to the council; and if you say, "You fool," you will be liable to the hell of fire.[73]

65. And he threatened he would demand an account for idle words. He also ordered us to do good, not just to friends but to enemies. For Scripture says: *But I say to you, Love your enemies and pray for those who persecute you.*[74] Then he shows the prize which transcends the merits of the contestants. For Scripture said: *so that you may be children of your Father in heaven; for he makes his sun rise on the evil and on the good, and sends rain on the righteous and on the unrighteous.*[75]

66. And setting down laws concerning oaths he altogether interdicts them, saying that Yes and No are sufficient confirmation of what one says.[76] He further states that the life of poverty is the more perfect condition: *So therefore, none of you can become my disciple if you do not give up all your possessions.*[77] And nevertheless, while instituting such a strict way of life of this kind, He does not promise that He will give any pleasure or satisfaction in this life but rather poverty, misery, injuries, blows, and wounds of every sort: *In the world you face persecution.*[78] And: *Blessed are you when people revile you and persecute you and utter all kinds of evil against you falsely on my account. Rejoice and be glad, for your reward is great in heaven.*[79]

67. He has indicated the toils and the dangers but has also promised to give in return prizes and crowns at the end of life. In another place Scripture says: *If they persecuted me, they will persecute you; if they kept my word, they will keep yours also.*

[80] And in yet another place: *If they persecuted me, they will persecute you; if they kept my word, they will keep yours also.*[81]

68. Such, then, are the laws of the Christians. It is truly just that we should admire those men and those who have believed in them. In fact, hearing those words and without having received either wealth or power, or bodily health, from the One who had called them, but trusting in these long-term, invisible promises they have endured dangers, journeyed round the earth, and carried their teaching to the nations.

69. It is no less appropriate to praise those who received them. In spite of the fact that they did not find anything brilliant or remarkable in preachers, but instead the language of fishermen and tentmakers, and the most extreme poverty, they in fact lacked the basic means of subsistence. Where would they get it, in that they had been forbidden to worry about tomorrow? But not only did people believe

in what they said, but they also made light of the laws that were then in circulation and they abandoned their ancestral traditions.

70. Those enjoyed such reverence for the ones who had been exposed to dangers, even unto death, that the tombs of those heroes were regarded by all as treasures which provided blessings of every sort.

71. See, then, my friends, reflect on the might of those laws. The Romans, Persians, and those who lived outside the empire showed their own weakness in trying to dissolve them. By attempting to do so they only made their strength all the more obvious. The laws of Lycurgus and Solon, without enduring any external attack, were destroyed by themselves.

72. Neither Pythian Apollo nor Athena Polias[82] was able to make the laws which they had established prevail; they were extinguished as soon as the Romans took over. Let any one of you, my friends, produce even one Spartan who endured death on behalf of the laws of Lycurgus. Or one Athenian who did so on behalf of those of Solon. Or a Locrian who did so for those of Zaleuchos. Or a Cretan who did so for those of Minos. But not one of you can point out even one. However, we can produce myriads of men and women ready to endure death on behalf of the laws of the fishermen and the tent-makers. The witnesses are the tombs of the martyrs, illustrious cities and distinguished places which bring benefits to their inhabitants and to strangers alike.

73. Since the difference has now been clearly demonstrated between both the laws and the legislators by the preceding comparative study—on the one hand, those that are the products of human device have been shown and, on the other, those that are heavenly, salutary products—receive, my friends, the divine gifts and do not dishonor the One who has donated to us this great and loving largess. And you will recognize their divine dimensions more accurately if you encounter them after expelling wretched prejudice from your souls.

Discourse 10

ON TRUE AND FALSE ORACLES

1. Those enamored of tyranny grab power, even though they have no right whatever to it. They surround themselves with external trappings of royalty—the purple robe, the crown, the throne, the chariot, the spear-bearers—but with no thought of seeking to have the other qualities of royalty. They desire to be called, not lovable fathers, but severe masters, not benign protectors, but extremely rigid chieftains. The result is that legitimate kings often dethrone them out of pity for the victims of their illegal authority, and often the people and the military strip them of power because they can no longer endure their arrogance.[1]

2. The all-wicked demons have been both active and passive in this regard. For they abandoned the rank which had been assigned them, ran away from the very gentle overlordship of the Creator, and seized upon tyranny, having appropriated the name of divinity. They called themselves gods and persuaded foolish individuals to offer them divine honor. Then, striving to maintain their power, their latest innovation is to foreknow and foretell the future, in this way deceiving men who are easily led astray.[2]

3. That is why everywhere on earth they founded workshops of deceit[3] and thought up the deception of oracles, those who prophesy with the help of a meal, or of ventriloquism, or of necromancy,[4] and the Castalian spring,[5] the fountain of Colophon,[6] the sacred oak and the bronze of Dodona,[7] the tripod of Cirrha,[8] and the cauldron of Thesprotia,[9] the oracle of Ammon in Libya,[10] and that of Zeus at Dodona,[11] and at Branchidai,[12] and in Delos,[13] and Delphi,[14] and Colophon, that of the Clarian, and the Pythian, and Delian, and Didymaian [Apollo],[15] and at Lebadia that of Trophonios,[16] and in Oropus that of Amphiaraos,[17] and in the land of the Tyrennian and the Chaldeans

the very obscure grottos of necromancy; at one place, the oracle of Amphilochus,[18] and in another, that of Glaucos,[19] and elsewhere, that of Mopsos,[20] and of other such individuals with odious names.

4. Sufficient proof that these oracles have been the work of maleficent demons, usurping the name of divinity, is the silence that now engulfs them. In fact, after the appearance of our Savior, those who offered this deception to human beings ran away, for the brilliance of the divine light proved unendurable to them.[21]

5. Plutarch of Chaeronea has given incontrovertible testimony to this.[22] He was not a Hebrew but a Greek, by both birth and language. Further, he was enslaved to Greek opinions and had a detailed knowledge of the error of oracles, doubtless because Delphi, Lebadea, and Oropus were places not far from Chaeronea but bordering on it, or practically so. Plutarch wrote at length on a wide variety of subjects. He was, in fact, a man of great learning and wide experience. He wrote also on the topic of oracles and, in particular, the work entitled *Concerning the Obsolescence of Oracles*.

6. In this work he says among many other things:

> That it is not the gods, said Heracleon, who are in charge of the oracles, since the gods ought properly to be freed of earthly concerns, but that it is the demigods, ministers of the gods, who have them in charge, seems to me not to be a bad postulate; but to take, practically by the handful, from the verses of Empedocles,[23] sins, rash crimes, and heaven-sent wanderings, and to impose them on the demigods, and to assume that their final fate is death, just as with men, I regard as rather too audacious and uncivilized.

7. It is not a prophet from the Christian side nor an apostle who has said these things, nor any of those who believed in them, and who were eager to formulate their teachings, but an individual who was well versed in the standard school curriculum and enslaved to the ancient deception of the philosophers. This man said, first, that it was not the gods who were giving oracles, but demons, and then that the guardians of their temples, seized by them and transported in Bacchic frenzy, emit oracles at a price, but without foretelling anything true; that even in those matters of which they brag with youthful insolence to have some inspiration and insight, they foretell many dire and haz-

ardous things, not just pests and errant paths but almost as many deaths for men, and that the words they utter are not the product of divine inspiration or possession, but rather mere plagiarisms from the poet Empedocles.

8. What follows contains the same idea. It goes like this:[24]

> In what concerns the mysteries, in which it is possible to discover the foremost indications of the truth concerning demons, let my mouth be silent, as Herodotus says.[25] As to the religious feasts and the sacrifices as well as the days of abstinence and days of mourning, in the course of which there are sacrificial slaughterings and eating of flesh, as well as fasts and breast-beating, and very frequently obscenities resound in the vicinity of the sanctuaries and such follies of the excited tossing their necks.[26] I would venture to say that these rites honored none of the gods, but were for the sake of averting the wicked demons as compensation for the ancient human sacrifices.

9. Then, in the passage which we have just examined, Plutarch said that the oracles did not issue from gods but from demons. Here he further characterized these demons as wicked, and produced their deeds as the clearest proofs of his statement. For who, I ask you, can derive pleasure from eating raw flesh and from tearing the flesh from the joints, and from shameful remarks and obscene actions, and the mad goings on of those in delirium who toss their necks, if it is not maleficent demons that are responsible for the misfortune of humanity?

10. To the foregoing words he has added the following:[27]

> When Ammonius had ceased speaking, I said, "Won't you rather tell us all about the oracle, Cleombrotus? For great was the ancient repute of the divine influence there, but at the present time it seems to be somewhat evanescent."

> As Cleombrotus made no reply and did not look up, Demetrius said, "There is no need to make any inquiries or to raise any questions about the state of affairs there, when we see the evanescence of the oracles here, or rather the total disappearance of all but one or two."

11. It was after the epiphany of our Lord and Savior that Plutarch wrote those words. The date also explains why the oracles had disappeared.

The Testimony of Porphyry: No Divine Prescience

Porphyry, for his part, in his treatise, *On the Philosophy from Oracles*, speaks as follows:[28]

> But already the exact knowledge of the movement of the stars and the conclusions derived therefrom are not comprehensible to human beings or even to some of the demons. And so they lie about many things when they are consulted.

12. Therefore, my friends, even if you do not believe us when we are critical of your oracles, at least believe the one who is our worst enemy and your best friend. For he is our implacable enemy, one who wages open war on (our) religion. Porphyry has affirmed that the demons who preside over the so-called oracles tell lies.

13. That he calls these gods and ascribes astrology rather than divine foreknowledge to them, he has made clear in this same work. For he has this to say:[29]

> In fact, what the gods say, if they speak knowing what has been fated, they reveal from the motion of the stars; and this almost all the gods who are not liars have confessed.

14. But those whom he here has called gods he elsewhere affirms are not gods, and this he has shown, not in some different work, but in this present one.[30] In fact, after having quoted the oracle of Apollo, which teaches that it is necessary to sacrifice to earthly gods, to gods beneath the earth, to marine gods, to gods in the heavens and in the air, he rejects this oracle as being no good.

15. He asserts that we should not regard as gods those who take pleasure in sacrifices of living beings: that human sacrifice is the most unjust of all, and unholy, shameful, and injurious, and for that reason cannot be acceptable to the gods. Then he introduces Theophrastus,

who asserts that sacrifices of human beings are appropriate not to gods but to demons. He makes fun of the human sacrifices of the ancients and gives an account of many of them from many regions.[31]

16. Then, having taught that the wicked demons have ordered these sacrifices to be performed, he adds:[32]

> That is why an intelligent, temperate man will be on guard against performing such sacrifices, but he will be eager to purify his soul completely. For they do not become attached to a pure soul.

17. But the Pythian Apollo has legislation quite the opposite to that of Porphyry. For he lays down, in fact, that anyone consulting the oracle should pay ransom to the evil demon: libations, a pyre, black blood, dark wine, and such things. And after other such remarks he has taught the prayer that should be made in offering the sacrifice:[33]

> O demon, who has received the diadem of wicked-minded souls, under the recesses of the heavens and earth.

And these remarks Porphyry has made in the same work where he had proved that this demon is not a god and where he maintained his own idea that those who take pleasure in such sacrifices are not real gods.

18. And, to prevent anyone saying that he has falsely stated these things, he has placed an oath at the beginning of his work:[34]

> I call upon the gods to witness that I have not added anything to or taken anything away from the sense of the oracles, except that I may have corrected an incorrect word, or have made a change for the sake of clarification or have filled out an incomplete meter.

Through these words he accuses the Pythian of ignorance. For not only does he correct incorrect words and clarify ambiguous passages, but he even provides remedies for limping meters which the Pythian has uttered through the mouths of the interpreters.

19. And Diogenianus also exposes the falsity of the gods who pronounce oracles. This is what he has to say:[35]

That in the majority of cases the so-called seers miss the mark is proved by the lives of almost all men and even the prophets themselves proclaim the mantic art.

20. And a little later he says:[36]

Now I will just add this to what I have said already, that in the few instances where the so-called prophets happen to get it right in their prophecies, this is due more to causality of chance than to scientific knowledge. For it is not the fact of what has been prophesied coming true, never, but rather seldom or hardly ever, or as a result of scientific knowledge, that a thing turns out as forecast, that is what we have decided to call a result of chance, we who have distinguished clear ideas under each category.

Men Compel the Gods to Speak

21. That Porphyry maintains that the gods who utter oracles foretell what they do simply because they are compelled to do so by men can easily be learned by anyone who consults the work which he wrote, *On the Philosophy from Oracles.* He has actually quoted the very words of the gods.

22. He says, for instance,[37] that Hecate replied to his invocation:

I have come hearkening to your prayer, which the nature
of mortals has found for consultations of the gods.

And elsewhere, reproaching the one who called upon her, she said:[38]

In need of what have you called on me, goddess Hecate,
with compulsions that tame the gods.

And Apollo, for his part, exclaims:[39]

Listen to me, though I am unwilling to speak, since you
have bound me by necessity.

And again:[40]

Release now the lord. For the mortal no longer retains the god.

23. Through these examples Porphyry has made plain, and those who have usurped the name of deity have also made plain, that the devices and constraints of men are more powerful than the gods themselves. For the wiles of men drag the gods down from the heavens and bind them here below. And they cannot return to heaven until they get their release from men. And one can find in this same writer countless other examples of the same kind which indict the gods for their weakness.

IMPOSTURE AND AMBIGUITY IN THE ORACLES OF APOLLO

24. How full of such horrific materials the oracles are, can easily be learned by anyone who reads about them. When the Athenians were once hit by plague the Pythian oracle responded[41] that the plague would not cease until the Athenians sacrificed seven youths and seven maidens to Minos.

25. And the ambiguity of the oracles has often provided a foreboding of disasters for many. For example, Aristomachos[42] did not comprehend the meaning of the word "narrows"; he left behind the strait and the triremes and lost his life while crossing the strait. The one expounding the oracle should not have concealed the oracle in obscurity, pretending to know the future; but in sheer malice he uttered an ambiguous prophecy in order that the lie would not be easily detected.

26. It was a similar ambiguity that portended disaster for Croesus. The oracle said:[43]

Croesus, having crossed the Halys, will destroy a great empire.

But it did not indicate whether the empire would be his own or that of the enemy, so that, win or lose, he could not blame the oracle. And that was what the Pythian did after receiving gifts worth many thousands from Croesus.[44] So one of two things is evident: the oracle was either fraudulent or very ungrateful. For he either preened himself about something of which he was ignorant, or he knew and deliberately acted unjustly toward those who were eager to serve.

27. Julian had a similar experience when he was about to set out on an expedition against the Assyrians:[45]

> Now we, all the gods, are preparing to bring the trophies
> of victory to the river which bears the name of a wild beast
> (i.e., the Tigris)
>   And I am their leader, Ares, the impetuous, who raises
> the din of war.

28. Something analogous to this happened to the Athenians when Xerxes attacked them with an army of tens of thousands. The seers of the Athenians ran to the god. And this is how he began his oracular response:[46]

> Unfortunate ones, why do you sit there?

A response which, from all the evidence, clearly proves his ignorance.

29. For if he had really foreseen the victory he would not have called them unfortunate, but rather thrice-blessed. In fact, the Greeks with two hundred triremes and three hundred men overcame thousands of triremes and countless thousands of men.[47]

30. Furthermore, Apollo advised them to flee after predicting the weakness of the guardian goddess of the fortification. He said:[48]

> Pallas cannot propitiate Olympian Zeus,
> in spite of invoking him with many prayers.

What resulted was exactly the opposite to this. After saying, in effect, that Zeus was not responsive to the prayers of Athena, he goes on to say, as if he had changed his mind:[49]

> Far-ranging Zeus gives a fortification to Tritogenes.

31. As for those whose hopes were poised on a razor's edge, he did not reveal in concise, clear-cut terms any way out of their

dilemma. He concealed his own ignorance in the ambiguity of his oracular utterances, fearing the consequences of his lying.

32. The conclusion of the oracle is along the same lines:[50]

O divine Salamis, you will destroy the children of women;
whether Demeter scatters or gathers.

He did not know, as you can deduce from the text, who would die, whether the Persians or the Athenians. That is why only women are mentioned by him, without any identification of their nationality. As to the words, "whether Demeter scatters or gathers," these are the words of one who is completely ignorant of the date of the victory. But, as it happened, Themistocles,[51] by his cleverness and courage, prevented the falsehood of the oracle from being completely obvious, and proved that the Athenians, far from being unhappy, were very fortunate.

33. As to the citizens of Sparta and Cnidus, the oracles of this one refer defeat to Sparta and slavery to Cnidus.[52] The oracle prided itself that it had given those most savage and most disgraceful laws to Lycurgus, the legislator. For it said to him upon his arrival at Delphi:[53]

You have come, Lycurgus, to my richly endowed temple,
a friend to Zeus and to all the occupants of heavenly Olympus.
I am not sure if I will prophesy that you are a god or a man.
But I rather hope that you are a god, Lycurgus.
You have come in search of good legislation.
That I will give to you.

34. Now we have shown in the previous discourse what laws Lycurgus had established. He legislated, for instance, the expulsion of strangers, unrestrained pederasty, illicit community of wives, and he upset the laws of marriage.[54] But the wisest, most cultivated prophet himself said that he had given these laws and named as god the one who introduced this legislation while admitting that he did not know whether he should address him as a god or as a man. And, wishing to give him the more honorable title, he did not actually give it as a god would but, as if a man, he said: "I rather hope."

IMMORALITY OF APOLLO'S ORACLES

35. This oracle praised the women of Sparta who had unrestrained intercourse with whomsoever they wished. And he said:[55]

Pelasgian Argos has primacy over the whole earth;
so have Thracian horses and Spartan women, and men who
drink the waters of lovely Arethusa.

36. Apollo also pronounced Archilochus, who was a very salacious poet,[56] worthy to be sung and immortal. He made this reply to the father of Archilochus:[57]

Telesicles, you will have a son immortal and worthy to be
sung among men.

37. And he said to Homer:[58]

Fortunate and unfortunate.

Unfortunate, because of the fact of being struck blind, and fortunate because of the poetry which he judged to be first-rate. But this same poetry Plato, having anointed with perfume, as he might the female pudenda[59] expelled from the Utopia which he was creating.

38. It was the oracle too who ordered the boxer Cleomedes to be hailed as worthy of divine honors. The oracle says:[60]

Cleomedes of Astypalea, last of heroes,
whom you honor with sacrifices
making him no longer mortal.

We have already spoken of the many murders which this one had previously dared to commit.

39. And this is the oracle which he delivered to the inhabitants of Methymna:[61]

But for the inhabitants of Methymna it would be far preferable
that they venerate the tip of the phallus of Dionysus.

Now the wisest of the gods, whom the poets have called Phoibos, did not blush in this oracle to give orders that a prepuce be honored as holy and without stain.

40. It was he, too, who instead of protecting his own temple when it was on fire,[62] announced that such was the lot allocated to it by the Fates, and he chanted a monody to bewail his sad experience. I will quote the closing lines of it:[63]

Endure with a patient heart the immortal designs of the Fates because Zeus in the heavens has promised with a favorable nod that what they determine with their threads will remain fixed.

41. One can find countless other examples of the ridiculous in the oracles of Apollo. These have been assembled, not only by Porphyry in his *On the Philosophy from Oracles*, but also by the cynic Oenomaos,[64] who demonstrated the falsity of oracles.

42. I have made mention of Oenomaos, Porphyry, Plutarch, Diogenianus, and the others because you regard them as worthy of credence in that they speak of what pertains to you. As for us, the facts speak for themselves, and in one clear voice facts denounce the oracles as false.

THE ORACLES HAVE BECOME SILENT
SINCE CHRIST'S COMING

43. In fact before the epiphany of our Savior, while darkness still encompassed, so to speak, the whole world, maleficent demons like bandits and marauders in their hunting down human nature used ambushes and snares, and nets of all sorts. But when the light of truth arose they all took to flight and abandoned their own holes.

44. That is why, when He was manifested to them, they exclaimed:[65] *Suddenly they shouted, "What have you to do with us, Son of God? Have you come here to torment us before the time?"* And others again implored him not to send them into the abyss. In Philippi the spirit of the python exclaimed concerning the apostles: *"These men are slaves of the Most High God, who proclaim to you a way of salvation."*[66]

45. That is why, having seen the proclamation of the truth circulating everywhere, they took to flight like runaway soldiers who

have committed many crimes and offenses, and then, when they saw the presence of the King, took to flight and deserted their posts.

46. But the sovereign King of the universe has destroyed their onslaughts. The water of Castalia is no longer a source of prediction; the fountain of Colophon no longer issues prophecies; the bronze of Thesprotia no longer is involved in divination; the tripod of Cirrha no longer issues oracles; the bronze of Dodona no longer talks nonsense nor does the much-vaunted oak tree speak any longer.[67] No, the god of Dodona is now silent, the god of Colophon is silent, so is the Pythian, the Clarian, the Didymaean, and the oracle of Lebadaia; Trophonios is silent, so is Amphilochus, Amphiaraos, Ammon, and the necromancy of the Chaldeans and of the citizens of Tyre.

47. For the one who rebuked the abyss has ordered them to keep silent. Drying it up, He said to the abyss, as the prophet reports: *Be dried up. And I will make your rivers run dry.*[68]

48. Apollo at Daphne, when he ordered us to transfer our remains [i.e., of Babylas],[69] was struck by a thunderbolt from the heavens. For the martyr of the Crucified did not in fact allow him to make his predictions or to lead men continually astray. But just as the mighty Paul rebuked the spirit of the python, so also the remains of the martyr bridled the falsehood of the oracle.

The Salvation of the Gentiles Preached and Realized

49. And so your own oracles have taught you what kind the oracles of your gods are. Anyone who has encountered the sacred Scriptures can learn accurately what sort of things the God of the universe foretells, and how these predictions are useful and profitable for life, and how they cause the brilliance of truth to shine forth. I will recall just some of them to show the difference between our predictions and yours by way of comparison.

ISAIAH PREDICTS THE DESTRUCTION OF THE IDOLS

50. I will quote those first prophecies which foretold the destruction of idols. Hear, now, the prophet, Isaiah: *In days to come the mountain of the Lord's house shall be established as the highest of the mountains, and shall be raised above the hills; all the nations shall stream to it. Many peoples shall come and say, Come, let us go up to the mountain of the Lord, to the*

house of the God of Jacob; that he may teach us his ways and that we may walk in his paths. For out of Zion shall go forth instruction, and the word of the Lord from Jerusalem. He shall judge between the nations, and shall arbitrate for many peoples; they shall beat their swords into ploughshares, and their spears into pruning-hooks; nation shall not lift up sword against nation, neither shall they learn war anymore.[70]

51. You have now heard what the prophet foretold. Now in the name of truth say if, in these oracles, there is anything which appears to you equivocal or ambiguous. But I know you will make no such claim on the basis of doubting the facts. In fact, you have before your eyes the testimony of the facts.

52. Or do you not see the sublimity of the Church, and how the majority genuflect before it and show it reverence, the majority willingly, although some answer back and serve against their judgment? Do you not see the tops of the mountains stripped of your abomination and adorned with the residences of the ascetics,[71] and the crowds coming from all quarters, proclaiming the divinity of the Logos who is manifest on Zion and embracing the law which has gushed forth from Zion? And do you not see that they have ceased from wars and that in place of weapons of war they have taken in hand the implements of agriculture?

53. Or do you not know that at the precise moment when this prophecy was uttered there was a king in Jerusalem, another in Samaria, another in Idumea, and another still in Moab, and yet another in Moab, and another in Ammon? And do you not know that the Arabs and Madianites and Amalecites were under other leaders? And Gaza, Ascalon, and Azotus, and indeed Sidon, Tyre, and Damascus, were under the direction of different leaders. For there were kings, not just over individual cities but even over individual towns.[72]

54. But at the very moment when our Savior became incarnate in the flesh Caesar Augustus was emperor over the universe, and after he had brought to naught the ethnarchs and the divided kingdoms he submitted them all to the government of Rome.[73] It was with a premonition of these events that the prophet made his predictions. A little later he made the tragic narration of the destruction of the idols which had been manufactured by man.

55. The Scripture says: *The idols shall utterly pass away. Enter the caves of the rocks and the holes of the ground, from the terror of the Lord, and from the glory of his majesty, when he rises to terrify the earth. On that day peo-*

ple will throw away to the moles and to the bats their idols of silver and their idols of gold, which they made for themselves to worship, to enter the caverns of the rocks and the clefts in the crags, from the terror of the Lord, and from the glory of his majesty, when he rises to terrify the earth.[74]

56. This is not the place to undertake an explanation of this prophecy, but you surely must admire the truth of this oracle, and confess the truth of the facts which you have often experienced.

57. But there is no need to blush, my friends; for it is proper to feel shame, not at the confession of sin, but at its commission. Even if you do not wish to say, everybody knows in that they were eyewitnesses that the gods were frequently buried in the earth and that they were drawn up from there by those instructed in piety and exposed to public view.

58. For those enslaved to impiety have interred them, thinking that thereby they come to the rescue of their gods. Others point out where they are hidden to those who investigate such things. Others excavate, and when they make a discovery, they expose it in the marketplaces, so that women and their offspring may make fun of their so-called gods.[75] Some were images of reptiles, others of quadrupeds. They also worshipped at that time images of bats and mice. They destroyed the actual animals—I mean snakes and scorpions, and mice and bats—but they deified their images.

59. Now we have already said more than enough on these matters. Let us now learn the accuracy of the other oracles. The following words come from the same prophet: *On that day people will regard their Maker, and their eyes will look to the Holy One of Israel; they will not have regard for the altars, the work of their hands, and they will not look to what their own fingers have made, either the sacred poles or the altars of incense.*[76]

60. These events had been foretold by the prophet more than a thousand years before the reign of Constantine, after which the temples of the demons were destroyed.[77] But this divinely inspired man saw in advance as if he were actually there, and he predicted what would happen long afterwards. By contrast, however, the oracle of Dodona and the Pythian did not announce how events which took place only three months later would turn out, but they gave responses which inclined to error on one side or the other.

61. But hear also what follows: *Turn back to him whom you have deeply betrayed, O people of Israel. For on that day all of you shall throw away your idols of silver and idols of gold, which your hands have sinfully made for you.*[78] And again: *I, the Lord, am first, and will be with the last. The coast-*

lands have seen and are afraid, the ends of the earth tremble; they have drawn near and come. Each one helps the other, saying to one another, "Take courage!" The artisan encourages the goldsmith, and the one who smooths with the hammer encourages the one who strikes the anvil, saying of the soldering, "It is good"; and they fasten it with nails so that it cannot be moved.[79]

62. But the statue cannot stand if it is not nailed together, nor can it move if it is not carried by others. Here is another passage: *Here is my servant, whom I uphold, my chosen, in whom my soul delights; I have put my spirit upon him; he will bring forth justice to the nations. He will not cry or lift up his voice, or make it heard in the street; a bruised reed he will not break, and a dimly burning wick he will not quench; he will faithfully bring forth justice. He will not grow faint or be crushed until he has established justice in the earth; and the coastlands wait for his teaching. Thus says God, the Lord, who created the heavens and stretched them out, who spread out the earth and what comes from it, who gives breath to the people upon it and spirit to those who walk in it: I am the Lord, I have called you in righteousness, I have taken you by the hand and kept you; I have given you as a covenant to the people, a light to the nations, to open the eyes that are blind, to bring out the prisoners from the dungeon, from the prison those who sit in darkness. I am the Lord, that is my name; my glory I give to no other, nor my praise to idols*[80]

63. Such are the words that the God of the universe addressed to Christ the Lord as to a man, calling him Jacob and Israel in accordance with His visible nature. For it is from the race of Jacob that He has come in His human nature. And He has clearly shown His gentleness and patience which He used when He was being insulted by the Jews. He said that He had been given as a testament of the race. Indeed He had promised salvation through Him to the patriarchs and to the Jews themselves.[81]

64. God said that Christ had arisen as a light for the Gentiles to open the eyes of the blind, and to break the bonds of those in chains, and to liberate from darkness those who sat imprisoned in the darkness of ignorance. Now God described as blind, and captives, and sitting in darkness those who were surrounded by the darkness of ignorance and enchained by the fetters of sin.

65. That he has so named those enslaved in the error of superstition is clear from the sequel: *I am the Lord, that is my name; my glory I give to no other, nor my praise to idols.*[82] And so at the same time as He manifested Himself He stripped those of the name which they had appropriated and applied to themselves; and again, a little later, He

said: *The Lord goes forth like a soldier, like a warrior he stirs up his fury; he cries out, he shouts aloud, he shows himself mighty against his foes.*[83] And then He teaches why He had not done this before, saying: *For a long time I have held my peace, I have kept still and restrained myself; now I will cry out like a woman in labour, I will gasp and pant. I will lay waste mountains and hills, and dry up all their herbage; I will turn the rivers into islands, and dry up the pools.*[84]

66. The first are the marks of patience, the second, those of philanthropy. For from the beginning God had been patient in not punishing. But then, after employing caution, He called upon those who were erring and scattered those who remained in their erring ways: *I will destroy*, He says, and lay bare. *I will lay waste the mountains and hills, and turn rivers into islands and make all their lakes dry up.*[85]

67. By these words He has indicated to them the sanctuaries of the idols which were found there. These, after His epiphany, He destroyed and dried them up like lakes: *I will lead the blind by a road they do not know, by paths they have not known.*[86]

For those of old who went astray did not know the way of truth. But, having taken the apostles as guides and conductors, rather as beacon-bearers, they abandoned the paths of error and discovered the highway of truth: *I will turn the darkness before them into light, the rough places into level ground.*[87]

68. Instead of the former darkness they enjoy intellectual light and, abandoning tortuous paths, they keep to the straight road. Then, since they still wander in error, he chastises them *They shall be turned back and utterly put to shame—those who trust in carved images, who say to cast images, "You are our gods."*[88] And a little later: *I am about to do a new thing; now it springs forth, do you not perceive it? I will make a way in the wilderness and rivers in the desert. The wild animals will honour me, the jackals and the ostriches; for I give water in the wilderness, rivers in the desert, to give drink to my chosen people, the people whom I formed for myself so that they might declare my praise.*[89] He has called His people those who have the faith and of whom he has been called the firstborn, because he has assumed human flesh.

THE SALVATION OF NATIONS IN ISAIAH

69. That he has spoken these things in Isaiah in reference to the Gentiles is attested by the following passage: *Listen to me, O coastlands,*

pay attention, you peoples from far away![90] Nothing in this refers to the Jews; the words "islands" and "gentiles" prove that. And elsewhere: *Listen to me, my people, and give heed to me, my nation; for a teaching will go out from me, and my justice for a light to the peoples. I will bring near my deliverance swiftly, my salvation has gone out and my arms will rule the peoples; the coastlands wait for me, and for my arm they hope.*[91]

70. Through all these statements God predicted the salvation of the nations, the law of the Gospel, and the light of knowledge which he proffered to all people by the holy apostles. "By the arm" naturally does not designate a bodily limb since the divine nature is simple and not composite, but in a figurative fashion he has expressed his power. In fact, since combatants make war with their hands, and tillers work with them, and likewise other manual laborers, he has rightly designated by the phrase "by the arm" this force in which we place our confidence when we exclaim: *I will fear no evil, for you are with me.*[92]

71. And again he exclaims: *See, I made him a witness to the peoples, a leader and commander for the peoples. See, you shall call nations that you do not know, and nations that do not know you shall run to you, because of the Lord your God, the Holy One of Israel, for he has glorified you.*[93] Seeing, then, Christ the Lord reigning over the world and all the nations gladly hymning his overlordship, both understand the prophecy and marvel at the truth.

72. But listen to what follows: *So those in the west shall fear the name of the Lord, and those in the east, his glory.*[94] And again: *I was ready to be sought out by those who did not ask, to be found by those who did not seek me. I said, "Here I am, here I am," to a nation that did not call on my name.*[95] And all prophecy is full of such words.

In Jeremiah, the Promises Are Transferred to the Gentiles

73. Now in order to demonstrate that the other prophets have made predictions similar to these, listen to Jeremiah who exclaims: *At that time Jerusalem shall be called the throne of the Lord, and all nations shall gather to it, to the presence of the Lord in Jerusalem, and they shall no longer stubbornly follow their own evil will.*[96]

74. Notice, my friends, the close correspondence of these statements. And see all those people coming from all sides into that city, in which the passion of the Lord and Savior occurred, and feeling a loathing for the deceit of the idols and instead offering their reverence to the Crucified.

75. Here is another passage from the same prophet: *Thus says the Lord: Stand at the crossroads, and look, and ask for the ancient paths, where the good way lies; and walk in it, and find rest for your souls. But they said, "We will not walk in it."' Also I raised up sentinels for you: "Give heed to the sound of the trumpet!" But they said, "We will not give heed." Therefore hear, O nations, and know, O congregation, what will happen to them.*[97]

76. The Jews were the first to be addressed by the prophets and apostles in the divine proclamations. But when they rejected the message the divinely given gifts were presented to all the Gentiles. The God of the prophet sometimes calls the prophets of old "routes," but it is the Lord and Savior Himself who is called the good way.

77. Just as byways from villages and the countryside converge on the imperial highway[98] so all the prophets have given signposts to this road to those who are willing to believe. And the Lord Himself exclaims in the holy Gospels: *I am the way, and the truth, and the life.*[99] That is why he encourages the Jews to read the oracles of the prophets and to investigate what was prophesied.

78. But, after they rejected the prophets, he brought as well the trumpet of the apostles. And when, as Luke reports in Acts, these latter repeated: *We will not hear you,* the divine men shouted at them: *'It was necessary that the word of God should be spoken first to you. Since you reject it and judge yourselves to be unworthy of eternal life, we are now turning to the Gentiles.*[100]

79. Then once again the prophet announces the salvation of the nations and exclaims to the God of the universe: *O Lord, my strength and my stronghold, my refuge on the day of trouble, to you shall the nations come from the ends of the earth and say: Our ancestors have inherited nothing but lies, worthless things in which there is no profit. Can mortals make for themselves gods? Such are no gods!*[101] What could be clearer than these words?

80. The prophet has written this oracle as if he were an eyewitness viewing the transformation of the world and hearing the repentance of the nations, and giving ear to those satirizing the inadequacy of the idols.

OTHER PROPHETS ANNOUNCE THE SALVATION OF THE GENTILES

81. And Amos, the prophet, or rather the God of the universe using the prophet as his mouthpiece, predicted not just the salvation of

the Gentiles but also the Diaspora of the Jews: *For lo, I will command, and shake the house of Israel among all the nations as one shakes with a sieve.*[102]

82. And a little later: *On that day I will raise up the booth of David that is fallen, and repair its breaches, and raise up its ruins, and rebuild it as in the days of old; in order that they may possess the remnant of Edom and all the nations who are called by my name, says the Lord who does this.*[103]

83. And if anyone wants to learn what is this tent, let him hear the inspired John saying: *And the Word became flesh and pitched his tent among us, and we saw his glory, the glory as of the only-begotten from the Father full of grace and truth.*[104]

84. Zephaniah also exclaims: *The Lord will be terrible against them; he will shrivel all the gods of the earth, and to him shall bow down, each in its place, all the coasts and islands of the nations.*[105] In fact, when he ordered the Jews to assemble in the temple of Jerusalem he gave the additional instruction of necessity that once the so-called gods had vanished, each should worship the true god without the necessity of coming to Jerusalem but should worship in houses and cities and villages and in the rural areas.

85. And a little later he adds: *At that time I will change the speech of the peoples to a pure speech, that all of them may call on the name of the Lord and serve him with one accord. From beyond the rivers of Ethiopia my suppliants, my scattered ones, shall bring my offering.*[106] The reference here is to the one language of the apostles, which was Galilean;[107] this was divided by God into all the languages of all the nations and he addressed to all the call to salvation.

86. By the mouth of Zechariah he prophesies in the same vein: *Sing and rejoice, O daughter Zion! For lo, I will come and dwell in your midst, says the Lord. Many nations shall join themselves to the Lord on that day, and shall be my people; and I will dwell in your midst. And you shall know that the Lord of hosts has sent me to you.*[108]

87. In those terms the only-begotten Son has accurately shown forth His own person and that of the Father. But He has said that He has been sent, since it is precisely not as God but as man that He has been made manifest. And since He has come, it behooves Him to fulfill all justice on behalf of humanity and to give an example of the submission that he lauded.

88. And elsewhere: *Rejoice greatly, O daughter Zion! Shout aloud, O daughter Jerusalem! Lo, your king comes to you; triumphant and victorious is he, humble and riding on a donkey, on a colt, the foal of a donkey. He will cut*

off the chariot from Ephraim and the warhorse from Jerusalem; and the battle-
bow shall be cut off, and he shall command peace to the nations; his dominion
shall be from sea to sea, and from the River to the ends of the earth.[109]

89. And a little further on: *And the Lord will become king over all the*
earth; on that day the Lord will be one and his name one. The whole land shall
be turned into a plain from Geba to Rimmon south of Jerusalem.[110] What, my
friends, is there in those oracles that is obscure or in any need of elu-
cidation? What is there in those expressions that does not loudly proclaim its testimony by facts?

90. Hear, then, the God of the universe speaking to Israel
through the mouth of Malachi: *I have no pleasure in you, says the Lord of*
hosts, and I will not accept an offering from your hands. For from the rising of
the sun to its setting my name is great among the nations, and in every place
incense is offered to my name, and a pure offering; for my name is great among
the nations, says the Lord of hosts. But you profane it when you say that the
Lord's table is polluted, and the food for it may be despised.[111]

91. Compare, then, my friends the words and the facts, and consider the rejection by the Jews and the acceptance by the Gentiles, and
the spiritual sacrifice to the Lord of the universe that is offered
throughout lands and seas. And chant the praise of him who has given
such a clear prediction of these things.

The Salvation of the Gentiles
in the Historical Books

92. And, if you wish, read also the oracles of Daniel, Ezekiel,
Joel, Micah, Hosea, and the other prophets. They all predicted the salvation of the Gentiles. Furthermore, when God made his covenant
with the patriarch Abraham He promised that He would bless the
Gentiles through his seed. He said: "*I will make of you a great nation, and*
I will bless you, and make your name great, so that you will be a blessing. I will
bless those who bless you, and the one who curses you I will curse; and in you
all the families of the earth shall be blessed."[112]

93. And this promise God has given him, not just once, but many
times. What is more, after the death of Abraham He gave the same
blessing to Isaac and after him he renewed it to Jacob. In fact, since it
is from their seed that the only-begotten Son has taken his human
nature in the Incarnation, and becoming incarnate and accomplish-

ing the economy for the whole world, he sent out his apostles and instructed them to teach all nations in the name of the Father, the Son, and the Holy Spirit, and the nations who believed would enjoy the blessings of salvation, it was only proper that He should confer this blessing on Abraham and on his descendants, both revealing to them what would come about and showing the greatness of their privilege, and consoling by the hope of salvation those who paid attention to the divine words.

94. When Jacob the patriarch, for his part, blessed Judah he recalled to memory the blessing of the Gentiles, saying: *The sceptre shall not depart from Judah, nor the ruler's staff from between his feet, until tribute comes to him; and the obedience of the peoples is his.*[113] The great Moses also exclaims: *Praise, O heavens, his people.*[114]

95. And who can easily collect the prophecies of the inspired David? For instance, in the second psalm he impersonates the Lord, saying: *I will tell of the decree of the Lord: He said to me, "You are my son; today I have begotten you. Ask of me, and I will make the nations your heritage, and the ends of the earth your possession."*[115] And he says in Psalm 8: *O Lord, our Sovereign, how majestic is your name in all the earth! You have set your glory above the heavens. Out of the mouths of babes and infants you have founded a bulwark because of your foes, to silence the enemy and the avenger.*[116] Now we see these things being fulfilled every day.

96. Further, in Psalm 9, he says to the God of the universe: *Rise up, O Lord! Do not let mortals prevail; let the nations be judged before you. Put them in fear, O Lord; let the nations know that they are only human.*[117] Since the human race had fallen into extreme irrationality, of necessity he demands that a legislator be given to them so that people could recover their humanity and abandon their bestiality.

97. In Psalm 21 also he says: *All the ends of the earth shall remember and turn to the Lord; and all the families of the nations shall worship before him. For dominion belongs to the Lord, and he rules over the nations.*[118] What follows contains the same idea: since David foretold the incarnation of a new people formed from all the nations.

98. And, so as to pass over a great number of texts, listen to David say in Psalm 45: *In the place of ancestors you, O king, shall have sons; you will make them princes in all the earth.*[119]

And again in Psalm 46:10: *"Be still, and know that I am God! I am exalted among the nations, I am exalted in the earth."*[120]

99. The following psalm announces the salvation of the Gentiles: *Clap your hands, all you peoples; shout to God with loud songs of joy. For the Lord, the Most High, is awesome, a great king over all the earth.*[121]

100. Psalms 7, 8, and 9 particularly, and indeed the whole psalms, so to speak, foretell the transformation of the world. They predict the election and faith of the Gentiles and besides the preexistence before all ages of our God and Savior, His generation from the Father, His birth from a virgin, His miracles, His sufferings, the incredulity of the Jews, His resurrection from the dead, His ascension to heaven, the coming of the Spirit, the concourse of the apostles on every land and sea.[122]

CONCLUSION

101. Notice furthermore that all the other prophets foretell these events. But I thought that it would be superfluous to assemble all their predictions because I would need many tomes to transcribe them all and to say what is appropriate about each. It will be enough for you, if you please, to deduce the truth of the others from the ones which we have examined. These are clear, true, and are, so to speak, accurate images of the events.

102. Just as the easiest way to understand the art of the master painters is to juxtapose the portrait and the original model, so you must juxtapose the facts that have already received fulfillment with what the prophecy has foretold in the outline traced beforehand by the Supreme Artist[123] so that you may see the exactness of the similarity.

103. For in former days, before the prophecy received its fulfillment, it was difficult to persuade people of that time that the prophecies were true. But when we now see fulfilled the prophecies of yesterday and yesteryear, and those words have now become realities, we have no trouble convincing our ears. For our ears have the corroboration of our eyes. We do not need Herodotus to tell us[124] that the ears are for men less credible than the eyes, since our eyes, in a manner of speaking, see what our ears hear.

104. Since then, my friends, you have already heard some few of the prophecies and have seen them corroborated by facts, compare the prophecies of our prophets with those of your own and exclaim

with the apostle: *Or what fellowship is there between light and darkness? What agreement does Christ have with Beliar? Or what does a believer share with an unbeliever? What agreement has the temple of God with idols?*[125]

105. In fact, the choirs of the prophets are the temples of God. But the idols which the pagans adore are deaf and dumb. It is of them that the spirit of God speaks: *Their idols are silver and gold, the work of human hands. They have mouths, but do not speak; eyes, but do not see. They have ears, but do not hear; noses, but do not smell. They have hands, but do not feel; feet, but do not walk; they make no sound in their throats. Those who make them are like them; so are all who trust in them.*[126,127] And may you, for your part, learn the truth of this and not share in the curse of the prophet.

Discourse 11

ON THE LAST END AND
FINAL JUDGMENT

1. Perhaps, my friends, you have heard mention of one Aristippus, who was, on his mother's side, the grandson of Aristippus, a disciple of Socrates. This man, in virtue of his association with his mother, had the greatest possible involvement in philosophy. In virtue of this he earned the sobriquet "metrodidact," which the whole world bestowed upon him.[1]

2. For this man, the lessons of his mother sufficed as an introduction to philosophy. But you, hearing as you do so many prophets and apostles, not to mention their successors who have been illustrious for their learning, refuse to learn the truth.

3. This is the state at which you have arrived, that you consider these teachings of no avail. In fact, it is not Sicilian luxury[2] on the grand scale, nor a life dissipated in a state of effeminacy that they promise; no more is it much-desired wealth and the violent strait of its conflicting currents, but rather perspiration, toils, and an existence rich in griefs.

4. That much is totally clear to you; but the net result of all this you cannot see. Doubtless, because you are accustomed to see only what is visible to your senses, you fail to recognize the nature of what is invisible. You do not possess those eyes which are created by faith.[3]

5. Now, insofar as your capacity and my ability allow, I will show you this, utilizing once more the light of the divine oracles. Accordingly I hope to show you now, by presenting to you in a comparative fashion the opinions of the philosophers and the dogmas of the divine evangelists, what are the views of the philosophers on our end in life, and what is the view of the divine evangelists.

Various Definitions of "End"

6. Epicurus has defined the end as living for the greatest pleasure.[4] Democritus of Abdera, however, who is the one who originated this doctrine, spoke of the joy of living, and not of pleasure, changing the terminology but not the teaching.[5]

7. Heraclitus of Ephesus also modified the terminology, but he has abandoned the basic concept, for in place of pleasure he has invoked contentment.[6] Now this definition has left something else unexplained. For it has invoked the term "satisfaction" without defining it. But people are divided about what its definition is; some think that temperance is the definition; for others, it is the opposing vice that is championed; some invoke incontinence; others continence; others still, a life that is ambitious and unjust; and finally others, a life of justice. But for Heraclitus, the end consists in what is pleasing to each one, that is to say, in what is agreeable and attractive, replacing the term "pleasure" with "contentment."

8. The famous Pythagoras imagined that the perfect science of numbers was the supreme good.[7] For Hecataeus, on the other hand, it was "self-sufficiency";[8] for Antisthenes, "modesty";[9] for Anaxagoras of Clazomenae, "reflection on life," with its concomitant freedom,[10] giving a definition worthy of philosophy because it is the greatest good to grasp the true nature of things and to set at naught the ephemeral, preserving one's soul free of all servitude.

Plato's Definition: Becoming Like the Divine

9. Now Plato, the son of Ariston, has eclipsed Anaxagoras by the grandeur and loftiness of his definition. For him, the supreme good consists in "becoming like the divine so far as we can."[11] This invitation to become like the gods is indeed praiseworthy, but the additional phrase, "so far as we can," makes the definition all the more praiseworthy. For it is certainly not within our power to make ourselves like God. For how, in fact, can a visible creature become like the invisible? How can something small and circumscribed in a small area become like the uncircumscribed which contains the created world? How can a being which is quite recent and cannot even create a heaven measuring a span become like to the eternal and to the Creator of the universe?

10. Consequently we cannot imitate this divine nature either in power or in wisdom. Assuredly it is possible to reproduce on a small scale some of the goodness, justice, gentleness, and benevolence. Indeed Christ the Lord has proposed such imitation to those who long for perfection. For He says: *Be merciful, just as your Father is merciful. For He makes his sun to rise on the wicked and the good, and to rain on the just and the unjust.*[12]

11. And for that matter Socrates, the son of Sophroniscus, Plato's teacher, was accustomed to call happy, not the person overflowing with riches and borne on a favorable breeze, but the person adorned with justice.[13] And he characterized as impious those who separated self-interest and justice. For he said that only what was just was advantageous.

12. The orators were unwilling to praise those words of his. For they said that justice was one thing and self-interest something else, showing in this way that what was advantageous was in no way compatible with what was nonadvantageous. For separation from what is just is, I presume, unjust. And injustice is harmful. And you would not rightly call what is harmful advantageous.

The View of Aristotle

13. In a word, Plato and Socrates were of one mind in saying what was admirable. But Aristotle, although he belonged to the school of Plato, did not profit from these teachings. Quite the contrary. The fullness of beatitude in his view came from a three-fold source of goods: goods of the soul, goods of the body, and external goods. He used to say that the happy man should not merely be adorned with virtue, but also have bodily strength, and be resplendent with beauty and inundated with riches.[14] If he lacked any one of these characteristics he could not be said to be happy.

14. Apparently Aristotle was more a follower of the poet Simonides, who said:[15]

To be healthy is best for man;
The second thing is to have a fair appearance,
and the third, to be wealthy without guile.

And Theognis likewise recommended that poverty should be avoided:[16]

We must flee poverty, Cyrnus, and hurl it into the teeming
sea down from the steep rocks.

THE VIEW OF THE STOICS

15. But the Stoics have cast their vote for quite the opposite viewpoints. They maintained that the end of man is to live according to nature and insisted that for the soul the body is neither an advantage nor a disadvantage because health cannot be a constraint to virtue or sickness cannot lead to evil, because, they said, these things are indifferent.[17] But they go even farther than that, since they assert that God and man possess the same virtue.

EPICURUS

16. Epicurus took the opposite route. He defined happiness as being neither hungry nor thirsty, and he said that one who enjoyed such a state could be a rival even for Father Zeus.[18] And so the love of pleasure has been for him a school exercise in impiety. And let no one see him confining his ridicule to that name alone—I mean the name Zeus—since it is clear that by such thoughts he dared to blaspheme the very God of the universe.

17. That was the experience of this thrice-wretched man who believed in mere chance and in the atoms, and thought that the universe was rudderless and uncared for and did not look forward to a judgment, since he believed that man's existence terminated with the tomb.

PLATO ON FINAL JUDGMENT AND RETRIBUTION

18. Plato, on the other hand, described the judgments and punishments of the next life. He says in Book 10 of the *Republic*:[19]

savage men of fiery aspect who stood by and took note of the voice laid hold on them and bore them away. But Ardiaeus and others they bound hand, foot and head, and flung down and flayed them and dragged them by the wayside, carding them on thorns.

19. In the *Phaedo* he expresses the same ideas:[20]

Halfway between these two a third river has its rise, and near its source issues into a great place burning with sheets of fire, where it forms a boiling lake of muddy water greater than our sea. From there it follows a circular course, flowing turbid and muddy, and as it winds round inside the earth it comes at last to the shore of the Acherusian lake, but does not mingle with its waters, and after many windings underground, it plunges into Tartarus at a lower point.

20. This is the river which is called Pyriphlegethon, whose fiery stream belches forth jets of lava here and there in all parts of the world. Directly opposite to this in turn the fourth river

breaks out, first, they say, into a wild and dreadful place, all leaden gray, which is called the Stygian region, and the lake which the river forms on its entry is called Styx. After falling into this, and acquiring mysterious powers in its waters, the river passes underground and follows a spiral course contrary to that of Pyriphlegethon, which it meets from the opposite direction in the Acherusian lake. This river too mingles its stream with no other waters, but circling round falls into Tartarus opposite Pyriphlegethon.

21. But, so as not to protract this discourse by quoting everything, it is easy, my friends, to consult this dialogue and learn clearly how he describes the judgment, and how he inflicts both proportionate punishments on those who commit minor wrongdoings and implacable punishments on those who have been guilty of grave and serious acts of impiety.

22. I will recall a few of his statements:[21]

Those who on account of the greatness of their sins are judged to be incurable as having committed many gross acts of sacrilege or many wicked and lawless murders or any other such crimes, these are hurled by their appropriate destiny into Tartarus, from where they emerge no more. As for those who are judged to have been guilty of sins which, though great, are curable—if, for example, they have offered violence to father or mother in a fit of passion, but spent the rest of their lives in penitence, or if they have committed manslaughter in the same fashion—these too must be cast into Tartarus, but when this has been done and they have remained there for a year, the surge casts them out— the manslayers down the Cocytus and the offenders against their parents down the Pyriphlegethon.

23. Plato teaches then how they cry and supplicate their victims for pardon. But if the victims are unrelenting they are sent back again into the lake and endure the same punishments. Having thus shown their punishments, he next reveals the places reserved for those who have led good lives. This is what he says:[22]

24. But those who are judged to have lived a life of surpassing holiness, these are they who are released and set free from confinement in these regions of the earth and, passing upward to their pure abode, make their dwelling on the earth's surface. And of these such as have purified themselves sufficiently by philosophy live thereafter altogether without suffering and reach habitations even more beautiful, which it is not easy to portray nor is there time to do so now. But the reasons which we have already described provide ground enough, as you can see, Simmias, for leaving nothing undone to attain during life some measure of goodness and wisdom, for the prize is glorious and the hope great.

25. In the *Gorgias* he says practically the same thing:[23]

Give ear, then, as they say, to a very fine story, which you, I suppose, will consider fiction, but I consider fact for what I am going to tell you I shall recount as the actual truth.

And a little further on he says:[24]

The man who has led a godly and righteous life departs
after death to the Isles of the Blessed and there lives in all
happiness exempt from ill, but the godless and unrighteous man departs to the prison of vengeance and punishment which they call Tartarus.

26. And again:[25]

Next they must be stripped naked of all these things before
trial, for they must be judged after death. And the judge
must be naked too and dead, scanning with his soul itself
the souls of all immediately after death, deprived of all his
relatives and with all that fine attire of his left on earth,
that his verdict may be just.

PLATO'S HEBREW SOURCES

27. That is exactly what Plato believes about the judgment seats
of Hades. For he encountered Hebrews in Egypt; he paid careful
attention to the oracles of the prophets. He knew the river of fire
which the divine Daniel contemplated and had learned the words of
the most divine Isaiah. For the latter had said about those who were
punished: *Their worm shall not die nor their fire be extinguished.*[26] And
again: *"Who among us can live with the devouring fire? Who among us can
live with everlasting flames?"*[27]

28. And it is possible to find many other such quotations in the
prophets. And the philosopher took some of his material from these
scriptural sources and mingled it with some from the Greek myths,
and so composed dialogues on these subjects. The following has the
same idea:[28]

As I said, then, whenever Rhadamanthus receives one of
these he knows nothing else about him, his name or origin, only that he is evil, and when he perceives this he dis-
patches him straight to Tartarus after first setting a seal
upon him to show whether he appears to him curable or

incurable, and on arrival there he undergoes the appropriate punishment. But sometimes a Greek, seeing another soul that has lived in piety and truth, that of a private citizen or any other, but especially I maintain, Callicles, the soul of a philosopher who has applied himself to his own business and not played the busybody in his life—and he is filled with admiration and sends him forthwith to the Isles of the Blest.

And after a brief period he continued:[29]

29. Now I have been convinced by these stories, Callicles, and I am considering how I may present to the judge the healthiest possible soul. And so I renounce the honors sought by most men, and pursuing the truth I shall really endeavor both to live and, when death comes, to die, as good a man as I possibly can be. And I exhort all other men thereto to the best of my ability, and you above all I invite in return to share this life and to enlist in this contest, which I maintain excels all other contests, and I reproach you in turn because you will not be able to help yourself when the trial and judgment will take place of which I spoke just now.

30. But when you come before your judge, the son of Aegina, and he seizes hold of you, you will gape and reel to and fro, no less than I do here, and perhaps someone will humiliate you by boxing your ears and will do you every kind of outrage. Now perhaps all this sounds to you like an old wives' tale and you despise it, and there would be nothing strange in despising it if our searches could discover anywhere a better and truer account, but as it is you see that you three who are the wisest Greeks of the day, you and Polus and Gorgias, cannot demonstrate that we should live any other life than this, which is plainly of benefit also in the other world.

31. Such things he discussed concerning these matters in this dialogue and counseled wisely that we should take precautions so as

to be free of such punishments. In the *Crito* also he introduced the laws addressing Socrates as follows:[30]

> Socrates, be advised by us your guardians and do not value more highly your children, your life, or anything else than you value what is right, so that when you enter the next world you may have all this to plead in your defense before the authorities there.

32. In the *Apology*, however, he said that death is good:[31]

> Let us think that there is a good hope that there is good in this. For death is one of two things: either it is annihilation and the dead have no consciousness of anything, or it is, as we are told, really a change, a migration of the soul from here to another place.

33. These words of his are praiseworthy even if they are adulterated with some illegitimate teachings, such as Rhadamanthus, and Minos, and the Islands of the Blest, and that only souls separated from their bodies are punished. For these views are at variance with the dogmas of truth. But Plato can be partially forgiven in that he did not participate in the teaching of the apostles.

34. But the doctrine of metempsychosis,[32] which he borrowed from the teachings of the Pythagoreans, must be completely avoided, my friends. For those teachings are completely ridiculous. For concerning the souls that are transmitted into bodies he says in the *Phaedo*:[33]

35. What sort of character do you mean, Socrates? Well, those who have cultivated gluttony, or selfishness, or drunkenness, instead of taking pains to avoid them, are likely to assume the form of donkeys and other such animals. Don't you think so?

> Yes, that is very likely.

> And those who have deliberately preferred a life of irresponsible lawlessness and violence become wolves and hawks and kites, unless we can suggest any more likely animals.

> No, what you mention are exactly right, Cebes.

36. Not to drag out the quotation any further, the one who consults the text will find him saying that the souls of those who have practiced the social virtues will pass into the bodies of bees, wasps, and ants,[34] or even back into the human race. Now these views are not just ridiculous; they clearly contradict what has been presented previously.

37. He said that the souls would be punished in that place, some indeed in Acheron, others in the Acerousian marsh, others still cast into the Styx, the Cocytus, and the Pyriphlegeton, and that those who had sinned incurably would be snatched from the waves of the Pyriphlegeton into Tartarus; and that those who sinned in a fashion that could be expiated could become suppliants as they were borne down the river to those whom they had formerly injured and whom they now saw on the river banks, and would be cast from the swell of the river into the marsh. And he said that those who had been slaves to pleasure would become donkeys, and that those who had espoused a life of rapine and tyranny would be turned into wolves, hawks, and kites. Finally, that those who had led a social life would enjoy a most happy life, turned into wasps, bees, and ants. The philosopher decreed such a life for those who were serious in the pursuit of virtue.

38. But these views are quite contradictory. In the first quotation he had sent them to the Isles of the Blessed and had stated that he could not put into words what would be the abodes of the philosophers. But in the second statement it is to those he assigns the lives of wasps, bees, and ants, and he says those who in the previous life had done no evil receive as recompense both to injure and to be injured by others.

39. For wasps and bees by nature strike with their sting, and ants pillage the meadows and take their share of the crops with the cultivators, even though they have not shared in their toils. Besides, the wasps are the enemy of the workers because they destroy the fruits of their crops. But the best of philosophers, far from being aware of any of this, merely kept as his goal to achieve a reputation for pioneering these doctrines.[35]

Revolutions of a Thousand Years
40. Yes, and elsewhere he produces other myths in these words:[36]

For a soul does not return to the place where she came
from for ten thousand years, since in no lesser time can

she regain her wings, save only his soul who has sought after wisdom unfeignedly, or has conjoined his passion for a loved one with that seeking. Such a soul, if with three revolutions of a thousand years she has thrice chosen this philosophical life, regains thereby her wings and speeds away after three thousand years; but the rest, when they have accomplished their first life, are brought to judgment and after the judgment some are taken to be punished in places of chastisement beneath the earth, while others are borne aloft by justice to a certain region of the heavens, there to live in such a manner as is merited by their past life in the flesh.

41. Now it is easy to grasp the absurdity of these expressions. For who, I ask you, could ever teach him the cycles of these myriads of years? And that after the passage of thousands of years each soul would then return to its own place. And that about what occurred in the intervening time it was inappropriate for even the most abandoned types to speak, so how could a philosopher? In fact he teamed up those who had practiced the pure philosophy with the impure and the pederasts and said that both were equally deserving of the same rewards.

42. But, forgetful once more of what he had said (for he had assigned heaven to these souls), in the *Republic* he said that the soul of Orpheus had obtained the body of a swan, that Agamemnon had become an eagle, Ajax a lion, Atalanta an athlete, and Thersites an ape.[37] I do not know why he undertook to introduce such foolish beliefs into his dialogues. But it is obvious that he was in a playful rather than a serious mood when he describes transmigrations of souls in them. For in many other places he describes the punishments in Hades.

43. I will return to these again, lest I seem to leave the philosopher in ridiculous statements of that kind. Hear him then speak in his own words:[38]

It is not the tale by Alcinous told[39] that I shall unfold, but the tale of a warrior bold, Er, the son of Armenius, by race a Pamphylian. He once upon a time was slain in battle and, when the corpses were taken up on the tenth day already decayed, was found intact, and having been brought home, at the moment of his funeral, on the twelfth day as he lay on the pyre, revived, and after coming to life related what he said he had seen in the world beyond.

44. He said that when his soul had gone forth from his body it journeyed with a great company and that they came to a mysterious region where there were two openings side by side in the earth; that judges were sitting between these, and that after every judgment they bade the righteous proceed to the right and upward through the heaven with tokens attached to them in front of the judgment passed on them, and the unjust to take the road to the left and downward, they too wearing signs behind of all that had befallen them, and that when he himself drew near they told him that he must be the messenger to mankind to tell them of that other world, and they charged him to give ear and to observe everything in the place.

45. These words are truly worthy of philosophy. For they do not send souls into the bodies of irrational animals, but rather send those who have lived well to heaven, and those who have by previous choice lived badly down to Hades. It is plain, then, that his earlier remarks were made in jest and those present remarks are said in seriousness.

PLUTARCH'S TEACHING

46. And Plutarch, in his *Concerning the Soul*, has depicted the judge and the attendants of the judge inserting this description in his work:[40]

We were present when Antyllus was conversing with Sositeles and Heracleon. He already seemed to the doctors to be lifeless, but shortly he was brought back from what seemed a not very deep sleep and said or did nothing that betrayed any symptoms of being mentally disturbed. And he told us that after dying he was brought back to life and that he would not die again from that disease, but that he had heard those who had led him away being reprimanded by their lord, because they had sent for Nicander and that they had mistakenly led him off instead of Nicander, who was a shoemaker.

Plutarch added that as soon as Nicander died Antyllos got well.

47. Such, then, are the teachings of the philosophers. For instance, some measure human happiness in terms of the pleasures of food and drink; others thought up more rational accounts. Some felt that human life extended as far as the grave; others dreamed up retributions for deeds done in this life and designated, as far as words could describe, places for punishment full of dread, not indeed leaving these accounts free of mythical elements, as you can gather from what we have already said.

48. Now it is time that you contemplate the teachings with reference to God in the sacred Gospels. The beginning of blessings, they say, is a praiseworthy fear of God. As Solomon and his father teach: *The fear of the Lord is the beginning of wisdom.*[41] And the end is a life adorned with the divine laws. For Scripture says: *Happy are those whose way is blameless, who walk in the law of the Lord. Happy are those who keep his decrees, who seek him with their whole heart.*[42]

49. The Savior of the universe has taught us this in the holy Gospels. For He calls blessed, not those who are wealthy and are swimming in pleasures and luxuries, but the poor in spirit, the meek, the merciful, and those who hunger and thirst for justice' sake, and who endure to suffer some evil for the sake of some good, and He promises the kingdom of heaven to those who direct themselves aright in these and similar ways. He promises the kingdom of the heavens.

50. But I think it would be beneficial if I quoted for you the actual laws written in the form of the Beatitudes: *Blessed are the poor in spirit, for theirs is the kingdom of heaven. Blessed are those who mourn, for they will be comforted. Blessed are the meek, for they will inherit the earth. Blessed are those who hunger and thirst for righteousness, for they will be filled. Blessed are the merciful, for they will receive mercy. Blessed are the pure in heart, for they will see God. Blessed are the peacemakers, for they will be called children of God. Blessed are those who are persecuted for righteousness' sake, for theirs is the kingdom of heaven.*[43]

51. And all the other directives, my friends, have the same import. But that should suffice to show the legislator's intent and the end to which He has directed our sight. For He did not command us to expect with eagerness wealth, or bodily health, beauty, but the perspiration involved in virtue and the hazards to be undertaken on its behalf, and its very great and ineffable prizes.

ETERNAL LIFE IN CHRIST JESUS

52. What words suffice to bear witness to the immortal, infinite kingdom of heaven and the life which will be free of old age, pain, and sorrows? Concerning this the blessed Paul has exclaimed: *"What no eye has seen, nor ear heard, nor the human heart conceived, what God has prepared for those who love him."*[44] But if the one who witnessed these things cannot describe those things of which he was deemed worthy to be an actual spectator, it would be very difficult for anyone else to hazard the task of describing the indescribable.

53. As proof that He defined the end of good things as eternal life, listen to what he wrote to the Romans: *When you were slaves of sin, you were free in regard to righteousness. So what advantage did you then get from the things of which you now are ashamed? The end of those things is death. But now that you have been freed from sin and enslaved to God, the advantage you get is sanctification. The end is eternal life. For the wages of sin is death, but the free gift of God is eternal life in Christ Jesus our Lord.*[45]

54. He says that the gift of freedom in and of itself is sufficient to show you the fruit of piety; but nevertheless out of his own generosity the munificent and bountiful Lord has bestowed on you eternal life so that you might recognize the difference between sin and justification. For the end of the one is death, but of the other, eternal life.

55. Then after very many other things he showed them the greatest of his blessings: *For all who are led by the Spirit of God are children of God. For you did not receive a spirit of slavery to fall back into fear, but you have received a spirit of adoption. When we cry, "Abba! Father!" it is that very Spirit bearing witness with our spirit that we are children of God, and if children, then heirs, heirs of God and joint heirs with Christ—if, in fact, we suffer with him so that we may also be glorified with him.*[46]

56. And in his Epistle to the Galatians he says something very similar: *So you are no longer a slave but a child, and if a child then also an heir, through God.*[47] And he has expressed similar sentiments in his letter to Timothy: *I know the one in whom I have put my trust, and I am sure that he is able to guard until that day what I have entrusted to him.*[48]

57. But in another letter to Timothy he has added this: *As for me, I am already being poured out as a libation, and the time of my departure has come. I have fought the good fight, I have finished the race, I have kept the faith. From now on there is reserved for me the crown of righteousness, which*

the Lord, the righteous judge, will give to me on that day, and not only to me but also to all who have longed for his appearing.[49]

THE RESURRECTION OF THE BODY

58. He has written similarly about the resurrection of the body to the Corinthians, the Thessalonians, the Philippians, and to many others. He says, for instance: *What is sown is perishable, what is raised is imperishable. It is sown in dishonour, it is raised in glory. It is sown in weakness, it is raised in power. It is sown a physical body, it is raised a spiritual body. If there is a physical body, there is also a spiritual body.*[50]

59. And again: The *trumpet will sound, and the dead will be raised imperishable, and we will be changed. For this perishable body must put on imperishability.*[51] And again: *But our citizenship is in heaven, and it is from there that we are expecting a Saviour, the Lord Jesus Christ. He will transform the body of our humiliation so that it may be conformed to the body of his glory, by the power that also enables him to make all things subject to himself.*[52]

THE FINAL JUDGMENT

60. And the Lord, speaking to the Jews, said: *Because he is the Son of Man. Do not be astonished at this; for the hour is coming when all who are in their graves will hear his voice and will come out—those who have done good, to the resurrection of life, and those who have done evil, to the resurrection of condemnation.*[53]

61. And again, when he discoursed about the last end, he added this: *Immediately after the suffering of those days the sun will be darkened, and the moon will not give its light; the stars will fall from heaven, and the powers of heaven will be shaken. Then the sign of the Son of Man will appear in heaven, and then all the tribes of the earth will mourn.*[54] By these words he showed the grief of those who were unbelievers.

62. Then, when he narrated the parable of the virgins in which some of them with their lamps entered into the wedding feast while the foolish remained outside because their lamps had run out of oil, and further told the parable of the talents—the industrious laborers and the one who was lazy and hid his talent in the ground and was expelled into the outer darkness, He added:

63. *When the Son of Man comes in his glory, and all the angels with him, then he will sit on the throne of his glory. All the nations will be gathered before him, and he will separate people one from another as a shepherd separates the sheep from the goats, and he will put the sheep at his right hand and the goats at the left. Then the king will say to those at his right hand, "Come, you that are blessed by my Father, inherit the kingdom prepared for you from the foundation of the world; for I was hungry and you gave me food, I was thirsty and you gave me something to drink, I was a stranger and you welcomed me, I was naked and you gave me clothing, I was sick and you took care of me, I was in prison and you visited me."*[55]

64. And when they replied that they had done none of these things (for it is characteristic of the athletes of virtue that they behave with modesty and conceal their riches) the King will say to them: I assure you, as often as you did it for one of my least brothers who believed in Me, you did it for Me.[56]

65. And having thus proclaimed them virtuous and given them the rewards for their toils, He will say to those on His left: *"You that are accursed, depart from me into the eternal fire prepared for the devil and his angels."*[57] He also explains to them the reasons for their punishments.[58] None of them had done any of the good deeds which had been done by the chorus of the just. Nor did they imitate their extreme modesty. Rightly, therefore, they will be convicted and given over to punishment.

66. Compare, my friends, these (scriptural) teachings with those of Plato, which are so loudly praised. The rest of the drivel of Plato and of others like him is worthy of that outside darkness. That part of his teaching which we found praiseworthy has some affinity with the teachings of Scripture.

67. For Plato also promised rewards for the good and punishments for the wicked, as are also promised to us in the Scriptures in both the Old and the New Testaments. He indeed has introduced other judges, Aeacus, Minos, and Rhadamanthus, men who are not completely praiseworthy, Minos in particular having had many charges made against him.[59] We, however, await as our judge our Creator, who also knew very well the nature which He created, and knew not just its words and deeds but also its every internal thought and movement.

68. He, therefore, will judge us, having donned the garment of our humanity. For the nature of divinity cannot be perceived by the eyes. Wherefore He calls Himself the Son of man, so that those who

are being judged will see this nature. This is why the divine apostle, when he was speaking to the people of Athens, said: *While God has over-looked the times of human ignorance, now he commands all people everywhere to repent, because he has fixed a day on which he will have the world judged in righteousness by a man whom he has appointed, and of this he has given assur-ance to all by raising him from the dead.*[60]

THE WORLD TO COME PREDICTED AND FULFILLED

69. If anyone disbelieves these words and regards as trifling the words of the apostles, for that very reason he will learn the truth of those words. For Christ the Lord predicted many things concerning the life to come, and also many things that pertained, not to the future life, but to the present life only. Examine, therefore, my friends, the prophe-cies concerning the present. And if you discover that they have been proved true and turned out as forecast then you should accept what has been prophesied about the future without any cavil.

70. This must be examined closely. Christ the Lord predicted that the siege of the city of Jerusalem and that its celebrated temple would be leveled to the ground and that the race which would crucify him would be scattered throughout the entire world.[61] Let us see if this prophecy has been fulfilled.

71. Now I do not think you can have any doubts about the Jews. They have been expelled from their city and have been made second-class citizens in every other country. You who have witnessed it confess the isolation of the temple and its destruction to its foundations.[62] The rest of you can believe the account of the eyewitnesses. I with my own eyes have seen its desolation[63] and the prophecy which I have heard with my ears I have seen fulfilled with my eyes, and I vouch for and bow down before its truth.

72. So, actual circumstances testify in the most eloquent terms to the truth of this prophecy. But let us verify the fulfillment of another prophecy. Christ the Lord foretold to the apostles the kind of strug-gles and dangers which they would have to undergo when they brought their teaching to the Jews and Gentiles. He said to them:

73. *See, I am sending you out like sheep into the midst of wolves.*[64] And again: *for they will hand you over to councils and flog you in their synagogues; and you will be dragged before governors and kings because of me, as a testi-*

mony to them and the Gentiles.[65] And a little later: *Brother will betray brother to death, and a father his child, and children will rise against parents and have them put to death; and you will be hated by all because of my name. But the one who endures to the end will be saved.*[66]

74. And furthermore: *If they have called the master of the house Beelzebul, how much more will they malign those of his household!* [67] And again: *Do not think that I have come to bring peace to the earth; I have not come to bring peace, but a sword. For I have come to set a man against his father, and a daughter against her mother, and a daughter-in-law against her mother-in-law; and one's foes will be members of one's own household.*[68]

75. All these things, my friends, we have seen fulfilled in detail. The apostles have run all those hazards in bringing the light of the Gospel to the world. And their successors have preserved the faith which they handed on. The tombs of the martyrs bear witness to this; they are resplendent throughout land and sea, and they confirm the truth of the divine preachings. But He did not merely foretell difficulties to them; He also foretold victory:

76. *And I tell you, you are Peter, and on this rock I will build my church, and the gates of Hades will not prevail against it.*[69] One can now see, in fulfillment of the prophecy, houses divided against themselves. For men who have been caught in the net of the faith are in contention with their wives who do not yet believe. Or wives, who have accepted the yoke of our religion, eagerly strive that their husbands who are still in error should be caught in the net. So a necessary separation produces a praiseworthy union.

FAITH IN THE WORD

77. Now, to pass over other predictions, there was the incident of the woman who brought an alabaster flask of myrrh to anoint his feet. When he saw her faith he said to his disciples: *Truly I tell you, wherever this good news is proclaimed in the whole world, what she has done will be told in remembrance of her.*[70] So wherever on land and sea that the Gospel is read, the faith of this woman is also preached.

78. Since, then, the Lord has predicted these things, and the things which will occur in this life and we have seen them come true, let us also receive without question the things which He prophesied about the world to come, advancing from what has been fulfilled to

what has yet to occur, and using the evidence of the one as a guarantee of the truth of the other.

CONCLUSION: CHRIST IS FAITHFUL TO HIS PROMISES

79. For this reason precisely Christ made the one set of predictions as a guarantee of the fulfillment of the other ones. And the honors which He did not promise to those who believed in Him He nevertheless generously bestowed. And He conferred much splendor not just on the living but also honored the dead with an abundance of glory, so that in giving what He had not promised we would believe that He would fulfill what He had promised.

80. For assuredly the one who gave what was not attached to his covenants and who in his generosity exceeded his promises will undoubtedly fulfill His promises and give the rewards that He has shown to the contestants. For it would be disgraceful if the ones in charge of the gymnastic contests gave the promised awards to the athletes and to fulfill pledges to workers on completion of their tasks but, on the other hand, for the Creator of the universe through whom out of sheer generosity had created what was nonexistent, and who had consummated the mystery of his dispensation, and had bestowed the light of divine knowledge on those who could not see, and after all that to say that He would not carry out what He had promised.

81. But if the promise is true, as indeed it is (for the promise is a divine promise), then, my good friends, the lessons of the divine teaching are not in vain. For He promised to those who believed a heavenly kingdom and a life without end, and an intellectual illumination and membership in the choir of the incorporeal ones, just as, at the other end, he threatened eternal punishments to the unbelievers.

82. This He has made clear in the parable of the good seed and the weeds. When He had finished explaining this, He added: *So will it be at the end of the age. The Son of Man will send his angels, and they will collect out of his kingdom all causes of sin and all evildoers, and they will throw them into the furnace of fire, where there will be weeping and gnashing of teeth. Then the righteous will shine like the sun in the kingdom of their Father. Let anyone with ears listen!*[71] And at the end of these words He said: *Let anyone with ears listen!*[72]

83. My good friends, I will use the same words in my exhortation to you. For of course we do not force you against your will to accept the divine gifts, but we exhort and beseech you, and show you the greatness of what He has promised. And so we conclude with this remarkable saying of the Lord: *Let the one who has ears to hear heed this.*

Discourse 12

ON PRACTICAL VIRTUE

THE OBJECT OF PHILOSOPHY

1. Roots produce trees and nourish them; branches and leaves adorn them, and fruit dangles aloft in their midst. If one lops the branches or strips the foliage, the trees become useless. They are despoiled of their beauty and the roots at the base are made to appear completely superfluous.

2. Likewise, the body is in need of eyes to see and direct the other senses; it is in need of feet to walk and to support itself. It is in need of hands to work and to procure for the other organs nourishment, drink, and the other necessities.

3. Tunics, cloaks, mantles, in fact all articles of dress are manufactured not only with the help of the weaver's warp; they also need the woof which is inwoven and combined with the warp.[1]

4. Why have I recounted these things? It is not, my friends, out of love for small talk, but rather to use these examples as a demonstration of the nature of philosophy, to use that word in its precise meaning. Knowledge of divine things, in fact, is truly and in all respects the supreme good. But knowledge does not suffice to accomplish what is considered worthwhile.

5. Without doubt, good behavior must be united to knowledge. In fact, what the root is to the tree, what the eye is to the body, what the thread is to the fabric, knowledge of truth is to souls, as faith testifies.[2]

248

THEORY AND PRACTICE

6. But it is not enough to know what it is appropriate to think about the divinity; one's life must be organized according to its laws. In fact, just as those who are taught painting,[3] or shoemaking, or any other craft, do not seek to be proficient merely for the sake of knowledge, but to produce something with their hands and to show in their works imitations of these masters, so too it is necessary that those who love religion should not confine themselves to the study of theology and natural philosophy, but should also study the laws of practical virtue and observe them to the best of their ability, and should try to fashion and model the type of their soul in accordance with these laws.

IMITATION OF THE DIVINE

7. For he who rules and shapes his soul in this way not merely imprints on it the characters of the divine laws, but actively becomes a living, rational image of the legislator himself. That is what the great herald of truth teaches when he exclaims: *Therefore be imitators of God, as beloved children.*[4] Elsewhere the Master gives this counsel: *that you may be children of your Father in heave.*[5] And again: *Be perfect, therefore, as your heavenly Father is perfect.*[6]

8. He imitates, as far as is possible, the God of the universe. He desires what God desires, and likewise hates what his Master hates. Now what pleases and displeases God is taught in clear terms in the divine laws.

9. We hear the godly David exclaim: *For you are not a God who delights in wickedness; evil will not sojourn with you. The boastful will not stand before your eyes; you hate all evildoers. You destroy those who speak lies; the Lord abhors the bloodthirsty and deceitful.*[7]

10. He has shown us in these passages what is the disposition of the legislator, and in another psalm he introduces a character who has those characteristics clearly imprinted on him, and who addresses this prayer to the legislator: *I will walk with integrity of heart within my house; I will not set before my eyes anything that is base. I hate the work of those who fall away; it shall not cling to me. Perverseness of heart shall be far from me; I will know nothing of evil. One who secretly slanders a neighbour I will destroy. A haughty look and an arrogant heart I will not tolerate. I will look with*

favour on the faithful in the land, so that they may live with me; whoever walks in the way that is blameless shall minister to me. No one who practises deceit shall remain in my house; no one who utters lies shall continue in my presence.[8]

11. Through these words he has taught us not only that it is possible to imitate the omnipotent and omniscient God, but he has also indicated to us the manner of imitation. But assuredly he has not ordered us to create heaven, earth, sun, moon, and so on, or to have a nature that is simple and infinite, but only to hate what he hated and to love what he loved.

12. Having achieved such virtue, the prophet exclaims with confidence: *Thy friends, O God, have been greatly honored by me.*[9] And a little later: *I hate them with perfect hatred; I count them my enemies.*[10] And again: *the bloodthirsty would depart from me.*[11] And again: *Go away from me, you evildoers, that I may keep the commandments of my God.*[12] And again: *I hate the double-minded, but I love your law.*[13] And again: *Oh, how I love your law! It is my meditation all day long.*[14] And again: *How sweet are your words to my taste, sweeter than honey to my mouth!*[15]

13. And you could find many other passages of the same tenor in this psalm. For all prophecy is filled with such lessons.

REWARD OF THE GOOD, PUNISHMENT OF THE WICKED

For his part, Moses indicates in his laws what is pleasing to the God of the universe and, on the other hand, what displeases Him. Besides, Isaiah, Jeremiah, Ezekiel, Daniel, and the whole choir of the prophets have taught us to make this distinction.

14. And their God Himself in the Gospels says: *"Not everyone who says to me, Lord, Lord will enter the kingdom of heaven, but only one who does the will of my Father in heaven."*[16] And again: *but whoever does them and teaches them will be called great in the kingdom of heaven.*[17] And again: *If you love me, you will keep my commandments.*[18]

15. Elsewhere, in the parable of the talents[19] He has explained that He will demand, not just the amount he is owed, but will also look for interest on it. And the one who cannot pay, he will strip of his grace, and deliver him bound to darkness. Likewise He left outside the nuptial chamber those virgins who had not brought oil with them, still calling them virgins.[20] Likewise the one who had not on a wedding garment He separated from guests and drove him out from the ban-

quet. And yet he had come because he was invited and had not come self-invited. But because he had availed himself of the invitation which was issued through the sole generosity of the married couple and had not got on a marriage garment he suffered what he suffered.[21]

16. That is why the divine apostle exclaims, saying: *For if we wilfully persist in sin after having received the knowledge of the truth, there no longer remains a sacrifice for sins, but a fearful prospect of judgement, and a fury of fire that will consume the adversaries.*[22]

17. Then he supports this parable with an example: *Anyone who has violated the law of Moses dies without mercy "on the testimony of two or three witnesses" How much worse punishment do you think will be deserved by those who have spurned the Son of God, profaned the blood of the covenant by which they were sanctified, and outraged the Spirit of grace? For we know the one who said, "Vengeance is mine, I will repay." And again, "The Lord will judge his people."*[23]

18. He causes fear to those who live in slothfulness and says: *It is a fearful thing to fall into the hands of the living God.*[24] And elsewhere He exclaims: *For all of us must appear before the judgement seat of Christ, so that each may receive recompense for what has been done in the body, whether good or evil.*[25]

ASSIMILATION TO THE BODY ACCORDING TO PLATO

19. All the aforesaid suffices to prove that knowledge has need of practical virtue.[26] Let us now examine the views of the Greek philosophers. For we will see that Plato and certain others who were in accord with his philosophy were in harmony with our views. In the *Laws* Plato speaks as follows:[27]

So he who would be loved by such a being must himself become such to the utmost of his might, and so, by this argument, he that is temperate among us is loved by God, for he is like God, whereas he that is not temperate is not like God.

20. Consequently Plato has said nothing which is contrary to our teaching but he too recognizes that in everything concerning good dispositions we must as far as possible imitate God the Creator. Accordingly, in this passage He did not call the man who is master of

his desires a wise man, but rather the one who keeps the rational part of his soul safe and sound.

21. He has written in almost identical terms in the *Theaetetus*:[28]

Evils can never be done away with, for the good must always have its contrary, nor have they any place in the world of the gods but they must haunt this region of our mortal nature. That is why we should with all speed take flight from this world to the other, and flight means becoming like to God insofar as is possible.

22. In these words, then, in a fashion that is very illuminating and wise, he has acquainted us with the means of imitating God.

First of all, he has prescribed the avoidance of certain things here below, not making us extraterrestrial, but merely separating us from terrestrial affairs. This he has made clear in what follows:[29]

Flight means becoming like to God.

23. This addition is worthy of our admiration. In fact, he has not prescribed that we assimilate ourselves, but "insofar as is humanly possible." Then he explains what is the nature of assimilation. "Assimilation," he says, "is becoming just and holy with wisdom." And this additional specification is admirable. For there are some people who have the greatest concern for justice, but pollute everything that is beautiful in the good by their maladroit behavior.

24. And then, this is all in the *Theaetetus*, he teaches at length the perfection of virtue, writing as follows:[30]

Let us speak of the leaders of philosophy. For what can one say of those who are unworthy practitioners of philosophy? From their youth up the leaders have never known the way to marketplace or council chamber, or any other place of public assembly; they never hear a decree read out or look at the text of a law. To take any interest in the rivalries of political cliques in meetings, dinners, and merrymaking with flute-girls never occurs to them, not even in dreams. Whether any fellow citizen is well- or ill-born or has inherited some defect from his ancestors on either side, the philosopher does not know any more than how many pints of water there are in the sea.

25. He is not even aware that he knows nothing of all this. For if he holds aloof it is not for reputation's sake, but because it is really only his body that sojourns in his city, while his thought, disdaining all such things as worthless, as Pindar says:[31]

"takes wings, beyond the sky, beneath the earth," searching the heavens, and measuring the plains, everywhere pursuing the course of the stars and seeking to explore the true nature of things."

26. In these lines Plato has depicted the mode of existence of our philosophers because he certainly did not find such types among the Greeks. For Socrates, the chief of the philosophers, spent his life in discussions in the gymnasia and the salons; on every occasion that he lingered in town he went down to the Peiraeus to watch the processions. When he served time with the hoplites he had a tour of duty at the battles of Potidaea and Delion.[32] Then, when he visited the dining hall he exchanged pleasantries over their cups with Aristophanes and Alcibiades, as we learn from Plato's *Symposium*.[33] He also went up to the theater and joined the crowds as a spectator.

27. The words of Plato are not strictly applicable to him. And if they are not applicable to him it would be difficult to find anybody else to whom they are applicable. But those who have become enamored of the philosophy of the Gospel have distanced themselves from political troubles. For having installed themselves on mountain tops, or enjoying the life in desert places, they have chosen a life spent in contemplating divine things and their chosen lot in life is in harmonizing themselves with this contemplation, with no care for wives, children, and material possessions, but directing their souls in accordance with the canon of divine laws and, like the best artists, they paint their spiritual image after the best models of virtue.

28. It is truly to those that the words of Plato really apply. He testifies to this himself when, among several other remarks, he says:[34]

A herdsman of this sort, penned up in his castle, is doomed by the sheer press of work to be as rude and uncultivated as the shepherd in his mountain fold. He hears of the marvelous wealth of some landlord who owns ten thousand acres or more, but that seems a small matter to one accustomed to think of the world as a whole.

29. But among the Greeks who cultivate philosophy no one of them has built a mountain shack and occupied it; a sufficient proof of that is provided by the writings of antiquity, and this is corroborated by you in your hostility to those who opt for such a life.

30. Yet Plato has said that this is worthy of the highest admiration. And he speaks similarly in Book 2 of the *Republic*:[35]

> And when we have set up an unjust man of this character, we must set the just man at his side, a simple and noble man, who, in the phrase of Aeschylus,[36] "does not wish to seem, but to be good." Then we must deprive him of the seeming. For if he is going to be thought just, he will have honors and gifts because of that esteem. We cannot be sure in that case whether he is just for the sake of justice or for the sake of the gifts and the honors.

31. So we must strip him bare of everything but justice and make his state the opposite of his imagined counterpart. Though doing no wrong he must have the repute of the greatest injustice, so that he may be put to the test as regards justice through not softening because of ill repute and the consequences thereof. But let him hold on his course unchangeable.

32. These traits apply equally to us athletes of virtue. For it is not, as in the case of Antisthenes, Diogenes, or Crates,[37] for the sake of empty glory, but for the sake of goodness itself that they do what they do. Accordingly they pass their lives far from cities and towns, concealing their virtue and only revealing it to the One who should be the judge.

UNDERSTANDING AND INDULGENCE IN JUDGMENT

33. But you are reluctant to view or marvel at those engaged in such contests. If you see some who partially surround themselves with this appearance but whose lives do not completely conform to the pattern, you immediately wag your tongues in abuse. And if you exclude only those, that would be somehow understandable. But when you go beyond those and try to make fun of and abuse those who are very different and who are true devotees of philosophy, you show how totally unjust your objection is. For then you are not excoriating the wicked but slandering the life that is worthy of emulation, acting like one who sees a monkey imitating a human, and because of this act of imitation deciding to hate humanity.[38]

34. I am not the only one to criticize such a view of things. So does Plato, who says in the *Theaetetus:*[39]

> Then let us treat our question somewhat in this fashion. Suppose that someone should commend goat-keeping, or the goat itself as a valuable animal, and another man, who had seen goats damaging lands under cultivation by grazing on them without a keeper, should denounce the brutes or find fault with any creature he had seen thus under no control or bad control. Can we say that censure of anything coming from such a quarter would have the least validity?

35. These are Plato's words, my friends, and not mine. He teaches us not to scoff at all the flocks of beasts merely because some of them are badly guided by wicked guardians or are completely bereft of a guardian. And he clearly teaches elsewhere that a flock of philosophers cannot be generated:[40]

> For there are many bearers of the narthex but few bacchants.

This Christ the Lord too has said: *Many are called, but few are chosen.*[41]

36. Plato is in accord with this sentiment when he further says in the *Epinomis:*[42]

My thesis is that attainment of bliss and felicity is impossible for humankind, with the exception of a chosen few. I would limit the statement to the term of a lifetime; when life is over, there is a fair hope that a person may achieve all.

37. Why, then, do you find it so hard to put up with the fact that you see some people in our community being untrue to the way of life which they profess? Why do you not rather marvel at those who have embraced the supernatural life and wage this contest in the body while pursuing with zeal a way of life that is incorporeal? But you had to do something quite different, on the one hand, excessively marveling at them because they transcended the limits of human nature and, on the other hand, having indulgence for those who have been swamped by their natural passions.

38. That these things are extremely difficult, you yourselves also know for, as the poet put it:[43]

You were not born from an oak tree nor from a pine tree.

That is what Plato has also shown in the *Republic*, Book 1 when he makes Cephalus remark in his discussion with Socrates:[44]

I know well that for my part as the satisfactions of the body decay, in the same measure my desire for the pleasures of good talk and my delight in them increase.

39. Then, as Sophocles demanded if his sexual drive was still vigorous, he is said to have interjected:[45]

Hush, man. Most gladly have I escaped this thing you talk of, as if I had run away from a raging and savage beast.

In this he is dilating on disgraceful passion.

40. In the *Gorgias* he has this to say about justice and injustice:[46]

For it is difficult, Callicles, and most praiseworthy to pass through life in righteousness when you have every license to do wrong. But men of this kind are few, though both here [in Athens] and elsewhere, there have been, and I fancy will yet be, honorable men and true, who possess the virtue of managing justly whatever is entrusted to them.

41. And again:[47]

But among all these arguments, while others were refuted, this alone stands steadfast, that we should be more on our guard against doing than suffering wrong, and that before all things a man should study not to seem good, but to be good.

42. There was also the exchange that Socrates had with Crito. After many remarks he added:[48]

Then in no circumstances must we do wrong. One must not even do wrong when one is wronged, which most people find acceptable. What, then, Crito? Should one do injuries or not?

Surely not, Socrates.

And is it right to do an injury in retaliation, as most people believe, or not?

Never.

For, I suppose, there is no difference between injuring people and wronging them?

Exactly.

So one ought not to return a wrong or an injury to anyone.

43. That is the teaching of Socrates and Plato on wrongdoing and on justice. It truly merits our admiration, and it is reasonable and in accord with human nature. For nature has been the teacher of ethical norms to all human beings. When the Creator was making the human race he planted in nature the knowledge of good and of what is not good. That is why, not just Socrates, Plato, Aristides, the son of

Lysimachus, and certain other Greeks, but many of the barbarians as well have led the life of justice.

THE GOOD PAGAN

44. For example, Hellanicus reports in his *Histories*[49] that the Hyperboreans dwell beyond the Ripaean mountains and lead a life of justice. They do not eat meat but live on hard-shelled fruits. According to other historians,[50] the Brahmans who live in forests, cover their bodies with leaves.

45. They say that the Scythian Anacharsis[51] was a philosopher. He was at this juncture so inflamed with love for philosophy that his fame and renown had spread far and wide. Not only did he war against the passions of the soul while he was awake. Even when he was asleep he showed signs of his continence. For instance, he was in the habit of holding his private parts with his left hand, and of pressing his lips with his right hand, showing that the battle against the tongue is tougher and needs more help to attain victory.[52]

46. Chiron, the Centaur, according to Hermippus of Berytus,[53] was a teacher of justice and Homer called him[54] the most just of the Centaurs. Truly, then, it is inappropriate that we be surprised when Hesiod maintains[55] that the path of virtue is rough, arduous, and difficult, or that Simonides has said that virtue inhabits inaccessible rocks.[56]

47. What Homer has attested about Chiron and the Hippomolgoi,[57] and what Anacharsis has effectively put into practice is precisely what the most illustrious poets have celebrated in verse. Antisthenes, the Cynic,[58] a follower of Socrates, maintained that madness was preferable to pleasure. That is why he exhorted his friends never to lift a finger for the sake of pleasure.

48. Diogenes of Sinope, who was a disciple of Antisthenes, was nominally a philosopher, but he became a slave to pleasure. He had intercourse in public with prostitutes, giving the worst kind of example to spectators. They say that when someone reprimanded him for his bad conduct, and asked him: "What are you making, Diogenes?" he replied with his customary grossness of expression:[59]

Offscouring, if I succeed, a person.

49. Crates of Thebes was a devotee of Diogenes' lifestyle; he crowned his virtue with many eulogies. This is one of his sayings:[60]

Those who are not bent and enslaved to servile pleasure
love the kingdom of immortality and freedom.

He used to say that hunger was the remedy for the sexual impulse, or, if not a remedy, a halter. But in a fit of passion, he publicly consorted with Hipparchia of Maronea and consummated his Dog-marriage[61] in the [Stoa] Poikile, having said farewell to his grandiloquent principles.

50. Aristippus of Cyrene, when he was reproached for his liaison with a mistress from Corinth, said:[62]

I possess Lais, but she does not possess me.

And the Peripatetics nominally spoke well of virtue but in reality praised pleasure. And this is not an accusation made by others about them; they themselves have written it about their own master.

51. In fact the Peripatetic philosopher, Aristocles, relates[63] that Lyko, the Pythagorean, had said concerning Aristotle that he bathed in a bath of hot oil and then sold the oil. He added that, upon his departure from Chalcis, the tax-gatherers who got on the ship to search it found on his person fifty-four plates of bronze, but that, according to others, he only had thirty flat earthen dishes.

52. In my opinion their account is not completely false. Because it is in things of this sort that happiness is stated by him to consist. He had the habit of saying that one could not be happy if he did not have a body in good condition and external goods in abundance, for without these nothing helped virtue. Atticus, the Platonist,[64] shows this clearly in his writings against Aristotle. The speeches confirm the statements made against him.

RULES TO FOLLOW IN TEMPTATION

53. Plato's teaching is diametrically opposed to this. In the *Republic*, Book 3, for instance,[65] he orders us to take care of the body

for the sake of the harmony of soul, through which it is possible to live and to live well, when the message of truth is announced.

54. This is also the advice of the divine apostle: *The night is advanced; the day has approached. Let us put aside the works of darkness and put on the weapons of light. Let us march honestly, as in the full day.*[66]

55. In fact we should not give such care to the body as to risk it dominating the soul, but so that it should collaborate with the soul, and in dependence upon it, so that it recognizes its least signs. Plato is in accord with us completely on this point, since his advice is that the body receive due care. He has also indicated the origin and development of the passion of lust:[67]

56. We can perhaps say, and not without reason, that love begins with a glance, that it increases with hope, that it is nurtured by memory, and that custom takes care of it.

And this is what he says of virtue:[68]

The first sprout of every plant, if it is well directed toward its own perfection, is most potent to achieve the consummation of its appropriate end.

SOCRATES NOT A SAINT

57. Socrates, for his part, has advised us[69] to resist the temptation to eat when we are not hungry and to drink when we are not thirsty, and to avoid glancing at, and kissing, fair creatures, since this is more dangerous than to approach the poison of scorpions and venomous spiders.

58. But these were only vain words, completely divorced from reality. He had in fact the habit of frequenting the gymnasia in search of young men, and he feasted his eyes on this licentious spectacle. *Philebus, Phaedrus, The Dream, Charmides,* and other dialogues which contain an account of his philanderings are my proof of this.[70]

59. The things which Alcibiades recounted about Socrates, Plato has written in the Symposium,[71] but for my part, to spare Socrates, I will not dare repeat them. For those words in that dialogue contain much about the eccentricities and drunken behavior of Socrates and his disgraceful propensity to stumble and fall.

60. Plato says that he dined and spent the whole night drinking, and when the others who had had enough wanted to sleep, he stayed awake and kept on drinking, all the while discussing, quite uselessly, what was suitable for Alcibiades, or for Aristophanes,[72] or the other revelers.

61. Porphyry in his *History of Philosophy*[73] narrates that Socrates was testy and short-tempered. His source was Aristoxenus, who wrote a life of Socrates.[74]

62. Porphyry[75] said that he never encountered any one more persuasive than Socrates. That was because of his voice, his appearance, his bearing, and especially because of a particular mannerism of his.

63. And this mannerism, he said, he indulged in when he was not angry. But when he was seized by this passion his ugliness was dreadful. For he abstained from no word or deed. And going through other such experiences, he shows himself to be also enslaved to sensual pleasures.

64. This is what he says:[76]

He was vigorously drawn toward sensual pleasure but without resorting to any wrongdoing, for he only had sexual intercourse with married women or with prostitutes. He had two women at the same time, Xanthippe, who was a citizen and more compatible, and Myrto, daughter of Aristides and granddaughter of Lysimachus. He took Xantippe, had intercourse with her and sired Lamprocles. And he was legally married to Myrto, to whom Sophroniscus and Menexenus were born.

65. These women did not stop from being in contention with each other. And whenever they stopped they turned on Socrates, because he never intervened in the course of their disputes, but merely laughed when he saw them fighting with one another and with him. And they say that he was sometimes contentious in social gatherings and abusive and arrogant.

66. This is what Porphyry further says of Socrates:[77]

It is told about him that while still an infant he was a bad boy and a disorderly one. First, they say that he constantly refused to obey his father and, when he ordered him to take the tools of his trade and go wherever he wished, he ignored his order and went around wherever he wished.

67. And when he was about seventeen years of age it was alleged that Archelaos,[78] the student of Anaxagoras, was his lover and that Socrates did not reject his approaches and attentions but was his constant companion for several years. And thus prepared by Archelaos, he turned to philosophy.

68. And then a little further on we read:[79]

Among other reproaches heaped on Socrates was the charge that he intruded himself into the crowd and passed his time at the gaming tables and the herms.

That is what Porphyry says of Socrates, with further details which I have deliberately omitted. From what I have quoted it is possible to discern that these men paid lip service to virtue, but in practice they abandoned themselves to pleasure and were resigned to be the slaves of their passions.

69. Now if, according to Porphyry, he was strongly attracted to sensual pleasures and was not satisfied even with two women at the same time but also shamelessly had recourse to prostitutes, and if, according to Plato, he enjoyed the sight of naked boys in the gymnasia, and if he was quick to anger and had difficulty in controlling his temper, and if his tongue was abusive and unrestrained, what kind of philosophy could he pursue?

PLATO'S WEAKNESSES

70. Some of the ancients accuse Plato of having done many things that were unworthy of philosophy. Listen to what Xenophon has to say in his *Letter to Aeschines*:[80]

They dearly loved Egypt and the monstrous wisdom of Pythagoras. Their luxury and lack of loyalty to Socrates were proved by their love of tyranny and the preference of their appetites for a Sicilian table to a regime of austerity.

71. In these words he makes an oblique reference to his stay in Sicily with the tyrant Dionysius.[81] In fact, when he left Athens, he stayed with Dionysius, enjoying the luxury of Syracuse, and after the tyrant's death, remained on with his son. He so benefited this tyrant with his advice that he was kept in confinement in the stone quarries, and later Dionysius sold him as a barbarian slave. And Plutarch informs us[82] that he imported oil into Egypt as a commercial venture.

72. Notwithstanding our awareness of these reproaches we greatly admire what has been well said by him and we insist that you derive benefit from such good utterances.

SOME PAGANS ARE MORALLY ADMIRABLE

73. Furthermore we hear that there were many admirable women among the Greeks. Lysidice, so they say,[83] took her bath without removing her shift because of her intense modesty. And as for Philotera [84] she got into her bath, uncovering her body bit by bit as the water covered it. And in getting out of the bath she followed a similar procedure. Theano, the female Pythagorean, when someone looked at her with the admiring remark: "What a splendid arm," replied,[85] "yes, but it is not public property." And on another occasion,[86] when asked after what interval can a woman go to the Thesmophoria after having intercourse with a man, replied, "immediately if it was with her own husband, but never if it was with somebody else's."

MARRIAGE AND CHASTITY

74. We praise these and similar sentiments and declare that they are worthy of philosophy. And we approve Plato when he includes marriage in the list of human blessings and hails it as an intimation of immortality and a guarantee of the survival of the race.[87] On the other hand, we strongly censure Democritus and Epicurus,[88] who take pleasure in avoiding marriage and procreation. Since they define pleasure as the supreme good, they completely exclude anything involving cares.

75. The philosophers of the Stoa[89] adopted a middle way, since they listed marriage and procreation in their catalog of indifferents. But the sacred Scriptures celebrate chastity, which philosophy pro-

poses as leading to a life of freedom from care. But they present the laws of marriage as the means to increase the human race and to free from debauchery those who wish to live chastely. They repudiate fornication and other sexual misbehavior as behavior fitting for pigs.

76. The divine apostle says: *Let marriage be held in honour by all, and let the marriage bed be kept undefiled; for God will judge fornicators and adulterers.*[90] And elsewhere: *for God will judge fornicators and adulterers.*[91] And again: *To the unmarried and the widows I say that it is well for them to remain unmarried as I am. But if they are not practising self-control, they should marry. For it is better to marry than to be aflame with passion.*[92] And elsewhere: *But fornication and impurity of any kind, or greed, must not even be mentioned among you, as is proper among saints.*[93] And in another place: *See to it that no one becomes like Esau, an immoral and godless person, who sold his birthright for a single meal.*[94]

77. And so our teachers have set forth a way of life adapted to rational beings, while the most outstanding of the pagan philosophers have themselves been enslaved to pleasure and have drafted laws to inculcate debauchery. Such are the laws of Plato concerning marriage and pederasty.[95] What is more, this is what Hippodamus, the Pythagorean, wrote about friendships:[96]

Some are born from the knowledge of the gods, others from the generosity of humans, and still others from animal pleasure.

78. Christ the Lord says in the holy Gospels: *No one has greater love than this, to lay down one's life for one's friends.*[97] And when He taught us the extremes of perfection, He ordained us to love even our enemies. But the one who has taught us the τετρακτύς of the Pythagoreans[98] has laid down generosity as a condition for human friendship.

79. But not only is this idea unjust but it is altogether inconsistent. For we find many who have become benefactors of their enemies and, on the other hand, many who have had good done them and who have become very ungrateful in return to their benefactors. Friendship, then, is not the offspring of generosity, but generosity is the fruit of friendship.

80. Having examined and recognized, my friends, the distance that separates divine and human matters, and using these like so many milestones, proceed on the road to perfection and, as the can-

ticle of the spirit says: *Do not turn my heart to any evil, to busy myself with wicked deeds.*[99]

81. For whenever we demonstrate the great superiority of the evangelical laws to Greek philosophy you approve those laws, but you freely bring forward those who transgress them and use that as an occasion to criticize the laws.

82. Those types had to be condemned but that does not entail condemning the laws. Bad grapes do not call for giving up good ones. Bitter almonds do not turn us against sweet ones. We do not criticize true gold because of gold that has an admixture of copper. Nor do we scoff at genuine clothes of purple because of those that are only imitation. Nor do we bring accusations against skilled painters because of those who are untrained. Neither do we hate upright men because of the immoral ones, nor, if we come across an incompetent physician, do we renounce the whole medical profession? But among painters and physicians, just as among shoemakers, coppersmiths, and goldsmiths, we marvel at those who are outstanding and dismiss those who are incompetent. But we do not blame the professions, even if we do not find a single skilled practitioner.

83. This would indeed be the height of absurdity because the blind criticize the sense of sight as useless, and those who have a speech impediment criticize the origins of speech as if they were unnecessary; and because the deaf declare the sense of hearing superfluous.

84. Thus, then, it is truly useless and wrong for the sake of those who transgress the laws to blame the laws themselves, and those who are eager to observe the laws. If a carpenter, in drawing a straight line, does not follow the rule but in using the adze in the wrong way destroys ink markings, either taking away from the inside further than the line, or leaving behind too much on the outside, should we on that account blame the carpenter's rule, which showed what was right. For what is blameworthy is the ignorance of the carpenter.

85. The laws take the place, so to speak, of a ruler[100] and among those who use them some direct their private lives better as a result, but others, preferring what is easier to what is better, walk outside the straight line which they have chalked up for themselves. That is why such people should be condemned but the laws should be praised.

86. In fact, if a very good physician prescribes for someone who is ill taking certain things and abstaining completely from others, but then the patient, giving little heed to the physician's prescriptions,

prefers his own pleasure to the treatment and eats and drinks what is forbidden, thus worsening his disease, we do not blame the physician for giving him bad advice.[101] For we know well that the disease has worsened as a result of the patient's immoderate behavior, not from the attention of the consultant.

DEGREES OF VOLUNTARY ACTS

87. Reflecting on these and similar facts let us chant the praise of the Author of those salutary laws and admire their utility and benefit for our lives. Then, like spectators at a great contest, let us applaud those who observe the laws, but let us not hold the same judgment against those who violate them, for all do not transgress with the same intention.

88. We ourselves, human as we are, commit inadvertently many sins which the laws themselves call involuntary.[102] For instance, one might intend to throw a stone at a dog or some other creature but might miss the target and kill a human being instead. Herodotus has accounts of similar happenings.[103]

89. It sometimes happens that one is chopping wood with a hatchet and hits a passerby with the blade unintentionally. Acts of this kind are condoned by the laws in that they are involuntary. There is no lack of variety in voluntary acts either. For instance, it is not the same thing to strike one's neighbor in a moment of anger and spurred on by temper and as a result cause his death, but without premeditation, or striking with that in mind, and, on the other hand, plan the death with calculation, and lying in wait and malice aforethought. The first act is a result of irrational anger, the second, a deed of sheer malice. In the first instance there is not full consent, but in the second there is.

90. Likewise, in sins of sensuality men do not always fall in the same way. Some, without being the least preoccupied, move around among attractive bodies and then one day they suddenly set eyes on somebody and succumb to passion, and reason loses its control. On the other hand, others think that life consists in feasting one's eyes on such spectacles.

91. There were others who do not gladly enjoy the pleasures of food or drink, but are defeated in combat because they are not will-

ing to resist as they should. Others overindulged and enjoyed luxuries and gave themselves to pleasure who imagined all sorts of pleasurable experiences and who aroused their desires by every species of discovery and who, at the end, were reduced to desolation when their desires were quenched.

92. That is why, the difference between sinners being so great, the same severity should not be displayed toward all; we should feel disgust at those who openly embrace the life of pigs, but to others we should offer good counsel, encouraging them, lavishing care upon them, and applying remedies for their return to health. As for those who live like pigs, if they continue in their swinish existence, let us lament for them as long as they live, but produce for them the epitaph of Sardanapalos upon their demise.

93. This was the epitaph on his tomb:[104]

> I am the sum of everything I have eaten, all my excesses,
> the pleasures of love which I have enjoyed. But I leave
> much behind me and all the good things, I, the king of
> great Nineveh, am but dust.

94. But those who composed the inscription have falsified the facts. For he did not consist of all he had eaten and drunk, since these had turned into foul-smelling waste. All he had was the evil stench of a sinful life, which continually tormented and grieved his soul, conscious as it was of the greatest immoralities and mindful of all its acts of transgressions.

95. That, my friends, is why I have composed this twelfth discourse. I have given an exposition on God, matter, creation, also on virtue and vice, the opinions of the Greeks, and the teachings which the sacred Scriptures have given us. I have also shown that their theories have been annihilated and fallen into the obscurity of forgetfulness, whereas our teachings have flourished and perdured.

96. That is exactly what Porphyry said in the writing which he directed against us:[105]

> One is astonished today at the fact that for so many years
> the city had been the prey of disease when Asclepius and
> the other gods were sojourning there, but now that Jesus is

held in honor it does not experience the least public benefit from any of the gods.

97. That is what Porphyry, our worst enemy, has to say. And he recognized clearly that once the true faith appeared, after the cross and the saving passion, neither Asclepius[106] nor any other of the so-called gods could further play the cheat on human beings, because the Light has risen and banished the lot of them like bats to darkness. It is my hope that you get a share of those rays. It was for this reason that I undertook this work and that I have prepared this cure for you from herbs which I have collected from far and wide.

NOTES

NOTES TO THE INTRODUCTION

1. J. Quasten, *Patrology* (Westminster Md., 1950–53), 3:543. M. F. A. Brok, "De waarde van de Graecarum affectionum curatio van Theodoretus van Cyrus als apologetisch werk," *StC* 27 (1952): 201–12, rightly contests G. Bardy's negative appraisal of the Curatio in *DTC* 15 (1946). See A. Dulles, *The History of Apologetics* (San Francisco, 2007), 71f.

2. In addition to the bibliographical items noted in ACW 49:160–65, see "Theodoret," in *Encylopedia of Early Christianity* (New York, 1987), 889–91; G. May, "Das Lehrverfahren gegen Euthyches im November des Jahres 448: Zur Vorgeschichte des Konzils von Chalkedon," *Annuarium Historiae Conciliorum* 21 (1989): 1–61; W. De Vries, "Das Konzil von Ephesus 449, eine 'Raubersynode'?" *OCP* 41 (1975): 357–98; Th. Sagi-Bunic, "'Deus perfectus et homo perfectus': A Concilio Ephesino (a. 431) ad Chalcedonense (a. 451)" (Rome, 1965), 167–204; M. Parmentier, "Non-medical Ways of Healing in Eastern Christendom: The Case of St. Dometios," *Fructus centesimus, FS. G. J. M. Bartelink* (Steenbrugis, 1989), 279–96, M. Parmentier, "A Letter from Theodoret of Cyrus to the Exiled Nestorius (CPG 6270) in a Syriac Version," *Bijdragen* 51 (1990): 234–45; P. B. Clayton, Jr., *Theodoret, Bishop of Cyrus, and the Mystery of the Incarnation in the Late Antiochene Christianity*, diss., Union Theological Seminary, New York, 1985; now published, Oxford, 2007; P. Gray, "Theodoret on the 'One Hypostasis': An Antiochene Reading of Chalcedon," *SP* 15 (1984): 301–4; A. de Halleux, "Le décret chalcedonien sur les prérogatives de la Nouvelle Rome," *EThL* 64 (1988): 288–323; J. N. Guinot, "Présence d'Apollinaire dans l'oeuvre exégetique de Théodoret," *SP* 19 (1989): 166–72; C. T. McCollough, "Theodoret of Cyrus as Biblical Interpreter and the Presence of Judaism in the Later Roman Empire," *SP* 18,1 (1985): 327–34, I. G. Tomkins, *The Relations between Theodoret of Cyrrhus and His City and Its Territory, with Particular Reference to the Letters and Historia religiosa*, diss., Oxford, 1993).

3. Quasten, *Patrology*, 3.544.

4. Quasten, *Patrology*, 3.538.

5. See D. S. Wallace-Hadrill, *Christian Antioch: A Study of Early Christian Thought in the East* (Cambridge, New York, 1982), 100–104.

6. See P. Pilhofer, *Presbyter Kreitton: Der Alterbeweis der Judischen und christlichen Apologeten und seine Vorgeschichte* (Tübingen, 1990); A. J. Droge, *Homer or Moses? Early Christian Interpretations of the History of Culture* (Tübingen, 1989).

7. J. Sirinelli, *Les vues historiques d'Eusèbe de Césarée durant la periode prenicéenne* (Dakar, 1961).

8. On the significance of Porphyry see P. Hadot, "Citations de Porphyre chez Augustin," *REAug* 6 (1960): 155f.; E. Te Selle, "Porphyry and Augustine" AugStud 5 (1974): 113–48; C. Evangeliou, "Porphyry's Criticism of Christianity and the Problem of Augustine's Platonism," *Dionysius* 13 (1989): 51–70; P. Pirioni, "Il soggiorno siciliano di Porfirio e la composizione del ΚΑΤΑ ΧΡΙΣΤΙΑΝΩΝ," *Rivista di storia della Chiesa in Italia* (Milan) 39 (1985): 502–8; F. Corsaro, "La reazione pagana nel IV secolo e l'Apocritico di Macario di Magnesia," *Quaderni catanesi di studi classici e medievali* 6 (1984): 173–95; R. Goulet, "Porphyre et Macaire de Magnesie," *SP* 15 (1984): 448–52. T. D. Barnes, "Porphyry, Against the Christians: Date and Attribution of Fragments," JThS 24 (1973): 424–42; Niketas Siniossoglou, *Plato and Theodoret: The Christian Appropriation of Platonic Philosophy and the Hellenic Intellectual Resistance*, Cambridge Classical Studies (Cambridge, 2008), 28, 77–78, 86, 101, 132.

9. See Quasten, *Patrology*, 3.538; also N. Festa, "Lo stilo di Teodoreto nella Terapia," *RAL* 6 ser. 4 (1928): 584–88.

10. P. Canivet, "Précisions sur la date de la Curatio de Théodoret de Cyr," *RechScR* 36 (1949:) 585–93. I. Pasztori-Kupan, *Theodoret of Cyrus* (London and New York, 2006), 86. N. Siniossoglou, *Plato and Theodoret*, 34–35; Clayton, *Theodoret, Bishop of Cyrus and the Mystery of the Incarnation in the Late Antiochene Christianity*, 76–87; A. Leroy Molinghen, "Naissance et enfance de Théodoret," in *L'enfant dans les civilisations orientales*, ed. A. Theodorides; P. Naster, and J. Ries (1984), 153–58.

11. On Epistle 113 see ACW 49.2 and 162, notes 15–17. Also G. F. Chesnut, "The Date of Composition of Theodoret's *Church History*," *VigChr* 35 (1981): 245–52.

12. M. Richard, "L'activité littéraire de Théodoret avant le Concile d'Ephèse," *RSPh* 24 (1935): 82–106.

13. On Basil cf. E. A. De Mendieta, "The Official Attitude of Basil of Caesarea as a Christian Bishop towards Greek Philosophy and Science" in *The Orthodox Churches and the West*, ed. D. Baker, SCH 13 (Oxford, 1976), 337–68.

14. On Newman cf. ACW 49.2.

15. See "Apologetik," *RAC* 1 (1950): 533–43. G. Bardy, "Apologetik. 1. Alte Kirche," *TRE* 3.371–411; L. W. Barnard, "Apologisti-Apologetica (caraterri generali)," *DPAC* 1.288–90; R. M. Grant, *Greek Apologists of the Second Century*

(Philadelphia, 1988), and "Forms and Occasions of the Greek Apologists,"
SMSR 52 (1986): 213–26, and "Early Christianity and Pre-Socratic Philosophy"
in *Harry Austryn Wolfson Jubilee* (Jerusalem, 1965), 357–84. B. Amata,
"L'apologia cristiana di Arnobio diSicca come ricerca della verità assoluta,"
Salesianum 51 (1989): 47–70; W. Kinzig, "Der 'Sitz im Leben' der Apologie in
der alten Kirche," *ZKG* 100 (1989): 291–317; L. Padovese, "Lo 'scandalum
incarnationis et crucis' nell'apologetica cristiana del secolo secondo e terzo,"
Laurentianum 27 (1986): 312–34; N. Z. van der Vorst, *Les citations des poètes grecs
chez les apologistes chrétiens du IIe siècle* (Louvain, 1972); A. J. Droge, "Justin Martyr
and the Restoration of Philosophy," ChH 56 (1987): 303–19; M. Rizzi, " 'Justitia'
e 'veritas': l''exordium' degli scritti apologetici di Giustino, Atenagora,
Tertulliano," Aevum 65 (1991): 125–49; L. W. Barnard "L'intolleranza negli
apologisti cristiani con special e riguardo a Firmico Materno," *CS* 11 (1990):
505–21, J.-M. Demarolle, "Un aspect de la polémique paienne a la fin du IIIe
siècle," *VigChr* 26 (1972): 117–29; U. Kuehneweg, "Die griechische Apologeten
und die Ethik," *VChr* 42 (1988): 112–20; C. Burini, *Gli apologeti greci, traduzione,
introduzione e note,* Collana di testi patristici 59 (Rome, 1986); P. Carrara, *I pagani
di fronte al cristianesimo: Testimonianze dei secoli I e II,* Biblioteca Patristica
(Florence, 1984).

16. *Saint John Chrysostom Apologist,*. trans. M. A. Schatkin and P. W.
Harkins, FOTC 73 (Washington, DC, 1983).

17. Quasten, *Patrology,* 3.543.

18. For illustrations see *Umanesimo e Padri della Chiesa,* Bibliotheca
Medicea Laurenziana (Rome, 1997), 390; also E. Garin, "La biblioteca di San
Marco," in *La chiesa e il convento di San Marco a Firenze* (Florence, 1989),
79–148.

Notes to the Preface

1. The word πίστις means both faith and persuasion. Rhetoric, the art
of persuasion, played a larger role than is generally realized as origin, source,
or analogue of early Christian faith; cf. J. L. Kinneavy, *Greek Rhetorical Origins of
Christian Faith: An Inquiry* (New York, 1987); *Plato and Theodoret: The Christian
Appropriation of Platonic Philosophy and the Hellenic Intellectual Resistance,* translation and commentary, Cambridge Classical Studies (Cambridge, 2008), 1–30.
On the changing role of reason in faith in the apologetic tradition see J.-H.
Walgrave, "Le grand malentendu apologetique," *Revue Catholique International
Communio* 3 (1978): 7–16. See also C. Gilmour, "Diognetus' Faith," *Prudentia*
19, 2 (1987): 34–43, which argues that the term πίστις as "the faith," i.e., an
identifiable body of Christian doctrine, places the *Letter to Diognetus* closer in
spirit to the apologists than to the Apostolic Fathers.

2. The "barbarian" aspect of the Scriptures, their lack of refined diction, is a subject that Theodoret returns to frequently. It is a charge that goes back to Celsus; cf. Origen, *C. Cels.* 1.62, 3.39, and passim. The rejection of the claims of the martyrs is returned to in Theodoret, *Affect.* 8.11.

3. See Discourse 1.30–32.

4. Cf. Clement, *Protr.* 2.24, who names, besides these three, Nicanor of Cyprus and Hippo of Melos. Diagoras of Melos is routinely depicted as a radical atheist instead of a mere skeptic about traditional religion; cf. M. Winiarczyk, "Diagoras von Melos: Wahrheit und Legende," *Eos* 67 (1979:): 191–213; 68 (1980): 51–75. When the Eleusinian Telesterion was being built, the secret of Eleusis was flagrantly violated by Diagoras.

5. Clement, *Protr.* 5.66, says: "Epicurus alone I shall gladly forget, who carries impiety to its full length and thinks that God takes no charge of the world," trans. *ANF* 2.191.

6. Cf. Clement, *Str.* 5.13.90: "And it occurred to Aristotle to extend Providence to the moon from this psalm [36 (35).6]: 'Lord, thy mercy is in the heavens, and thy truth reacheth to the clouds,'" trans. ANF 2.465. See *Affect.* 6. 7, and n. 10.

7. For Plato cf. *Affect.* 6.26–48; and for Plotinus cf. *Affect.* 6.59–73.

8. The fishermen (cf. Matt. 4:18) are Peter and Andrew; the tentmaker is Paul (cf. Acts 18.3), and the tax collector, Matthew (cf. Matt. 9.:9). This is a recurring triad in Theodoret; cf. *Affect.* 6.61; 8.4; 9.20; *Haer.* 1.1. Also in Chrysostom; cf. *Dem. contra pag.* 5.3.

Notes to Discourse 1

1. Clement sounds a similar keynote in the *Paidagogus* 1.1.3: "Just as our body needs a physician when it is sick, so too when we are weak our soul needs the Educator to cure its ills."

2. [= Clement, *Str.* 1.27.171; FOTC 85, pp. 148–49]. See also Clement, *Protr.* 10.109; also Salvian, *Gub. Dei*, 6.16.

3. Cf. Chrysostom, *Pan. Bab.* 55 : "When their brain becomes inflamed and they kick and bite those who wish to deliver them from their infirmity, then their disease becomes incurable," trans. FOTC 73.107. Athenaeus, *Deip.* 1.24de, describes head fomentations.

4. See n. 3; Chrysostom, *Pan. Bab.* seems here, as at many other points, to be a source for Theodoret.

5. Under the Greek word διυλιστήρ, "sieve," the *PGL* notes the present instance, as well as Epiphanius, *De mensuris* 24. Theodoret's source, however, is probably Clement, *Paed* 1.6.32, for the translation of which "filtration" (ANF 2.217) is preferable to "dematerialization" (FOTC 23.31). See also Clement,

Eclog. prophet. 7, and *Str.* 2.20.116. On filtering cf. W. R. Schoedel, *Ignatius of Antioch* (Philadelphia, 1985), 166–67.

6. Clement, *Str.* 1.9.43, similarly combines agricultural and medical terminology: "We must lop, dig, bind and perform the other operations. The pruning knife and the pick ax and the other agricultural instruments are necessary for the culture of the vine....And, as in husbandry, so also in medicine." See also Philo, *Quod deter.* 29, and Chrysostom, *Hom. in Gen 2.2:* "Let us imitate the farmers: when they see the land scarified and cleared of the obstruction of weeds, they sow the seed liberally," trans. FOTC 74.29.

7. Cf. Clement, *Str.* 7.16.93: "But the chief thing is to get rid of self-conceit, taking a position midway between exact science and rash opinionativeness." For the treatment of the ailment cf. *Str.* 7.16.98. At *Str.* 7.16.99 Clement tells us that of the three mental conditions—ignorance, conceit, knowledge—ignorance is the characteristic of the heathen, knowledge of the true Church, and conceit of the heretics. See also *Str.* 2.11: "As, then, philosophy has been brought into evil repute by pride and self-conceit, so also gnosis by false gnosis called by the same name."

8. Clement, *Str.* 1.21.142, identifies Attic as one of the five Greek dialects, with Ionic, Doric, Aeolic, and Koine.

9. Cf. *Affect.* 1, n. 45. Pherecydes is frequently cited in Eusebius, *P.e.* cf. SC 206.321f. He was Pythagoras's teacher. See H. S. Schibli, *Pherekydes of Syros* (New York, 1990).

10. For Pythagoras's travels cf. Iamblichus, *Life of Pythagoras,* cc. 2–4, translated in K. S. Guthrie, *The Pythagorean Sourcebook and Library* (Grand Rapids, MI, 1987), 58–63. See also Clement, *Str.* 1.15.66, FOTC 85, p. 72.

11. On Thales cf. Herodotus, 1.170; Aetius, *Plac.* 1.3.1; and K.R.S., 79. Diogenes Laertius 1.24 quotes Pamphila saying that he learned geometry from the Egyptians; cf. Clement, *Str.* 1.15.66.

12. Diogenes Laertius 1.50 has Solon visiting Egypt, Cyprus, and the court of Croesus. See also Herodotus, 1.29–32.

13. Cf. Clement, *Str.* 1.15.66: "Plato does not deny importing from abroad the best parts into his philososphy, and admits a visit to Egypt." See also Apuleius, *De Platone,* 1.3.

14. Cf. Clement, *Str.* 1.21.134: "Among the Egyptians also we find former human beings deified by human delusion: Hermes of Thebes, Asclepius of Memphis, and again in Thebes, Teeiresias and Manto, as Euripides says," FOTC 85, 122.

15. See *Affect.* 1.24 and 1.69.

16. Cf. Origen, *C.Cels.* 1.15.

17. Plutarch, *Sol.* 2, *De Is. et Osir,* 10.

18. On Porphyry, see R. Wilken, *The Christians as the Romans Saw Them* (New Haven, 1984), 126–63. See also R. M. Grant, "Porphyry among the Early

Christians," in *Romanitas et Christianitas: Studia Iano Henrico Waszink* (Amsterdam, 1973), 82.

19. Numenius, fr. 7, [=Clement, *Str.* 1.22.150], on which see Armstrong, ed., CHLG 96–06; de Vogel, *GP* 3.421–33. Numenius was a second-century Pythagorean who had a preference for the books of Moses. Of his work *On the Good* important fragments are preserved in Eusebius *P.e.* books 11, 14, and 15.

20. [=Clement, *Str.* 1.15, 66.] Clement says that Pythagoras, like Thales, consorted with the prophets of the Egyptians, by whom he was circumcised, that he might enter the adytum and learn from the Egyptians the mystic philosophy. See also Iamblichus, *Vita Pythag.* 2: "The purpose of his Egyptian visit, at the prompting of Thales, was to get in touch with the priests of Memphis and Zeus." *Vita Pythag.* 4 adds: "He thus passed twenty-two years in the sanctuaries of temples studying astronomy and geometry, and being initiated in no casual or superficial manner to all the mysteries of the gods."

21. Cf. Gen. 17:12; Exod. 12:48.

22. Cf. Gen. 17:10f. and Exod. 2:5–6. Theodoret expands on this in his *Quaest 3 in Exod.* Here Theodoret is summarizing Clement, *Str.* 1.23.151–55, who in turn is utilizing Philo, *Vita Moysis,* 1.16–17.

23. Diotima is "the Mantinean woman" in Plato, *Symp.* 201–212b.

24. Plato, *Menex.* 235de.=Clement, *Str.* 4.19 (a chapter devoted to the topic that women as well as men are capable of perfection). Theodoret mentions Aspasia here and draws on Clement later for his anecdotes about Lysidica, Philotera, and Theano, in *Affect.* 12.73.

25. On Homer's *Iliad* as school text cf. H.-I. Marrou, *A History of Education in Antiquity* (New York, 1956), 9–13, 359–61. We can deduce from this reference to Homer and the one to Hesiod at 2.95 that Theodoret pursued the normal Greek education; cf. Canivet, *Entre,* 35f.

26. Cf. Clement, *Str.* 1. 23, 153, Philo, *Mig.* 178, Canivet, *Entre,* 299–300. Tatian, *Orat.* 1.1–2, opens with a long catalog of such Greek practices with foreign origins.

27. Cf. Clement, *Str.* 1.16, 74: "The Phrygians were the first who attended to the flight of birds. And the Tuscans, neighbors of Italy, were adept at the art of the haruspex." On the Phrygians, cf. Gregory Nazianzus, *Orat.* 4.209.

28. Clement, *Str.* 1.16.74: "The Etruscans invented the trumpet and the Phrygians the flute."

29. [=Clement, *Str.* 1.16, 75]. Cf. Athanasius, Gent. 18, for a similar listing. On the alphabet see L. H. Jeffery, *The Local Scripts of Archaic Greece,* 2d ed. (Oxford, 1961), 1–41.

30. [=Clement, *Str.* 1.16, 75].

31. Cf. Clement, *Str.* 1.16, 75: "Atlas, the Libyan, was the first who built a ship and navigated the sea."

32. For Plutarch, see note 17 *supra.* Diodorus (a historian from Sicily),

1.96, 4–5 [= Eusebius *P.e.* 10.8.4]. Clement, *Str.* 1.15, 66 says that Orpheus was from Odrysae or Thrace. On the trip to Egypt see M. L. West, *The Orphic Poems* (Oxford, 1983), 26 and n. 68. For the connection with Dionysus see I. M. Linforth, *The Arts of Orpheus* (Berkeley, 1941), 206f.

33. See Demosthenes, *Against Aristogeiton*, 11.

34. [=Eusebius, *P.e.* 10.8.4]. Cf. Clement, *Paed* 3.4.28; Tatian, *Orat.* 8: "Rhea, also called Demeter," Athenagoras, *Leg.* 20.1, trans. Schoedel, who notes 41 n.1: Rhea, according to the Orphics, became known as Demeter after she had given birth to Zeus. On Rhea/Cybele see Burkert, *S & H,* 102–5.

35. Clement, *Protr.* 2.14, says: "Then there are the mysteries of Demeter and Zeus's wanton embraces of his mother and the wrath of Demeter."

36. Cf. Clement, *Protr.* 2 : "That Phrygian Midas who having learned the cunning imposture from Orpheus."

37. On Pythagoras's supposed association with Pherecydes cf. K.R.S., 52–53, Pasztori-Kupan, *Theodoret of Cyrus* (London and New York, 2006), 92 and esp. 238, n.16. Tatian, *Orat.* 3, also links them. Clement, *Str.* 6.7.57: "But if I come to Pythagoras and Pherecydes and Thales and the first wise men, I come to a standstill in my search for their teachers."

38. [= Clement, *Str.* 1.14.62] Aristoxenus, fr. 14, Diogenes Laertius 1.118 (DK 14.8), K.R.S., 222. See F. Amory, "Socrates the Legend," *Classica et Mediaevalia* 35 (1984): 19–65.

39. Leander, fr. 2, [=Clement, *Str.* 1.14.62, FOTC 85, 68–69].

40. Herodotus, 1.170.

41. Stagyra, on the coast of Chalcidice, Macedonia.

42. On Diogenes of Sinope in Asia Minor (cf. also 1.50, 3.53, 6.20, 48, 49) see H. D. Rankin, *Sophists, Socratics and Cynics* (Totowa, NJ, 1983), 229–34. Sinope was in Asia Minor. Diogenes was a Cynic philosopher; cf. Diogenes Laertius, 6.20–21.

43. [= Clement. *Str.* 1.16.78.] Alcmaeon of Croton (c. 500), a pupil of Pythagoras, was a physician and scientist. Empedocles (494–434 B.C.) from Agrigento in Sicily was a poet, philosopher, and statesman, a follower of Pythagoras and Parmenides.

44. Zamolxis (or Zalmoxis), a runaway slave who came to Thrace from Samos, was regarded by the Thracian Getae as the only true God. For them death was "going to Zamolxis" and conferred immortality of the soul. See Herodotus 4.76–77 and Lucian, *Zeus Rants,* 42. Iamblichus, *Vita Pythag.*, trans. Guthrie, *HGP,* I.100, says he was a slave of Pythagoras. See also Clement, *Str.* 4.8; Origen, *C. Cels* 2.55, 3.34, 3.54, Lucian, *Dial. D.* 9; Chrysostom, *Pan. Bab.* 10. Cf. Clement, *Protr.* 2: "Others say that Melampus, the son of Amythaon, imported the festivals of Ceres from Egypt into Greece."

45. According to Herodotus 4.76–77, Anacharsis was a Scythian who traveled widely in Greece and brought back Greek customs. Lucian, *Scyth.* 1: "Anacharsis was not the first to come from Scythia to Athens out of a longing

for Greek culture." See A. MacC. Armstrong, "Anacharsis the Scythian," *G &*
R 17 (1948): 18–23; J. F. Kindstrand, *Anacharsis: The Legend and the*
Apophthegmata (Stockholm, 1981).

46. Origen, *C. Cels.* 1.24, speaks of "the Brahmans or Samanaeans
among the Indian philosophers." Cf. Clement, *Str.* 1.15.70–72; A. Dihle,
"Indische Philosophen bei Clemens Alexandrinus," in *Antike und Orient*
(Heidelberg, 1984), 78–88. See also Tertullian, *Apol.* 42, *Adv. Marc.* 1.13;
Augustine, *Civ. Dei* 4.16.

47. Porphyry, *Hist. phil. fr.* 11.

48. Porphyry, *Hist. phil. fr.* 11.

49. Plato, *Apol.* 17bc.

50. Ibid. 18a.

51. Plato, *Statesman* 261e.

52. [= Clement, *Str.* 1.19.93] Cf. Plato, *Resp.* 5.475de.

53. Clement, *Str.* 1.19.93. The Platonic definition of philosophy is taken
over by Clement.

54. [=Eusebius, *P.e.* 12.8.2]. Plato, *Leg.* 3.689cd.

55. For the proverb "neither read nor swim" see E. B. England, *The Laws*
of Plato 1 (New York, 1921), 378–79, who notes variants in Theodoret's read-
ings, due to "perhaps quoting from memory."

56. [=Eusebius, *P.e.* 12.29.9]. Plato, *Theaet.* 174de. Theodoret's citation
is faulty; cf. SC 57.114 n. 2.

57. Cf. Tatian, *Orat.* 26, jibing at astronomers in general: "Gaping at the
sky, you tumble into pits."

58. [=Eusebius, *P.e.* 12.29.9]. Plato, *Theaet* 174de.

59. [=Eusebius, *P.e.* 12.29.17]; ibid., 176c.

60. Theophilus, *Ad Autol.*, 1.1 sounds a similar note: "Fluent speech and
euphonious diction produce delight and praise resulting in empty glory. The
man who loves truth, however, pays no attention to defiled language but exam-
ines the facts behind the word to see what it is and what it means," OECT,
trans. R. M. Grant (Oxford, 1970). For similar sentiments cf. Clement, *Protr.*
8.99, Arnobius, *Adv. nat.* 1.58–59 (=ACW 7.104–7); Minucius Felix, *Oct.*
(=ACW 39.16–23); Paulinus of Nola, *Carm.* 20.28f (= ACW 40.158).

61. On the seniority of the Hebrews, see Clement, *Str.* 1.21, 101, P.
Pilhofer, *Presbuteron kreitton: Der Alterbeweis der judischen und christlichen*
Apologeten und seine Vorgeschichte (Tübingen, 1990).

62. On the "barbarous" style see n. 2 *supra*, also Acts 4:13.

63. Porphyry, *De philos. ex orac.* 147=Eusebius, *P.e.* 9.10. See also ps.-
Justin, *Coh. Gr.* 24; R. L. Wilken, "Pagan Criticism of Christianity: Greek
Religion and Christian Faith," in *Early Christianity and the Classical Tradition in*
Honorem R. M. Grant (Paris, 1979), 117 f.

64. Dan. 2–3:7.

65. See Herodotus 1.46.

66. On the annexation of Lydia see Herodotus, *CAH* 3.222, 520–26.
67. *To Boetos, On the Soul* [=Eusebius, *P.e.* 14.10.3; SC 338.102–4].
68. *To Anebo* [=Eusebius, *P.e.* 14.10.1; SC 338.102].
69. [= Clement, *Str.* 1.14.62; FOTC 85. p. 68 and n. 293].
70. He means Aristotle; cf. *Affect.* 1.24 and n. 49.
71. Diogenes; cf. *Affect.* 1.24.
72. On Solon cf. *Affect.* 1.12.
73. [= Clement, *Str.* 1.15.69= Eusebius, *P.e.* 10.4.19–20], Plato, *Tim.* 22b; also quoted ps.-Justin, *Coh. Gr.* 12, Cyril, *Juln,* Hippolytus, *Ref.* 6.22.
74. On the proverb cf. Raeder, *RhMus* 57 (1902): 449–59. Cf. Clement, *Str.* 1.14.62; Theodoret, *H.e.* 3,4; N. Demand, "Pythagoras, son of Mnesarchos," *Phronesis* 18 (1973): 91–96.
75. On the Pythagorean silence cf. *Stanford Encyclopedia of Philosophy* (Stanford, Calif., 2005–6), *Affect.* 1.127; Clement, *Str.* 1.14.62, 5.11.67; Hippolytus, *Ref.* 6.22; Porphyry, *Vita Pythag.* 19. Gregory Nazianzus, *Orat.* 27.10, in disqualifying some from the role of theologian, advises as an alternative: "Attack the silence of Pythagoras, and the Orphic beans, and the novel brag about 'the Master said.'"
76. See *The Pythagorean Sourcebook and Library* 58–59. On Pythagoras's sect, see K.R.S., 216–19.
77. Plato, *Tim.* 40de [=Eusebius, *P.e.* 2.7.1, 13.1.1; 14.5]. Cf. *Affect.* 3.34–35.
78. On Plato against Homer and Hesiod see *Rep.* 2.377b–378e.
79. This is dealt with more fully at *Affect.* 5.10f. Cf. Aetius, *Plac.* 392–93, 329–32.
80. Plato, *Gorgias,* 524ab [=Eusebius, *P.e.* 12.6.1–4].
81. [=Eusebius, *P.e.* 12.1.2]. Plato, *Leg.* 1.634d.
82. Theognis, lines 77–78 [= Eusebius, *P.e.* 12.2.2].
83. [=Clement, *Str.* 5.14.115, Eusebius, *P.e.* 13.42].
84. [=Clement, *Str.* 5.3.18]. Empedocles, fr. 5.1–2. See M. R. Wright, *Empedocles: The Extant Fragments* (New Haven, 1981), 95.
85. [=Clement, *Str.* 1.14.64]. Parmenides, fr. 4.1. See K.R.S., 239–62.; D. Gallop, *Parmenides of Elea Fragments: A Text and Translation* (Toronto, 1984), 16; 36, n. 45; 56–57.
86. [=Clement, *Str.* 5.12.81]. Solon, fr. 16. M. L. West, *Iambi et Elegi Graeci* (Oxford, 1992), 2:151. This is an Orphic fragment (Kern 245).
87. [= Clement, *Str.* 5.12.81]. Empedocles, fr. 133; see Wright, *Empedocles: The Extant Fragments* (New Haven, 1981), 131, 252–53, On the Empedocles fragment [B 83] see J. Barnes, *Early Greek Philosophy* (Harmondsworth, 1987), p. 164: for the divine cannot be...grasped...by human hands, by which the surest path to persuasion leads to the human mind, as translated from Clement, *Str. Str.* In Abb pp. ix–x, V, 12, 81. See also Clement, *Str.* 3, 14, 2, and n. 50:

I wept and wailed when I saw the unfamiliar face
And again:
Oh! Oh! Unhappy race of mortals, unblest!
Out of what strife, what groans were you born.
88. [= Clement, *Str.* 5.14.108]. Antisthenes, fr. 24; cf. Clement, *Protr.* 6.71
[= Eusebius, *P.e.* 13.13.35].
89. [=Clement, *Str.* 5.14.108=Eusebius, *P.e.* 13.13.35]. Xenophon, *Mem.*
4.3.13; cf. Clement, *Protr.* 6.71.2.
90. [= Clement, *Str.* 5.11.68, on which cf. SC 279. 238–39]; trans., ANF
2.460; Bacchylides, fr. 5, ed., H. Maehler, *Bakchylides* (Berlin, 1968), 116.
91. For ἐποπτεία as initiation cf. C. Kerenyi, Eleusis, 45–47. Cf. Clement,
Str. 1.28.176 (GCS 2.108): "The Mosaic philosophy is divided into four parts—
the fourth, the department of theology, insight, which Plato predicates of the
truly great mysteries." See also Eusebius, *P.e.* 5.10.2.
92. [=Clement, *Str.* 5.6.33]; Plato, *Theaet.* 155e.
93. [=Clement, *Str.* 4.7.45]; Epicharmus, fr. 246.
94. [=Eusebius, *P.e.* 13.6.1]; Plato, *Crat.* 46b.
95. [=Clement, *Str.* 5.3.17]; Plato, *Alc.* 109c.
96. [=Clement, *Str.* 5.4.19]; Plato, *Phaedo* 67b.
97. [=Eusebius, *P.e.* 13.13.5]; Orpheus, fr. 245.1 Cf. N. Zeegers-
Van der Vorst, *Les citations des poètes grecs* (Louvain, 1972), 261.
98. Bacchae 472; [=Clement, *Str.* 4.25.162].
99. Phoenissae 471–72; [=Clement, *Str.* 1.8.40].
100. fr. 432 [=Clement, *Str.* 6.2.10]. Cf. Clement, *Str.* 5.3.16.
101. [=Clement, *Str.* 2.5.24]; Epicharmus, fr. 249.
102. [=Clement, *Str.* 2,4,17]; Heraclitus, fr. 18.
103. [=Clement, *Str.* 4.2.4]; Heraclitus, fr. 22.
104. Aristotle, *Top.* 5.3. Cf. Clement, *Str.* 1.8.39. See Canivet, *Entre* 43–44,
A. Quacquarelli, in *Complementi interdisciplinari di patrologia* (Rome, 1989),
117–18.
105. [=Clement, *Str.* 2.4.16–17]; Epicurus, fr. 255.
106. Cf. Irenaeus, *Adversus haereses* 1.20.1: "They [i.e., the Marcosians]
bring forward that false and wicked story which relates that our Lord, when he
was a boy learning his letters, on the teacher saying to him, as is usual,
'Pronounce Alpha,' replied, 'Alpha.' But when again, the teacher bade him
say, 'Beta,' the Lord replied, 'Do thou first tell me what Alpha is, and then I
will tell you that Beta is.' " See also Theophilus, *Ad Autol.* 1.8.
107. On differences in distances in astronomy cf. Aetius, *Plac.* 362–63.
108. Aetius, *Plac.* 351.
109. Aetius, *Plac.* 351.
110. Aetius, *Plac.* 351. Cf. C. H. Kahn, *The Art and Thought of Heraclitus*
(Cambridge, 1979), 163–64 and 320, n. 193.
111. Cf. Theodoret, *On Divine Love*, in *A History of the Monks of Syria*, ed.

and tr. R. M. Price (Kalamazoo, Mich.: Cistercian Publications, 1985), 190. "It is possible in the same way, too, to test the other men of skill, not to mention them individually: athletes, runners, actors of tragedy, pilots, shipwrights, doctors, peasants, and in a word, all the others who put their hand to some skill."

112. Cf. *History of Monks*, 30.7: "Just as jointers straighten their planks with a measuring cord and remove what is excessive to the point where, applying the rule, they see the plank is equal, so too one who wishes to emulate a particular life must apply it to himself in place of a rule." For faith needed by apprentices cf. Theophilus, *Ad Autol.* 1.8.

113. [=Clement, *Str.* 1.9.44]. The "touchstone" image recurs in Theodoret, *Carit.*, tr. Price, 190.

114. Cf. Theodoret, *History of Monks* 9.6.8 for a similar elaborate dress worn by Theodoret's mother in her youth. The following passage owes much to Clement, *Str.* 2.2.8–9; FOTC 85, p. 162.

115. Heb. 11:6.

116. The hierophant in question is probably the one at the Eleusinian mysteries. Aristides, *Apol.* 12 speaks of the hierophant at Isis/Osiris. See Clement, *Protr.* 12.1, 14.1 and C. Riedweg, "Die Mysterien von Eleusis in rhetorisch geprägten Textes des 2./3/ Jahrhunderts nach Christus," *Illinois Classical Studies* 13 (1988): 127–33.

117. Priapus, originally worshiped as a god of fertility, is Iampraeus, son of Dionysus and Aphrodite or a local nymph. See Diodorus, Siculus 4.6.4; *OCD*, s.v. 876; A. Richlin, *The Garden of Priapus: Sexuality and Aggression in Roman Humor* (New Haven, 1983). He was adopted as a god of gardens, in which his ithyphallic statue acted as a combined scarecrow and guardian deity. See Pausanias, 9.31.2.

118. On similar pleasure, Aphrodite, intoxication, Dionysus, see *infra* 3.49. For a similar listing cf. Theodoret, *Provid.* 1.7 (ACW 49.11 and 166, n. 6).

119. Φαλλός is poorly attested in LSJ, s.v. Theodoret probably means the imitation phallos carried in procession. See J. Henderson, *The Maculate Muse: Obscene Language in Attic Comedy* (New Haven, 1975), 35: "Phallos is simply the uncathected organ, while 'πεος' is the embodiment of raw sexuality." For possible pagan-Christian continuity in Symeon the Stylite (cf. Theodoret, *Hist. Rel.* 26) see D. T. M. Frankfurter, "Stylites and Phallobates: Pillar Religions in Late Antique Syria" *VigChr* 44 (1990): 168–98.

120. Cf. Clement, *Protr.* 34, for the lengthy Prosymnos episode; cf. *Affect.* 3.80. The festival of Phallagogia was also censured in Gregory Nazianzus, *Orat.* 39, *In s. lumina*, PG 36.337. For accounts of the festival cf. Burkert, *Homo necans*, 69–72, and notes; also "Genitalien," *RAC* 10 (1976): 1–52, esp. 12–14, 38–39.

121. On the dismemberment of Osiris by Typhon and search by Isis cf. Plutarch, *De Is. et Osir.*, Athenagoras, *Leg.* 22.8–9; Theophilus, *Ad Autol.* 1.9, Clement, *Protr.* 4.48; Minucius Felix, Oct. 22.1 (on which, ACW 39.278, n.

287); Arnobius, *Adv. nat.* 1.36; Lactantius, Div. inst. 1.21.21; Synesius, *De prov.,* PG 66.1212–80.

122. F. W. Norris, "Isis, Serapis and Demeter in Antioch of Syria," *HThR* 75 (1982): 189–207 has a useful check-list of archaeological data.

123. On Orpheus imported from Egypt see Linforth, *Arts of Orpheus*, 207.

124. Pindar, fr. 180 [=Clement, *Str.* 1.10.49], Pasztori-Kupan, *Theodoret of Cyrus,* 105 and 239, n. 70; FOTC 85, 59.

125. Plato, *Resp.* 2.314a [=Eusebius, *P.e.* 12.7].

126. Orpheus, fr. 245, ed. Kern [=Eusebius, *P.e.* 13.12.5]. See M. L. West, *The Orphic Poems,* 34 and n. 104.

127. Plato, *Laws* 5.730c [=Clement, *Str.* 2.4.18, FOTC 85, p. 168, and n. 53].

128. Phaedo 69c. Cf. Clement, *Str.* 3.3.17, FOTC 85, 266–67.

129. On preliminary initiation cf. Clement, *Protr.* 2.2.2. The entirety concerns pagan mysteries; for a description of the rites see 2.15 and for the Christian alternative see 12, 119–20. Theodoret is clearly less enthusiastic than Clement about the role of philosophy in Christian teaching.

130. Cf. Clement, *Str.* 1.3.22: "The wretched sophists, babbling away in their own jargon, show themselves greater chatterers than turtle doves." Tatian, *Orat.* 1.3, explaining why he abandoned Greek philosophy, says: "For according to the comic poet these things are 'baubles and chitter-chatter, swallows' music schools, a disgrace to art (Aristophanes, *Frogs* 92–93), and the devotees of this wisdom croak and caw like crows," trans. M. Whittaker, *Tatian Oratio ad Graecos* (Oxford, 1982).

131. Acts 14:16f.

132. A guide through nature and creation is a Patristic topos: cf. D. S. Wallace-Hadrill, *The Greek Patristic View of Nature* (New York, 1978).

133. Cf. Clement, *Str.* 1.7.37, Basil, *Hex.* 3.6.

134. On the thorns/roses motif see Clement, *Str.* 2.1.3, F. W. Norris "Of Thorns and Roses: The Logic of Belief in Gregory Nazianzen," *ChH* 53 (1984) 455–64. On the bee cf. Clement, *Str.* 1.6.33 and, for "the Sicilian bee," *Str.* 1.1.11; Basil, *Leg. Lib. Gent.,* 4, 8. "Honig," *RAC* 15, 122/123 (Stuttgart, 1992), 433–73. For tastes cf. Theodoret, *Provid.* 6.17 (ACW 49.79, 201, n. 17). On the selective use of the classics by Christians see C. Gnilka, "Usus iustus: Ein Grundbegriff der Kirchenväter im Ungang mit der antiken Kultur," *Archiv für Begriffsgeschichte* 24 (1980): 34–76.

NOTES TO DISCOURSE 2

1. Cf. Theophilus of Antioch, *Ad Autol.* 1.2; Clement, *Paed.* 1.6.26; *Str.* 7.3.13.

2. The night birds and the luminous rays of the sun appear again, ring-composition-wise, in the last discourse: cf. 12.97. See D'Arcy W. Thompson, *Glossary of Greek Birds* (Oxford, 1895), 119. Cf. Basil, *Hex.* 7.7, 9.4, 8.7. For bats cf. Homer, *Od.* 24, 1–8; Basil, *Hex.* 8.3, 8.7; art. "Fledermaus," *RAC* 7.1097–1105.

3. For the Sun of Justice cf. Mal. 3:20.

4. Homer, *Il.* 8.68.

5. For "self-conceit" (Greek οἴησις) cf. Clement, *Str.* 7.16.95. Clement also prescribes how it should be cured (*Str.* 7.16.98).

6. For the need for seafood to be cooked in salt cf. Clement, *Str.* 1.8.41, p. 53.

7. Plato, *Resp.* 3.398a. On χελίδονες=*pudenda muliebria,* cf. LSJ. s.v., 5 and Supplement, 313, and see J. Henderson, *The Maculate Muse* (New Haven, 1975): 128–29, 147. This piece of vulgarity is repeated at 5.9 and 10.37.

8. On Plato's criticism of Homer (e.g., *Resp.* 2.7, 4–7) cf. R. Lamberton, *Homer the Theologian* (Berkeley, 1986), 16–21 and Stefan Weinstok, "Die platonische Homerkritik und seine Nachwirkung," *Philologus* 82 (1926–27): 121–53. Plato's banishing of the poets won St. Augustine's approval also: *Civ. Dei,* 2.14. See also Cyril of Alexandria, *Juln.* 2.4 (SC 322. 216), Tertullian, *Apol.* 14: *Exinde quis non poeta ex auctoritate principis sui: dedecorator invenitur deorum?* For Homer in Theodoret see G. J. M. Bartelink, "Homère dans les oeuvres de Théodoret de Cyr," *Orpheus* 2 (1981): 6–28; Bartelink, "Homer," *RAC* XVI (Stuttgart: Hiersmann, 1994), 121, 1991, 116–47, esp. 139.

9. Cf. Theodoret, *Provid.* 1.6. On the king's highway cf. Theodoret, *Haer.,* Intro., PG 83.337.

10. There are several patristic parallels for the following doxographical account: e.g., Minucius Felix, *Oct.* 19.4; ps.-Justin, *Coh. Gr.* 3, 4, 5. Here Theodoret is most dependent on Aetius, *Plac.,* I.3,1, Eusebius, *P.e.* 14. 1, I. 8 [= Clement, *Str.* 1.14.59].

For Thales, see Tatian, *Orat.* 41.4. On the date (730–700) of the *Theogony* cf. M. L. West, *Hesiod Theogony* (Oxford, 1966), 40–48.

11. Homer, *Il.* 14.201, quoted also in Aetius, *Plac.* 1.3.2, Theophilus, *Ad Autol.* 2.5; Athenagoras, *Leg.* 18; Hippolytus, Haer. 10.7. Diodorus of Sicily, 1.12.5, since, as he tells us, the Egyptians considered Oceanus to be their River Nile. See Guthrie, *HGP* 1.60.

12. Aetius, *Plac.* I. 3, 3. Diels, *Dox.* 277. Cf. ps.-Justin, *Coh. Gr.* 3; Clement, *Str.* 1.14. 63; *Protr.* 5.66. See E. Asmus, "What Is Anaximander's Apeiron?" *JHPh* 19 (1981): 279–97, R. M. Dancy, "Thales, Anaximander and Infinity," *Apeiron* 22 (1989): 279–97. Clement quotes Parmenides (Diels-Kranz I. 230, fr.

1.29–30) on the two ways: "The one is the dauntless heart of convincing truth, the other is in the opinions of men, in whom is no true faith" (*Str.* 5.9.59.6).

13. [=Clement, *Str.* 1.11,52]. Aetius, *Plac.* 1.3, 4. For Diogenes of Apollonia in Crete (fl. c. 440), see J. Zafiropulo, *Diogène d'Apollonie* (Paris, 1956); J. Barnes, *The Presocratic Philosophers* (London, 1979), 2:265–81. See also Diog. Laert. 9.57, K.R.S., 434–52, A. Laks, *Diogène d'Apollonie: La dernière cosmologie presocratique* (Leiden, 1983), N. Siniossoglou, *Plato and Theodoret: The Christian Appropriation of Platonic Philosophy and the Hellenic Intellectual Resistance*, Cambridge Classical Studies (Cambridge, 2008), 129; Derek Krueger, "Diogenes the Cynic among the Fourth Century Fathers" *VigChr* 47 no. 1 (1993): 29–49.

14. [=Aetius, *Plac* 1.3, 11 (Diels, *Dox.* 283)=Clement, *Protr.* 5. 64; cf. *Str.* 1.11.52]. Hippasos of Metapontus in Magna Graeca (sixth century, B.C.), an early Pythagorean; cf. Hippolytus, Haer. 10.6. Hippasos and Heraclitus are also linked ("both from Metapontus") in ps.-Justin, *Coh. Gr.* 3.

15. [=Aetius, *Plac* 1. 1, 3, 20 (Diels, *Dox.* 286–87) = Clement, *Protr.* 5.64]; cf. *Str.* 5.2.15. See also Hermias, *Irrisio*, 8; Hippolytus, Haer. 10.6.

16. Diels-Kranz, I.135 fr. 27D: "For all come out of earth and unto earth come all" quoted also in Hippolytus, Haer. 10.7.

17. [=Clement *Str.* 1.14. 64].

18. Democritus of Abdera in Thrace. [=Clement, *Protr.* 5.66]; cf. Guthrie, *HGP* 1.382 f.

19. For Epicurus cf. ps.-Justin, *Coh. Gr.* 4.

20. For Metrodorus of Chios [=Clement, *Protr.* 5.66, *Str.* 1.14.64], see K. Freeman, *The Pre-Socratic Philosophers: A Companion to Diels, Fragmente der Vorsokratiker*, 2nd ed. (Oxford, 1959), 327–29; Freeman, *Ancilla to the Pre-Socratic Philosophers: A Complete Translation of the Fragments in Diels Fragmente der Vorsokratiker* (Oxford, 1956), 120–21; Cicero, N.D. 1.3186. Zeno of Elea [=Clement, *Str.* 1.14.64]; also cf. Tertullian, *Apol.* 21. Diogenes of Smyrna was taught by Metrodorus of Chios, pupil of Epicurus.

21. Plato, *Phaedo* 96a [=Eusebius, *P.e.* 1.8.17]. On its significance cf. D. Furley, The Greek Cosmologists (Cambridge and New York, 1987), 1:9.

22. *Phaedo* 96c [=Eusebius, *P.e.* 1.8.18].

23. *Theaet.* 180ac [=Eusebius, *P.e.* 14.4.4–5].

24. *Theaet.* 180de [=Eusebius, *P.e.* 14.4.6].

25. Parmenides, fr. 8.38, reads: οὐλον ἀκίνητον τεμεναι τοι παντ ονομ εσται. However, more recently D. Gallop, *Parmenides of Elea: Fragments. A Text and Translation* (Toronto, 1984), 70 [following Burnyeat, *Philosoph. Rev.* 91 (1982): 3–40] constitutes the text differently and translates it as: "To be whole and changeless; / wherefore it has been named all things."

26. On Melissus see Furley, *The Greek Cosmologists*, 1:110–14, J. E. Raven, *Pythagoreans and Eleatics* (Cambridge, 1948; repr. Amsterdam, 1966), 78–92. Cf. *Affect.* 4.8, 4.15, and 5.65.

27. Plato, *Sophist* 242c–d [=Eusebius, *P.e.* 14.4. 9], on which cf. M. Bordt, "Der Seinsbegriff in Platons *Sophistes*: Eine Untersuchung zu 242b6–249d5," *ThPh* 66 (1991): 493–529.

28. On the Eleatic sect originating with Xenophanes cf. Clement, *Str.* 1.64. 2; K.R.S., 163–66; M. J. Edwards, "Xenophanes Christianus?" *GRBS 32* (1991): 219–28; J. H. Lesher, *Xenophanes of Colophon, Fragments: A Text and Translation with a Commentary* (Toronto, 1992).

29. Empedocles was a native of Acragas in Sicily. On love and strife, cf. fr. 25 (22), Diogenes Laertius 9.12, Hippolytus, Haer. 7.29, 10.7; C. Mugler, "Sur quelques fragments d'Empèdocle" *RPh* 25 (1951): 33–65; M. R. Wright, *Empedocles: The Extant Fragments* (New Haven, 1981), 106 and 192–94; M. C. Stokes, *The One and the Many in the Presocratics* (Cambridge, MA, 1971), 161–72.

30. Plato, *Soph.* 246a [=Eusebius, *P.e.* 14.4. 9].

31. For Timon of Phlius (c. 320–230 B.C.) see *Affect.* 5.16; also Diogenes Laertius, 9.12.109–11; *Timone di Fliunte, Silli,* a cura di M. Di Marco (Rome, 1989); I. Gallo, "Il giudizio di Timone di Fliunte su Socrate (Diog. Laert. II,19)," in *Filologia e Forme Letterarie: Studi offerti a Francesco della Corte,* ed. S. Boldrini et al., 5 vols. (Urbino, 1987). On his satyric work, *On the Silloi*, lampoons, which he dedicated to Tiberius Caesar, cf. Clement, *Str.* 1.14.63; Eusebius, *P.e.* 14.18.28 (SC 338.160–63 and notes); Clement, *Str.* 3.14. For Pyrrho (c. 360–270 B.C.) see Diogenes Laertius, 9.11.61–108. On Pyrrho and Timon cf. C. L. Stough, *Greek Scepticism: A Study in Epistemology* (Berkeley, 1969), 5–6; R. Pratesi, "Timone, Luciano e Menippo: Rapporti nell'ambito di un genere letterario," *Prometheus* 11 (1985): 40–68.

32. Timon, fr. 10 [=Eusebius, *P.e.* 14.18.28]; cf. *Tim.* 48c. [=Clement, *Str.* 5.14.89 = Eusebius, *P.e.* 13.13.3].

33. For Anaxagoras cf. ps.-Justin, *Coh. Gr.* 3.

34. See Photius, *Life of Pythagoras* 8 [= *Biblioth. cod.* 249], as quoted in K. S. Guthrie, *Pythagorean Sourcebook* (Grand Rapids, MI: 1988), 138. Cf. ps.-Justin, *Coh. Gr.* 19.

35. "Empedocles became a pupil of Anaxagoras and Pythagoras," Diogenes Laertius, *Life of Pythagoras.* For disputed dates of Anaxagoras cf. K.R.S., 352–55.

36. Theano is described in Clement, *Str.* 1.16.80 as the first woman philosopher and writer of poetry. See *Affect.* 12.73; Freeman, *The Pre-Socratic Philosophers,* 84, 214. Teleuges as teacher of Empedocles (Diogenes Laertius, 8.43, Eusebius, *P.e.* 10.15) is discounted by Wright, *Empedocles,* 5.

37. For Archelaos of Athens see Diels-Kranz 60A1; Diogenes Laertius, 11, 16; K.R.S., 385–89.

38. On Pythagoras in Egypt see Iamblichus, *Life of Pythagoras* 3, as quoted in Guthrie, *HGP* 1.60–61; also Cyril of Alexandria, *Juln.* 1.40.

39. Plutarch, *Sol.,* 2.

40. Ps.-Xenophon, *Ep. 1 to Aeschines* [=Eusebius, *P.e.* 14.12]. The same excerpt is found at *Affect.* 12.70.

41. For Pythagoras in Sicily see Clement, *Str.* 1.15.66.

42. On Sicilian luxuries cf. Theodoret, *Provid.* 9.6. (cf. ACW 49, 121, and 207, n. 4).

43. Plato, *Crat.* 397c–d [=Eusebius, *P.e.* 1.9.12, where it is described as ἐπισφράγισμα τοῦ λόγου, following on quotation of Porphyry, *De Abstinentia*, 2.7; cf. *Affect.* 7.39).]

44. For the etymology, θεός, θέειν see Theophilus of Antioch, *Ad Autol.* 1.4.

45. *Theogony* 116f. [=Eusebius, *P.e.* 2.7.2; 13.1.2; 14.5]. See also Theophilus of Antioch, *Ad Autol.* 2.5.

46. Homer, *Il.* 14.201=302; already quoted *supra*, 2.9.

47. Homer, *Il.* 14.247.

48. Plato, *Ion* 534b [=Clement, *Str.* 6.18.168].

49. Fr. 246, Kern [=Eusebius, *P.e.* 13.12.5]. Cf. ps.-Justin, *Coh. Gr.* 13. See M. L. West, *The Orphic Poems* (Oxford, 1983), 33–35.

50. Fr. 247, Kern [=Eusebius, *P.e.* 13.12.5, 13.13.51]. Cf. Clement, *Str.* 5.14.124, 127. The translation is from J. B. Friedman, *Orpheus in the Middle Ages* (Cambridge, MA, 1970), 15.

51. For the coating with honey, cf. Lucretius, *De rerum natura* 1.935–50, ed. Cyril Bailey (Oxford, 1947); Lactantius, *Div. inst.* 5.1.

52. See Friedman, *Orpheus in the Middle Ages*, 35–36, quoting a similar reprimand of Orpheus in Augustine, Contra Faustum 13, 15.

53. *Tim.* 27e–28a [=Eusebius, *P.e.* 11.9.4].

54. *Tim.* 37e–38a [=Eusebius, *P.e.* 11.9.7]. Stobaeus 1.8.45.

55. *Crito* 47c–d [=Eusebius, *P.e.* 13.6.8].

56. *Crito* 48a [=Eusebius, *P.e.* 13.6.11].

57. Clement, *Protr.* IV, 62, 1 ; Theophilus, *Ad Autol.* 1,5, 2, 36, quoting *Oracula Sibyllina*, fragment 1; W. Burkert, *Homo Necans* (Berlin and New York, 1972), 8, and n. 36.

58. *Ep.* 13, 363b [=Eusebius, *P.e.* 11.13.4].

59. [=Clement, *Str.* 5.12.78]; *Tim* 28c, much quoted by the Fathers; cf. J. Geffcken, *Zwei griechische Apologeten* (Leipzig, 1907), 174f.

60. On the seniority of Moses cf. Tertullian, *Apol.* 19.1 (Fragmentum Fuldensis, CCL 1.119); Tatian, *Orat.* 31.1–4; Clement, *Str.* 1.21.101, 105–7; Origen, C. Cels. 6.7, 7.30; ps.-Justin, *Coh. Gr.* 9; Justin, *1 Apol.* 44, Cyril of Alexandria, *C. Juln.* 1.4–5.

61. Porphyry, *Contra Christianos* 4. [=Eus. *P.e.* 1.9.21]. See also R. Goulet, "Porphyre et la datation de Moise," *RHR* 184 (1977): 137–64; A. Smith, "Porphyrean Studies since 1913" *ANRW* II.36.2, 717–73, esp. 731–37.

62. For a good survey of the scholarship on the Sanchuniathon / Philo of Byblos question see J. Ebach, *Weltentstehung und Kulturentwicklung bei Philo*

von Byblos (Stuttgart, 1979), 4–21. Also see West, *Hesiod Theogony*, 24–30; Sanchuniathon (which Theodoret spells Sanchòniathon) is mentioned also at 2.94 and 3.25. See H. W. Attridge and R. A. Oden, *Philo of Byblos: The Phoenician History* (Washington, DC, 1981); M. J. Edwards, "Philo or Sanchuniathon? A Phoenician Cosmogony," *CQ* 41 (1991): 213–20, maintains that the cosmogony in Philo cannot possibly be dated to any older period than that of Archaemenids.

63. Semiramis, queen of Assyria, Mesopotamia (mentioned only at 2.45–47) is described in Athenagoras, *Leg.* 30 as "a licentious and murderous woman, regarded as the Syrian goddess and the Syrians venerate...doves on behalf of Semiramis (for the impossible is related that the woman turned into a dove—the myth is found in Ctesius)," trans. W. Schoedel, OECT 73. The sanctuaries are mentioned in Eusebius, *P.e.* 1.9.26. On the "writings" (γράμματα) see Attridge and Oden, *Philo of Byblos* 73 n. 11.

64. Cf. Clement, *Str.* 1.15.73, Tertullian, *Apol.* 19.2: "Troiano denique proelio ad mille annos ante est." See also Tatian, *Orat.* 32.2.

65. On Moses before, and Homer after, the Trojan War, see Clement, *Str.* 1.21.117; Theophilus, *Ad Autol.*; Tatian, *Orat.* 31.1–4; Cyril of Alexandria, *Juln.* 1.4–5. Also A. J. Droge, *Homer or Moses? Early Christian Interpretations of the History of Culture* (Tübingen, 1988). On Porphyry's interest in chronology, despite Theodoret's assessment, cf. J. Pépin, *La tradition de l'allégorie: De Philon d'Alexandrie à Dante* (Paris, 1987), 57f.

66. [=Eusebius, *P.e.* 10.11.28–29=Clement, *Str.* 1.21.131]. On Orpheus participating in the Argonaut expedition cf. West, *The Orphic Poems*, 4 n. 4, p. 4, n. 3, quoting Bacch 28(b), Aesch., *Agam.* 1630, Euripides, *Bacch.* 562, *IA* 1212. See also Theophilus. *Ad Autol.* 2.30. For Hercules in the Argonautica see K. Galinsky, *The Herakles Theme* (Totowa, NJ, 1972), 108–16.

67. For Euneus, see Homer, *Il.* 7.467.

68. On Sarpedon at Troy cf. Tatian, *Orat.* 41.1.

69. For Helen's τειχοσκοπία, cf. Homer, *Il.* 3.236. *Il.* 5.628.

70. For Linos, Musaios [=Clement, *Str.* 1.21, 107]; cf. Tatian, *Orat.* 41.1–2. For Thamyris see Lucian, *Fisherman*, 6.

71. On Moses/Homer, cf. J. Pépin, "Le challenge Homère-Moise aux premiers siècles du christianisme," *RSR* 29 (1955): 105–22; Pépin, *La tradition de l'allégorie*, 48–49.

72. Homer, *Il.* 21.196.

73. Cf. Clement, *Protr.* 7.74. On philosophers irrigating their genius from Moses, see Clement, *Str.* 1.21, and Tertullian, *Apol.* 47.

74. Cf. Clement, *Str.* 1.14.6, 1.17.87, 5.14.99.

75. Exod. 20:2.

76. Exod. 20:4–5.

77. Deut. 6:4.

78. Cf. Isaiah 1:2, 44:24, 49:5, and see A. C. Vrame, "Theodoret Bishop

of Cyrus as an Exegete of Isaiah I: A Translation of his Commentary with an Introduction" *GOTR* 34 (1989): 127–47. For the charge that the Jews were uneducated cf. Origen, *C. Cels.* 4.36. For Theodoret's anti-Judaism cf. Entre. 51–79 and C. T. McCollough, "Theodoret of Cyrus as Biblical Interpreter and the Presence of Judaism in the Later Roman Empire," *SP* 18, 1 (1985): 327–34.

79. Deut. 6:4.
80. Isa. 6:3; cf. Rev. 4:8; Gen. 1:26.
81. Gen. 1:27.
82. Gen. 1:26.
83. Gen. 1:27.
84. Gen. 9:3–6; cf. Lev. 7:11 and 17:14.
85. Gen. 11:7.
86. Gen. 19:24.
87. Ps. 32:6.
88. Ps. 109:1.
89. Ps. 109:3.
90. Ps. 44:7.
91. Plato, *Ep.* 6.323d.
92. *Epin.* 986c [=Eusebius, *P.e.* 11.16.1].
93. *Ep.* 2.312d–e [=Eusebius, *P.e.* 11.20.2]. Cf. H. Dörrie, "Der König: Ein platonisches Schlüsselwort, von Plotin mit neuem Sinn erfüllt," *Rev. Internat. Philos.* 24 (1970): 217–35 [=*Platonica Minora* (Munich, 1976), 390–405].
94. *Tim.* 48c [=Eusebius, *P.e.* 13.13, 3]. See Siniossoglou, *Plato and Theodoret*, 69.
95. Numenius, fr. 10, ed. Lemans [=Eusebius, *P.e.* 11.18.6]. Cf. Siniossoglou, *Plato and Theodoret*, p. 83 and n. 132. Cf. Origen, *C. Cels.* 1.14. See *The Neoplatonic Writings of Numenius*, collected and translated from the Greek by K. Guthrie, with a foreword by M. Wagner (Lawrence, KS, 1987), 28–29; J. M. Dillon, *The Middle Platonists: 80 B.C. to A.D. 220* (Ithaca, 1977), 361–79, esp. 365–72; R. Lamberton, *Homer the Theologian: Neoplatonist Allegorical Reading and the Growth of the Epic Tradition* (Berkeley, 1986), 54–77; F. L. Lisi, "Los tres niveles de la divinidad en Numenio de Apamea" *CFilos* 17 (1977): 111–30; M. Frede, "Numenius" *ANRW* II.36.2, 1034–75, esp. 1047f.
96. Plotinus, Ennead V.1, 6 [=Eusebius, *P.e.* 11.17, 7]. Cf. M. Atkinson, *Plotinus: Ennead V. 1, On the Three Principal Hypotheses, A Commentary with Translation* (Oxford University Press, 1983); P. Kalligas, Traces of Longinus' Library in Eusebius' *Praeparatio Evangelica*, CQ 51 (2002): 584–98. "Propos du titre du Traité de Plotin ΠΕΡΙ ΤΩΝ ΤΡΙΩΝ ΑΡΧΙΚΩΝ ΥΠΟΣΤΑΣΕΩΝ (*Enn.* V,1)" *REG* 105 (1992): 253–61; Siniossoglou, *Plato and Theodoret*, p. 66 and n. 41. J. Dillon, "Logos and Trinity: Patterns of Platonist Influence on Early Christianity," in *The Philosophy in Christianity*, ed. G. Vesey (Cambridge, 1989),

1–13, reprinted in Dillon, *The Great Tradition: Further Studies in the Development of Platonism and Early Christianity* (Aldershot, 1997), 251.

97. Plotinus, *Ennead* 5.1. 6–7 [=Eusebius, *P.e.* 11.17.8].

98. On alleged Neoplatonic "borrowings" from Christian theology cf. P. Aubin, *Plotin et le Christianisme: Triade plotinienne et Trinité chrétienne* (Paris, 1992); K. Kraemer, "Bonum est diffusivum sui. Ein Beitrag zum Verhältnis von Neoplatonismus und Christentum" *ANRW* II.36.2, 994–1032, esp. 1008f.

99. Cf. H. Blumenthal, "Nous and Soul in Plotinus," in *Atti del Convegno internazionale sul tema: Plotino e il Neoplatonismo in Oriente e in Occidente (Roma, 5–9 ottobre 1970)* (Rome, 1974), 203–19.

100. Ps. 32:6.

101. On Amelius see H. Dörrie, "Une exégèse Neoplatonicienne du Prolog de l'Évangile selon saint Jean," *Épektasis: Mélanges patristiques offerts au cardinal Jean Daniélou* (Paris, 1972), 75–87 [=*Platonica Minora*, 491–507]; L. Brisson, "Amélius: Sa vie, son oeuvre, sa doctrine, son style," *ANRW* II.36.2, 793–860, esp. 840f. On Plutarch see J. Whittaker, "Plutarch, Platonism and Christianity" in *Neoplatonism and Early Christian Thought*, ed. H. J. Blumenthal and R. A. Markus (London, 1981), 50–63, esp. 63, n. 25.

102. [= Eusebius, *P.e.* 11.19.1]

103. John 1:1.

104. John 1:14. On the interpretation of this text cf. *Theodoret, Eranistes*, ed. G. Ettlinger (Oxford, 1975), 9–13, 91–94.

105. John 1:5.

106. Sanchuniathon was a legendary chronicler of ancient Phoenicia, a literary creation of Philo of Byblos, who lived in the reign of Hadrian (117–138). See Attridge and Oden, *Philo of Byblos;* Eusebius, *P.e.* 10.9.12.

107. Manetho, fr. 74 ed. Müller. He was an Egyptian priest who wrote in the time of Ptolemy II Philadelphus, 285–246 B.C. His *Aegyptiaca* was a history of Egypt from the beginning to the death of Alexander the Great, 323 B.C. Theophilus, *Autol.* 3.21 says that he "expressed much nonsense in Egyptian fashion and actually uttered outrageous slanders about Moses." See C. Scott Littleton, "The 'Kingship in Heaven' Theme," in *Myth and Law among the Indo-Europeans: Studies in Indo-European Comparative Mythology*, ed. Jaan Puhvel (Berkeley, 1970), 83–21, esp. 100–102.

108. See A. Burton, *Diodorus of Sicily: Book I, A Commentary* (Leiden, 1972), 16, 44–47.

109. On the popularity of Hesiod (from Ascra, Boeotia) in the school curriculum cf. West, ed. *Hesiod Theogony*, 50–52, R. A. Pack, *The Greek and Latin Literary Texts from Greco-Roman Egypt* (Ann Arbor, 1965), 46–48.

110. For Orpheus on the rites of initiation see *Affect.* 2.32.

111. On Cadmus see *Affect.* 1.20.

112. Cornutus, a Stoic philosopher and commentator on Aristotle, was born in Leptis Magna, Libya, c. A.D. 20 He was the teacher of the satirist

288 THEODORET OF CYRUS: *A CURE FOR PAGAN MALADIES*

Perseus. See G. W. Most, "Cornutus and Stoic Allegoresis: A Preliminary Report," *ANRW* II.36.3, 2014–65.

113. Plutarch and Aetios are here acknowledged as sources by Theodoret. See *Affect.* 4.31 and nn. 78, 79.

114. On Porphyry cf. Eusebius, *P.e.* 1.9, 20–22, SC 202, 176–79, and further, Attridge and Oden, *Philo of Byblos,* 4–5.

115. Homer, *Il.* 8.16.

116. Here Eusebius is named by Theodoret as one of his few acknowledged sources. There is no acknowledgement of his equally considerable debt to Clement of Alexandria, *Stromata;* cf. Haer. 1 (PG 83.340).

117. *On The Phoenician History of Philo,* see n. 118.

118. An example of Theodoret's use of apophatic terminology. Cf. G. A. Maloney, "Apophatic theology," *NCE* 18.23–24, and A. C. Pegis, "Penitus manet ignotum," *Mediaeval Studies* 27 (1965): 212–26.

119. On the Trinity one in essence, cf. Canivet, *Entre,* 337–38.

120. Timaeus of Locri (in southern Italy) [=Clement, *Str.* 5.14.115 =Eusebius, *P.e.* 13.13.42]. See T. H. Tobin, ed., *Timaios of Locri: On the Nature of the World and the Soul* (Chico, CA, 1985). See also Guthrie, *Pythagorean Sourcebook,* 287–96.

121. Cf. Parmenides, fr. 8.4; Diels-Kranz I. 235. Cf. Hippolytus, *Ref* 1.11.1.

122. Plutarch, *Concerning the E at Delphi* [=Eusebius, *P.e.* 11.11].

123. On Parmenides cf. *Affect.* 4.7.

124. On Plato's Demiurge cf. *Affect.* 4.32–38. On Plutarch, *Epitome,* cf. Diels, *Dox.* 297.

125. See Eusebius, *P.e.* 14. 16,1 (SC 338.134, n. 1) for the source of Theodoret's error on Diagoras's place of origin, *pace* Canivet, SC 79.169, n. 1. The place was not Miletus, but the island of Melos.

126. For the Stoic "corporeal" God cf. *Affect.* 4.46.

127. Protagoras, fr. 2 [=Eusebius, *P.e.* 14.3.7], on which see R. K. Sprague, *The Older Sophists* (Columbia, SC, 1972), 4, 20, 2; C. W. Müller, "Protagoras über die Götter," *Hermes* 95 (1967) 148–59.

128. Numenius, fr. 10, Lemans [=Clement, *Str.* 1.22, 150]. See D. Ridings, "Μωϋσῆς ' Ἀττικίζων," *SP* 20 (1989): 132–36; M. J. Edwards, "Atticizing Moses? Numenius, the Fathers and the Jews," *VigChr* 44 (1990): 64–75.

129. Theodoret's digging for gold metaphor pretty well expresses his views on the strengths and weaknesses of Hellenism; cf. P. Allen, "Some Aspects of Hellenism in the Early Greek Church Historians," *Traditio* 43 (1987): 368–81, esp. 376f.

Notes to Discourse 3

1. Cf. Plato, *Resp.* 9.576d, *Leg.* 3.693, 11.942c; Gregory Nazianzus, *Orat.* 29.2.

2. Homer, *Il.* 2.204–5. Cf. Origen, *C.Cels.* 8.68 and H. Chadwick, trans. (Cambridge and New York, 1980), 504, n. 2.

3. On "atheists" see M. Winiarczyk, "Wer galt im Altertum als Atheist," *Philologus* 128 (1984): 157–83, and Winiarczyk, *Diagorae Melii et Theodori Cyrenaei reliquiae* (Leipzig, 1981). Athenagoras, *Leg.* 4, says that the Athenians judged Diagoras "guilty of atheism in that he not only divulged the Orphic traditional doctrine and published the mysteries of Eleusis and the Cabiri and chopped up the wooden statue of Heracles to boil his turnips, but openly declared that there was no god at all." His atheism is known only through such anecdotes; cf. W. Burkert, *Greek Religion* (Cambridge, MA, 1985) 316.

4. Cf. *Affect.* 2.112. Theodore of Cyrene (460 B.C.), a celebrated mathematician who was a teacher of Plato and Theaetetus (cf. Plato, *Theaet.* 147d).

5. Euhemeros, the best known of this trio, is mentioned in Clement, *Protr.* 2.24; Theophilus of Antioch, *Ad Autol.* 3.7; Minucius Felix, *Oct.* 21.1. See F. Jacoby, FGrH 1. 300–313.

6. Ps.-Plut. *De placit. philos.*1.7 [=Eusebius, *P.e.* 14.16.1].

7. On the sensuality of the gods of Homer and Hesiod see Xenophanes, fr. 11: "Homer and Hesiod have ascribed to the gods all deeds that among men are a reproach and disgrace: thievery, adultery, and mutual deception" (trans. Guthrie, *HGP* 1.71). See also Plato, *Euthyphro* 6b; Clement, *Protr.* 2.33; Theophilus of Antioch, *Ad Autol.* 2.5–7; Basil, *Leg. lib. gent.* 4, ed. N. G. Wilson (London, 1975), 22 and 47, n. 16.

8. Diodorus, 1.11 [=Eusebius, *P.e.* 1.9.1]. Diodorus is called "your most famous historian" in ps.-Justin, *Coh. Gr.* 9.

9. For the identification of Osiris/Helios and Isis/Selene cf. Plut. *De Is. et Os.* 372d; Eusebius, *P.e.* 1.9; Firmicus Maternus, c. 8; ACW 37.63 and 171, n. 185, n. 186. For Zeus's various metamorphoses cf. Aristides, *Apol.* 9; Athenagoras, *Leg.* 22; Athanasius, *Gent.* 12; Lactantius, *Div. inst.* 1.11; Arnobius, *Adv. nat.* 5.22.

10. See note on Tyre and Sidon at 10.53.

11. Plato, *Crat.* 397 c–d [=Eusebius, *P.e.* 1.9.12].

12. For the θεός/θεῖν etymology cf. Theophilus of Antioch, *Ad Autol.* 1.4; Clement, *Protr* 2.26.1; *Str.* 4.23; Eusebius, *P.e.* 1.9.

13. Theodoret returns to this at *Affect.* 4.34.

14. Gen. 1:14, Clement of Rome, *1 Clem.* 24.3–5, 25.1–4; Basil, *Hex.* 6.2; John Chrysostom, *Hom. 6.10 in Gen.*

15. Theodoret discusses the sun and moon also in *Provid.* 1.23–26.

16. Cf. Rom. 1:25, Athenagoras, *Leg.* 16; Chrysostom *Hom. 6.12 in Gen.*

17. Cf. Theodoret, *Provid.* 2.5–8; ACW 49.25–27 and notes.

18. Cf. Clement, *Str.* 2.20.115; Gregory of Nyssa, *C. Eunom.* 3.20; John Chrysostom, *Hom.* 6.14 in Gen.

19. On air breathing pestilence cf. Clement, *Str.* 5.7.43: "For the dogs are symbols (to the Egyptians) of the two hemispheres, which, as it were, go round and keep watch; the hawk, of the sun, for it is fiery and destructive (so they attribute pestilential diseases to the sun), the ibis of the moon."

20. For built-in deficiencies cf. Theodoret, *Provid.* 2.5–6; ACW 49.26 and 177, n. 8; John Chrysostom, *Hom.* 2.12 in Gen.; FOTC 74.3–6.

21. Wisd. 13:5, Rom. 1:20.

22. More generally the goldsmith is censured by the Fathers for elaborate creations; cf. Clement, *Paed.* 2.3.

23. Rom. 1:20.

24. Rom. 1:20–23.

25. Rom. 1:22–23.

26. Plutarch, *De Is. et Osir.* 32.

27. For Sanchuniathon cf. *Affect.* 2. 44–45 and notes.

28. On the deification of Hercules cf. Justin, *1 Apol.* 21, Lactantius, *Div. inst.* 1.21.

29. Cf. Eusebius, *P.e.* 11.2.17–34.

30. Cf. Clement, *Str.* 1.16.75.

31. The death of Hercules is noted in Cicero, *ND* 3.41, 3.70; Minucius Felix, *Oct.* 22.6 (on which cf. ACW 39.287, n. 319); Tertullian, *Ad nat.* 2.14. 9; Theophilus, *Ad Autol.* 1.9; Athenagoras, *Leg.* 29; Justin, *1 Apol.* 21, 2; Lactantius, *Div. inst.* 1.18.6, 4.39. See also Athenagoras, *Leg.* 22.6; Cyril H. *Catech.* 6.10; Aristides, *Apol.* 10.

32. Asclepius and Hercules are similarly linked in Tertullian, *Ad nat.* 2.14.9: *hunc vos de pyra in coelum suble<vastis, ipsa> facilitate qua et alium igni sed divino confectum*; also *Apol.* 14. See also Justin, *1 Apol.* 21; Theophilus, *Ad Autol.* 3.2; Athenagoras, *Leg.* 29 (Markovich, ed. [Berlin and New York, 1990], 94 and citations); Origen, *C.Cels.* 3.22 (Chadwick, trans., 141, n. 6); Lactantius, *Div. inst.* 1.20; Ambrose, *De virg.* 3.2.7; Arnobius, *Adv. nat.* 1.41, 4.24.

33. Diodorus of Sicily wrote a universal history in forty books, of which books 1–4 and 11–20 survive, as well as fragments.

34. For the Dioscuri cf. Origen, *C.Cels.* 3.22; Lactantius, *Div. inst.* 1.5, where they are linked with Heracles and Orpheus.

35. For Orpheus and his lyre cf. M. L. West, *The Orphic Poems* (Oxford, 1983), 32; Tatian, *Orat.* 1.1; Gregory Nazianzus, *Orat.* 4.

36. Cf. Athanasius, *Gent.* 24: "The Indians worship Dionysus, calling him symbolically wine."

37. See Athenagoras, *Leg.* 32, Chrysostom, *Pan. Bab.* 77–78 (FOTC 73.120–21 and n. 76). Cinyras, a mythical king of Cyprus, established the worship of Aphrodite on the island. See Clement, *Protr.* 2.44 and 3.45 where Ptolemy, Book 1 on Philopator is quoted to the effect that Cinyras and his

descendants were interred in the temple of Aphrodite at Paphos. Her cult at Paphos included sacred prostitution.

38. Homer, *Il.* 20.234. See also Justin, *1 Apol.* 21, 25; ps.-Justin, *Disc.* 2; Tatian, *Orat.* 10.1, Athanasius, *Gent.* 11, Lactantius, *Div. inst.* 1.11.

39. See Euripides, *Or.* 1633–37 for the *deus ex machina* rescue. See also Tatian, *Orat.* 10, ed. and trans. M. Whittaker, OECT (Oxford and New York, 1982), 21 and note; Clement, *Str.* 2.20, quoting Euripides, *Andr.* 629, and *Paed.* 3.2.13, quoting Euripides, *IA* 71–77.

40. For deification of the emperors see D. L. Jones, "Christians and the Roman Imperial Cult," *ANRW* II.23.2 (1980) 1023–54, esp. 1029–32 (Nero), 1033–35 (Domitian) and 1040–41 (Commodus). For Nero's immoralities cf. Suetonius, *Nero,* 26–29. For deification of Nero cf. L. Kreitzer, "Apotheosis of the Roman Emperor," *Biblical Archaeologist* 53 (1990): 211–17; of Commodus see art. "Commodus," *RAC* 3:255–66; also *CAH* 12, 12 and n. 16.

41. *Tim.* 40de [=Eusebius, *P.e.* 2.7.1–2, 13.1. 1 and 14.5].

42. See Theophilus, *Ad Autol.* 2.5, quoting *Theogony,* 116–23, 126–33; also 2.6 and 2.7. On Hesiod see K.R.S., 34–37. Cyril of Alexandria, *Juln.* 2.25 suggests that even Julian might possibly blush at the fables of Hesiod.

43. For Cronus and Uranus see P. Hadot, "Ouranos, Kronos and Zeus in Plotinus' Treatise against the Gnostics," in *Neoplatonism and Early Christian Thought,* ed. H. J. Blumenthal and R. A. Markus (London, 1981), 124–37. See also Cicero, *ND* 2.64 and Pease, ed. 2.708; Tatian, *Or.* 21.3; Athenagoras, *Leg.* 20, 2 (ed. Marcovich, 60); Clement, *Protr.* 14, 2; Origen, *C.Cels.*1.17; M. L. West, *Hesiod, Theogony* (Oxford, 1966), 18–30; P. Walcot, *Hesiod and the Near East* (Cardiff, 1966), 1–54.

44. For Zeus's various incestuous marriages, see Athenagoras, *Leg.* 32.1; ps. Justin, *Disc.* 2; Lactantius, *Div. inst.* 1.13. For his varied amours cf. his own confessions to his wife, Hera: Homer, *Il.* 14.315–29. See also Theophilus, *Ad Autol.* 1.9; Tatian, *Orat.* 8.4; Athanasius, *Gent.* 1.12; Cyril of Alexandria, *Juln.* 2.11; Firmicus Maternus, *Err. prof. rel.* 12.2, 12.4.

45. For the gelding of Cronos see Plato, *Tim.* 40e; Hesiod, *Theogony.* For the devouring of his own children cf. *Euthyphro* 6a; for dethroning of Cronus *Resp.* 2.377e; for illicit amours, *Phaedrus* 255c.

46. *Resp.* 2.377e–78a [=Eusebius, *P.e.* 2.7.4; 13.3.4–5].

47. *Resp.* 3.378a–c [=Eusebius, *P.e.* 2.7.5–6; 13.3.4–5].

48. *Resp.* 11.378d [=Eusebius, *P.e.* 2.7.7; 13.3.6].

49. *Crat.* 396b.

50. See *Affect.* 3. 54. Diodorus 1.11–12 [=Eusebius, *P.e.* 3.2.5–7]; cf. A. Burton, *Diodorus* (Leiden, 1972), 54–70.

51. The source is surely Diodorus Siculus, 1.21, filiated through Eusebius, *P.e.* 3.13. Cf. Athanasius, *Gent.* 24; Lactantius, *Div. inst.* 4.10. Mnevis was a sacred bull worshiped as the incarnation of the sun-god, Re' Atum at

Heliopolis; cf. Diodorus Sic., 1.84, 4 and Burton, *Diodorus*, 242; Eusebius, *P.e.* 3.13.1–2.

    52. *Antiq. Rom.* 11.19 [=Eusebius, *P.e.* 11.8.4]. See E. Cary, ed., *The Roman Antiquities of Dionysius of Halicarnassus* 2.19, LCL, 7 vols. (Cambridge, MA, 1937–50), 1 (1937): 362–67.

    53. For a similar passage cf. Theodoret, *Provid.* 1.6; ACW 49.166, n. 6. For Eros and Aphrodite as sexual desire cf. Plato, *Symp.* 203b–e; cf. V. Pirenne-Delforge, "Eros en Grèce: Dieu ou Démon" in *Anges et démons: Actes du Colloque de Liège et de Louvain-la-Neuve* (Louvain-la-Neuve, 1989), 223–39. For Athena as reason cf. Origen, *C.Cels.* 8.67, ed. Chadwick, 503, n. 2. For anger, Ares cf. Gregory Nazianzus, *Orat.* 4. 122. For Hermes as theft cf. Theodoret, *Provid.* 1.6; ACW 49.166, n. 6.

    54. For a similar *reductio ad absurdum* cf. Theophilus, *Ad Autol.* 1.9.2, 2.2–3, 3.3; Athanasius, *Gent.* 9. For the proverb see Leutsch-Schneidewin, *Corpus Paroemiographorum Graecorum*, 3 vols. (Hildesheim, 1958–61), 1.314, 45.

    55. Antisthenes, fr. 35 [=Clement, *Str.* 2.20.107]. In Clement it is clear that Helen is the real target. Rankin, *Sophists, Socratics, and Cynics* (Totowa, NJ, 1983), 220, says that it is chronologically doubtful whether Diogenes could have been taught by Antisthenes. For Antisthenes see further D. R. Dudley, *A History of Cynicism* (London, 1937), 1–6; art. "Diogenes von Sinope," *RAC* 3.1063–75, H. Kusch.

    56. Plato, *Crat.* 404c.

    57. Plutarch, *De Daedalis Plataeensibus*, 4 [=Eusebius, *P.e.* 111, proem.].

    58. Orpheus, fr. 302 [=Eusebius, *P.e.* 3.3.5]. Cf. Clement, *Str.* 5.12.78.

    59. Plato, *Epin.* 980c [=Eusebius, *P.e.* 2.2.25].

    60. This is a wrong attribution; actually *De Is. et Osir.* 25 [=Eusebius, *P.e.* 5.5.1, SC 262.272].

    61. Plutarch, *De def. orac.* 21 [=Eusebius, *P.e.* 5.5.3]. The Solymoi were legendary warriors of Asia Minor who were finally subdued by Bellerophon.

    62. Actually Porphyry, *De abstin.* 4. 9 [=Eusebius, *P.e.* 3.4.10–11].

    63. On magical incantations cf. G. Luck, *Arcana Mundi* (Baltimore, 1985). For the connection between demons and sacrifices cf. Chrysostom, *Pan. Bab.* 74; FOTC 73.118–19 and n. 163, quoting J. Geffcken, *Zwei griechische Apologeten* (Berlin, 1907), 219f.

    64. Porphyry, *De abstin.* 2. 41–42 [=Eusebius, *P.e.* 4.22.10–12].

    65. Homer, *Il.* 4.49 [=24.70].

    66. Porphyry, *De philos. ex orac.* 147 [=Eusebius, *P.e.* 4.23.1] For the continued vitality of the cult of Sarapis cf. Theodoret, *H.e.* 5.22, which describes the destruction of a statue of Sarapis by Theophilus, bishop of Alexandria.

    67. Porphyry, *De philos. ex orac.* 150 [=Eusebius, *P.e.* 4.23.6]. See also Eunapius, *Lives,* quoted in G. Luck, *Arcana Mundi* (Baltimore, 1985), 303. See also art. "Hecate," *RAC* Lief. 106/7, 310–38, A. Kehl.

    68. Judg. 14:14.

69. Num. 22:12.

70. Porphyry, *Ad Aneb.* 38 [=Eusebius, *P.e.* 5.10.1–5], on which see SC 262.304–6 and notes. Cf. Luck, *Arcana Mundi,* 125.

71. Abydos, not the Milesian city on the Hellespont, but a town in Lower Egypt, site of an oracle and one of the claimants to the site of Osiris's tomb; cf. Diodorus of Sicily, 1.85 and Burton, *Diodorus,* 244–48; Plutarch, *De Is. et Osir.,* 13–18; and J. G. Griffiths, *The Origins of Osiris and His Cult* (Leiden, 1980), 25f.; Firmicus Maternus, *Err. prof. rel.* 2.6; ACW 37.46 and 146, n. 34.

72. For Chaeremon see P. W. van der Horst, *Chaeremon, Egyptian Priest and Stoic Philosopher: The Fragments* (Leiden, 1984); M. Frede, "Chaeremon der Stoiker," *ANRW* II.36.3 (1987) 2067–2103; A. Barzan, "Cheremone di Alessandria" *ANRW* II.32.3 1981–2001), esp. 1992–96. He was a first-century A.D. Stoic, the tutor of Nero, who wrote on astronomy, history, and grammar. See also Origen, *C.Cels.* 1.59 and Chadwick, trans. 54, n. 1.

73. Plato, *Tim.* 41b [=Eusebius, *P.e.* 11.32.4; 13.18. 10].

74. Homer, *Il.* 5. 341–42.

75. Cf. Basil, *Leg. lib. gent.* 22, ed. N. G. Wilson, p. 34: "Pheidias and Polycleitus, one of whom made the Zeus for the Elians and the other, Hera for the Argives"; see also Theophilus of Antioch, *Ad Autol.* 1.10, Athenagoras, *Leg.* 17, 4, which contains a longer list, on which cf. ACW 23.48 and 143, n. 134; Origen, *C.Cels* 8.17.18, Athanasius, *Gent.* 35; Tertullian, *Idol.* 3; Lactantius, *Div. inst.* 2.4.

76. Xenophanes, fr. 14 [=Clement, *Str.* 5.14.109].

77. Xenophanes, fr. 15 [=Clement, *Str.* 5.14.109=Eusebius, *P.e.* 13.13.36].

78. Fr. 16 [=Clement, *Str.* 7.4.22] and cf. K.R.S. 168–69; Guthrie, *HGP* 1.371.

79. [=Clement, *Str.* 5.11.76]. Cf. Arnim, *SVF* 1.264. Zeno of Citium, in Cyprus (335–263 B.C.) was founder of the Stoic school of philosophy. See 4.12, 4.15.

80. Cf. 3.38, *supra.* Plato's fear of the hemlock is also invoked in ps.-Justin, *Coh. Gr.* 20: "Thus, in fear of the hemlock Plato composed an artfully ambiguous dissertation on the gods." See also *Coh. Gr.* 22. For the friendship cup cf. Lucian, *Sat.* 18, [Gk. Φιλοτσία (κύλιξ)].

81. *Laws* 12. 955e–956a [=Clement, *Str.* 5.11.76=Eusebius, *P.e.* 3.8.2].

82. Isa. 40:20.

83. Isa. 44:16–17.

84. Isa. 44:20.

85. Canivet, *L'entre,* 13–15, understands these "Hellenists" not just as humanists but as attached to pagan practices. See also Gregory Nazianzus, *Contra Jul.* 102 and Eusebius, *Vita Const.* 2.44 and ελληνίζω, s.v., Lampe, PGL 451.

86. Cf. Clement, *Protr.* 4.53, quoting from Posidippus, *On Cnidus,*which describes the nude Aphrodite of Cnidus by Praxiteles, who apparently used

his mistress, Cratine, as his model. Clement is reproduced in Arnobius, *Adv. nat.* 6.13 (ACW 8.464 and 595, n. 108); see also Lactantius, *Div. inst.* 1.17. On Aphrodite Pandemos see art. "Dirne," *RAC* 3.1177. See also M. Robertson, *A History of Greek Art,* 2 vols. (London, 1975), 1.390–94, and pl. 127b. 548–50.
    87. For Europa's depiction in art cf. Robertson, *A History of Greek Art,* 1.67, 81, 118, 193.
    88. For the lithsome and effeminate portrait of Dionysus cf. Callistratus, *Descriptions,* 8; *On the Statue of Dionysus;* V. J. Hutchinson, "The Cult of Dionysos/Bacchus in the Graeco-Roman World," *JourRoman Arch* 4 (1991): 222–30.
    89. For Pan (returned to at *Affect.* 7.8 and 7.12) see Herodotus 2.46, 2.145; Gregory Nazianazus, *Orat.* 4.77. He was a woodland god and god of pastures and flocks, the son of Dionysus and Aphrodite. See Philostratus, *Imagines* 2.2, also M. Robertson, *A History of Greek Art,* 1.556 for the Aphrodite/Pan at Delos. Pan. 14 [=Clement, *Str.* 14.109=Eusebius, *P.e.* 13.13.36]. For Xenophanes see Guthrie, *HGP* 1.371, K.R.S. 168.
    90. For Zeus's metamorphoses cf. Isocrates, *Helen,* 59; as eagle descending on Ganymede cf. Homer, *Il.* 20.232–35, Clement, *Protr.* 2.33, 4.49, 12.2; Gregory Nazianzus, *Orat.* 4.22; Firmicus Maternus, *Err. prof. rel.* 12.2; Minucius Felix, *Oct.* 23.7 and ACW 39.290. n. 334. For Zeus and Ganymede in art cf. Robertson, *A History of Greek Art,* 1. 277 and plate 60b.
    91. For the swan and Leda cf. Aristides, *Apol.* 9.7; Tatian, *Orat.* 10.1; Athenagoras, *Leg.* 22; Clement, *Protr.* 4.59; G. Becatti, *The Art of Ancient Greece and Rome: From the Rise of Greece to the Fall of Rome* (Englewood Cliffs, NJ, 1968), 213 and fig. 189. Apollodorus, *The Library,* trans. Sir J. G. Frazer, 2 vols. (London, 1921), 2:23–24; Robertson, *A History of Greek Art,* v.1. 402, and pl. 129d.
    92. For Zeus showering impregnating gold in the lap of Danae cf. Aristides, *Apol.* 9.6; Clement, *Protr.* 4.58, also 4.61; Arnobius, *Adv. nat.* 4.26, Lactantius, *Div. inst.* 1.2, Augustine, *Civ. Dei* 18.13. See A. B. Cook, *Zeus: A Study in Ancient Religion,* 2 vols. in 3, illus. (New York, 1964–65) 3.460–61, for artistic depictions of the event. Danae was the daughter of Acrisius of Argos and Eurydice. She was seduced despite the fact that she was imprisoned by her father in a bronze underground chamber to prevent intercourse with men. For other body counts of Zeus's victims cf. ps.-Justin, *Disc. to Greeks* 2, Origen, *C.Cels.* 1.37; Pausanias, 9. 31 (Pausanias, *Guide to Greece,* ed. P. Levi, 2 vols. [New York, 1971], 1. 374); Diodorus of Sicily, 1.88, 4.6.
    93. For Priapus cf. Lactantius, *Div. inst.* 1.21.
    94. For the *Phallagogia* see Clement, *Protr.* 2.14, 2.34. Clement, after narrating the unconsummated homosexual encounter between Dionysus and Prosymna and the subsequent shaping of the phallus from the fig tree, concludes: "As a mystic memorial of this incident phalloi are raised aloft in honor

of Dionysus." See Pickard-Cambridge, *The Dramatic Festivals of Athens* (Oxford, 1968), 43, for *phallaphoros* at the Rural Dionysia.

95. For the feminine "comb" (μηνις) in the feast of Thesmophoria cf. Clement, *Protr.* 2.15–17. For κτείς=*pudenda muliebria* cf. LSJ s.v., quoting Callimachus, *Fragmenta* 308 in *Anthologia Palatina* 5.131 (Philodemus), et al.

96. For a full treatment of theriomorphic worship in Egypt cf. K. A. D. Smelik and E. A. Hemelriüjk, "Opinions on Egyptian Animal Worship in Antiquity," *ANRW* II.17.4 (1984) 1853–2000, 2337–57. See also Cicero, *ND* 1.43 and ed. Pease, 1.289–91. Theodoret is here relying on Clement, *Protr* 2.39. See also Aristides, *Apol.* 12, 7 (Syriac); Geffcken, *Zwei griechische Apologeten,* 75; Justin, *1 Apol.* 24. It is a frequent motif already in the Greek Apologists; cf. Athanasius, *Gent.* 24. On the goat cult (actually a ram cult) cf. Diodorus Siculus, 1.84, 4 and Burton, *Diodorus,* 243. Mendes was the Egyptian god Khnum-Ré, worshiped at Busiris, more usually called Mendes, a town in the Nile delta, mentioned also in Clement, *Protr.* 2.39. See also Athenagoras, *Leg.* 14.2, 28.4. For similar catalogs of strange gods in Egypt see Philo, *Decal.* 76–79, Lucian, *Zeus Rants,* 42.

97. For lion worship at Leontopolis cf. Diodorus Siculus, 84, 4 and Burton, *Diodorus* 243; also Strabo XVII,1.40. For the *latos,* or perch, at Latopolis, cf. D'Arcy W. Thompson, *A Glossary of Greek Fishes* (London, 1947), 144–45. For the ibis cf. K. A. D. Smelik, "The Cult of the Ibis in the Greco-Roman period, with special attention to the data from the Papyri," in *Studies in Hellenistic Religions,* ed. M. J. Vermasseren (Leiden, 1979), 225–43. There is an amusing portrait of crocodile worship in Clement, *Paed.* 3.2.4; see also Origen, *C.Cels.* 5.34 and 51, Chrysostom, *Hom. 7.18 in Gen.* The crocodile god was Sobek, associated with Lake Moeris.

98. On angels and archangels cf. J. Daniélou, *Anges et leur mission d'après les pères de l'église* (Paris, 1953).

99. On Cherubim and Seraphim cf. Clement, *Str.* 5.6.36.

100. On the asexuality of angels cf. Theodoret, *Haer.* 5.7.1. *RAC* 5.118, quoting Justin, *Dial.* 128, 4; St. Justin Martyr, *Dialogue with Trypho,* ed. Michael Slusser (Washington, D.C., 2003), 194.

101. Angels may be called "sons of God" collectively; cf. Job 1:6.

102. On angels called saints cf. art. "Heilig," *RAC* 5.115–16; cf. Clement, *Str.* 5.36.4, 7.86.6.

103. Heb. 1:14, also quoted in Origen, *C.Cels.* 5.4.

104. On the angelic nature of the monastic life cf. Theodoret *Hist. Rel.* 3.15, 21.3, 26.23, trans. Price; Daniélou, *Anges et leur mission,* 119–22.

105. See the vivid description of the mountaintop monastic retreat of Eusebius of Teleda in Theodoret, *Hist. Rel.* 26. 4, trans. Price, 49–50. For those who lived in groups of twos and threes cf. Marcianus, in Theodoret, *Hist. Rel.* 3.4. On the threefold nature of the monastic life see further P. Canivet, *Le monasticisme syrien selon Théodoret de Cyr* (Paris, 1977).

106. The Persian propensity to unnatural vices is already castigated in Herodotus, 3.31. See also Lucian, *De sacr.* 5. Among the Fathers it became a commonplace: Tatian, *Orat.* 28, Minucius Felix, *Oct.* 31.3 (ACW 39.338, n. 512); Tertullian, *Apol.* 9.16; Origen, *C.Cels.* 5.27.

107. On Zeus's polygamy cf. Homer, *Il.* 14.307–28. See Eusebius, *P.e.* 2.3.19; Athenagoras, *Leg.* 20,2. On Perrepphata (=Persephone) cf. Athenagoras, *Leg.* 20.3.

108. Cf. Justin *1 Apol.* 21, ps.-Justin, *Disc.* 2, Athenagoras, *Leg* 21.5.

109. On demons cf. Lactantius, *Div. inst.* 2.14 4.27; art. "Démon, II. Dans la littérature ecclésiastique jusqu'à Origène," *DSp* 3.152–89; Daniélou, "III. Dans la plus ancienne littérature monastique," *Anges et leur mission,* 189–212, A. et C. Guillaumont. See also Lactantius, *Div. inst.* 2.14, 4.27.

110. Cf. Epistle of Barnabas, 18,1; Theophilus of Antioch, *Ad Autol.* 2.28; Origen, *C.Cels.* 6.44. See also J. Giblet, "La Puissance Satanique selon l'Évangile de saint Jean," in *Anges et démons: Actes du Colloque de Liège et de Louvain-la-Neuve,* 291–300.

111. On the voluntary fall of the angels see J. Daniélou, "The Demons and the Problem of Evil," *Anges et leur mission,* 187–92.

112. Ibid., 358–62. E. Pagels, "Christian Apologists and the Fall of the Angels: An Attack on Imperial Power?" *HThR* 78 (1985): 301–25, R. Bauckham, "The Fall of the Angels as the Source of Philosophy in Hermias and Clement of Alexandria," *VigChr* 39 (1985): 313–30.

113. For guardian angels cf. art. "Anges 3.B," *DSp* 1.586–98; J. Duhr, "Angelo, 1. Angelologia," *DPAC* 1.195–202.

114. *Laws* 10.896d–e [=Clement, *Str.* 5.14.92=Eusebius, *P.e.* 13.13.8].

115. The role of the Demiurge of evil governing the heavens is exaggerated here; cf. Canivet, SC 57.201, n. 1. Cf. Plato, *Resp.* 2. 379b, *Tim.* 41d.

116. On the Paraclete cf. John 14:16, 26.

117. Eph. 2:2. For the thought cf. Tertullian, *Apol.* 23, Eusebius, *H.e.* 7.10.

118. *Phaedrus* 240b [=Clement, *Str.* 5.14.93=Eusebius, *P.e.* 13.13.9].

119. For the same metaphor cf. Chrysostom, *Pan. Bab.* 2, FOTC 73.76. It is applied to the smooth style of the philosophers in ps.-Justin, *Exhort* 36.

NOTES TO DISCOURSE 4

1. Democritus, fr. 33, Diels-Kranz 2.133=Clement, *Str.* 4.23.149. Cf. Stobaeus *Ecl.* 11,31,149. For commentary on *Affect.* 4 there is a scholarly monograph: Marco Ninci, *Aporia ed entusiasmo: Il mondo materiale e i filosofi secondo Teodoreto e la tradizione patristica greca* (Rome, 1977).

2. Porphyry, *Hist. phil. fr.* 12, see *Porphyrii philosophi Platonici Opuscula selecta,* ed. A. Nauck (Leipzig, 1886), p. 9, 11. 20–32.

3. Cf. Matt. 9.10; Luke 7.36–50; Luke 23:39–43.

4. For the same image cf. Clement, *Paed.* 3.9.47–48.

5. Wisd. 9:14. For the night battle image cf. Basil, *Ep.* 69: we shall hereafter know those who are united with us and not, as in a night battle, be unable to distinguish between friends and foe. For a classic description of one cf. Thucydides, 7.44.

6. Cf. Aetius, *Plac.* 2.4.11, and Diels, *Dox.* 284. Xenophanes, a Greek philosopher from Colophon, Asia Minor, c. 570–c. 480 B.C., disciple of Anaximander and founder of the Eleatic school. Cf. Cicero, *Acad.* 2. 118; Diels-Kranz I.123, A34; Sextus Empiricus, *Pyrrh. hypotyp.* 1.224, Hippolytus, *Ref.* 1.14; J. Mansfeld, *Studies in the Historiography of Greek Philosophy* (Assen, 1990), 80, n. 192, n. 193.

7. Xenophanes, fr. 27; cf. FOTC 85, p. 71; cf. Aetius, *Plac.* 2.4.11, p. 284 [=Diels-Kranz, A36]; Cf. Eusebius, *Praeparatio Evangelica,* quotations from which can be read in *Theodoret of Cyrus: On Divine Providence,* trans. T. Halton, ACW 49 (New York and Mahwah, NJ, 1988), p. 85. James Lesher, *Xenophanes of Colophon: Fragments: A Text and Translation with Commentary* (Toronto, 1992), p. 124; also Niketas Siniossoglou, *Plato and Theodoret: The Christian Appropriation of Platonic Philosophy and the Hellenic Intellectual Resistance,* Cambridge Classical Studies (Cambridge, 2008), pp. 51, 71.

8. An example of sorites illustrating Theodoret's skill in logic.

9. Parmenides, fr. 8,4 [=Clement *Str.* 5.14.112=Eusebius, *P.e.* 1.8.5, 13.13. 39]. See Diels-Kranz 1.235. For text and trans. of the whole fragment see K.R.S., 248–49, where text is persuasively emended and translated: "whole and of a single kind, and unshaken and perfect"; see also *CQ* 20 (1970): 32–34; Hippolytus, *Ref.* 1. 11,12; Diogenes Laertius, 9.21–23 (Diels-Kranz I.217, 28A1).

10. For the combination of earth and fire cf. *Xenophanes,* 287.

11. Melissos (cf. *Affect.* 2.15) was a pantheist and an opponent of the atomist theories; cf. K.R.S., 390–401; Guthrie, *HGP* 1.337

12. Aetius, *Plac.* 2.1.6, p. 328; Stobaeus, 7–9.

13. See Diogenes Laertius, 9.34; Aetius, *Plac.* 1.3.18, p. 285, on which cf. D. Furley, *Greek Cosmologists* (Cambridge, 1987), I.117–22; K.R.S., 402f; also Hippolytus, *Ref.* 2.

14. On Metrodorus of Chios, pupil of Democritus, see K. Freeman, *The Pre-Socratic Philosophers: A Companion to Diels, Fragmente der Vorsokratiker,* 2d ed. (Oxford, 1959), 120–21; Freeman, *Ancilla to the Pre-Socratic Philosophers: A Complete Translation of the Fragments in Diels Fragmente der Vorsokratiker* (Oxford, 1956), 327. Aetius, *Plac.* 1.3.18, pp. 285–86.

15. [=Aetius, *Plac.* 1.3.18]. See Diels, *Dox.* 285.

16. [=Aetius, *Plac.* 1.3.19] For Ekphantus of Syracuse, a Pythagorean, cf. Diels, *Dox.* 286; Hippolytus, *Ref.* For his fragments see K. S. Guthrie, *The*

Pythagorean Sourcebook (Grand Rapids, 1987), 257–59, Stobaeus, *Flor.* 48, Guthrie, *HGP* 1.323–37.

17. [=Aetius, *Plac.* 1.3.21].

18. [=Aetius, *Plac.* 1.3.22]. Cf. Aristotle, *De anima* 1.2. On privation cf. Aristotle, *Metaph.* 1019a27.

19. On the fifth element see Aristotle, *De anima* 1.2, and D. E. Hahm, "The Fifth Element in Aristotle's *De philosophia*: A Critical Reexamination," in *Essays in Ancient Greek Philosophy*, vol. 2, ed. J. P. Anton and A. Preuss (Albany, NY, 1983), 404–28.

20. Xenocrates of Chalcedon succeeded Speusippus as head of the Academy and remained head for twenty-five years (399–314 B.C.); see Diels, *Dox.*, p. 288; G. Reale, *A History of Ancient Philosophy*, vol. 3: *The Systems of the Hellenistic Age*, ed. and trans. from the 3rd Italian ed. by J. R. Catan (Albany, N.Y., 1985), 73.

21. [=Aetius, *Plac.* 1.3.25]. On Zeno of Citium, son of Mnaseus, see Diels, *Dox.* 289; A. Graeser, *Zenon von Kition: Positionen und Probleme* (Berlin, 1975), 7; Hippolytus, *Ref.* 1.13.2.

22. [=Aetius, *Plac.* 1.3.19–26; 1.7.26, which assigns ἀκίνητον καί πεπρασμένον to Parmenides.] For Hippasos of Metapontus see Diels, *Dox.* 168, 192, ps.-Justin, *Exhort. ad Graec.* 3.

23. Cf. Aetius, *Plac.* 1.9.2 (Diels, *Dox.* 307–8).

24. [=Aetius, *Plac.* 1.9.2].

25. [=Aetius, *Plac.* 1.9.3]. Cf. Diels, *Dox.* 308.

26. Cf. Aetius, *Plac.* 1.4–5 (Diels, *Dox.* 308). See H. A. Wolfson, "Plato's Pre-existent Matter in Patristic Philosophy," in *The Classical Tradition: Literary and Historical Studies in Honor of H. Caplan*, ed. L. Wallach (Ithaca, NY, 1966), 409–20.

27. Aetius, *Plac.* 1.9.4–5.

28. Aetius, *Plac.* 1.9.7; cf. Diels, *Dox.* 283 and 141.

29. Aetius, *Plac.* 1.18.3; cf. Eusebius, *P.e.* 15.34.1.

30. Empedocles, fr. 13; cf. Furley, *Greek Cosmologists*, 1.80, Aetius, *Plac.* 1.18.2 (Diels, *Dox.* 316).

31. Aetius, *Plac.* 1.18.5.

32. Aetius, *Plac.* 1.18.4. See F. Wehrli, *Die Schule des Aristoteles: Texte und Kommentare*, vol. 5: *Straton von Lampsakos*, 10 vols. in 4 (Basel, 1967–69), fr. 54. See further D. Furley, "Strato's Theory of the Void," in *Aristoteles Werk und Wirkung Paul Moraux Gewidmet*, ed. J. Wiesner, 2 vols. (Berlin and New York, 1985–), 594–609.

33. Aetius, *Plac.* 2.1, 2 (for one), Diels, *Dox.* p. 327. Theodoret omits Ekphantos and Empedocles from the Aetios list. See Charles Mugler, *Deux thèmes de la cosmologie grecque: Devenir cyclique et pluralité des mondes* (Paris, 1953); also, W. Jaeger, *Theology of Early Greek Philosophy*, chap. 2. For Melissus see L.

Obertello, "Melissus of Samos and Plato on the Generation of the world," *Dionysius* 8 (1984): 3–18.

34. Aetius, *Plac.* 2.1.3; Diels, *Dox.* 32; Aetius, *Plac.* 2.14.2.

35. On many unlimited worlds cf. ACW 49.168, n. 2. On Diogenes and Epicurus cf. Cyril, *Juln.* 2.14; SC 322 (Paris, 1985), 232–34.

36. On shapes cf. Aetius, *Plac.* 2.2.1–4 (Diels, *Dox.* 329). See Theophilus, *Ad Autol.* 2.32, and SC 20.183, n. 2, which cites *Phaedo* 98, and Aristophanes, *Clouds*, and states that the first to teach that the world was spherical were the Pythagoreans, if not Pythagoras himself, at least Pirolaos.

37. Aetius, *Plac.* 2.2.1–4.

38. *Loc. cit.*

39. Aetius, *Plac.* 2.4.1–12. On the eternity of the world see D. T. Runia, "Philo's *De aeternitate mundi:* The Problem of Its Interpretation," *VigChr* 35 (1981): 105–51.

40. Aetius, *Plac.* 2.4.1–12, pp. 330–32.

41. Aetius, *Plac.* 2.13.1. Cf. Eusebius, *P.e.* 15.30.1.

42. Aetius, *Plac.* 2.13.3; Diels, *Dox.* 341. Cf. Eusebius, *P.e.* 15.30.3.

43. Aetius, *Plac.* 2.13.4. See Diels, *Dox.* 341.

44. Aetius, *Plac.* 2.13.5. Cf. Eusebius, *P.e.* 15.30.4, on which Guthrie, *HGP* 2.370–71.

45. Aetius, *Plac.* 2.13.7; Diels-Kranz 12A, 10–11; cf. Furley, *The Greek Cosmologists*, 1.25.

46. Aetius, *Plac.* 2.13.9; Diels, *Dox.* 342; Eusebius, *P.e.* 15.30.4.

For the event at Aegispotami, 405 B.C., cf. Plutarch, *Epit. apud Eusebium, P.e.* 1.8.12; Plutarch, *Lysander* c. 12; F. M. Cleve, *Giants of Pre-Sophistic Greek Philosophy: An Attempt to Reconstruct Their Thoughts* 2 (The Hague, 1973), 291D; Furley, *The Greek Cosmologists*, 74; M. L. West, "Anaxagoras and the Meteorite of 467 B.C.," *Journal of the British Astronomical Association* 70, no. 8 (1960): 368–69.

47. Aetius, *Plac.* 2.13.12; Diels, *Dox.* 342. Plutarch adds the phrase "like glue."

48. Aetius, *Plac.* 2.13.13; Diels, *Dox.* 343, is spherical, like the cosmos and the stars; 15.26.1: Anaximander, like a chariot wheel (on which see Guthrie, *HGP* 1.93–94).

49. Aetius, *Plac.* 2.13.14; Diels, *Dox.* 343. Cf. Eusebius, *P.e* 15.30.7.

50. Aetius, *Plac.* 2.13,15; Diels, *Dox.* 343. Cf. Eusebius, *P.e.* 15.30.8, which has fuller information on Heracleides (SC 338, 376). See F. Wehrli, *Die Schule*, V. fr. 113b. For Heracleides see also IV.23, V.18, and H. B. Gottschalk, *Heraclides of Pontus* (Oxford, 1980), esp. chaps. 3 and 4.

51. Aetius, *Plac.* 2.14.1; Diels, *Dox.* 343. Cf. Eusebius, *P.e.* 15.31.1, which attributes this view to the Stoics.

52. For Democritus as the source of the teachings of Epicurus, cf. Cicero, *ND* 2.66 and Pease, ed. (Cambridge, MA, 1955–58) 1.230–31 for a host of references. Diels, *Dox.* 344. On Cleanthes the Stoic see also 5.27.

53. Aetius, *Plac.* 2.20.3; Diels, *Dox.* 348.

54. Aetius, *Plac.* 2.20.6–7; Diogenes Laertius 2.8 and 15. See Cleve, *Giants of Pre-Sophistic Greek Philosophy,* 291.

55. Aetius, *Plac.* 2.20.9; Eusebius, *P.e.* 15.30.1.

56. Aetius, *Plac.* 2.20.10; Stobaeus, *Ecl.* 1.508. Cf. Eusebius, *P.e.* 15.30.4.

57. Aetius, *Plac.* 2.20.11. Cf. Eusebius, *P.e.* 15.23.6. See P. Moraux, "Quinta essentia," *RE* 24 (1963): 1196f., Simplicius, *Comm. on Aristotle De anima,* ed. Hayot, p. 68, 5, and Anaximenes (cf. Diels-Kranz, 1.199). See also Cyril, *Juln.* 2.15.

58 Aetius, *Plac.* 2.20.5. Cf. Eusebius, *P.e.* 15.23.4. See Plato, *Timaeus* 41d.

59. Aetius, *Plac.* 2.20, 12 (Diels, *Dox.* 349–50). Cf. Eusebius, *P.e.* 15.23.7. On Philolaus see K. Guthrie and T. Taylor, *The Pythagorean Writings* (Grand Rapids, MI, 1987),102–3; K. Freeman, *Ancilla,* 73–77; C. A. Hoffman, *Philolaos of Croton* (Cambridge, U.K., 1993) 266–70.

60. Aetius, *Plac.* 2.22, 3–5, *Plac.* 2.22, 2 (boat) and 2.20, 1 (chariot wheel). Cf. Eusebius, *P.e.* 15.25.2: Heraclitus says that it is curved, boat-shaped; 15.25.3.

61. Aetius, *Plac.* 2.20,1, Diels, *Dox.* 351; cf. Eusebius, *P.e.* 15.23.1, "twenty-eight times" 26,1 "twenty-seven times." On Anaximander cf. C. H. Kahn, *Anaximander and the Origins of Greek Cosmology* (New York, 1964).

62. For Empedocles cf. Eusebius, *P.e.* 15.23.8, on which see Guthrie, *HGP* 2.192–94.

63. For Anaxagoras cf. Eusebius, *P.e.* 15.24.2.

64. Aetius, *Plac.* 2.21.4; cf. Eusebius, *P.e.* 15.24.3, 6.31.

65. Aetius, *Plac.* 2.25.8; cf. Eusebius, *P.e.* 15.

66. For Anaximenes cf. Aetius, *Plac.* 2.25.1.2.

67. Aetius, *Plac.* 2.25.9; cf. Eusebius, *P.e.* 15.26.5.

68. Aetius, *Plac.* 2.25.9.

69. Aetius, *Plac.* 2.25.13; cf. Eusebius, *P.e.* 15.26.6.

70. Aetius, *Plac.* 2.26.1, 2. Eusebius, *P.e.* 15.27.1: The Stoics say that it is larger than the earth, like the sun. 27.2: Parmenides says that it is similar in size to the sun.

71. Aetius, *Plac.* 2.20–22.

72. Lucian, *Icaromenippus,* starts out with a satirical calculation on Menippus's journey from the earth to the moon, and then from the moon to the sun and to heaven.

73. Aeschylus, *Prometheus Vinctus* 44 [=Clement, *Str.* 5.1.5]. See Canivet, *Entre,* 205.

74. Theodoret uses the same two similes in *De providentia,* 9.5. Cf. Plato, *Resp.* 2.363d.

75. Xenophon, *Mem.* 4.7.6 [=Eusebius, *P.e.* 14.1. 5].

76. See *Affect.* 1.97 and note.

77. Xenophon, *Mem.* 1.1.11–14 [=Eusebius, *P.e.* 15.62.1–4].

78. Theodoret is here uncharacteristically forthcoming about his sources. On the importance of his remark on Aetios cf. Guthrie, *HGP* 1, pp. xiii–xiv.

79. This is now regarded as pseudo-Plutarch; cf. K. Ziegler, "Plutarchos," *RE* 21 (1951) 636–962.

80. Porphyry, *Hist. phil. fr.*, Nauck. See *supra*, Disc. 1, 27 and 2, 95.

81. *Timaeus*, 29de [=Eusebius, *P.e.* 11.21.2].

82. =Clement, *Str.* 5.11.75, but not Plato. [Cf. GCS 2.376].

83. Plato, *Resp.* 509b [=Eusebius, *P.e.* 11.21.5].

84. Plato, *Tim.* 28bc [=Eusebius, *P.e.* 11.29.3–4].

85. Plato, *Tim.* 28c [Eusebius, *P.e.* 11.29.4].

86. Plato, *Tim.* 38c.

87. Euripides, *Phoen.* 546–547 [=Eusebius, *P.e.* 11.31].

88. Plato, *Tim.* 29a [=Eusebius, *P.e.* 11.31.1].

89. Plato, *Tim.* 29a [=Eusebius, *P.e.* 11.31.1].

90. Plato, *Tim.* 32b [=Eusebius, *P.e.* 11.32.2].

91. Plato, *Tim.* 38b [=Eusebius, *P.e.*11.32.3].

92. Plato, *Polit.* 269d–e [=Eusebius, *P.e.* 11.32.6]. Also quoted in Athenagoras, *Leg.* 16.4.

93. Plato, *Polit.* 272e–273a [=Eusebius, *P.e.* 11.34.1–2].

94. See *supra*, 4.11 and 12.9

95. Plato, *Polit.* 273bc [=Clement, *Str.* 3.3.19].

96. Plato, *Tim.* 31a [=Clement, *Str.* 5.12.79=Eusebius, *P.e.* 11.13.2].

97. Cf. Hesiod, *Theogony*, 116, and Hesiod, *Theogony*, ed. M. L. West (Oxford, 1966), 192–93, for notes on "Chaos" (best translated as "Chasm").

98. The interdependency of the arts and crafts is also stressed in Theodoret, *Provid.* 6.31. Cf. ACW 49.54 and 192, n. 39.

99. Cf. Ps. 134:6.

100. Cf. Irenaeus, *Adversus haereses* 2.8 and 9 for proof of one Creator of one universe.

101. On the banishment of the fallen angels cf. Isa. 14:12.

102. Cf. Job 38:11; Jer. 5:22.

103. On the seasons borrowing from one another cf. Theodoret, *Provid.* 1.33 and ACW 49.174, n. 50.

104. On the Nile cf. Philo (*De vita Moyses*, 1.114–15): "Egypt is almost the only country, apart from those in southern latitudes, which is unvisited by one of the year's seasons—winter.... The river begins to rise as the summer opens, and ceases when it ceases" (trans. F. H. Colson, *Philo*, vol. 6 [Cambridge, MA, 1959], 333, 335). On its flooding and various theories to explain it cf. Aetius, *Plac.* 4.1.1–6 [=Diels, *Dox.* 384–85]; Hippolytus, *Ref.* 1.8.5, ed. Markovich, who gives Hippolytus's sources as Aristotle, fr. 248, ed. Rose; Seneca, *Quaest. nat.* 4a, 2.17, and Diodorus, 1.38.4. Herodotus, [Bk. 2.19–27, and A. B. Lloyd, *Herodotus Book II Commentary*, vol. 2 (Leiden, 1976), 91–125.

105. Cf. Clement, *Protr.* 4.58.

106. For the lityerses cf. Athenaeus, *Deip.* 415b. Lityerses was a bastard son of Minos, who challenged wayfarers to a reaping match and, if they lost, bound their heads to his sheaves. The dithyramb was a form of poetry first cultivated by Doric writers to celebrate the birth of Dionysus. For the paean cf. Clement, *Protr.* 1.1, Thucydides, 7.44. For the oupingos cf. Athenaeus, *Deip.* 619b.

107. Ps. 103:22.

108. For the cicadas cf. Clement, *Protr.* 1.1; Basil, *Hex.* 8.7; Gregory Nazianzus, *Orat.* 28.24. For the farewell to Sirens and Muses cf. *Affect.* 8.1.

109. On God as shipbuilder and pilot cf. Theodoret, *Provid.* 2.1–3 (ACW 49.24 and 175, n. 1).

110. Cf. 1 Cor. 14:25.

NOTES TO DISCOURSE 5

1. For the magnet image cf. Clement, *Str.* 2.6.26 and 7.2.9, quoting Plato, *Ion* 533d, where Plato compares its attractive powers with those of the Muses. See also Augustine, *Civ. Dei* 21.4; Palladius, *De gentibus Indiae et Bragmanibus*, ed. J. Duncan M. Derret; *C&M* 21 (1960): 109; A. Radl, *Der Magnetstein in der Antike: Quellen und Zusammenhängen* (Stuttgart, 1988).

2. 1 Cor. 1:18.

3. Isa. 1:19, on which see A. C. Vrame, "Theodoret Bishop of Kyros as an Exegete of Isaiah I: A Translation of His Commentary with an Introduction," *GOTR* 34 (1989): 129–49. For Theodoret's stress here and elsewhere on free will, cf. Nemesius, *De nat. hom.*, on which cf. P. B. Clayton, Jr., *Theodoret, Bishop of Cyrus and the Mystery of the Incarnation in the Late Antiochene Christianity*, diss. Union Theological Seminary, New York, 1985; now published, Oxford, 2007), pp. 240–42; W. Telfer, *Nemesius of Emesa* (Philadelphia, 1955); T. Halton, "The Five Senses in Nemesius, *De nat. hom.*, and Theodoret, *De Providentia*," *SP* 20 (1987): 94–101.

4. Ps. 33 [34]:12–13.

5. Ps. 33 [34]:14–15. 6. Ps. 33 [34]:16.

6. Ps. 33 [34]:17.

7. John 7:37.

8. Matt. 11:28.

9. Hesiod, *Works and Days*, 410 and 413 [=Eusebius, *P.e.* 14.27.1].

10. Plato, *Resp.* 3.398a, also cited with the same comment at Discourse 2, 6, note 7.

11. For the legend of Cadmus, founder of Thebes, sowing the dragon's teeth cf. Plato, *Laws* 2.663e.

12. Cf. Origen, *C. Cels.* 4.36 and Chadwick, ed., 211 and n. 1. Theodoret's source here is Eusebius, *P.e.* 15.5.1, on which see J. Sirinelli, *Les vues historiques d'Eusèbe* (Dakar, 1961), 353.

13. Homer, *Od.* 18.310.

14. Theognis, 11.425–27 [=Clement, *Str.* 3.3.15, FOTC 85, p. 265, n. 53]

15. Euripides, fr. 449 [=Clement, *Str.* 3.3.15, 2; FOTC 85, p. 265, n. 54]. See Plutarch, 2.899a.

16. Herodotus 1.32 [=Clement, *Str* 3.3.16; FOTC 85, p. 266, n. 56].

17. Cf. Plato, *Phaedo* 81–82a [=Eusebius, *P.e.* 13.16.4–6]. See Canivet, *Entre*, 209.

18. Plato, *Crat.* 400b–e [=Clement, *Str.* 3.16.3, FOTC 85, p. 266, n. 59]. See C. J. de Vogel, "The Soma-Sema Formula: Its Function in Plato and Plotinus Compared to Christian Writers," in *Neoplatonism and Early Christian Thought*, ed. H. J. Blumenthal and R. A. Markus (London, 1981), 79–95.

19. Philolaus, fr. 14 [=Clement, *Str.* 3.3.17, FOTC 85, p. 267, n. 60]. See also Athenagoras, *Leg.* 6.1. For a discussion of the fragment see Guthrie, *HGP*. 1.331. Philolaos was a Pythagorean from southern Italy, either Croton or Tarentum; cf. F. M. Cleve, *The Giants of Pre-sophistic Greek Philosophy: An Attempt to Reconstruct Their Thoughts*, 2 vols. (The Hague, 1973), 2.451f.; T. A. Dorandi, in *ANRW* II. 36.5, 3777–84.

20. Plato, *Resp.* 3.410c [=Clement, *Str.* 4.4.18].

21. Not Timaeus but, apparently through a lapse of memory, Timon, author of the *Silloi*. This is Timon, fr. 22 [=Clement. *Str.* 5.1.11=Eusebius, *P.e.* 15.62.14]. See Canivet, *Entre*, 209–10, on this citation from memory.

22. For Plutarch he is using ps.-Plutarch, *On the Opinions of the Philosophers*, Bk. 4, c. 2. For Porphyry he may be using his lost *On Miscellaneous Questions*, cf. Telfer, trans. *Nemesius* (LCC), 260, 268. Aetius, *Plac.* furnishes most of the data found in paragraphs 17–23; cf. Diels, *Dox.*, 45–49, 273–444.

23. Aetius, *Plac.* 4.2.1, Diels, *Dox* 386. But see too *Plac.* 1.11.6. On Thales cf. Guthrie, *HGP* 1.45–72.

24. Aetius, *Plac.* 4.2.2. Alcmaeon was a junior fellow citizen of Pythagoras at Croton; cf. *CAH* 4.548, Guthrie, *HGP* 1. 350f, Aristotle, *De anima*, 405a30.

25. Aetius, *Plac.* 4.2.3 for Pythagoras's self-moving number.

26. Aetius, *Plac.* 4.2.4. For Xenocrates cf. Nemesius, *De natura hominis* 2; Cicero, *ND*, 1.34, ed. Pease, 1.245.

27. Aetius, *Plac.* 4.2.5; cf. Plato, *Theaetetus* 153b–c.

28. Aetius, *Plac.* 4.2.6, Diels, *Dox.* 387. For Aristotle's entelechy cf. Aristotle, *De anima* 412a, 27–28; Hippolytus, Ref. 7 and E. Osborn, *La morale dans la pensée chrétienne primitive* (Paris 1984):, 280–82. For Porphyry's refutation cf. Eusebius, *P.e* 15.11.4.

29. Clearchus is here apparently a mistake for Dikaiarchos, pupil of

Aristotle; cf. Aetius, *Plac.* 4.2.7, Diels, *Dox.* 387, Guthrie, *HGP* 1.315; Nemesius gets it wrong too: Deinarchos, *De Nat. hom.*, 2.

30. Aetius, *Plac.* 4.3.2. Somewhat differently Stobaeus *Ecl.* 1.49 lists Anaximenes, Anaxagoras, Archelaus, and Diogenes; Diels, *Dox.* 387.

31. Aetius, *Plac.* 4.3.3. Diels, *Dox.* 388.

32. Aetius, *Plac.* 4.3.3 names only Parmenides and Hippasos.

33. Aetius, *Plac.* 4.3.6. Heracleides Pontikos, fr. 113b; F. Wehrli, *Die Schule des Aristoteles* (Basel and Stuttgart, 1950), 7:34.

34. Aetius, *Plac.* 4.3.11. For the soul in Epicurus see A. A. Long and D. N. Sedley, *The Hellenistic Philosophers* (Cambridge and New York, 1987), vol. 1, 14C, p. 67, vol. 2, 68.

35. Diels, *Dox.* *389.* On Empedocles, see Guthrie, *HGP* 1. 313–14, D. B. Claus, *Toward the Soul* (New Haven, 1981), 114–15.

36. On Critias see Diels, *Dox.* 213–14, 389; D. N. Levin, in Sprague, *Older Sophists*, 241–70, esp. 249, no. 23., citing Aristotle, *De anima*, 1.2.405b. Others, like Critias, claim that [the soul is] blood, and Philoponus, on Aristotle, *De anima*, Intro. 9.19: Critias, one of the Thirty. For he stated that the soul was blood. "For blood flowing around the heart," he says, "is what perception is for men" [=*Critias* fr. 8, ed. Bach]. Critias is also mentioned in Tertullian, *De anima* 5.2, Nemesius, *De nat. hom* c. 2: *De anima*, PG 40.536.

37. [=Eusebius, *P.e.* 15.60.1] Cf. Tertullian, *De anima* 14.2.16; ps.-Justin, *Exhort.; c.* 6; Guthrie, *Sourcebook*, 32–33.

38. On Xenocrates see Diels, *Dox.* 389.

39. On Aristotle cf. Tertullian, *De anima*,14.2.

40. [=Eusebius, *P.e.* 15.60.2] Cf. Tertullian, *De anima*, 14, 2. Aetius, *Plac.* 4.21.1–4 (*SVF* 2.836). What Aetius says is: From the commanding faculty there are seven parts of the soul that grow out and stretch out into the body like the tentacles of an octopus; IV. 21, 1–2. Cf. C. J. de Vogel, *GP*, 3.88, Long and Sedley, *The Hellenistic Philosophers*, vol. 1, no. 53H, 315, vol. 2, 314, M. E. Reesor, *The Nature of Man in Early Stoic Philosophy* (New York, 1989), 137–47.

41. The successors of Pythagoras who added ether to the four elements.

42. For a similar summary of different viewpoints cf. Sextus Empiricus, *Against the Logicians* 1.313.

43. [Aetius, *Plac.* 4.5.2=Eusebius, *P.e.* 15.61.2] Strato, fr. 18, *Die Schule des Aristoteles*, vol. 5, V, ed. F. Wehrli (Basel and Stuttgart, 1950). Strato of Lampsachus succeeded Theophrastus as head of the Lyceum (cf. Clement, *Str.* 1.14.63), which he directed from 287 to 269 B.C. He wrote a work, now lost, called *On Discoveries* (cf. *Str.* 1.14.61, 1.16.77). See de Vogel, *GP*, v. 2.724, quoting Plutarch, *De libidine et aegritudine*, c. 4 on one central organ. See also Tertullian, *De anima* 14.5, 15.5.

44. [=Aetius, *Plac.* 4.5.3=Eusebius, *P.e* 15.61.3] Erasistratus was a Greek anatomist and physician, fl. c. 300 B.C. He founded a school of anatomy at Alexandria that studied the convolutions of the brain Aetius, *Plac.* 4.5.3

(Diels, *Dox.* 391. Cf. Tertullian, *De anima* 15.5. For the epikranis, membrane of the brain, cf. Theodoret, *Provid.*, 27–28, ACW 49.43 and notes, 188–89.

45. [Aetius, *Plac.* 4.5.4 = Eusebius, *P.e.* 15.61.4] Herophilus, an outstanding physician of Alexandria, third century B.C., who is credited with the discovery of the nervous system and the function of the brain; cf. de Vogel, *GP*, 3.948, Tertullian, *De anima* 15.5.

46. [Aetius, *Plac.* 4.5.5] On Epicurus, cf. Tertullian, *De anima* 15.5: "within the structure of the breast."

47. See M. R. Wright, *Empedocles:The Extant Fragments* (New Haven, 1981), 252.

48. [Aetius, *Plac.* 4.5.8; cf. Diels, *Dox.*, 391.]

49. Cf. Clement, *Str.* 5.13.88: "The Pythagoreans say that mind comes to man by divine providence." See also Minucius Felix, *Octavius* 19.6. For belief in the soul's indestructibility in Anaxagoras see Diels-Kranz 59 A96 [=Aetius, *Plac.* 7.], which, however, is characterized by D. Furley, *The Greek Cosmologists* (Cambridge and New York, 1987), 1.154 and n. 6 as "one solitary and very unreliable report." For Diogenes of Apollonia see D. B. Claus, *Toward the Soul*, 139–40.

50. For Heraclitus see Diels, *Dox.* 392, Guthrie, *HGP*, 1.433.

51. For Stoic doctrine of universal conflagration (Gk. 'ἐκπυρωσις) cf. Diogenes Laertius, 10.101–2; Justin, *1 Apol.* 20; Tatian, *Orat* 3.1; Athenagoras, *Leg.* 1. Philolaus was a Pythagorean from southern Italy, either Croton or Tarentum. See Cleve, *The Giants*, 2:451f. Theophilus, *Ad Autol.* 2.37, M. Spanneut, *Le stoicisme des pères de l'église de Clément de Rome à Clément d'Alexandrie* (Paris, 1957)

52. See Diels, *Dox.* 393.

53. Cf. Plato, *Tim.* 77b [=Clement, *Str.* 8.4.10]

54. Cf. Aetius, V. 26. For a careful source study of this passage on Plato, Aristotle and the Stoics cf. J. Mansfeld, "Doxography and Dialectic" in *ANRW* II.36.5 (1990) 3056 ff. esp. 3188–90, who identifies *Stromata* 8.10.3–4 as the source.

55. Aristotle, *De anima*, 2.2 [=Clement, *Str.* 8.4.10]. See further D. J. O'Meara, "Remarks on Dualism and the Definition of Soul in Aristotle's *De Anima*," *Museum Helveticum* 44 (1987): 168–74.

56. Cf. Clement, *Str.* 8.4: "But, according to the Stoics a plant is neither animate nor an animal."

57. For Zeno of Citium cf. Eusebius, *P.e.* 15.20.1; Diels, *Dox.* 470, Diogenes Laertius 7.

58. According to H. Raeder, "De Theodoreti Graecarum Affectionum Curatione Quaestiones criticae," diss. (Halle, 1900), 109, this is a wrong reference, which should be assigned to Arius Didymus. See Canivet, *Entre*, 211 and 311; also Eusebius, *P.e.* 15.20.6 (SC 338.326) and H. Diels, *Dox.* (Berlin, 1958), 471. See also D. E. Hahm, "The Ethical Doxography of Arius Didymus,"

ANRW II.36.4, 2935–3055. W. Telfer, *Cyril of Jerusalem and Nemesius of Emesa*, LCC 4 (Philadelphia, 1955). See also Athenagoras, *Leg.* 20.3, Nemesius of Emesa, *De nat.hom.*, trans. Telfer, 262–63 for Numenius's definition of soul, on which cf. A. Tripolitis, *The Doctrine of the Soul in the Thought of Plotinus and Origen* (New York, 1968), 26–30.

59. Longinus, fr. 7 [=Eusebius, *P.e.* 15.21.3]. This is part of a longer fragment in Eusebius; cf. SC 338.328 and n. 1. See also de Vogel, *GP*, 3.1363, quoting Porphyry, *Vita Plotini*, 20, a review of the philosophers. For Cleanthes cf. Minucius Felix, *Oct.*, 19.10, ACW 39, 86, and 270 n. 253. Tertullian, *Apol.* 21. Longinus was a disciple of Ammonius Saccas, and is not to be confused with ps.-Longinus, author of *On the Sublime*.

60. Cf. Aetius, *Plac.* 4.6,1.

61. See E. Bréhier, *Chrysippe* (Paris, 1910), 164–71.

62. Cf. Plato, *Laws* 10.898e–900a. For the claims of fate and the arguments against astral determinism see Origène, *Philocalie 21–27: Sur le libre arbitre* (SC 226, Paris, 1976), 130–40.

63. Plato, *Laws* 1.626e [=Eusebius, *P.e.* 12.27.2]. On free will cf. A. Dihle, *The Theory of Will in Classical Antiquity* (Berkeley, 1982).

64. Plato, *Laws* 1.644e [=Eusebius, *P.e.* 12.27.4].

65. Plato, *Laws* 10.904bc [=Eusebius, *P.e.* 12.52.26].

66. Plato, *Laws* 10.904de [=Eusebius, *P.e.* 12.52.27].

67. Plato, *Resp.* 2.379bd [=Eusebius, *P.e.* 13.3.9–14].

68. Homer, *Il.* 24. 527–28, 530.

69. Plato, *Resp* 2. 380b–c [=Eusebius, *P.e.* 13.3.17–18].

70. Plato, *Alc.* 1.133c [=Eusebius, *P.e.* 11.27.5; Tertullian, *De an.* 1.2–4 does not think much of Socrates' ability to philosophize on the soul.

71. Plato, *Phaedo* 79a–c [=Eusebius, *P.e.* 11.27.6–8].

72. Plato, *Phaedo* 80a [=Eusebius, *P.e.* 11.27.13].

73. Plato, *Phaedo* 80b–c [=Eusebius, *P.e.* 11.27.14].

74. Plato, *Phaedo* 80d–e [=Eusebius, *P.e.* 11.27.16–17].

75. Eusebius, *P.e.* 2.13 suggests that in the gnostic sects, unlike the orthodox hierarchies in the chief episcopal sees, succession did not guarantee uncontaminated transmission of teaching.

76. Cf. Clement, *Protr.* 5.66.

77. Cf. Aetius, *Plac.* Eusebius, *P.e.* 15.5.1, 15.34.2, Clement. *Str.* 5.14.90 [=Eusebius, *P.e.* 13,13,4]. See Athenagoras, *Leg.* 25, 2, ed. M. Markovich, *Legatio pro Christianis* (Berlin and New York, 1990) for a host of references. On Aristotle not countenancing providence this side of the moon, cf. *Affect.* 6.7, and n. 10.

78. Gen. 2:7.

79. Cf. Exod. 21:22.

80. Job 10:9–12.

81. Ps. 118:73.

82. On the unity of the human race cf. Gen. 1:27, 2:24.

83. On the similar potential of women and men for philosophy cf. Clement, *Str.* 4.19.122.

84. Anacharsis, ep. 1 [=Clement, *Str.* 1.16.77]. See J. F. Kinstrand, *Anacharsis: The Legend and the Apophthegmata* (Uppsala, 1981), esp. 17–32.

85. For the Brahmans, the highest caste in India; cf. Clement, *Str.* 1.15.68, 3.7.60. See also Chrysostom, *Jud. et Gent.* 12.4.

86. Homer, *Il.* 13.5–6. Cf. Clement, *Paed.* 1.6.36.

87. Xenophon, *Cyropaidia*, passim. The four cardinal virtues are also dealt with in Aristotle, *De virt. et vitiis*, 2.1–6.

88. [=Clement, *Str.* 1.14.59]. Clement tells us there were "four from Asia – Thales of Miletus, Bias of Priene, Pittacus of Mitylene, and Cleobulus of Lindos; two from Europe – Solon, the Athenian, and Chilon, the Lacedaemonian. And the seventh, some say was Periander of Corinth, others, Anacharsis, the Scythian, others, Epimenides, others have enumerated Acusilaus, the Argive, and others, Pherecydes of Syros. And Plato substituted Myso, the Chenian." See Diogenes Laertius 1.13.41, Augustine, *Civ. Dei*, 18.25.

89. Plato, *Protag.* 343a.

90. See n. 72 and n. 73. For a similar attack on the Hellenists cf. "croaking and cawing like crows," Tatian, *Orat.*1.2–3. See R. Dostalova, "Christentum und Hellenismus: Zur Herausbildung einer neuen Kulturellen Identität im 4 Jahrhundert," *Byz Slav* 44 (1982): 1–12. In his *History of Monks*, 27.4, Theodoret describes Baradatus: "he sometimes syllogizes better and more powerfully than those well versed in the labyrinths of Aristotle." In the same work, 2.21, he focuses on one Asterius "who had been reared in sophistic falsity and then made his way into the church of the heretics…craftily advocating falsehood and using artifice against the truth…covering over his falsehood with a smooth tongue as if with a decoy and spreading out the web of his syllogisms like nets." *Theodoret of Cyrrhus A History of the Monks*, trans. R. W. Price, Cistercian Studies 88 (Kalamazoo, MI, 1985); Symeon Stylites, 26, 13, p. 167. Earlier the syllogisms of Aristotle and Chrysippus had been downplayed by Basil in Basil, *Contra Eunomium*, SC 299.172–73 and n. 1.

91. Lucian also castigates those with little Greek except the occasional swear-word. See also Gregory Nazianzus, *Orat.* 4.102.

92. Most of these questions are answered in Clement, *Str.* 1.14.64–65, which deals with the διαδχη among Greek philosophers. Parmenides succeeded Xenophanes, Zeno succeeded Parmenides, Speussipus was the successor of Plato, and was succeeded by Xenocrates and then by Polemo. Zeno of Citium, founder of the Stoics, was succeeded by Cleanthes and Chrysippus. On Speusippus cf. T. A. Dorandi, in *ANRW* II.36.5, 3761–92, esp. 3763–66.

93. On the translations of the Bible cf. B. M. Metzger, *The Early Versions of the New Testament* (Oxford, 1977); art. "Bibelübersetzungen," *TRE* 6: 160–216; "Bible, IV (Texts and Versions), *NCE* 2.414–61; E. Tov, "Die griechische

Bibelübersetzungen," ANRW II.20.1 (1987) 121–89. J. N. Guinot, " 'Le Syrien' dans les commentaires de Théodoret," *SP* 25 (Leuven, 1993), 60–91 notes the strange absence here of any reference to a Syriac translation.

94. Cf. Justin, *1 Apol.* 16.8; *2 Apol.* 10.8, Athenagoras, *Leg.* 11.3; Clement, *Str.* 4. 59; Origen, *C.Cels.* 7.41; Gregory Nyssa, *Deit.*: "You enter a bakeshop and ask for bread. Instead of selling you the bread, the baker wants to talk to you about the 'begotten' and the 'unbegotten' son," PG 46.557; Tertullian, *Apol.* 46: *Deum quilibet opifex Christianus et invenit et ostendit et exinde totum quod in deum quaeritur re quoque adsignat.*

95. Anacharsis, *Ep.* 1 [=Clement, *Str.* 1.16.77]. On Anacharsis, a Scythian prince, see Kinstrand, *Anacharsis*; S. K. Stowers, *Letter-Writing in Greco-Roman Antiquity* (Philadelphia, 1986), 118–21, and A. J. Malherbe, *The Cynic Epistles,* trans. A. M. McGuire (Missoula, Mont., 1977). On Scythians speaking Greek see R. A. Greer, *Broken Lights and Mended Lives: Theology and Common Life in the Early Church* (University Park, Pa., 1986), 187. On Theodoret's knowledge of Greek and Syriac cf. SC 79, nos. 9—10. On Hebrew, N. Fernandez Marcos, "Teodoreto de Ciro y la lengua hebrea" *Henoch* 9 (1987): 39–54.

96. 1 Cor. 14:11.

97. On the Illyrians see c. 26, "The Romans in Illyria," *CAH* 7, 822–55. The land of Paeonia lies north of Macedonia and west of Thrace. The Taulantii were subdued by Octavian; cf. *CAH* 10.85. 88. Atintania is in the central part of the valley of the river Aous, east of Epirus.

98. On Persian eloquence cf. Plato, *Laws* 3.693d–694a.

99. For the labyrinths of the logic of Chrysippus cf. SVF 2.76–94.

100. The Ishmaelites, Arab tribesmen of the Syrian desert, also known as Saracens, are frequently mentioned in Theodoret's *Religious History,* e.g., 6.4; 26.13, 18, 21. In 26.13, for instance, we are told: "the Ishmaelites, who were enslaved in their many tens of thousands in the darkness of impiety have been illuminated by his (i.e., Symeon Stylites) standing on the pillar....The Ishmaelites, arriving in companies, two or three hundred at a time, sometimes even a thousand, disown with shouts their ancestral imposture." Trans. Price, 166–67 and n. 18.

101. On Roman conciseness cf. Eusebius *P.e* 10.4.13–20. On the knowledge of Latin see W. V. Harris, *Ancient Literacy* (Cambridge, MA, 1989), 175–85.

102. On the languages of Syria cf. Harris, *Ancient Literacy,* 187f.

103. Cf. Plato, *Phaedrus* 253c. See K. T. Ware, "The Meaning of 'Pathos' in Abba Isaias and Theodoret of Cyrus" *SP* 20 (Leuven, 1987): 315–22.

104. Ps. 138:6.

105. Hippocrates was born on the island of Cos c. 460 and became known as the father of medicine. A corpus of Hippocratic writings was preserved in the library of Alexandria. Galen (ca. A.D. 130–200), philosopher and physician, was a native of Pergamum, lectured at Rome (A.D. 162), and was a pro-

lific writer on all branches of knowledge. Theophrastus (372–287 B.C.) was a disciple of Plato and Aristotle, a philosopher and naturalist, author of, among other titles, *A History of Plants.*

NOTES TO DISCOURSE 6

1. Discourse 6 occupies a central place and role in the *Curatio* and is one of the best composed; cf. Canivet, *Entre,* 215–22. Theodoret, *Provid.* 3 begins with a similar nautical *prosopopoiia,* a familiar topos, but here it may have been suggested by the passage from Plato, *Polit.* 269d–e, quoted at 4.44.

2. For similar fault-finding, cf. Theodoret, *Provid.* 7.4–7.

3. On Fate, ειμαρμένη, see D. Amand, *Fatalisme* (Louvain, 1943, repr. Amsterdam, 1973); esp. 4–6 for Plato and 6–13, for Stoicism. On Destiny, πεπρωομένη, cf. A. Magris, *The Cult of Τύχη,* 2 vols. (Trieste, 1984); *Entre.,* 312f. For Τύχη see art. "Fortuna," *RAC,* 182–97. The cult of Τύχη was especially in vogue in Antioch. On the Moirai, or Moerae (Lat. *Parcae*), see W. C. Greene, *Moira: Fate, Good and Evil in Greek Thought* (Cambridge, MA, 1944). The three sisters identified with the Fates were, in Hesiod, *Theog.,* 217–22, Clotho, Lachesis, and Atropos, the first spinning the thread of life, the second, measuring it out, and the third, severing it. On 'ανάγκη, especially associated with the Atomists Leucippus and Democritus, cf. Aetius, *Plac.* 1.25.3.

4. Theodoret returns to the question of necessity/free will in 12.87f. See A. Dihle, "Liberté et destin dans l'antiquité tardive," *RThPh* 121 (1989): 129–47.

5. Cf. Homer, *Il.* 16.431f.

6. Homer, *Od.* 1.68f. Chrysippus likes to quote Homer too; cf. Eusebius, *P.e.* 6.8, SC 266.182–87, quoting N. Zeegers-Vander Vorst, *Les citations des poètes grecs* (Louvain, 1972), 94: "Chrysippe est, parmi les auteurs anciens, le plus grand citateur de poètes."

7. Cf. Eusebius, *P.e.* 14.16.1. Diagoras of Melos was the best known of the "atheists" to the Fathers: see *Affect.* 3.4 and n. 3.

8. Protagoras, Fr. 2 [=Eusebius, *P.e.* 14.3.7, 19.10]. Protagoras of Abdera in Thrace was a sophist notorious for his agnosticism, especially in his treatise *On the Gods,* which opened with the sentiment quoted here (and also at 2.113) and for which he was banished from Athens; cf. *CAH* 5. 378–79.

9. *Sent.* 1, fr. 359. Epicurus was criticized by many of the Fathers for denying divine providence; cf. Eusebius, *P.e.* 15.34.1; Hippolytus, *Ref.* 1.22.3, "Epikur" *RAC* 5.681–819, esp. 791ff.; Dessi, "Elementi epicurei in Clemente Alessandrino," *Athenaeum* 60 (1982): 402–35; D. Obink, "The Atheism of Epicurus," *GRBS* 30 (1989): 187–223.

10. [=Eusebius, *P.e.* 15.5.1]. On Aristotle's limiting Providence to the

310   THEODORET OF CYRUS: *A CURE FOR PAGAN MALADIES*

moon cf. Theodoret, *Provid.* 2.3 (ACW 49.170, n. 14), A. J. Festugière, *L'idéal religieuse des Grecs et l'Évangile* (Paris, 1981), Excursus C, 221–63 and D. T. Runia, "Festugière Revisited: Aristotle in the Greek Patres," *VigChr* 42 (1988): 1–34; L. J. Elders, "The Greek Christian Authors and Aristotle," *Doctor Communis* 43 (1990): 26–57.

11. On Oenomaus of Gadara, a second-century Syrian Greek, a Cynic philosopher, and critic of oracles in his *The Charlatans Exposed,* see D. Amand, *Fatalisme,* 75 and 129–34; D. R. Dudley, *A History of Cynicism* (London, 1937), 162f., G. Reale, *A History of Ancient Philosophy,* trans. J. Caton (Albany, NY, 1990), 4:153–54; J. Hammerstaedt, *Die Orakelkritik des Kynikers Oenomaus* (Frankfurt am Main, 1988); Hammerstaedt, *ANRW* II.36.5, 2834–65. For a convenient French translation of the fragments cf. L. Paquet, *Les Cyniques Grecs* (Ottawa, 1975), 233–63. Most of the fragments are found in Eusebius, *P.e.,* for which cf. SC 266.30–109). Theodoret mentions him by name only here and at 10.42. See F. Gasco Lacalle, "Cristianos y cínicos: Una tipificación del fenómeno cristiano durante el siglo II," *Memorias de Historia Antigua* 7 (1986): 111–19.

12. Oenomaus, fr.14 [=Eusebius, *P.e.* 6.7.2–3], SC 266.162–65; Paquet, *Les Cyniques Grecs,* 257. For Democritus cf. Aristotle, *De gen. anim.,* 5.8.789; for Chrysippus, *SVF* 2.978, see R. MacMullen, *Paganism in the Roman Empire* (New Haven, 1981), 10 and 145, n. 42.

13. Oenomaus, fr. 14.

14. Oenomaus, fr. 14 [=Eusebius, *P.e.* 6.7.20]. See H. W. Attridge, "The Philosophical Critique of Religion in the Early Empire," *ANRW* II.16.1 (1978): 45–78, esp. 56–59.

15. Here begins a lengthy borrowing from Eusebius, *P.e.* 6.8.8–10 (SC 266.186), which in turn is a borrowing from Diogenianus, *Adv. Chrysippum.* Diogenianus is not identified here by Theodoret, but he is mentioned at 10.19–20 and 42 in connection with oracles. See M. Isnarde Parente, "Diogeniano, gli Epicurei e la Tuvch," *ANRW* II.36.4, 2424–45.

16. This definition of Necessity is characterized in Greek by a series of puns difficult to match in English; cf. Eusebius, *P.e.* 6.8.8–9; N. D. Robertson, *Nemesis: The History of a Social and Religious Idea in Early Greece,* University Microfilms (Ann Arbor, MI, 1969), 16.

17. See L. Pearson, *Popular Ethics in Ancient Greece* (Stanford, CA, 1962), 39–48, 69–73.

18. For Obligation (Gk. χρέος) and Destiny (ειμαρμένη) see Aetius, *Plac.* 1.27–28c.

19. See B. C. Dietrich, *Death, Fate, and the Gods* (London, 1965).

20. Cf. Stobaeus, *Ecl.* 1.79, quoted in *SVF* 2. 264. Plato, *Resp.* 10. 617bc, 620d, *Leg.* 12.960c.

21. Cf. Eusebius, *P.e.* 15.15.6. See also Plotinus, *Enn.* 3.2.13; Amand, *Fatalisme* 6–13. Theophilus of Antioch, *Ad Autol.* 2.4 lumps Chrysippus with

Epicurus in denying the existence of providence. On adrasatea, cf. Adravsteia, LSJ, p. 24 and *Supplement*, p. 7.

22. For Pythagoras, cf. Aetius, *Plac.* 1.25.2; Eusebius, *P.e.* 6.7.17–18. For Democritus and Chrysippus Eusebius, *P.e.* 6.7.17–18.

23. For Parmenides cf. Aetius, *Plac.* 1.25.3.

24. For Heraclitus, cf. Aetius, *Plac.* 1.27.1.

25. For Chrysippus on Fatality see Aetius, *Plac.* 1.27.2, and Diels, *Dox.* 32.

26. [=Aetius, *Plac.* 1.27.5]. Zeno of Citium in Cyprus, 335 B.C.–263 B.C., studied philosophy under the Cynics but founded his own school in the Painted Porch, or Stoa Poikile, whence the name Stoicism.

27. [=Aetius, *Plac.* 1.25.4].

28. On τύχη in Plato [=Aetius, *Plac.* 1.29.1].

29. On τύχη in Aristotle [=Aetius, *Plac.* 1.29.2] see G. Verbeke, "Happiness and Chance in Aristotle," in *Aristotle on Nature and Living Things*, ed. A. Gotthelf (Pittsburgh, 1985), 247–58.

30. Aetius, cf. Diels, *Dox.*, 321–26. Anaxagoras cf. Aetius, *Plac.* 1.29.7.

31. Philemon, fr. 137 [=Clement, *Str.* 5.14.128=Eusebius, *P.e.* 13.13, 55]. He seems here to have forgotten his decision (6.4 and 5) to leave the poets out of consideration.

32. Philemon, fr. 100 [=Clement, *Str.* 7.4.25]. On sneezing cf. Origen, *C.Cels.* 4.94.

33. Menander, fr. 109 [=Clement, *Str.* 7.4.24].

34. For Antiphon, see Diels-Kranz, A7 no. 87, K. Freeman, *The Pre-Socratic Philosophers: A Companion to Diels, Fragmente der Vorsokratiker*, 2d ed. (Oxford, 1959), 371–404; J. S. Morrison, in *The Older Sophists*, ed. K. S. Sprague (Columbia, S.C., 1990), 106–240, esp. 128. Clement has a clarifying line: Antiphon "noticing that the sow was thin with lack of food through the meanness of the owner." See Lucian, *True Stories*, 2.33.

35. Bion, fr. 45 [=Clement, *Str.* 7.4.24]. Bion of Borysthenes was an itinerant satiric poet; cf. A. Pennacina, "Il cibo e il corpo nella diatriba e nella satira," *Homo edens: Regimi, miti e pratiche dell'alimentazione nella civiltà del Mediterraneo*, A cura di O. Longo and P. Scarpi (Milan, 1989), 1.75–79. On Archesilaus cf. 5.65.

36. Diogenes, fr. 282 [=Clement, *Str.* 7.4.25]. On Diogenes of Sinope (400–325 B.C.), also mentioned at 1.24. He became a professor of philosophy, emphasizing an attitude of indifference. Some of his lectures have been preserved by his pupil Appian. See *CAH* 11.694–95; M.-O. Goulet-Cazé, "Le livre VI de Diogène Laërce: Analyse de sa structure et réflexions méthodologiques," *ANRW* II.36.6 (1992): 3880–4048, F. G. Downing, *Cynics and Christian Origins* (Herndon, Va., 1992).

37. Diogenes, fr. 118 [=Clement *Str.* 7.4.26]. Cf. Diogenes Laertius 6.39 and 6.50.

38. Fr. 266, ed. Kaibel [=Clement, *Str.* 5.14, 100]. Epicharmus, c. 540 B.C., was a writer of comic farces in the Dorian dialect, fragments of which are extant. See Aristotle, *Poetics* 5.1449b.

39. [=Clement *Str.* 5.14,121=Eusebius, *P.e.* 13.13.47].

40. Philemon fr. 246 Kock. The translation of the verses is by Attridge, *Old Testament Pseudepigrapha*, II, 828. Cf. also Canivet's note. 40. [=Clement, *Str.* 5.14.121] Diphilus, a contemporary of Menander, c. 350 B.C, and like him a poet of the New Comedy, on whose works Plautus and Terence based some of theirs. The "eye of justice" in this citation is a very hoary metaphor that may predate both Diphilus and Philemon.

41. Pindar, fr. 142 (106) [=Clement, *Str.* 5. 708=Eusebius, *P.e.* 13.13.25].

42. Plato, *Leg.* 4. 715e–716b [=Clement, *Protr.* 6.69.4=Eusebius, *P.e.* 13.13.5]. See also Stobaeus 1.3.55.

43. Plato, *Gorgias* 525 a–c [=Eusebius, *P.e.* 12.6.9–11].

44. Exod. 9:16.

45. For the analogy of the public executioner cf. John Chrysostom, *Catech.* 1.28, 7.19, SC 50.122, 238, where Chrysostom is thinking of the δῆμιος in his hated role as public executioner of the Christians, which Theodoret may also have in mind, and which would intensify his unpopularity.

46. On Israel's punishment by the Assyrians, 722 B.C., see Isa. 10: 1–27 and Théodoret de Cyr, *Commentaire sur Isaie*, SC 295.24f.

47. Plato, *Philebus* 28c [=Eusebius, *P.e.* 12.51.35].

48. Ibid.

49. Ibid., 30c.

50. Prov. 3:19.

51. Plato, *Leg.* 1.631b–d [=Eusebius, *P.e.* 12.16.3–5].

52. Plato, *Leg.* 2.661a–c [=Eusebius, *P.e.* 12.21.2–4].

53. Plato, *Leg.* 2.661c–d [=Eusebius, *P.e.* 12.21.5].

54. 1 Sam. 16:7.

55. Plato, *Theaet.* 176c [=Eusebius, *P.e.* 12.29.16].

56. Plato, *Leg.* 10.899d–e [=Eusebius, *P.e.* 12.52.1].

57. Plato, *Leg.* 10.900c–d [=Eusebius, *P.e.* 12.52.5].

58. Plato, *Leg.* 10.902e–903a [=Eusebius, *P.e.* 12.52.19].

59. Plato, *Leg.* 10.903a [=Eusebius, *P.e.* 12.52.20].

60. Plato, *Laws* 10.905b [=Eusebius, *P.e.* 12.52.30].

61. For the mutual interdependence of the rich and poor, cf. Theodoret, *Provid.* 6.31–35 (ACW 49.83–84).

62. For the sounds of the lyre cf. μέση, s.v., LSJ, 1105; νεάτη, s.v. LSJ, 1164; Aristotle, *Probl.* 19, 25, Plato, *Philebus* 17c–d; *Gorgias*, 452a–d; *Resp.* 443d.

63. For shapes cf. Aetius, *Plac.* 4.19. 2, Stobaeus, ed l. I. 14 , Diels. For similar reflections (in conjunction with treatment of the τετρακτύς, cf. 12.78) cf. Hippolytus, *Ref.* 1.2.6–10, ed. Markovich, 59, who refers to W. Burkert, *Wisdom and Science in Ancient Pythagoreanism* (Cambridge, MA, 1972); A.

Delatte, *Etudes sur la littérature pythagoricienne* (Paris, 1915), 249; Diophanti, *De arithmetica* 1, ed. Tannery, Teubner 80, p. 2f., G. Roeper, *Philolologus* 7 (1852): 532.

64. Croesus was a sixth-century B.C. king of Lydia in Asia Minor who, despite his wealth, was told by Solon of Athens, "Account no man happy before his death." Midas, a mythical Phrygian king, was granted his wish by Dionysus that anything he might touch would be turned into gold. The epitaph on his tomb is quoted in Plato, *Phaedrus*, 264d. Darius I, king of Persia, was called "the Huckster" because of his preoccupation with taxes, trade, and industry, on which cf. *CAH* 4.198–201.

65. The interdependence of craftsmen is also stressed in Theodoret, *Provid.* 6.33, 7.34.

66. For Theodoret's attitude toward slavery see R. Klein, "Die Sklavenfrage bei Theodoret von Kyrrhos: Die 7 Rede des Bischofs ueber die Vorsehung," in *Romanitas–Christianitas, Untersuchung zur Geschichte und Literatur der römischen Kaiserzeit, Johannes Straub zum 70. Geburstag gewidmet*, ed. G. Wirth (Berlin and New York, 1982), 586–633.

67. Cf. *Resp.* 2.379b–c [=Clement, *Str.* 5.14, 136].

68. Plato, *Resp.* 10.617e; "God is blameless" is much quoted by the Fathers: e.g., Justin, *1 Apol.* 44; Clement, *Str.* 5.14.136. See J. Geffcken, *Zwei Griechische Apologeten* (Leipzig, 1907), 103 n. 4.

69. Plato, *Apol.* 41c–d.

70. On Atticus see J. Dillon, *The Middle Platonists: 80 B.C. to A.D. 220* (Ithaca, NY, 1977). Plotinus taught at Rome from about A.D. 253 to A.D. 270.

71. Plotinus, *Enneads*, 3.2.1.

72. *Enneads*, 3.2.2.

73. John 1:3.

74. He lists the Emperors Tiberius (A.D. 14–37), Gaius (Caligula, 37–41), Nero (54–68), Vespasian (69–79), Titus (79–81), Domitian (81–96), Nerva (96–98), Trajan (98–117), Hadrian (117–138), Antoninus Pius (138–161), Lucius Verus (161–69), and Commodus (177–192), but omits Claudius (41–54), Galba, Otho, and Vitellius (68–69) and Marcus Aurelius (161–80). Cf. Eusebius, *P.e.* 15.34.2.

75. On Ammonius Saccas cf. Eusebius, *H.e.* 6.19; Reale, *A History of Ancient Philosophy*, 4.297–302 and 521–22; and H. Crouzel, *Origen*, Eng. trans. (San Francisco, 1989), 10–12; H. Dörrie, "Ammonios, der Lehrer Plotins," *Hermes* 83 (1955): 439–77, F. H. Kettler, "Origenes, Ammonius Saccas und Porphyrius," in *Kerygma und Logos*, Festschrift für K. Andresen (Göttingen, 1979), 322–28; F. M. Schroeder, "Ammonius Saccas" *ANRW* II.36.1, 493–526, esp. 494–509; "Ammonios Sakkos," *RAC* Supplement Lief. 3 (1985), 323–32, M. Balthes.

76. For the notion that Plotinus had access to Christian Scripture cf. *Affect.* 2.87 and n. 100.

77. Plotinus, *Enneads* 3.2.3.

78. Ps. 18:2.

79. Plotinus, *Enneads* 3.2.3.

80. *Enneads* 3.2.4.

81. *Enneads* 3.2.4–5.

82. *Enneads* 3.2.5.

83. *Enneads* 3.2.5.

84. *Enneads* 3.2.7.

85. *Enneads* 3.2.8.

86. *Enneads* 3.2.9.

87. *Enneads* 3.2.9.

88. *Enneads* 3.2.11.

89. Epictetus, mentioned only here by Theodoret, was a Greek Stoic philosopher, c. 50–120 A.D. Born in Hierapolis in Phrygia, he went to Rome as a slave in the house of Epaphroditus, freedman and favorite of Nero. After emancipation he became a philosopher, lecturing in Rome until A.D. 94. See Reale, *A History of Ancient Philosophy* 4:105–25; A. Jagu, "La Morale d'Epictète et le christianisme" *ANRW* II.36.3, 2164–99, esp. 2175f.

90. A patristic commonplace; cf. Basil, *Hex.* 5.6–10; SC 26 bis, 300–322; FOTC 46.74–82. Gregory Nazianzus, *Orat.* 28.26.

91. Cf. Chrysostom, *Hom. in Gen.* 5.9–12 and *Hom. in Gen.* 6.9 (FOTC 74.70–72, 82). D. S. Wallace-Hadrill, *The Greek Patristic View of Nature* (Manchester, 1968).

92. On the virgin birth in Theodoret cf. *De Provid.* 10.15 (ACW 49.140 and 211, n. 31), *Eranistes*; also the Excursus on Theodoret's Christology in Canivet, *Entre*. On the humanity of Christ cf. K. McNamara, "Theodoret of Cyrus and the Unity of Person in Christ," *IThQ* 22 (1955): 313–28.

93. On Christ, cf. Eusebius, *P.e.* 15.15.6=Clement, *Str.* 7.3.20]. Here Theodoret simply takes two sentences from Eusebius and inverts them! Clement says: "Now we are made to be obedient to the commandments if our choice be such as to will salvation."

94. The salvation of humankind achieved through Christ's Incarnation is obviously the centerpiece of Theodoret's apologetic. Cf. *Affect.* 10.93.

95. On the relative lateness of the Incarnation cf. Theodoret, *Provid.* 10.44, ACW 49.148 and 212, n. 69. This was a problem raised by Porphyry; cf. Augustine, *Predestination of the Saints*, 9 (17). On the providential spread of Christianity cf. E. Gabba, "The Holy Spirit, the Roman Senate, and Bossuet," in Ancient Studies in Memory of Elias Bickerman, *Journal of the Ancient Near East Society* 16–17 (New York, 1985). The same question is raised and left unanswered in Theodoret, *Provid.* 10.44. See A. Stötzel, "Warum Christus so spät erschien: Die apologetische Argumentation des frühen Christentums," *ZKG* 92 (1981): 147–60.

96. This elaborate but overly optimistic obituary notice by Theodoret on

the death of Hellenism is quoted in W. E. Kaegi, "The Fifth-Century Twilight of Byzantine Paganism," *Classica et Mediaevalia* 27 (1966): 243–75, also Isidore of Pelusium, *ep.* 1, 270: "Hellenism [=paganism] which time, labors, riches, arms and words strengthened, has vanished." See also J. Holland-Smith, *The Death of Paganism* (London, 1976), 32, 48. F. Thélamon, "Destruction du paganisme et construction du royaume de Dieu d'après Rufin et Augustin," *CrSt* 11 (1990): 523–41.

    97. On the Gospels as the fulfillment of the Prophets, see B. E. Daley, "Origen's *De Principiis:* A Guide to the Principles of Christian Scriptural Interpretation," *Nova et Vetera: Patristic Studies in Honor of Thomas Patrick Halton,* ed. J. Petruccione (Washington, D.C.: 1998), 3–21.

    98. On Jewish incredulity, diaspora and servitude cf. McCollough, in Disc. 2, n. 78.

    99. Euripides, *Oenomaus,* fr. 574, ed. Nauck [=Clement, *Str.* 6.2.18], 100. Euripides, *Phoenix* , fr. 811, ed. Nauck.

    100. Hyperides, fr. 195.

    101. Diels, *Dox.* 324.

    102. Andocides, *On the Peace,* 2 Isocrates, *Panegyricus.*

Notes to Discourse 7

    1. Cf. Matt. 7:13–14. This also echoes the Two Ways, described in *Didache* 5.2, and *Epist. ad Barn.* 18 and 19, also the story of the apparition of the two women, Virtue and Vice, at the crossroads to Heracles: Xenophon, *Mem.* 2.1, 21–34; Basil, *De legendis libris Gentilium* 5; Gregory Nazianzus, *Poemata de seipso,* 45, ll. 229–76 (PG 37.1369f.); Lactantius, *Div. inst.* 6, 4.

    2. See Chrysostom, *Pan. Bab.,* 3 : "If demons ever were able to delude and deceive people a little, it was when the source of light was still unknown to the multitude. And even then it was obvious that demons had wrought the works from the duplicity, especially the sacrifices," trans. Schatkin, FOTC 73.77 and nn. 8 and 10, which, pertinently cite Athanasius, *De Incarnatione* 12.6, 14.3; also Eusebius, *P.e.* 4. 5–21.

    3. Clement similarly moves (*Protr.* 4.46) from the seductive powers of literature to those of the plastic arts. See J. Pépin, "*Ut scriptura pictura:* Un thème de l'esthétique médiévale et ses origines," in *From Augustine to Eriugena: Essays in Honor of John J. O'Meara* (Washington, DC, 1991), 168ff., quoting this passage, as well as Eusebius, *P.e.* 3.7.1, and Porphyry, *De cultu simulacrorum,* fr. 2.

    4. The pattern of erotic art in the homes of the well-to-do is well exemplified by Hadrian's villa at Tivoli, on which cf. R. Bianchi Bandinelli, *Rome: The Center of Power 500 B.C. to A.D. 200* (New York, 1970), 264–74. The Antioch

mosaics were nearer home for Theodoret. Clement, *Protr.* 4.59, 4.61 tells us that the Greeks put Philaenic *schemata* (derived from Philaenis, Περι σχημάτων συνουσιας) on their bedroom walls.

5. He has Zeus chiefly in mind; cf. Athenagoras, *Leg.* 20; Minucius Felix, *Oct.* 23, 4 (ACW 39.30 and 289, n. 329); Tertullian, *Apol.* 21: *Non de sororis incesto nec de stupro filiae aut coniugis alienae deum patrem passus est squamatum aut cornutum aut plumatum, amatorem in auro conversum Danaidis. Iovis ista sunt numina vestra.*

6. The reference is to the famous entrapment of Ares and Aphrodite by her husband, Hephaistos, described in Homer, *Od.* 8.263–367, and often dwelt upon by the Fathers; cf. Aristides, *Apol.* 10, 7; Tatian, *Orat.* 8.1; Clement, *Protr.* 4.59, 4.61; Chrysostom, *Pan. Bab.* 110; Minucius Felix, *Oct.* 23,7 (ACW 39.91 and 290, n. 334). See J. Geffcken, *Zwei Griechische Apologeten* (Leipzig, 1907), 70.

7. For Zeus as eagle scooping off Ganymede cf. Homer, *Il.* 20, 232; Minucius Felix, *Oct.* 23, 7 (ACW 39.91 and 290, n. 354); M. Robertson, *A History of Greek Art*, vol. 1, 460, 578. For examples of the widespread depiction of Europa and the bull see the Pompeian painting from the House of Jason (first quarter of the first century A.D.) and the detail of a mosaic pavement (fourth century A.D.) in a villa at Lullingstone, Kent, England in *The Oxford History of the Classical World* (Oxford, 1986), 360, 634. For the Stoics Europa and the bull and Zeus as the swan with Leda represent the mixture of air and earth, cf. Athenagoras, *Leg.* 22.11 (SC 379). Cf. M. Robertson, *A History of Greek Art*, col. I.402 and vol. 2 (London, 1975), pl. 129d for a Hellenistic expression of Leda and the swan.

8. In Hippolytus, *Ref.* 5.7.29, we are told that the Naasenes equated the Logos with Hermes.

9. In Herodotus 2.46 we read that the Mendesians reckon Pan among their gods and in their painting and sculpture his image is made as among the Greeks with the head and the legs of a goat. See also Minucius Felix, *Oct.* 22.5, Lactantius, *Div. inst.* 1.21; P. Borgeaud, *The Cult of Pan in Ancient Greece*, trans. K. Atlass and J. Redfield (Chicago, 1988), 163f., for the celebration of his festival. See Hymn to Pan in Eusebius, *P.e.* 5.13.2.

10. The loves of Apollo are catalogued in Clement, *Protr.* 32.3, and also include Sterope, Aithousa, Arsinoe, Zeuxippe, Prothoe, Marsippa, Hypsiple.

11. For the story of Daphne, the virgin, pursued by Apollo but escaping his attentions thanks to Zeus, who transformed her into a laurel tree, cf. Clement, *Protr.* 32.3; ps-Justin, *Disc.* 2, Tatian, *Orat.* 8.4; Libanius; Chrysostom, *Pan. Bab.* 68 (where her mother is her rescuer); art. "Daphne," *RAC* 3.585–93, esp. 590.

12. For a mosaic from Daphne, suburb of Antioch, of the transformation into the laurel tree (third century A.D.) see G. Downey, *Ancient Antioch* (Princeton, 1963), fig. 31.

13. Clement, *Protr.* 2.17: "This mythological story the women celebrate variously city by city in the festivals called Thesmophoria, Scirophoria, and Arretophoria, dramatizing in many forms the tragic rape of Pherephatta (by Pluto). On the rape of Kore, i.e., Persephone, cf. C. Kerényi, *Eleusis: Archetypal Image of Mother and Daughter*, trans. R. Manheim, Bollingen Series 65 (New York, 1967).

14. For the wandering of Deo, i.e., Demeter, mother of Persephone, cf. Minucius Felix, *Oct.* 22.2 (ACW 39.88; 191, n. 68; and 282, n. 295).

15. Pandia was a daughter of Zeus and Selene. For the festival, which occurred on Elaphebolion 17, following the City Dionysia, cf. L. Deubner, *Attische Feste* (Hildesheim and New York, 1969), 176f.; H. W. Parke, *Festivals of the Athenians* (Ithaca, NY, 1977), 136; A. K. Michels, *The Calendar of the Roman Republic* (Princeton, NJ, 1967), 137; Burkert, *Homo necans: The Anthropology of Ancient Greek Sacrificial Ritual and Myth* (Berkeley, 1983), 182–83. The Diasia, the festival of Zeus Meilichios, occurred on Anthesterion 23; cf. Michels, *Calendar*, 117, 120, 187, quoting a scholiast on Aristophanes, *Clouds*, 408. See Thucydides 1.126; E. Simon, *Festivals of Attica: An Archaeological Commentary* (Madison, WI, 1983), 12–15.

16. "The sacrificial calendar of Erkhia designates for this day [Metageitnion 20] a sacrifice to Hera Thelkinia in Erkhia," Michels, *Calendar*, 42.

17. The Panathenaia, in honor of Athena, comprised two festivals, the Greater, and the Smaller (cf. Thucydides, 5.47). The Greater was celebrated in the third year of each Olympiad in the month Hekatombaion, generally extending over 23–30, or at least the three days 28 (the most important), 29, and 30. See Michels, *Calendar*, 34; A. W. Pickard-Cambridge, *The Dramatic Festivals of Athens*, 2 ed., rev. by J. Gould and D. M. Lewis (Oxford, 1969); Parke, *Festivals*, 33–50.

18. The Dionysia was the festival of Dionysus of which there were four in Athens; cf. LSJ. s.v. 374, Parke, *Festivals*, 125–36.

19. For the Eleusinia cf. *supra*, I. 21–22, G. E. Mylonas, *Eleusis and the Eleusinian Mysteries* (Princeton, NJ, 1961), 281–85; W. Burkert, *Homo necans*, 248–97. For the Thesmophoria, a women's three-day festival in honor of Demeter, celebrated in the Fall in Pyanopsion 11, 12, and 13, see Deubner, *Attische Feste*, 50f.; W. Burkert, *Structure and History in Greek Mythology and Ritual* (Berkeley, 1979), 139 and 210, n. 11; W. Burkert, *Greek Religion*, trans. J. Raffan (Cambridge, Mass., 1985), 242–46; Michels, *Calendar*, 71–74, Cook, *Zeus*, 3.165; Parke, *Festivals*, 33–50; art. "Demeter," *RAC* 3.685–86.

20. For the Delia, a quinquennial festival of Apollo at Delos, see Thucydides, 3.104; Xenophon, *Mem.* 4.8,2. The Pythia were the Pythian games celebrated every four years at Pytho or Delphi in honor of Pythian Apollo. See Tertullian, *Spect.*11.

21. Pausanias 8.4, 19 reports that in Pheneus, Arcadia, they have a temple of Hermes and hold Hermaian games. The Hermaia, mentioned in Plato,

Lysis 206c, was celebrated on Day 4 of each month and was devoted to three deities: Heracles, Hermes, and Aphrodite. See Deubner, *Attische Feste*, 217.

22. The Kronia, feast of Kronos, celebrated at Athens on Hekatombaion 12; cf. Michels, *Calendar*, 28. Later the Kronia became the Roman Saturnalia.

23. On the Poseidonia, feast of Poseidon, see Deubner, *Feste*, 214–15; Athenaeus, *Deip.* 590F.

24. The Heracleia, festival of Hercules, celebrated on Mounichion 4. Cf. Deubner, *Feste*, 226f.; Mikalson, *Calendar*, 17, 138; Aristophanes, *Frogs* 651.

25. For Asclepeia see E. J. and L. Edelstein, *Asclepius: A Collection and Interpretation of the Testimonies* (Baltimore, 1945), 1.312–20. Ion, whose home was in Ephesus, is coming from the festival of Asclepius in Epidaurus at the beginning of Plato, *Ion* 530, having just won first prize in the competition for rhapsodes.

26. On the Anakeia, the festival of the Dioscuri, Pollux, and Castor, also called Anakes, see Pausanias, 10.38; Deubner, *Feste*, 216; art. "Dioskuren," *RAC* 3: 1124–38.

27. Also stated in Clement, *Protr.* 2.19; Hippolytus, *Ref.* 5.8.39. On the κτείς see Burkert, *Homo Necans*, Eng. trans., 270, n. 21 for the scholarly literature on the interpretation of this passage.

28. For the Phallagogia see Clement, *Protr.* 2.34, and *Affect.*, I. 113–14 and nn. 122 and 123. On the priests inciting to gross behavior cf. ps.-Justin, *Disc.* 4. For an imitation phallus used at the Rural Dionysia cf. Aristophanes, *Acharn.* 243, 265f.

29. For a vivid portrait of a young satyr holding the drunken Silenus on the marble Borghese krater in the Louvre see G. Becatti, *The Art of Greece and Rome*, trans. J. Ross (New York, 1967), fig. 261. See also M.-C. Villaneuva Puig, "Images de Dionysus et de son cortege dans le ceramique grecque du IVe siè-cle en provenance de la Peninsula Iberique," *REAnc* 89 (1987) 297–317.

30. See Philostratus, *Imagines* 1.20, 1.22; also Callistratus, *Descriptions*, 1. See Burkert, *Homo necans*, 233, n. 12 for revelers at the Anthestheria, specifi-cally the night of transition from the Choes to the Chytroi. For Pan, son of Hermes, see Philostratus, *Imagines* 2. 11: "Pan...his garment extended...tries to make love to the nymphs." For Pan and the nymphs see Robertson, *A History of Greek Art*, vol. 1, 376. For Pan as pedagogue of Dionysus cf. Eusebius, *P.e.* 5.5.8, 5.6.1, quoting Porphyry, *De phil. ex orac.* 1.

31. Homer, *Il.* 1.423f.

32. Homer, *Il.* 1.39f.

33. Cf. *Ep. to Diog.*, 2; Clement, *Protr.* 4.51, *Str.* 7.6.31. Tertullian, *Apol.* 22.6, Dionysiis, mysteriis Atticis cocorum dilectus indicitur 39, Athenagoras, *Leg.* 25.1; Origen, *C. Cels.* 8.60.

34. On Egypt's cult of animals see *Affect.*, 3.85 and notes.

35. For the Scriptural prohibition of pork cf. Lev. 11.7: On eating pork cf. Clement, *Str.* 7.33.

36. Ps. 50:9–11.
37. Ps. 50:12.
38. Ps. 50:13.
39. Ps. 50:14–15.
40. Ps. 50:23.
41. Ps. 40:6.
42. Ps. 69:30–32.
43. Isa. 1:11–12.
44. Isa. 1:13–14.
45. Isa. 1:16; cf. Theodoret, *Haer.* 5.18.
46. Isa. 1:16.
47. Isa. 43:22–24.
48. Isa. 43:25.
49. Eph. 2:8–9.
50. Jer. 7:21–22.
51. Jer. 6:20.
52. Amos 5:23.
53. See *Porphyrius, "Gegen die Christen," 15 Bucher,* ed. A. von Harnack (Berlin, 1916). See also R. L. Wilken, *The Christians as the Romans Saw Them* (New Haven, 1984), 137, citing Eusebius, *H.e.* 6.19.2. For Porphyry's involvement with the Scriptures see M. Anastos, "Porphyry's Attack on the Bible," in *The Classical Tradition, Studies in Honor of Harry Caplan* (Ithaca, NY, 1966), 421–50.
54. Cf. Lucian, *Apol.* 4. For parrots imitating human speech; cf. Hippolytus, *Ref.* VI, and Osborne, 233. For the case for and against Porphyry's use of Christian exegesis see P. M. Casey, "Porphyry and the Origin of the Book of Daniel," *JThS* 27 (1976):15–33; Casey, "Porphyry and Syrian Eexegesis of the Book of Daniel" *ZNTW* 81 (1990): 139–42.
55. See Porphyry, *De abstin.* 2.5. [=Eusebius, *P.e.* 1.9.7–8] On the quotation from Theophrastus cf. A.-J. Festugière, *La Révelation d'Hermès Trismegiste* 2 (Paris, 1949), 190–91; Porphyry, *De abstin.* 2.7 [=Eusebius, *P.e.* 1.9.11].
56. The long development is in *De abstin.* 2.34ff. The additional remark is *De abstin.* 2.11 [=Eusebius, *P.e.* 4.14.2]. See *Select Works of Porphyry,* trans. T. Taylor (London, 1823; repr. Lawrence, KS, 1988), 69–70 and 52.
57. Porphyry, *De abstin.* 2.12 [=Eusebius, *P.e.* 4.14.3].
58. *De abstin.* 2.13 [=Eusebius, *P.e.* 4.14.3].
59. *De abstin.* 2.54 [=Eusebius, *P.e.* 4.16.1–11]. The feast of Saturnalia was in June. For demons as the instigators of human sacrifices cf. Chrysostom, *Pan. Bab.* 3, FOTC 73. 77 and n. 10; also *Pan. Bab.* 74.
60. On human sacrifices cf. Clement, *Protr.* 3.42, where some of these examples are recorded, a chapter devoted by Clement to proving that the pagan gods are inhuman demons because of their love of human sacrifice. See also Chrysostom, *Pan. Bab.* 3, and FOTC 73. 77 n. 10.

61. [=Eusebius, *P.e.* 4.16.12, on which see SC 262.170]. This is not from Philo, and Eusebius assigns it to Clement, *Protr.* 3.42, 2, who tells us that Theopompus, king of Sparta, was one of the victims. On the summit of Mt. Ithome in Messenia there was a precinct of Zeus. See J. Sirinelli, SC 206.205 and 315–321; also P. Nautin, "Trois autres fragments du livre 'Contre les Chrétiens,' " *Revue Biblique* 57 (1950): 409–16.

62. Plutarch, *De def. orac.* 14 [=Eusebius, *P.e.* 5.4. 2].

63. Menoecus, father of Creon and Jocasta, gave his life to dispel the plague by leaping from the walls of Thebes.

64. Codrus, Athenian king, died to preserve the kingdom for his sons; cf. Plato, *Symp.* 208d. Leo, an eponymous hero of an Attic deme; his daughters obeyed an oracle during a famine by running against the enemy's ranks; cf. Aristotle, *Athen. Const.* 18.3.

65. Ps. 106:37–38.

66. Ezek.16:20, 22.

67. Ps.-Sophocles, fr.1025, *TGF*, ed. Nauck, [=Clement, *Protr.* 7.74, *Str.* 5.14, 113]. This is also quoted in ps.-Justin, Coh. Gr. 18, Athenagoras, *Leg.* 5 (Markovich, ed., 31); Eusebius, *P.e.* 13.13.39, Cyril, *CJuln.* 1.44.

68. See Plato, *Phaedo* 118a; Xenophon, *Mem.* 1.1; Justin, *1 Apol.* 61; Tertullian, *Apol.* 46; Origen, *C. Cels.* 4.67; Lactantius, *Div. inst.* 3.20, 5.14; Artemidorus, *Oneiroc.*, V.9. Charges were brought against Socrates by Anytus on behalf of the professional men and politicians, and by Meletus on behalf of the poets; Plato, *Apol.* 23e.

69. Cf. Chrysostom, *Pan. Bab.* 103 (of Julian): "It is as if the ruler reigned at that time for the express purpose of consuming all the beasts of the inhabited world—so lavishly did he slay sheep and oxen upon his altars; and he reached such a pitch of madness that many of those in their midst still considered philosophers called him "cook," "butcher," and all such names," trans. M. Schatkin, FOTC 73.135.

70. Some see in this an allusion to a precise law against paganism of Theodosius II in 435 (cf. Theodoret, *H.e.* 5.37, 3) which would help to pinpoint the date of the *Curatio*, 435–37. See also *Affect.* 9.32, M. Ninci, *Aporia ed entusiasmo: Il mondo materiale e i filosofi secondo Teodoreto e la tradizione patristica greca* (Rome, 1977), 11, n. 2.

DISCOURSE 8

1. [=Clement, *Str.* 1.10.48, FOTC 85, p. 57]. For the Sirens cf. Homer, *Od.* 12. 154–200. Clement's explanation is that Pythagoras teaches us to cultivate wisdom apart from pleasure. In *ep.* 31 (27) Theodoret flatters a sophist he is writing to by comparing his Attic style with the charm of the Sirens (SC 40.97).

2. [=Clement, *Str.* 2.18.79, FOTC 85, p. 211]. Most of the examples are found in Diogenes Laertius, *Life of Pythagoras*, 17 (Diels-Kranz 58c6). For a translation, with equivalences, of the Pythagorean symbols or maxims, see K. S. Guthrie, *Pythagorean Source-Book and Library* (Grand Rapids, MI, 1987), 159–61. See also ps.-Justin, *Exhort.* 19; Hippolytus, *Ref.* 6.27; Plutarch, *De pueris educandis* 17 in *Plutarch's Moralia*, vol. 1, ed. F. C. Babbitt, LCL (Cambridge, MA, 1936); Porphyry, *VP* 42; K. R. S., 231–32; W. Burkert, *Lore and Science in Ancient Pythagoreanism* (Cambridge, MA, 1972), 166–72.

3. Canivet notes (SC 57.310, n. 1) that this explanation is neither that of Porphyry nor of Clement. See *Entre*, 223. Theodoret's source may be Porphyry, *Life of Pythagoras*. On these *akusmeta* cf. Burkert, *Lore*, 166–92.

4. For a very similar sentiment cf. Chrysostom, *De Sac.* 5. See also *Orat.* 4.92. For Theodoret's knowledge of Demosthenes cf. art. "Demosthenes," *RAC* 3. 731.

5. Theodoret, *Hist. Rel.* 8, describing the monk Aphraahat as "knowing just a few phrases of the Greek language," says "nonetheless who of those who plume themselves on their eloquence, knit their eyebrows, speak pompously, and embark with zest on syllogistic traps has ever surpassed the voice of this uneducated barbarian," cf. *Theodoret of Cyrrhus: A History of the Monks of Syria*, trans. R. W. Price, Cistercian Studies 88 (Kalamazoo, MI, 1985), 73.

6. On the nonelitist nature of early Christianity cf. Chrysostom, *Demonstratio* 2: "I shall not present an explanation carefully embellished with words and phrases. I shall speak in such a way that the house-servant, the lady's maid, the widow, the peddler, the sailor, and the farmer will find my arguments simple and easy to understand," trans. Harkins, FOTC 73.187.

7. The absence of "Hellenic brilliance" in the Scriptures had already been discussed by Origen in reply to the criticism of Celsus. Cf. Tatian, *Discourse*, 29, 32. See Minucius Felix, *Oct.* 5.4, ACW 39.56 and 183, n. 29.

8. Cf. Chrysostom, *Pan. Bab.* 65: "But God, who is a philanthropist...provides us with countless opportunities to be saved...by leaving the relics of the saints in our midst," trans. Schatkin, FOTC 73.112 and nn. 138–40, also her Intro., 37–44, for a good treatment of the veneration of martyrs and their relics. On the cult of martyrs cf. art. "Martyre. 1.3. Le culte des Martyrs," *DSp* 10. 723–26, W. Rordorf; also his "Aux origines du culte des Martyrs," *Irenikon* 45 (1972): 315–31. On the power of the relics cf. F. Pfister, *Der Reliquienkult im Altertum* (Giessen, 1912); Botting, "Reliquienverehrung, ihre Entstehung und ihre Formen," *Trier ThZ* 67 (1958): 321–24; T. Klauser, "Christlicher Märtyrerkult, heidnischer Heroenkult und spätjüdische Heiligenverehrung," *JbAC* (1974): 221–29.

9. The pagan repudiation of the cult of martyrs is already prominently mentioned by Theodoret in the Proemium, 1, of c. 1, v. I. Pasztori-Kupan, *Theodoret of Cyrus* (New York, 2006), p. 86.

10. Cf. Herodotus 2.43; Isocrates, *Helen* 59 for Zeus impersonating Amphitryon. See W. Burkert, *S & H*, 78–98; K. Galinsky, *The Heracles Theme* (Totowa, NJ, 1972). The proof that Heracles was a mere mortal is already taking shape in ps.-Justin, *Disc.* 3, and Clement, *Protr.* 2.30, 6, with many physiognomic details.

11. Plato, *Theaet.* 175 ab [=Eusebius, *P.e.* 12.29.10].

12. Isocrates, 1.50. Isocrates presented Heracles as a suitable model for Philip of Macedon; cf. G. K. Galinsky, *The Heracles Theme,* 103.

13. Cf. Clement, *Protr.* 2.24. Eurystheus of Argos was the person for whom Heracles performed the Labors. See also Eusebius, *P.e.* 2.2.31–32.

14. See L. R. Farnell, *Greek Hero Cults and Ideas of Immortality,* Gifford lectures delivered at the University of St. Andrews in the Year 1920 (1921; repr., Chicago, 1995), chap. 5; J. Fontenrose, *Python: A Study of Delphic Myth and Origins* (Berkeley, 1959), chap. 12; P. Bernard, "Vicissitudes au Gré de l'Histoire d'une Statue en Bronze d'Heracles entre Seleucie du Tigre et la Méssene," *Journal des Savants* (1990): 3–67.

15. For Hercules' connection with Tyre in Phoenicia cf. Herodotus, 2.44. For his cult, W. Burkert, *Greek Religion*, trans. J. Raffan (Cambridge, Mass., 1985), 210–11. See also B. Bergquist, *Herakles on Thasos: The Archaeological, Literary, and Epigraphic Evidence of his Sanctuary, Status, and Cult* (Uppsala, 1973), esp. 28, 29, 30, 36.

16. The joke is not original; Tatian, *Disc.* 21, Clement, *Protr.* 2.33, Tertullian, *Ad nat.* 2.14, 7, Gregory Nazianzus, *Contra Jul.* 1.122: "This thirteenth exploit, I don't know how it was passed over in the enumeration of his labors."

17. For an extended account of the love potion of Deianira see Diodorus Siculus, 4.36–39, esp. 38. Heracles' death and apotheosis is detailed in 4.39.

18. Sophocles, *Trachiniae* 960f. gives a different version of Hercules' end. For a good survey of the diversity of scholarly views on this question see P. Holt, "The End of the Trachiniai and the Fate of Herakles," *JHS* 109 (1989): 69–80. See also W. Burkert, "Greek Tragedy and Sacrificial Ritual," *GRBS* 7 (1966): 87–121 Clement, *Protr.* 2.30.6 places the pyre on Mt. Oeta and gives fifty-two as the age at death.

19. Cf. Plato, *Theaet.* 180a: "When you put a question, they pluck from their quiver little oracular aphorisms to let fly at you."

20. See *Le Bibliothèque d'Apollodore*, trans. J. Carrière and B. Massonie (Paris, 1991); Apollodorus, *Gods and Heroes of the Greeks: The Library of Apollodorus*, trans. M. Simpson (Amherst, MA, 1976), 185, nn. 8–9.

21. For full details on the doubts about the maternity cf. J. G. Frazer, ed. *Apollodorus: The Library* (Cambridge, MA, 1921), 2.13–15. Pausanias 2.26 reports that Coronis, pregnant by Apollo, was brought by her father, Phlegyas, to the Peloponnese, and at Epidaurus secretly gave birth to Asclepius. Ovid,

Met. 2.534–47, 598–632 reports that the angry Apollo shot her through the heart.

22. [=Eusebius *P.e.* 4.16.12, quoting Clement, *Protr.* 42, *Str.* 1.15.73]. See Pindar, *Pyth.* 3.1–6. Epidaurus, in Argolis, was famous for its fourth-century theater and its cult of the god of medicine, Asclepius, which claimed miraculous cures. Celsus speaks of Asclepius, "who did good and foretold the future to whole cities which were dedicated to him such as Tricca, Epidaurus, Cos, and Pergamum," Origen, *C. Cels.* 3.3. Tricca is a town in Thessaly.

23. Already reported *Affect.* 3.27. On Zeus τερικεραυνος, of the thunderbolt, cf. Homer, *Il.* 419; Eusebius, *P.e.* 15.7.7.

24. See Homer, *Il.* 11.832. Machaon, son of Asclepius, was himself a physician; cf. Homer, *Il.* 2.731–32. He was a leader of the contingent from Tricca, Ithome, and Oechalia in Homer's Catalog of Ships, *Il.* 2.

25. Paion is mentioned in Homer, *Il.* 5.900.

26. Homer, *Il.* 11.832 [=Clement, *Str.* 1.15.73].

27. On Semele, mother of Dionysos by Zeus, cf. Homer, *Il.* 14.325, Euripides, *Bacch.*, 28–43.

28. The frustrated sexual encounter between Dionysus and Prosymnos is told at length in Clement, *Protr.* 2.34. See art. "Feige I (Ficus carica)," *RAC* 7.677. Notice the hypocritical *aposiopesis* of Theodoret in calling attention to the phallic ritual.

29. For Castor and Pollux, mere men, as gods cf. Athenagoras, *Leg.* 29,2; Justin, *1 Apol.* 21, 2; Clement, *Protr.* 30, Lactantius, *Div. inst.* 1.10, 1.15. The sons of Tyndareus are called Ephestioi only in Theodoret. See art. "Dioskuren," *RAC* 3.1122–38.

30. Demosthenes, *Embassy* 158. The temple was actually in Thessaly.

31. For the Leocorion see *supra*, 7.43. See also Pausanias, 10.10, 1; Cicero, *ND* 3.19, 50; *PECS,* 485, which says that the Leocorion may be identified with the round building, 18 meters in diameter, near the Altar of the Twelve Gods in the new Agora, uncovered when a trench for the Athens-Piraeus railroad was opened up; see also J.Travlos, *Pictorial Dictionary of Ancient Athens* (New York, 1971), 3, 5, 578, fig. 5.

32. Oenomaos, fr. 12; cf. Eusebius, *P.e.* 5.34.2–4. See Canivet, *Entre,* 224. Cleomedes, the boxer, was from Astypalaia, in the South of the island of Cos; cf. *PECS,* art. "Kos," 466.

33. Antinous, the handsome Bithynian favorite of the emperor Hadrian, was drowned in the Nile, in A.D. 130 For his apotheosis cf. Origen, *C. Cels.* 3.36, ed. Chadwick, 152 and n. 1. See A. Hermann, "Zur Typologie des Heiligen-Unheiligen in der Spätantike," in *Mullus: Festschrift Theodor Klauser,* ed. A. Stuidber and A. Hermann, *JbAC,* supplementary vol. 1 (Munster, 1964), 155–67, and for his portraits see C. W. Clairmont, *Die Bildnisse des Antinous: Ein Beitrag zur Portraetplastik unter Kaiser Hadrian* (Rome, 1966). His statues are everywhere to this day, e.g., in Delphi and Naples Museums: *Enciclopedia*

THEODORET OF CYRUS: *A CURE FOR PAGAN MALADIES*

dell'Arte Antica (Rome, 1958), s.v. "Antinoo." Pausanias 8. 9, 7, reports on a shrine to him in Mantineia, Arcadia. Antinous is constantly mentioned by the Fathers: e.g., Athenagoras, *Leg.* 30.2 (and Marcovich, ed. 83); Tatian, *Orat.* 10.2; Justin, *1 Apol.* 29.4; Theophilus, *Ad Autol.* 3.8; Clement, *Protr.* 4.49.1–3; Origen, *C. Cels.* 5.63, 8.9; Tertullian, *Apol.* 13.9.

34. For Hyacinthus, the Spartan boy favorite of Apollo, a three-day festival was celebrated in Amyclae, during three days of July; cf. Athenaeus, *Deip.* 4.139f; Lucian, *Dial. D.* 14; Ovid, *Met.* 10.219; Pausanias. 3.1.10 (*Pausanias Guide to Greece*, trans. P. Levi, Penguin Books 2 [Harmondsworth and New York, 1979], 33 and n. 62) also 3.10.8, 3.16.2, 3.18.6; art. "Huakinthia," Pauly-Wissowa, *RE* 9.1.1–2.

35. Antiochus, fr. 15 ed. Müller. [=Clement, *Protr.* 3.45=Eusebius, *P.e.* 6.2–5].

36. Acrisios, a legendary king of Argos, was husband of Eurydice and father of Danae; cf. A. B. Cook, *Zeus: A Study in Ancient Religion* 2 (New York, 1964–65), 1115; art. "Danae," *RAC* 3.567–71.

37. Leander, fr. 5 [=Eusebius, *P.e.* 2.6.2–5.] See Canivet, *Entre*, 224. For Cleomachus (or Kleochus) at Didyma, cf. J. Fontenrose, *Didyma* (Berkeley, 1988), 165f.

38. Lycophron was a priestess of Artemis. For the temple in Magnesia see Strabo, 14. 1, 40. For Zeno of Myndos, a Greek grammarian, see H. Gärtner, *RE* XA, 143f.

39. The town of Telmessos was on the borders of Lycia and Caria, noted for its oracle of Apollo, which was consulted by Croesus. Its ancient theater is well preserved.

40. For the burial of Patroclus cf. Homer, *Il.* 23.236–54.

41. Thucydides, 2.34. For the battle of Marathon cf. *CAH* 4, chap. 8, 2nd ed.

42. Homer, *Od.* 11. 24–37. This is the oldest literary account of necromancy; cf. G. Luck, *Arcana Mundi: Magic and the Occult in the Greek and Roman Worlds: A Collection of Ancient Texts* (Baltimore, 1985), 176–77.

43. Aristocles, fr. 7 [=Eusebius, *P.e.* 15.2.8]. Aristocles, second-century A.D. philosopher from Messina, Sicily, was the teacher of Alexander of Aphrodisias. See Diogenes Laertius, 5.4. where the story goes awry.

44. Pindar, fr. 132 [=Clement, *Str.* 4.26.167] See I. Opelt, "Die christliche Spätantike und Pindar," *ByzF* 2 (1967[=Polychordia]): 284f., esp. 290.

45. Empedocles, fr. 146 [=Clement, *Str.* 4.23.150].

46. Heraclitus, fr. 24 [=Clement, *Str.* 4.4.16].

47. Heraclitus, fr. 25 [=Clement, *Str.* 4.7.49].

48. The sons of Oedipus, Eteocles and Polyneices, fought in internecine warfare in Aeschylus, *Seven against Thebes.*

49. In 514 B.C. Harmodius and Aristogeiton, who had migrated to

Athens from Tanagra, conspired against Hippias and his brother, Hipparchus, apparently not so much for political principle, but simply because of a private wrong inflicted by Hipparchus. See Thucydides, 1.20, 6.54–60, *CAH* 4.79, and now C. Gafforini, "Armodio e Aristogitone e la propaganda seleucide," *Aevum* 63 (1989): 17–23. Statues in their honor, the first in the Agora, were set up in 510, near the orchestra, honoring them as liberators of the city; cf. J. Travlos, *Pictorial Dictionary of Ancient Athens* (London and New York, 1971), 3, 301, and figs. 5, 29. See also Pausanias 1.29.2.

50. Heraclitus fr. 27 [=Clement, *Str.* 4.22.144].

51. Plato, *Phaedo* 114b [=Clement, *Str.* 3.3.19].

52. Plato, *Phaedo* 114c [=Clement, *Str.* 4.6.37].

53. Plato, *Phaedo* 62b [=Clement, *Str.* 3.3.19, FOTC 85, p. 268].

54. Plato, *Phaedo* 67c and *Resp.* 1. 330e [=Clement, *Str.* 4.22.144].

55. Plato, *Phaedo* 64a. [=Clement, *Str.* 3.3.17; FOTC 85, p. 266].

56. Plato, *Resp.* 5.468e [=Eusebius, *P.e.* 13.11.1].

57. Plato, *Resp.* 5.469ab [=Eusebius, *P.e.* 13.11.1].

58. Plato, *Crat.* 398b–c. 51. Plato, *Phaedo* 114b [=Clement, *Str.* 3.3.19, FOTC 85, p. 268].

59. Hesiod, *Op.* 121–23.

60. Plato, *Epin.* 973c [=Clement, *Str.* 3.1.10, 5.1.7].

61. Eccles. 11:28.

62. Prov. 4:18.

63. Wisd. 3:1.

64. Plato, *Resp.* 2.361e –362a [=Clement, *Str.* 5.14.108=Eusebius, *P.e.* 13.13.35].

65. Plato, *Laws* 11.926e –927a [=Eusebius, *P.e.* 12.3.1].

66. Plato, *Apol.* 28d [=Eusebius, *P.e.* 13.10.3].

67. Plato, *Apol.* 29a [=Eusebius, *P.e.* 13.10.5].

68. Plato, *Apol.* 29b [=Eusebius, *P.e.* 13.10.6].

69. Plato, *Apol.* 41c.

70. Plato, *Apol.* 30cd.

71. Meletus and Anytos (along with Lycon) were the judges of Socrates. See 7.47, also *CAH* 5. 391–96.

72. Theodoret criticizes some of Plato's errors at *Affect.* 12.70f.

73. [=Clement, *Str.* 4.8.56]. Anaxarchus of Abdera, a pupil of Democritus. For the anecdote cf. K. Freeman, *The Pre-Socratic Philosophers: A Companion to Diels, Fragmente der Vorsokratiker,* 2d ed. (Oxford, 1959), 330; Diogenes Laertius 9.58–59, which was often invoked by the Fathers, e.g., Tertullian, *Apol.* 50 (and the excellent note in F. J. A. Hort and J. B. Mayor, *Clement of Alexandria, Miscellanies,* Book 7 [London and New York, 1902], 475–76); Origen, *C. Cels.* 7.53 (and Chadwick, ed., 439, n. 8). See more recently, Paul Bernard, "Le Philosophe Anaxarque et le roi Nicocréon de Salamine," *Journal des Savants* (1984): 3–49.

74. [=Clement, *Str.* 4.8.56]. Tertullian, *Apol.*, 50, juxtaposes a similar incident with the pounding of Anaxarchus but makes the character an Attica meretrix. See Mayor-Souter edition, 477. Erathosthenes, 275–195, born in Cyrene, in Africa, and based in Alexandria, has been called the founder of astronomical geography and of scientific chronology. Zeno of Elea was a student of Parmenides and noted for his paradoxes, especially that concerning Achilles and the turtle. See G. Vlastos, "Plato's Testimony concerning Zeno of Elea," *JHS* 95 (1975): 136–62.

75. For Timotheus of Pergamon cf. Pauly-Wissowa, *RE* VI A 2 (1937) col. 1358.

76. Achaicos was a Peripatetic philosopher.

77. Miltiades (c. 550 B.C.–489 B.C) was the Athenian hero of the decisive battle of Marathon in 490 B.C., in which the Athenians repelled the Persian invasion, with six thousand Persian losses. Cimon (c. 512–449 B.C.), son of the aforementioned Miltiades, was commander-in-chief of the Athenian forces and head of the Delian confederacy from 476 to 462 B.C. but fell from power for his Spartan sympathies and was ostracized, 461; cf. *CAH* 5.46–49, 69–72. Pericles was the great Athenian leader, 461–429 B.C. under whom the beautification of Athens reached its greatest heights and became "the school of Hellas." See *CAH* 5.72–75, 91–94, 166–69. Themistocles, c. 528–462 B.C. as archon of Athens, 493 B.C. fortified the new harbor of Peiraeus and orchestrated the great sea victory over Persia at Salamis in 480 B.C; he was ostracized in 471 and had to flee to Persia. A *Life* by Plutarch is extant. Aristides, surnamed the Just (c. 520–c. 468 B.C), was one of the ten Athenian generals at Marathon. He was a rival of Themistocles and was ostracized in 483, but after being recalled he commanded eight thousand Athenian foot-soldiers at the battle of Plataea in 479 B.C. He earned the nickname for his scrupulous fairness in assessing membership dues in the Delian League.

78. Brasidas, a Spartan commander, active in the Archidamian wars of 431–421, also attacked and captured the Athenian colony in Amphipolis, Thrace in 424, but was himself killed in 422.

79. King Agesilaus II, a Spartan king (c. 443–c. 358), who campaigned in Asia Minor to free the Greeks from the Persians. Xenophon wrote *Agesilaus* as a panegyric. See C. D. Hamilton, *Agesilaus and the Failure of Spartan Hegemony* (Ithaca, NY, 1991). Lysander, a famous Spartan navarch, defeated the Athenians at the battle of Aegospotami, 405 B.C. See *CAH* 5.358–67.

80. Pelopidas and Epaminondas initiated a period of Theban supremacy in Greece, 371–362. With the defeat of Sparta at the battle of Leuctra and the refoundation of Messenia as an independent state, the creation of a new federal Arcadian state was created, with a capital at Megalopolis. See J. Buckler, *The Theban Hegemony, 371–362 B.C.* (Cambridge, MA, 1980).

81. Scipio the Elder (c. 236–c. 183 B.C.) fought at Cannae (216 B.C.), was proconsul in Spain (210 B.C.), and consul in Sicily (205 B.C.) and

defeated Hannibal at Zama, in 202 B.C. Scipio the Younger (c. 185–129 B.C.) fought in the battle of Pydna (168 B.C.) was consul in Africa (147 B.C.), and stormed Carthage in 146 B.C. Marcus Portious Cato the Elder, also known as Cato the Censor (234–149 B.C.), fought in the Second Punic War (218–201 BC) and won acclaim in the battle of the Metaurus (207). After much political experience, he was elected consul in 195, suppressed a rebellion in Spain in 194, and in 191 as military tribune was central in the defeat of Antiochus III at Thermopylae. Sulla, Roman general and dictator (c. 138 B.C.–78 B.C.), fought memorably in the Numidian War as quaestor under C. Marius in 107, and he fought again, in 104 and 103, under Marius against the Germans. He is known especially for his military occupation of Rome in 88 and his reign as dictator until he resigned shortly before his death in 79. Gaius Marius (ca. 157–86 B.C.) fought at Numantia under Scipio the Younger in 133 and was responsible for reforming the Roman method of recruiting for and discharging from the army in the last decade of the second century B.C. He became the opponent of Sulla in the 80s. For Caius Julius Caesar, Roman general, statesman, orator, and historian (100 B.C.–Ides of March, 44 B.C), see *CAH* 9. 691–740.

82. Cyrus the Great, who reigned from ca. 557 to 530 B.C., conquered Media, Sardis, Lydia, Babylonia, and central Asia. See P. Briant, *Histoire de l'empire perse: De Cyrus à Alexandre* (Paris, 1996), chaps. 1–2. Darius, king of the Persians ca. 522–486 B.C., came against the Greeks in the Persian war and suffered defeat at Marathon in 490, which stopped the extension of his empire to the west. See Briant, *Histoire de l'empire perse,* chap. 4. He died in 486 B.C. Xerxes, son of Darius, ruled over Persia 486–465 B.C. He continued his father's campaign against the Greeks and met defeat at the battle of Salamis (September 480). See Briant, *Histoire de l'empire perse,* chap. 13. Alexander the Great became king of Macedon in 336, defeated Darius, the Persian king, at Issos, in 333, and again at Gaugamela in 331, also conquering Afghanistan and India, and died at Babylon at the age of thirty-two in 323 B.C. See Peter Green, *Alexander of Macedon, 356–323 B.C.: A Historical Biography* (Berkeley, Calif., 1974), passim.

83. On Hadrian, A.D. 117–138, cf. *ANRW* II, 23, 1, 287–92. On Antoninus Pius, Roman emperor, 138–161; see *RAC* 1:477–80. For a similar listing cf. Theophilus, *Ad Autol.* 3.27.

84. Cf. John Chrysostom, *Hom. 26.5 in 2 Cor.*, quoted by M. A. Schatkin, FOTC 73. 34–35: "For that, whilst alive one should win battles and victories, being a king and having armies at his disposal, is nothing marvelous, no, nor startling or novel; but that after Cross and Tomb one should perform such great things throughout every land and sea, that it is which is most especially replete with such amazement and proclaims His divine and unutterable Power. And Alexander indeed after his decease never restored again his kingdom which had been rent in pieces and quite abolished: indeed how was it

likely he, dead, should do so? But Christ then most of all set up His after He was dead."

85. Augustus had prepared his own tomb by building a mausoleum as early as 28 B.C. between the Flaminian Way and the Tiber. When he died A.D. August 19, 14, he left three scrolls, one of which contained a record of his reign, which he directed to have engraved on bronze and posted at the entrance to the mausoleum; cf. *CAH* 10.571f. and Map facing p. 582, Plan 2, and Suetonius, *Vita Aug.* 100–101. Still surviving is the Gemma Augustea, a sardonyx cameo dating from A.D. 14–37, one register of which shows the deified Augustus looking over approvingly at his chosen successor, Tiberius, stepping from his chariot.

86. The Seleucid king Antiochus III (223 B.C.–187 B.C.) captured the city of Teos from the Attalids and in return the city established a cult that related Antiochus and his wife to Dionysus, the chief god of the city; cf. *The Oxford History of the Classical World* (Oxford and New York, 1986), 336.

87. On Gaius Caligula, Roman emperor, A.D. 37–41 cf. Suetonius, *Gaius (Caligula)*, c. 22: "And he nearly assumed a royal diadem then and there, turning the semblance of a principate into an autocracy. However, after his courtiers reminded him that he already outranked any prince or king, he insisted on being treated as a god—sending for the most revered or artistically famous statues of the Greek deities (including that of Jupiter at Olympia), and having their heads replaced by his own, trans. R. Graves (Penguin Classics, 1957). On Vespasian (69–79), cf. *CAH* XI. 19: "It is significant too that he completed the Temple of Divus Claudius on the Caelian and restored his cult. It was a fitting reward that he should take his place next after them on the roll of deified emperors; that, after Divus Augustus and Divus Claudius, Divus Vespasianus should be handed down to the gratitude of posterity." Hadrian, a Spaniard, who succeeded Trajan as emperor, was an indefatigable traveler throughout the empire, an aficionado of Hellenism and patron of the arts and also of jurisprudence. On the mausoleum Hadrian built for himself, which still exists as the Castel sant'Angelo, cf. *CAH* 11.797–99, G. Becatti, *The Art of Ancient Greece and Rome: From the Rise of Greece to the Fall of Rome* (Englewood Cliffs, NJ, 1968), 340. See also K. Scott, *The Imperial Cult under the Flavians* (Stuttgart, 1936; repr., New York, 1975), art. "Consecratio II (Kaiserapotheose)," *RAC* 3.284–94.

88. On the sanctuaries of the martyrs cf. A. Grabar, *Martyrium: Recherches sur le culte des reliques et l'art chrétienne antique* (Paris, 1946), esp. v.1.214–27 (Antioche). This eloquent statement on martyrdom is quoted in the article "Martyr," *DACL* 10.2.24–51.

89. On pilgrimages see E. D. Hunt, *Holy Land Pilgrimage in the Later Roman Empire, A.D. 312–460* (Oxford, 1982); G. Stemberger, *Juden und Christen im Heiligen Land: Palaestina unter Konstantin und Theodosius* (Munich, 1987); H. Donner, *Pilgerfahrt ins Heilige Land: Die ältesten Berichte christlicher*

Palästinapilger (4–7 Jahrhundert) (Stuttgart, 1979). See also Basil, *in hon. S. Mamas*, PG 31.589, *ep.* 155, 164, 165 (for relics of Sabas).

90. See art. "Reliques et reliquaires," *DACL* 14.2. 2294–2359. E. D. Hunt, *Holy Land Pilgrimage in the Later Roman Empire*, 128–36. On replicas of eyes cf. B. Kotting, *Peregrinatio religiosa*, 49 and n. 257 and esp. 398–99. For *ex-votos* see art. "Ex-Voto," *DACL* 5.1.1037–49; art. "Votive und Weihegaben," *LThK* 10.2.897–98; Gregory Nazianzus, *Contra Jul.* 1.86. For pagan background, cf. F. van Straten, "Votives and Votaries in Greek Sanctuaries," in *Le sanctuaire grec entretiens sur l'antiquite classiqué* 28 (Geneva, 1990), 247–90.

91. On priests and sacristans (νεωχωροι) erecting their τροπαιον cf. J. Bernardi, "Le mot τροπαιον appliqué aux Martyrs," *VigChr* 8 (1954): 174–75.

92. See Peter Brown, *The Cult of the Saints* (Chicago, 1981), 50, who uses this paragraph as his launching pad for c. 3: "The Invisible Companion," On Martyrs' Names Given to Children." Cf. H. Delehaye, *Les orgines du culte des martyrs* (Brussels, 1933), 50–140; art. "Noms Propres," *DACL* 12.2.1481–1553, esp. 1551f.

93. The most obvious contemporary example was Babylas replacing Apollo at Daphne in Antioch; cf. Chrysostom, *Pan. Bab.* 126. See also Theodoret, *History of the Monks of Syria*, c. 28, Thalelaeus, trans. Price, 182, and n. 3. Also Theodoret, *H.e.* 5.21 for the destruction of the temple of Zeus at Apamea. See W. H. C. Frend, "Monks and the End of Greco-Roman Paganism in Syria and Egypt" *CrSt* 11, 1 (1990): 469–84. F. Paschoud, "Christian Intolerance as It Was Seen and Judged by Pagans" *CrSt* 11, 1 (1990): 545–77.

94. Theodoret invokes other martyrs' names in *ep.*131. Those named here were specially venerated in the Antioch area, a point used by Canivet to argue for a date of composition prior to Theodoret's move to Cyrus; cf. P. Canivet, "Précisions sur la date de la Curatio de Théodoret," *RechScR* 36 (1949): 588–92. See also Delehaye, *Les origines du culte des martyrs*, 219–22.

95. Cf. Chrysostom, *Pan. Bab.* 72: "for most people revelry alone was no longer the reason for the ascent to the suburb but also desire for the saint." Also *Pan. Bab.* 104: [Replying to Libanius's complaint that the destruction of Daphne's temple has taken away a resting place from worldly turmoil] "How is the temple more devoid of turmoil and a harbor sheltered from the waves, where there are flutes, kettle-drums, headaches, revelry and drunkenness," trans. Schatkin, 117, 136. The sideswipe at dances may be aimed at the Messalians or Meletians; cf. Theodoret, *Haer.* 4.7, 4.11

NOTES TO DISCOURSE 9

1. The Eunomians are constantly attacked by the orthodox for preferring prettiness of style to substance; cf. Gregory Nazianzus, *orat.* 27, 1–2;

Gregory of Nyssa, *C. Eunom.* 1.34 (NPNF ser. 2, 5. 79); A. Meredith, "Traditional Apologetic in the *Contra Eunomium* of Gregory of Nyssa," *SP* 14, 3, (=TU 117): 315–19. See also Theodoret's attack on a sophist named Asterius in *A History of the Monks*, 2.21.

2. On the harvesting of pearls see Aristotle, *H. A.* 1.5. 490a, Clement, *Str.* 21.3; Origen, *Comm. in Matt.*10.7, Basil, *Hex.* 7.3, 7.6; C. Nardi, "Quid de margaritarum origine Iohannes Chrysostomus senserit," *Latinitas* 28 (1980): 95–99.

3. On storing gold and silver cf. J. F. Healy, *Mining and Metallurgy in the Greek and Roman World* (London, 1978). On simplicity in the Christian message cf. Basil, *Hex.* 3.8–9.

4. For Minos, son of Zeus and Europa and legendary king and legislator of Crete cf. Clement, *Str.* 1.26.170, who tells us that the law writing took nine years, echoing Plato, *Leg.* 1.624b. See G. R. Murrow, *Plato's Cretan City: A Historical Interpretation of the Laws* (Princeton, N.J., 1960). Minos supposedly received the laws from Zeus in a cave; cf. Herodotus, 1.173, 3.122, 7.169–71. Also cf. Tertullian, *Apol.* 25; Lactantius, *Div. inst.* 1.22.

5. [=Eusebius, *P.e.* 12.49.5] Zaleuchos of the Italian Locri is always associated with Charondas, a lawgiver at Catania, Sicily, whose code was also adopted at Rhegium in southern Italy. Charondas may have been the pupil of Zaleuchos. Strabo records (XII. p. 539) that in his day (*pace* Theodoret!) the laws of Charondas were in force in Mazaca, a town of Cappadocia; cf. *CAH* 4.116, 355, 356 n.

6. [=Clement, *Str.* 1.26.170]. What Clement says is: Chamaeleon of Heraclea, in his work *On Drunkenness* and Aristotle, *On the Constitution of Locri*, record that Zaleuchos of Locri got his laws from Athena. Zaleuchos was author of the first Greek codification of laws, c. 650 B.C.; cf. *CAH* 4.115–16.

7. Oenomaos, fr. 10 [=Eusebius, *P.e.* 5.27. 8]. On Lycurgus as lawgiver see Plato, *Leg.* 1. 630d–632d, *Resp.* 10.599d.

8. Oenomaos, fr. 10 [=Eusebius, *P.e.* 5.27. 8]. This oracle is duplicated *infra*, 10. 33. Cf. Herodotus 1.65; Diodorus Siculus, 7.14,1; Clement, *Protr.* 10.108. For details on the association between Sparta and Delphi on the Lycurgan constitution cf. H. W. Parke, D. E. W. Wormell, *The Delphic Oracle* (Oxford, 1956), 1. 85–89. On the text of the oracle used here cf. Canivet, *Entre*, 232–33.

9. Phlius was a town in Phliasia, Peloponnesus, about fourteen miles southwest of Corinth, founded by Dorians from Argos.

10. For Apis of Argos cf. Clement, *Str.* 1.21.106. He was a legendary hero, son of Apollo, who went from Naupactus to Argos, whence he expelled all the serpents, so that Argos was sometimes called the "Apian" land. For Mnason in Phocis cf. Pauly-Wissowa, *RE* 15 2, 2257, 2248. Demonax of Mantinea in Arcadia was named arbitrator for Cyrene, Libya, when that city consulted the Delphic oracle on what form of government would be prefer-

able; cf. Herodotus 4.161. Pagondas of Achaia took part in the battle of Delium, 424, Thucydides, 4.91, 93. Archias is designated legislator of Cnidus instead of Eudoxos; cf. Clem. *Str.* 1.15.69. Philolaus of Thebes is mentioned in Aristotle, *Pol.* 2.9, 5–7. Pittacus (Aristotle, *Pol.* 2.12) rescued his native Mytilene from civil war, c. 595 B.C. Plato (*Hipp. maj.* 281c) tells us that Pittacus took no active role in politics.

11. Nestor is so described in Homer, *Il.* 1.249.

12. Solon, Athenian legislator, poet and statesman, c. 638–c. 559 B.C.

13. Cf. Clement, *Str.* 1.16. 80. "Draco has left laws but he adapted them to a constitution which already existed and there is no peculiarity in them worth mentioning except the greatness and severity of the punishments," Aristotle, *Ath. Pol.* 4,1. 2.12, 1274b and see further M. Gagarin, *Drakon and Early Athenian Homicide Law,* Yale Classic Monographs 3 (New Haven, 1981).

14. Cleisthenes, or Clisthenes, Athenian statesman and legislator, who initiated constitutional reforms in Athens in 508 B.C., developing in a democratic spirit the constitution of Solon, breaking up the power of the landed aristocracy, expanding the Boule to five hundred members and substituting for the old four tribes ten new ones; see *CAH* 4.141–72. Solon (c. 640–560 B.C.) was an Athenian statesman, legislator, and poet, elected chief magistrate in 595. His new legislation mainly codified existing practice; cf. *The Oxford History of the Classical World* (Oxford and New York, 1986), 32–35. Cf. Theophilus, *Ad Autol.* 3.23. For Trajan in Persia and Scythia see *CAH* 11, chap. 6.

15. The list of barbarian states is more decorative than substantive. Cf. Herodotus, 1.201–5; Basil, *Ep.* 324.

16. Theodoret is fond of these cumulative listings; cf. *H.e.* 4.3; also 1.10, where he is quoting the letter of Constantine.

17. For the places in Athens mentioned see J. Travlos, *Pictorial Dictionary of Ancient Athens* (New York, 1971), s.v. For the Eleven cf. Aristotle, *Ath. Pol.* 52.

18. The expulsion of strangers (ξενηλασια) is criticized by Plato, *Leg.* 12.949e–950c, *Protag.* 342b–d. The license of Spartan women is alluded to in *Leg.* 1. 637c. On the new citizens, the Νεοδαμωδεις, cf. A. H. M. Jones, *Sparta* (Cambridge, MA, 1967), 9, 80, 82.

19. On the laws on sexual behavior of Lycurgus, the Spartan legislator c. 600, see Plutarch, *Lycurgus.*

20. Cf. Plato, *Leg.* 9.858e.

21. The emperor Gaius Caesar Augustus Germanicus (Caligula) (37–41) succeeded Tiberius (A.D.14–37), and Claudius (41–54) followed. Claudius was poisoned by his wife, Agrippina, to pave the way for Nero (54–68).

22. On Vespasian (69–79), see Frend, *MPEC,* 181f; on Titus (79–81); on Domitian (81–96), cf. E. M. Smallwood, *CPh* 51 (1956): 1–13, ANRW II, 23,1, 257–72, Tertullian, *Apol.* 5.4, Hegesippus, *apud Eusebium,* *H.e.* 3.19–20, Frend, *MPEC,* 211–15.

23. On Trajan (98–117) see P. Keretsztes, "Rome and the Christian Church," ANRW II, 23, 1, 273–87, Frend, *MPEC*, 217–22. On Hadrian (117–38) cf. ANRW II, 23,1, 287–92.

24. For Trajan's campaigns against Persia and Scythia cf. Jerome, *Chron. Euseb.* sub anno 2118. "We have, therefore, evidence that under Trajan at the latest the unit was thirty cohorts , suggesting that it had extensive patrolling duties" (cf. *CAH* vol. 10, p. 223). For clarifying details on the Chronicle's synchronizations and its translation by Jerome see T. D. Barnes, *Constantine and Eusebius* (Cambridge, MA, 2006), 111–20.

25. For Hadrian's treatment of Jerusalem and for the building of its replacement, Aelia Capitolina, cf. *CAH* 11.313–14; S. Perowne, *Hadrian* (London, 1960) c.XIX. For Hadrian's toleration of the Christians cf. Frend, *MPEC*, 223–25.

26. For Antoninus Pius (138–61) see Eusebius, *H.e.* 4.26,10; Lucius Verus (161–169); Eusebius, *H.e.* 5.5.

27. On Commodus (180–192) see *ANRW* II.23.1, 304–9. On Maximian (235–38) and Carinus (283–85), Frend, *MPEC* 443f. T. D. Barnes, *Constantine and Eusebius* (Cambridge, MA, 1981), pp. 8–27 provides a masterly account of how the East/West division of the empire was administered; see esp. p. 8: "In 293 Diocletian and Maximian who, as Augusti, styled themselves brothers, adopted Galerius and Constantius as their sons." Theodoret's *Ecclesiastical History* (on which see Istvan Pasztori Kupan, *Theodoret of Cyrus,* Early Church Fathers [Routledge, 2006]), pp. 18 and 226, note 20) covers the years 325–428 and begins with Maximian and Galerius. Eusebius, *The Ecclesiastical History*, LCL 153, trans. Kirsopp Lake (Cambridge, Mass., 1926, repr. 1998), vol. 2, VIII, XIII, 10 pp. 298–99: *The whole principate was rent in twain* and n. 5. The meaning of this sentence is that the Empire was divided in respect of its treatment of Christians: persecution continued in the East.

28. For the anti-religious policy of Diocletian (284–306) see Frend, *MPEC,* c. 15: "The Great Persecution, 303–312." Theodoret begins his *H.e.* with the overthrow of Maximinan and Maxentius. See Frend, *MPEC,* 517–18. For Licinius, cf. Frend, *MPEC* 510–13, 520. For Maxentius, see Barnes, *Constantine and Eusebius,* 25–26, 29–34, 37–43. On the recent Persian persecution, cf. Theodoret, *H.e.;* M. Brok, *MSR* 10 (1953):181–94.

29. On the Sunday destruction of the churches in 303 cf. Theodoret, *H.e.* 5.38; Eusebius, *H.e.* 82.4.

30. The eyewitness accounts of Julian's persecutions, A.D. 362, underscore the urgency of Theodoret's apologetic. They are detailed by him in *H.e.* 3.11–14. See R. Browning, *The Emperor Julian* (Berkeley, 1976), 159–218. The earlier view, however, that the *Curatio* is a response to Julian's *Contra Galilaeos* has rightly been abandoned. Cf. Canivet, *Entre,* 113, and SC 57, Intro., no. 27.

31. Exod. 3:2.

32. Cf. Tertullian, *Apol.* 50.13.

33. On the prematureness of obituary notices like this see P. Allen, "Some Aspects of Hellenism in the Early Greek Church Historians," *Traditio* 43 (1987): 368–81.

34. The choirs of ascetics are dealt with at length by Theodoret in his *Religious History*.

35. On the spread of Christianity as a testimony to its divine origin cf. Eusebius, *H.e.* 1.

36. A pointer to the date of composition, perhaps; the Persian persecution, dated to 426/427; cf. Theodoret, *H.e.* 5.3, 2.

37. These harrowing details are duplicated in Theodoret. *H.e.* 5.39.

38. On Zoroaster cf. H. Chadwick, "The Relativity of Moral Codes: Rome and Persia in Late Antiquity," in *Early Christian Literature and the Classical Intellectual Tradition, in honorem R. M. Grant,* ed. W. R. Schoedel and R. L. Wilken (Paris, 1979).

39. Cf. Eusebius, *P.e.* 1, 4, 6, 6.10, 16, 6.10, 38, and Canivet, *Entre,* 296–97. The accusation of incestuous practices among the Persians is rampant among the Fathers. See *The Octavius of Marcus Minucius Felix,* trans. G. W. Clarke, ACW 39 (New York, 1974), pp. 64–65: "They gather for a feast with all their children, sisters, mothers—all sexes and all ages. There, flushed with the banquet after such feasting and drinking, they begin to burn with incestuous passions." Also, pp. 338–39: "illustrations in discussions on the variations in the moral code": Origen, *C. Cels.* 5.27 (mothers, daughters); Tatian, *Orat.* 28 (mothers), Lucian, *De sacrif.* 5 (sister); Tertullian , *Apol.* 9.16 : *Persas cum suis matribus misceri Ctesias refert.*

40. The immorality of Zoroaster's laws cf. Clement, *Str.* 3.30, 3.48. Porphyry, *VP* 12.23 states that Pythagoras was a pupil of Zoroaster.

41. The Massagetai, also mentioned at 5.55 and 8.6, were a savage race occupying the great plain to the east of the Caspian sea; cf. Herodotus, 1.201, 205, 212, 214–16.

42. Tertullian, *Apol.* 9.9, reports that some of the Scythians eat corpses.

43. [=Eusebius, *P.e.* 1.4.7]. The Tibareni lived in N. Pontus, along and behind the southeast shores of the Black Sea; cf. *CAH* 4.195.

44. The Hyrcanians were northeast Caucasians, located on the southeastern shores of the Caspian Sea, and constituted a Persian satrapy with the Parthians; cf. Herodotus, 3.117, 7.62. See *Der kleine Pauly* (Stuttgart, 1967), s.v. "Hyrkania."

45. Scythia as a Roman province comprised the lands immediately south of the mouths of the Danube.

46. Plato, *Resp.* 5.457b [=Eusebius, *P.e.* 13.19.1–2].

47. Plato, *Leg.* 7.804de [=Eusebius, *P.e.* 13.19.5].

48. The words are from the famous farewell scene of Hector and Andromache, Homer, *Il.* 6.490–92.

49. Plato, *Leg.* 11.925a [=Eusebius, *P.e.* 13.19.12]

50. For Candaulos, king of Lydia cf. Herodotus, 1.7–12 (where the speaker is Gyges), Clement, *Paed.* 2.10, 100; 3.5, 33.

51. Plato, *Leg.* 6.771e–772a [=Eusebius, *P.e.* 13.19.13].

52. Plato, *Resp.* 5. 457c–d [=Eusebius, *P.e.* 13.19.14].

53. Plato, *Resp.* 5. 458c–d [=Eusebius, *P.e.* 13.19.15].

54. See n. 53.

55. Plato, *Resp.* 10. 595c [=Eusebius, *P.e.* 12.49. 2].

56. Plato, *Resp.* 5.460e [=Eusebius, *P.e.* 13.19.17].

57. Plato, *Resp.* 5. 461bc. [=Eusebius, *P.e.* 13.19.18].

58. Echetus was a mythical king of Epirus who crushed his daughter's eyes with bronze spikes and confined her to a dungeon to grind grains of bronze, with the cynical promise that he would restore her eyes when she had transformed the bronze into corn. Phalaris, tyrant of Agrigentum, Sicily, c. 570–554 B.C., was notorious for his cruelty, especially for human sacrifices in a heated brazen bull. They are coupled in Gregory Nazianzus, *Orat.* 4.91 (PG 35.624 and note (13), quoting Homer, *Od.* 18.82, and Ovid, *Ibis,* 439). For the execution of Peter and Paul under Nero cf. Jerome, *De viris illustribus,* 1.

59. On abortifacient drugs cf. art. "Abtreibung," *RAC* 1.33, 55–60, W. Schaefke, "Frühchristlicher Widerstand. II, 2. Abtreibung und Aussetzung Neugeborener," ANRW II, 23, 1 (1979): 526–27; A. Keller, *Die Abortiva in der römischen Kaiserzeit* (Stuttgart, 1988).

60. Plato, *Phaedrus* 256d–e [=Eusebius, *P.e.* 13.20.6].

61. Plato, *Phaedrus* 256d–e [=Eusebius, *P.e.* 13.20.6].

62. Nero was emperor A.D. 52–64. His follies, crimes, and immoralities are detailed in Suetonius, *Nero,* 20–38. For Sardanopoulos, cf. Clement, *Paed.* 3.11, 70, writing on adultery of the eyes, says: "The effeminate Sardanapulus, king of the Assyrians, is pictured to us as such a man, reclining on his couch, smoothing down his purple dress, and showing the whites of his eyes." For a fuller description cf. Athenaeus, *Deip.* 12.528F–529D.

63. For Plato's laws on homicide cf. *Leg.* 9.865–69. [=Eusebius, *P.e.* 13.21. 2–7].

64. Matt. 5:28.

65. Matt. 5:32.

66. 1 Cor. 7:1–2.

67. 1 Cor. 7:4–5.

68. 1 Cor. 7:5.

69. 1 Cor. 7:5.

70. 1 Cor. 7:5.

71. Cf. 1 Cor. 7:32.

72. 1 Cor. 7:32–33.

73. Matt. 5:22.

74. Matt. 5:44. On Christians' love of enemies cf. Tertullian, *Apol.* 37, 1; Athenagoras, *Leg.* 10; Eusebius, *H.e.* 9.8.13–15.

75. Matt. 5:45.
76. Cf. Matt. 5:27.
77. Luke 14:33.
78. John 16:33.
79. Matt. 5:11–12.
80. John 15:20.
81. Matt. 10:25.
82. For Athena Polias cf. E. des Places, *La religion grecque* (Paris, 1969), 45–46.

Notes to Discourse 10

1. For general background to this chapter cf. S. Levin, "The Old Greek Oracles in Decline," *ANRW* II. 18.2, 1989, 1599–1649; R. Lane Fox, *Pagans and Christians* (New York, 1987), c. 2, 168–261. The devil as tyrant enslaving the human race was also the opening theme of *Affect.* 7. Cf. *Anges et demons: Actes du Colloque de Liege et de Louvain-la-Neuve* (Louvain-la-Neuve, 1989), esp. J. Ries, "Cultes paiennes et demons dans l'Apologétique chrétienne de Justin à Augustin," 337–52; G. J. M. Bartelink, "Les démons comme brigands" *VigChr* 21 (1967): 12–24. For the deposition of tyrants cf. Chrysostom, *Pan. Bab.* 2.

2. The devils continue to be depicted as tyrants and false prognosticators throughout paragraphs 1–44. Cf. Chrysostom, *Pan. Bab.* 3, FOTC 73, p. 77; Cyril H., *Catech.* 4.1.

3. "Workshops of deceit" is a common description of oracular sites; cf. Chrysostom, *De Laudibus Pauli*, 4.8, and n. 21 infra.

4. [=Eusebius, *P.e.* 2.3.1–4], on which cf. Canivet, *Entre*, 291–92. Eusebius acknowledges that he is using Clement, *Protr.* 2.1.23: "And bring and place beside the Pythian those that divine by flour, and those that divine by barley, and the Aelian, *Nat. an.*ventriloquists still held in honor by many." On prophecy by meal cf. 8.5; Pollux 7.188, Theocritus *Id.* 2.18; Tertullian, *Apol.* 23.1. On ventriloquism cf. Isa. 44.25–26 (LXX). On necromancy cf. Cyril Hierosol., *Catech.* 4.37; see also art. "Divinatio," *DSp* 2.1.292–319; "Mantik," *Lexikon der alten Welt* (Zurich, 1965), 1842–45, R. Bloch, *Les prodiges dans l'antiquité classique*, 1963.

5. The fountain of Castalia is signposted by Pausanias in his description of Delphi: "If you go up from the training grounds to the sanctuary, on the right of that road is the delicious water of Kastalia," 10. 8,4., trans. P. Levi, vol. 1. 425 and n. 54. Cf. Origen, *C. Cels.* 7.3. The Pythia, before being escorted by the priests to the temple of Apollo in Delphi, was required to bathe in either the Castalian spring or the one named Cassotis. See J. Pouilloux and G. Roux, *Enigmes à Delphes* (Paris, 1963), J. Fontenrose, *The Delphic Oracle: Its*

Responses and Operations (Los Angeles: University of California Press, 1981), 224 and n. 37.

6. Colophon, in Ionia, Turkey, twenty-five miles south of Izmir, was near Claros, near the coast between Smyrna and Ephesus, which was the seat of a famous sanctuary and oracle of Apollo Clarios; cf. *PECS*, 233. Claros is mentioned in the *Homeric Hymn to Apollo* and Iamblichus, *De mysteriis*; see "L'oracle de Claros," in G. Roux, *La civilisation grec*, 1 (1960). The whole oracular section beneath the temple is well preserved and the most flourishing period, according to the newest discoveries, was in the second and even the third century A.D. See *PECS*, 226. Apparently the seer drank the water of a secret well at Claros and pronounced the oracles in verse; cf. R. Graves, *The Greek Myths* (London, 1955), 1.179, R. Lane Fox, *Pagans and Christians*, 171–80. See Origen, *C. Cels.* 7.3.

7. Dodona is in Epirus, about twelve miles south of Ioannina. See Pausanias, 7.21, who mentions its wild doves and the oak trees, echoing Homer, *Il.* 16.234 and 14.327. In Plato, *Phaedrus* 275c, Socrates says: "The authorities of the temple of Zeus at Dodona said that the first prophetic utterances came from an oak tree. A legend said that two black doves flew from Egyptian Thebes, one to Libyan Ammon, the other to Dodona, both landing on oak trees, henceforth oracles of Zeus. At Dodona the priestesses listened to the cooing of doves, or the rustling of oak leaves, or the clanking of brazen vessels suspended from the branches"; cf. Graves, *The Greek Myths*, v. 1. 178. See Origen, *C. Cels.* 7.7.

8. Kirrha, the port town of Delphi, is mentioned in Pausanias as having a temple to Apollo and Artemis and Leto, 10.37, 5. The tripod to the Delphic oracle was six or seven miles away.

9. The oak of Thesprotia appears in Herodotus 2.56. Under it a woman, carried off by the Pelasgians from the temple of Theban Zeus in Egypt, built a shrine to Zeus, and after she had learned Greek, she established an oracle. On the cauldron cf. Athanasius, *Gent.* 1.10, 4; Gregory Nazianzus, *Orat.* 5.

10. On the temple and oracle of Zeus Ammon, ram-god of Egypt, near the Greek colony of Cyrene, Libya, cf. Origen, *C. Cels.* 7.6; H. W. Parke, *The Oracles of Zeus* (Oxford, 1967), 194–241; Lane Fox, *Pagans and Christians*, 230. It was visited by Alexander the Great; cf. Herodotus, 2.55. Plato considers it in the same breath as Delphi and Dodona: *Leg.* 5.738c. Alexander claimed Ammon as his father and is represented by his horn on coins; cf. M. Robertson, *A History of Greek Art* (London, 1975), 507 and pl. 156e.

11. See note 7 above and H. W. Parke, *The Oracles of Zeus: Dodona, Olympia, Ammon* (Oxford, 1967), 34–163. Herodotus 2.55, 57.

12. The Branchides were a priestly family in Asia Minor who controlled and operated the great temple and oracle of Apollo in Didyma, near Miletus. See J. Fontenrose, *Didyma Apollo's Oracle, Cult and Companions* (Berkeley, CA,

1988), 77–78, art. "Didyma or Branchidai," *PECS* 272–73. See also Herodotus, 1.92; Origen, *C. Cels.* 7.3 where Celsus is quoted on the predictions of the Pythian priestess, or those of the prietesses of Dodona, or of the Carian Apollo, or of those at Branchidai, or at the shrine of Zeus Ammon.

13. In Delos there was a great sanctuary of Apollo. Cf. Theodoret, *H.e.* 3.16, 21, which is not accurate information; see Fontenrose, *Didyma*, 24 and n. 42. On the Pythian Apollo at Delphi see Pausanias 10.5.3–5.

14. For Delphi see H. W. Parke and D. E. Wormell, *The Delphic Oracle*, 2 vols. (Oxford, 1956), J. Fontenrose, *The Delphic Oracle* (Berkeley, CA, 1978).

15. For these epithets of Apollo cf. Pauly-Wissowa, *RE s.v.;* Lane Fox, *Pagans and Christians*, 180–83.

16. This is straight from Clement, *Protr.* 2.23: "Recount to us also the useless oracles of that other kind of divination, or rather madness, the Clarian, the Pythian, the Didymaian, that of Amphiaraus, of Apollo, of Amphilochus." Didyma, unlike Delphi, remained fairly active in the third and fourth centuries, A.D.; cf. Fontenrose, *Didyma*, 22–25. It is significant because of Diocletian's envoy consulting it concerning the proposed persecution of the Christians, 206–8.

17. For the hero, Amphiaraos, a mythical king of Argos, and his sanctuary and oracle at Oropus on the east coast of Attica, looking across toward Eretria in Boeotia, see Robertson, *A History of Greek Art*, 1.121f., 376, and pl. 84b. Oropians, Pausanias tells us (1.34), "were the first to believe that Amphiaraos was a god, but since then all Greece has come to think him one." He adds: "I think Amphiaraos was particularly good as an arbiter of dreams; obviously, since he was recognized as a god for having instituted oracular dreams." See Herodotus 8.134. See also Justin, *1 Apol.* 18.

18. For Amphilochus see n. 20.

19. Glaucos, a Boeotian fisherman, because of discovering a marvelous herb, was divinized as a god of the sea.

20. Mopsos, a prophet, and Amphilochus jointly founded the oracular shrine at Mallos, but later fought and killed each other. Pausanias simply reports: "Amphilochus has at Mallos in Cilicia the best oracular shrine of these times," 1.34, trans. P. Levi, v. 1.98 and n. 206. Amphiaraos was in Boeotia, famous for its oracle of Trophonius from the sixth centiry B.C. and consulted by Croesus (550 B.C.), Mardonius (480), and Paulus Aemilius (168 B.C.). See "Lebadeia," *PECS*, 492; H. D. Betz, "The Problem of Apocalyptic Genre in Greek and Hellenistic Literature: The Case of the Oracle of Trophonius," in *Apocalypticism in the Mediterranean World*, ed. D. Hellholm (Tübingen, 1983) 577–97. Amphiaraus and Mopsus are linked by Celsus as "not deceitful impostures but true manifestations," Origen, *C. Cels.* 7.35.

21. Theodoret for the moment overlooks the revival of oracles under Julian; cf. Chrysostom, *Pan. Bab.* 76: "Orders were dispatched all over the world to repair the temples of the idols, to set up their altars, to render the

ancient honors to the demons, and to enrich them with tribute from many sources. 77. Whereupon magicians, sorcerers, soothsayers, augurs, mendicant priests, and entire workshops of the occult assembled from all quarters of the world," trans. Schatkin, FOTC 73.120.

22. Cf. Y. Verniere, "Nature et fonction des demons chez Plutarque," in *Anges et démons: Actes du Colloque de Liège et de Louvain-la-Neuve* (Louvain-la-Neuve, 1989), 241–51; Plutarch, *On the Obsolescence of Oracles*, 378–89, 111–15, 301–3. Plutarch, *De def. orac.; On the Obsolescence of Oracles*, LCL, vol. 5 (Cambridge, MA, 1936), chapter xxi: "If we call some of the demigods by the current name of gods, that is no cause for wonder; for each of them is wont to be called after that god from whom he has derived his portion of power and honor."

23. Cf. Empedocles, fr. 115.

24. Plutarch, *De def. orac.*

25. Herodotus, 2.7.1.

26. Pindar, fr. 208.

27. Plutarch, *De def. orac.* 5 [=Eusebius, *P.e.*]

28. Porphyry, *De philos. ex orac.* [=Eusebius, *P.e.* 6.5.1].

29. Porphyry, *De philos. ex orac.* [=Eusebius, *P.e.* 6.1.1].

30. Porphyry's demythologizing the oracles is well analyzed in R. L. Wilken, *The Christians as the Romans Saw Them* (New Haven, CT, 1984).

31. Porphyry, *De abstin.* 2.34–36 [=Eusebius, *P.e.* 4.10. 2–4.] Cf. Athenagoras, *Leg.* 27; Tertullian, *Apol.* 23. On Theophrastus cf. *Affect.* 7.38.

32. Porphyry, *De abstin.* 2.43=Eusebius, *P.e.* 4.18]

33. Porphyry, *De philos. ex orac.* 152–54 [=Eusebius, *P.e.* 4.20.1].

34. Porphyry, *De philos. ex orac.* 109 [=Eusebius, *P.e.* 4.7.1].

The limping meters are also satirized in Lucian, *Zeus Rants*, 6; Lucian, *Iup. Trag.* 18, 22, 32. See Attridge, *ANRW* II, 16,1, 54.

35. Diogenian, fr. 4 [=Eusebius, *P.e.* 4.3.5–6]. For Diogenianus cf. D. Amand, *Fatalisme*, 120–26; M. Isnardi Parente, "Diogeniano, gli epicurei e la τύχη," *ANRW* II, 36, 4 , 2424–45. His *De Fato* is excerpted in Eusebius, *P.e.* 4.3.1–13.

36. *Loc. Cit.*

37. Porphyry, *De philos. ex orac.* 154–58 [=Eusebius, *P.e.* 5.8.5–7].

38. Porphyry, *De philos. ex orac.* 154–58 [=Eusebius, *P.e.* 5.8.5–7].

39. Porphyry, *De philos. ex orac.* 158 [=Eusebius, *P.e.* 5.8.7].

40. Porphyry, *De philos. ex orac.* 162 [=Eusebius, *P.e.* 5.9.1].

41. On the plague at Athens, 420–419 B.C., see *CAH* 5.200f. Porphyry, *De philos. ex orac.* 162 [=Eusebius, *P.e.* 5.19.1]. See L. Paquet, *Les cyniques grecs* (Ottawa, 1975), 233.

42. cf. Oenomaos, fr. 2 [=Eusebius, *P.e.* 5.20.1–3]. The account in Eusebius is lengthier than here. See Fontenrose, *The Delphic Oracle.*

43. Cf. Herodotus 1.47, 53. Oenomaus, fr. 2 [=Eusebius, *P.e.* 5.20.10]. See

also Tertullian, *Apol.* 22: "*quo ingenio ambiguitates temperant in eventus sciunt Croesi*"; Chrysostom, *Pan. Bab.* 88; L. Paquet, *Les cyniques grecs*, 234. For the crossing of the Halys, cf. Herodotus, 1.6; Fontenrose, *The Delphic Oracle*, 67, 302.

44. The many-talented gifts of Croesus are itemized in Herodotus; cf. Parke and Wormell, *The Delphic Oracle*, 1.130–31; G. Roux, "Riches ofrandes dans le sanctuaire de Delphes: II. Le lion de Cresus et son socle de <mi-briques>," *Journal des Savants* (1990): 234–45.

45. For Julian's expedition to Assyria cf. Theodoret *H.e.* 3. 21, of which this is a duplicate.

46. Oenomaus, fr. 6=Eusebius, *P.e.* 5.20.10. See Paquet, *Les cyniques grecs*, 239–40.

47. For interesting precisions on the figures in the Athenian victory at Salamis (and literature) cf. A. Trevor Hodge, "Marathon: The Persians' Voyage," *TAPA* 105 (1975): 155–73.

48. cf. Herodotus, 7. 141; Oenomaus, fr. 6 Paquet, *Les cyniques grecs*, 240.

49. Tritogenes is variously derived; cf. LSJ, s.v.

50. See *Affect.* 369, n. 3.

51. Themistocles, 528–462 B.C., interpreted the ambiguous oracle about "the wooden wall" as meaning the ships, and "Holy Salamis" meant a naval victory there, which he brilliantly achieved in 480 B.C.

52. A Persian fleet under the Athenian admiral Conon defeated the Spartan fleet in 394 at Cnidus in Caria, which slowed but did not yet end Sparta's ambitions in Asia Minor.

53. Oenomaus, fr. 10 [=Eusebius, *P.e.* 5.27, 8]. Cf. Paquet, *Les cyniques grecs*, 245–46. On Lycurgus see Herodotus, 1.65–66; Parke and Wormell, *The Delphic Oracle*, 1.82, 86.

54. The laws of Sparta on ξενηλασία (the expulsion of foreigners) are criticized in Plato, *Leg.* 12.950b, 953e; *Protag.* 342c.

55. Oenomaus, fr. 10 [=Eusebius, *P.e.* 5.29, 4]. Cf. Paquet, *Les cyniques grecs*, 247.

56. The documentation of Archilochus for salacious verse has been strengthened by the publication of the Cologne papyrus fr. 196a discovered in 1974. (For text and translation, see *Greek Iambic Poetry*, ed. and trans. D. E. Gerber [Cambridge, MA, 1999], 210–15.) He was frequently castigated for his obscene verses: Plutarch, *Mor.* 520b; Clement, *Str.* 1.1.2; Eusebius, *P.e.* 5.32.2; Origen, *C.Cels.* 3.25.

57. Oenomaos, fr. 11 [=Eusebius, *P.e.*]; cf. Paquet, *Les cyniques grecs*, 249. "Archilochus is the first private individual whose contact with the Delphic oracle is beyond doubt," Parke and Wormell, *The Delphic Oracle*, 396, Fontenrose, *The Delphic Oracle*, 286.

58. *Loc.cit.*

59. On χελιδωηες=*pudenda*, cf. J. Henderson, *The Maculate Muse, Obscene Language in Attic Comedy* (New Haven, CT, 1975), 128–29, 147.

60. Oenomaos, fr. 12 [=Eusebius, *P.e.* 5.34.2–4]. On Cleomedes' prowess, cf. *Affect.* 8.27.

61. Oenomaos, fr. 13 FPhG II. 378–79=Eusebius, *P.e.* 5.36, 1]; cf. Paquet, *Les cyniques grecs,* 256, Parke and Wormell, *The Delphic Oracle,* 1.332–33, 2. 136–37, J. Fontenrose, *The Delphic Oracle,* 347. For clarification see also Pausanias, 10.19, 2, where we learn that "the Methymnian fishermen brought up in their nets a wooden face made out of olive wood. They brought it to Delphi for identification and were instructed to worship it as Dionysus Phallenos"; they kept this wooden head from the sea for themselves and honored it with prayers and sacrifices, while they sent a bronze one to Delphi. Theodoret departs from the explanation of Eusebius, which is, that cities vary in what they offer: marble heads, bronze heads, golden heads. Instead Theodoret reads more phallic intent here than the text warrants; cf. the remarks of E. des Places (SC 266.107, n. 1): "Malgré Théodoret, qui se gausse de ce 'bout de phallos,' il n'y a sans doute ici rien de phallique." See further G. Roux, *Delphes, son oracle et ses dieux* (Paris, 1976), 183–84 and, most recently, M. Casevitz and F. Frontisi-Ducroux, "Le Masque du 'Phallen': sur une epiclèse de Dionysos à Methymna," *RHR* 206 (1989): 115–27, which clearly shows that all that is being discussed is a mask made of olive wood. Methymna (modern, Molyvo) is on the north side of the island of Lesbos.

62. The temple was burned in 548 B.C. and again in 398 A.D. It was destroyed by earthquake in 373 and finally closed by Theodosius II. Cf. Libanius, *Antiochikos,* 228.

63. *De phil. ex or.,* pp. 171–72 [=Eusebius, *P.e.* 6.2.2–3.1.

64. The cynic Oenomaos is known to us chiefly through the fragments of his *The Charlatans Exposed,* preserved by Eusebius, but he may have been a source for the criticism of oracles in Origen, *C. Cels.* 7.5–6; cf. H. Chadwick, *JTS* 48 (1947).

65. Matt. 8.29. On the silence of the oracles cf. Minucius Felix, *Oct.* 26.5, Clarke, ed. ACW 39.310, n. 419.

66. Acts 16:17. The girl at Philippi was possessed of a divining spirit, here equated with the Python of Delphi.

67. Cf. Clement, *Protr.* 2.11. Note the fivefold epanaphora.

68. Ps. 106:9; cf. Isa. 44:27.

69. On St. Babylas see M. Schatkin, ed. and tr., *Saint John Chrysostom the Apologist,* FOTC 73 (Washington, DC, 1985), 120–37, N. C. Lieu, ed., *The Emperor Julian Panegyric and Polemic* (Liverpool, 1986), 44–89 (for *Pan. Bab.* XIV–XIX). For a fuller account of Julian and the oracle cf. Theodoret *H.e.* 3.10, 11. See also J. Fontenrose, *The Delphic Oracle,* 352.

70. Isa. 2:2–4.

71. On the aea (Gk. name for Edom) see further J. R. Bartlett, *Edom and the Edomites* (Sheffield, 1989), 115–61.

72. For the various kings see G. W. Bromiley, ed., *The International*

‍

Standard Biblical Encyclopedia, 4 vols. (Grand Rapids, MI, 1986): s.v. Arabia, I:220–26; Amalekites: Amalek, Amalekites, I:104; Ashkelon, I:318–19; Azotus, I:376; Ashdod, I:314–16; Ammon, I:111–12; Gaza, II:415–18; Idumea, II:800; Midian(ites), III:349–51; Sidon, IV:500–502; Tyre, IV:932–34. On Gaza v. Niketas Siniossoglou, *Plato and Theodoret: The Christian Appropriation of Platonic Philosophy and the Hellenic Intellectual Resistance*, Cambridge Classical Studies (Cambridge, 2008), translation and commentary.

73. For Caesar Augustus, Imperator, 14. A.D.–37A.D., and his expansion of the Roman empire cf. *CAH* 10. cc. 12, 13, and 18. For an account of his relations with his client kings (very different from that presented by Theodoret) see c. 4, pp. 113–15.

74. Isa. 2:18–21. See Theodoret, *Comm. in Isaïae* (SC 276), 206–8.

75. On making fun of the false gods cf. Canivet, *L'Entre*, 15.

76. Isa. 17:7–8.

77. On destruction of the temples under Constantine cf. Robin Lane Fox, *Pagans and Christians* (San Francisco, 1986), 663–81.

78. Isa. 31:6–7.

79. Isa. 41:4–7.

80. Isa. 42:1–8.

81. On salvation first cf. G. Koch, *Strukturen und Geschichte des Heils in der Theologie des Theodoret von Kyrrhos. Eine dogmen- und theologeschichtliche Untersuchung* (Frankfurt am Main, 1974); Siniossoglou, *Plato and Theodoret*, pp. 86–87.

82. Isa. 42:8.

83. Isa. 42:14.

84. Isa. 42:14–15.

85. For interpretation see Canivet, *L'Entre*, 59–61, and Guinot, *Comm. sur Isaïae* II (SC 295).

86. Isa. 42:16.

87. Isa. 42:16.

88. Isa. 42:17.

89. Isa. 43:19–21.

90. Isa. 49:1.

91. Isa. 51:4–5.

92. Ps. 23:14.

93. Isa. 55:4–5.

94. Isa. 59:19.

95. Isa. 65:1.

96. Jer. 3:17.

97. Jer. 6:16–18.

98. For image of imperial highway cf. Theodoret, *Haer.*, Preface (PG 83. 337) and Augustine, *Civ. Dei* 10. 32.

99. John 14:6.

342 THEODORET OF CYRUS: *A CURE FOR PAGAN MALADIES*

100. Acts 13:46.

101. Jer. 16:19–20.

102. Amos 9:9.

103. Amos 9:11–12.

104. John 1:14

105. Zeph. 2:11.

106. Zeph. 3:9–10.

107. For the reference to "Galilean" cf. Matt. 26:73, Acts 2:7.

108. Zech. 2:10–11.

109. Zech. 9:9–10.

110. Zech. 14:9–10.

111. Mal. 1:10–12.

112. Gen. 12:2–3, 22:18. Notice how he telescopes the books of Daniel, Ezekiel, Joel, Micah, and Hosea for uniform testimony to the salvation of the Gentiles. This does not show much awareness of, or reaction to, Porphyry's broadside on the prophecy of Daniel; cf. Wilken, *The Christians as the Romans Saw Them,* 141; C.T. McCollough, "Theodoret of Cyrus as Biblical Interpreter and the Presence of Judaism in the Later Roman Empire," *SP* 18, 1 327–44.

113. Gen. 49:10.

114. Deut. 32:43.

115. Ps. 2:7–8.

116. Ps. 8:1–3.

117. Ps. 9:19–21.

118. Ps. 22:27–28.

119. Ps. 45:17.

120. Ps. 46:10.

121. Ps. 47:1–2.

122. For the christological interpretation of the O.T., see McCollough, "Theodoret of Cyrus as Biblical Interpreter"; F. Rossiter, "Messianic Prophecy according to Theodoret of Cyrus," diss. (Rome, 1950).

123. On God as supreme artist cf. Gregory Nazianzus, *Orat.* 28.25.

124. Herodotus 1.8.10–11.

125. 2 Cor. 6:14–16.

126. Ps. 115:4–8.

127. On the silence he is merely borrowing Clement, *Protr.* 2.13. On Clement's premature exaggeration of the silence cf. J. Geffcken, *Der Ausgang des Griechisch- Römischen Heidentums* (Heidelberg, 1929), 10.

NOTES TO DISCOURSE 11

1. [=Clement, *Str.* 1.180.4, FOTC 85, p. 84, n. 393=Eusebius, *P.e.* 14.18.2]. Here Clement is listing female scholars to prove that women and men are equally capable of perfection. Aristippus of Cyrene, in North Africa, fl. c. 435–386 B.C., was a pupil of Socrates, and is also mentioned in Clement, *Paed.* 2.8, 64, 69. See also Diogenes Laertius, 2.83, and for his fragments, see E. Mannebach, ed., *Aristippi et Cyrenaicorum Fragmenta* (Leiden, 1961).

2. On Sicilian luxury cf. Plato, *Gorgias* 518b, *Resp.* 404c.

3. Chrysostom, *Bapt. hom.* 2.9 stresses the need for eyes of faith prior to baptism.

4. Epicurus, fr. 450 [=Clement, *Str.* 2.21.127].

5. Democritus, fr. 4 [=Clement, *Str.* 2.21.130]. Clement quotes Democritus, *On the Chief End* [Diels-Kranz 68 B 4]: "For delight [Gk. Τέρψις] and its opposite form the boundary of those who have reached full age." See D. McGibbon, "Pleasure as the 'Criterion' in Democritus," *Phronesis* 5 (1960): 75–77, M. Rill, *Morality and Self-Interest in Protagoras, Antiphon and Democritus* (Leiden, 1985), 75–84.

6. [=Clement, *Str.* 2.21.130]. Cf. Heraclitus, fr. 110D.

7. [=Clement, *Str.* 2.21.130]. Clement cites Heraclides of Pontus as his authority. fr. 110.D.7. For Pythagoras's scientific knowledge of the perfection of numbers cf. W. Burkert, *Lore and Science in Ancient Pythagoreanism* (Cambridge, MA, 1972), 433.

8. [=Clement, *Str.* 2.21.130]. On αὐτάρκεια see further A. J. Festugière, *Freedom and Civilization*, trans. P. T. Brannan (Allison Park, PA, 1987), 69–76.

9. Antisthenes, fr. 59=Clement, *Str.* FOTC 85. 244 translates "arrogancelessness."

10. For Anaxagoras of Clazomenae see Diogenes Laertius 2.6–15.

11. Plato, *Theaet.* 176b=Clement, *Str.* 2.22.131.

12. Luke 6:36; Matt. 5:5.

13. [=Clement, *Str.* 2.22.133].

14. Aristotle, *Eth. Nic.* 1.8.

15. Simonides, fr. 190A, Schol. 8 [=Clement, *Str.* 4.5.23].

16. Theognis, 175–76 [=Clement, *Str.* 4.5.23]. Theognis of Megara was the most notable of the early elegiac poets, c. 600 B.C. Many of his poems are addressed to his friend Cyrnus.

17. For Stoic 'αδιάφορα see Clement, *Str.* 2, 21, 129, 23, 138; C. J. de Vogel, *Greek Philosophy* (Leiden, 1963) 3.1018–22.

18. Epicurus, fr. 602 [=Clement, *Str.* 2.21.127].

19. Plato, *Resp.* 10.615e–616a [=Clement, *Str.* 5.14.90=Eusebius, *P.e.* 13.13.5].

20. Plato, *Phaedo* 113a–c [=Eusebius, *P.e.* 11.38.2–3].

21. Plato, *Phaedo* 113e–114a [=Eusebius, *P.e.* 11.38.4–5].

22. Plato, *Phaedo* 114b–c [=Eusebius, *P.e.* 11.38.6=Clement, *Str.* 3.3.19; 4.6.37].

23. Plato, *Gorgias* 523a [=Eusebius, *P.e.* 12.6.1]. See R. L. Enos, "Socrates Questions: The Rhetorical Vector of Plato's *Gorgias*," *Argumentation* 5 (1991): 5–15.

24. Plato, *Gorgias* 523a–b [=Eusebius, *P.e.* 12.6.1–2].

25. Plato, *Gorgias* 523e [=Eusebius, *P.e.* 12.6.3].

26. cf. Dan. 7:10; Clement, *Exc. ex Theod.* 38; Isa. 33.14. For Plato in Egypt cf. Clement, *Protr.* 6.70; *Str.* 1.15.66.

27. Isa. 33:14.

28. Plato, *Gorgias* 526b–c [=Eusebius, *P.e.* 12.6.15–16].

29. Plato, *Gorgias* 526d–527b [=Eusebius, *P.e.* 12.6.18–22].

30. Plato, *Crito* 54b [=Eusebius, *P.e.* 13.9.6].

31. Plato, *Apol.* 40c [=Eusebius, *P.e.* 13.0.9].

32. On metempsychosis or transmigration of souls cf. Plato, *Leg.* 10.903d; *Resp.* 10.617.

33. Plato, *Phaedo* 81e–82a [=Eusebius, *P.e.* 13.16.4–6].

34. Cf. Plato, *Phaedo* 82b; Theophilus *Ad Autol.* 3.7.

35. I.e. Pythagoras; cf. *supra*, n. 7.

36. Plato, *Phaedrus* 248e–249b [=Eusebius, *P.e.* 13.16.8], also quoted in R. P. C. Hanson, D. Joussot, et al., *Hermias Satire des philosophes païens*, Sources Chrétiennes 388 (Paris, 1993).

37. cf. Plato, *Resp.* 10. 620ac [=Eusebius, *P.e.* 13.16.9–10].

38. Plato, *Resp.* 10. 614b–d.[=Eusebius, *P.e.* 11.35.2–5].

39. Hom. *Od.* Bks. IX–XII.

40. Plutarch, *De anima*, fr. 3 [=Eusebius, *P.e.* 11.36.1].

41. Prov. 9:10; Ps. 110:10.

42. Ps. 119:1–2.

43. Matt. 5:3–10.

44. 1 Cor. 2:9.

45. Rom. 6.:20–23.

46. Rom. 8:14–17.

47. Gal. 4:7.

48. 2 Tim. 1:12.

49. 2 Tim. 4:6–8.

50. 1 Cor. 15:42–44.

51. 1 Cor. 15:52–53.

52. Phil. 3:20–21.

53. John 5:27–29.

54. Matt. 24:29–30.

55. Matt. 25:31–36.

56. Matt. 25:40.

57. Matt. 25:41.

58. Cf. Matt. 25:42–45.

59. Cf. Plato, *Gorgias* 526b–c; Tatian, *Orat.* 6.1.

60. Acts 17:30–31.

61. Cf. Luke 21:5–6, 21:20–24.

62. See *Affect.* 10.73. For Theodoret's attitude toward the Jews, cf. C. T. McCollough, "Theodoret of Cyrus as Biblical Interpreter and the Presence of Judaism in the Later Roman Empire," *SP* 18, 1 (1985): 327–34.

63. On Theodoret's visit to Jerusalem cf. Theodoret *Commentaire in Isaia* 1. 381–86 (SC 276); Canivet, SC 57. no. 9, E. D. Hunt, *Holy Land Pilgrimage in the Later Roman Empire, A.D. 312–460* (Oxford, 1982).

64. Matt. 10:16.

65. Matt. 10:17–18.

66. Matt. 10:21–22.

67. Matt. 10:25.

68. Matt. 10:34–36.

69. Matt. 16:18.

70. Matt. 26:13.

71. Matt. 13:40–43.

72. Matt. 13:43.

NOTES TO DISCOURSE 12

1. For description of weaving cf. Plato, *Leg.* 5.743e; Clement, *Str.* 1.8.41; 6.11, 91.

2. Cf. Clement, *Str.* 6.8.69. For the tree-roots analogy of truth and the soul cf. Basil, *Leg. lib. gent*, 3.

3. Clement, *Str.* 6.6.45, and 6.7.56 also state that the philosophers imitate the truth after the manner of painters.

4. Eph. 5:1.

5. Matt. 5:45.

6. Matt. 5:48.

7. Ps. 5:4–6.

8. Ps. 101:2–7.

9. Ps. 139:22.

10. Ps. 139:21–22.

11. Ps. 138:19.

12. Ps. 119:115.

13. Ps. 119:113.

14. Ps. 119:97.

15. Ps. 118:103.

16. Matt. 7:21.

17. Matt. 5:19.

18. Cf. John 14:15 and John 14:21.

19. Cf. Matt. 25:14–30.

20. Cf. Matt. 25:1–13.

21. Cf. Matt. 22:1–14.

22. Heb. 10:26–27.

23. Heb. 10:28–30.

24. Heb. 10:31.

25. 2 Cor. 5:10.

26. Cf. Clement, *Eclog. prophet.* 37, *Paed.* 1.3.

27. Plato, *Leg.* 4. 716cd [=Clement, *Str.* 2.22.132–33].

28. Plato, *Theaet.* 176ab [=Eusebius, *P.e.* 12.29.14–15].

29. Not identifiable in Plato; cf. Clement, *Str.* 2.14.12.

30. Plato, *Theaet.* 173c–174a [=Eusebius, *P.e.* 12.29.2–3]. On the importance of this text cf. H. Dörrie, Überlegungen zum Wesen antiker Frömmigkeit, *JbAC* Erg. Bd. 8, 3–13, esp. 8–9, also E. Osborn, *La morale dans la pensée chrétienne primitive* (Paris, 1984): 287–89; Niketas Siniossoglou, *Plato and Theodoret: The Christian Appropriation of Platonic Philosophy and the Hellenic Intellectual Resistance,* Cambridge Classical Studies (Cambridge, MA, 2008), pp. 112–13.

31. Pindar, fr. 292 (226), ed. B. Snell, Teubner (Leipzig, 1964), 147.

32. The battle of Amphipolis, as a result of which it became an Athenian settlement, occurred in 437/36, and Socrates may have participated as a hoplite. Amphipolis was situated on the river Strymon in Thrace. On the battle of Potidaea in 432 B.C. see Plato, *Symp.* 219e–220d, *Apol.* 28e, ed. Burnett, note, *CAH* 5.387. Potidea was on the isthmus of Pallene beside the Thermaic gulf, which the Spartan Brasidas captured; see *CAH* 5.38. At the battle of Delium (in northeast Boeotia) in 424, when the Boeotians defeated the Athenians, Socrates exhibited remarkable presence of mind in the retreat; cf. *CAH* 5. 240–42, 387.

33. Plato, *Symp.*, passim.

34. This passage was already quoted in *Affect.* 1.38.

35. Plato, *Resp.* 2.361 bd [=Eusebius, *P.e.* 12.10.2–3]. Cf. V. Saxer, "Le juste crucifié de Platon et Théodoret," *RSLR* 19 (1983): 189–215.

36. Aeschylus, *Sept.* 592.[=Eusebius, *P.e.* 12.10.2–3]

37. Antisthenes, c. 455–c. 360 B.C, founder of the Cynic school of philosophy. For the Cynic attitude cf. Justin *2 Apol.* 3. For Diogenes, a pupil of Antisthenes, cf. *infra,* 12.49 and n. 59. For Crates, a successor of Plato at the Academy, see *infra,* n. 61.

38. The monkey analogy has already been used of Porphyry in *Affect.* 8.37.

39. Not from *Theaet.* but *Leg.* 1.639a [=Eusebius, *P.e.* 12.33.1].

40. Matt. 20:16.

41. [=Clement, *Str.* 5.3.17]. *Orphica*, fr. 235, *The Orphic Poems*, ed. M. L. West (Oxford, 1983).

42. *Epinomis* 973c [=Clement, *Str.* 5.1.7].

43. Homer, *Od.* 19.163.

44. Plato, *Resp.* 1. 328d [=Clement, *Str.* 3.3.18]

45. Plato, *Resp.* 1. 329b–c.

46. Plato, *Gorgias* 526a–b [=Eusebius, *P.e.* 6.14].

47. Plato, *Gorgias* 527b [=Eusebius, *P.e.* 12.6.22].

48. Plato, *Crito* 49b–c [=Eusebius. *P.e.* 13.7.2–3].

49. Hellanicus, fr. 96.

50. On the Brahmans see *Disc.* 5, n. 86.

51. On Anacharsis cf. 1. n. 45.

52. Cf. Clement, *Str.* 5.8.44.

53. Hermippus, fr. 82 [=Clement, *Str.* 1.15.73]. Hermippus lived in Berytus (not the modern Beirut) in the time of Hadrian.

54. Homer, *Il.* 11.832.

55. Hesiod, *Op.* 289–92, already cited in 7.1–2.

56. Simonides, fr. 58 [=Clement, *Str.* 4.7.48].

57. The Hippomolgoi, the Mare-milkers, were a Scythian or Tartar tribe; Homer, *Il.* 13.5, cf. Strabo 296f.

58. Antisthenes, fr. 65 [=Clement, *Str.* 2.20.121]. Antisthenes was associated with both Socrates and the Cynics. See G. Vlastos, *Socrates: Ironist and Moral Philosopher* (Ithaca, NY, 1991), 208.

See also *Affect.* 1.75; 3.53; 11.8.

59. Neither Raeder nor Canivet can give a source for this crude remark. See *Socraticorum reliquiae*, ed. G. Giannantoni, vol. 2 (Rome, 1983–85), 409–691 where it is listed as no. 48. For Diogenes of Sinope, founder of the Cynic school, cf. G. Reale, *A History of Ancient Philosophy*, v. 3. 21–38, 378–84, *RAC* 3.1063–75; H. Kusch, Tertullian, *Apol.*46.6: *Novi et Phrynen meretricem Diogenis supra recumbentis ardori subantem.* For Phryne cf. Diogenes Laertius, 6.60. Diogenes is often cited by John Chrysostom, sometimes favorably; cf. P. R. Coleman-Norton, "St. Chrysostom and the Greek Philosophers," *CPh* 25 (1930): 308–9; K. von Fritz, "Antistene e Diogene," *Studi Italiani di Filologia Classica* 5 (1927): 133–49; D. Krueger, "Diogenes the Cynic among the Fourth Century Fathers" *VigChr* 47 (1993): 29–49.

60. Crates, fr. 5 [=Clement, *Str.* 2.20.21].

61. [=Clement, *Str.* 2.20.121] For the Dog-Marriage cf. Clement, *Str.* 4.9.121: "I also recollect a female Cynic—she was called Hipparchia, a Maronite, the wife of Crates—in whose case the so-called dog-wedding was celebrated in the [Stoa] Poikile." See also Diog. Laert. 6.85; Sextus. Empiricus, *Pyrrh. hypotyp.* 153; Tatian, *Orat.* 3.3; Gregory Nazaianzus, *Panegyric on Basil,* 60; John Chrysostom, *Pan. Bab.* 48, FOTC 73.102–3; H. D. Rankin, *Sophists, Socratics and Cynics* (London: 1983), 237; D. R. Dudley, *History of*

Cynicism (London, 1937), 49–52, 221, Stowers, *Letter-Writing in Greco-Roman Antiquity* (Philadelphia, 1986), 37–38, 89–90. Crates of Thebes lived in the last quarter of the fourth and first quarter of the third century B.C. See Diogenes Laertius, 6.85–93; Gregory Nazianzus, *Orat.* 7, *on Caesarius*, mentions his simplicity, *Contra Jul.* 4. For Theodoret's positive attitude toward marriage cf. G. W. Ashby, "Theodoret of Cyrrhus on Marriage," *Theology* 72 (1969): 482–91.

62. Aristippus, fr. 30. [=Clement, *Str.* 2.20,118]; cf. Diog. Laert. 2.74–75, Athenaeus, *Deip.* 12.544d, Lactantius, *Div. inst.* 3.15, 15; A. Guzzo, *Rendiconti dell' Accademia dei Lincei,* 12 (1937): 31–38. For the loves of Lais, the Corinthian courtesan, born in Hyccara, Sicily, see Diogenes Laertius, 2.78, *Gnom. Vat.* 41, Athenaeus, *Deip.* 13.588, Sextus Empiricus, *Pyrrh. hypotyp.* 3.204. She is much pilloried by the Fathers: Tatian, *Orat.* 2.1 and Whittaker, ed., n. 34; Tertullian, *Apol.* 13; Chrysostom, *Hom. 33, 4 in Matt.*

63. Aristocles fr. 7 [=Eusebius. *P.e.* 15.2.8–9], on which see P. Moraux, "La composition de la vie d'Aristote chez Diogene Laerce," *REG* 68 (1955): 124–63, esp. 151–52.

64. Atticus fr. 2 [=Eusebius *P.e.* 15.11.4]. Atticus is chiefly known through the fragments in Book XV of Eusebius. *P.e.*, on which see SC 338.16–18. See also J. M. Dillon, *The Middle Platonists* (Ithaca, NY, 1977).

65. Plato, *Resp.* 3.410c; 9.591d [=Clement, *Str.* 4.4.18].

66. Rom. 13:12–14.

67. This is not from Plato, but is lifted from Clement, *Str.* 6.2.23.

68. Plato, *Leg.* 6765e [=Clement, *Str.* 6.2.24].

69. Xenophon, *Mem.* 1.3.6, 12–13 [=Clement, *Str.* 2.20, 120].

70. Charmides is one of the apocrypha in the Corpus Platonicum.

71. Plato, *Symp.* 223c.

72. "Aristophanes, whose whole life is devoted to Dionysus and Aphrodite," Plato, *Symp.* 177e.

73. Porphyry, *Hist. phil. fr.* 10.

74. Aristoxenus, fr. 17, ed. Müller; cf. F. Wehrli, *Die Schule des Aristoteles.* Vol. 2, *Aristoxenus* (Basel, 1945). C. J. de Vogel, *Greek Philosophy* (Leiden, 1963v. 3. 245–48, G. Giannantoni, ed., *Socrate: Tutte le Testimonianze da Aristofane e Senafonti ai Padri cristiani* (Bari, 1971), 283–87.

75. Porphyry is obviously a major preoccupation with Theodoret throughout; cf. A. Meredith, "Porphyrius and Julianus against the Christians," *ANRW* II, 23, 2, 1119–49; B. Kötting, *Christentum und heidnische Opposition am Ende des 4 Jahrhunderts* (Münster, 1961). On the durability of Porphyry's attacks see P. Courcelle, *Greek Letters* (Cambridge, MA, 1969), 394f., de Labriolle, *Réaction paienne* (Paris, 1934), 223f.

76. Porphyry, *Hist. phil. fr.* 12. See C. J. de Vogel, *Greek Philosophy*, 2:246 (700d). See also Diog. Laert. 8.4, Plutarch, *Aristides* 27.

77. Porphyry, *Hist. phil. fr.* 12.

78. Archelaos, student of Anaxagoras, spent time in Samos with the

young Socrates, according to the *Epidemiai* of Ion of Chios (fr. 11, ed., Blumenthal). See also Clement, *Str.* 1.14.63, Plutarch, *Cimon*, 4. Archelaos Phil, fr. 10.

79. See H. Marrou, *History of Education in Antiquity* (New York, 1956), 57–60.

80. Ps.-Xenophon, *Ep. ad Aesch.* already cited at 2.24; also quoted in Cyril of Alexandria, *Juln.* 6.185; cf. de Vogel, *Greek Philosophy* 2:246 (700c).

81. Dionysius, tyrant of Syracuse, 405–367 B.C. Dionysius II was the nephew, not the son, of the first.

82. Plutarch, *Sol.,* 2.

83. Lysidice [=Clement. *Str.* 4.19]. Anacreon, 326, a shiftless woman playing the Dorian, *Lyrica Graeca Selecta*, ed. D. L. Page (Oxford, 1968), 160] provides a stark contrast.

84. Philotera [=Clement, *Str.* 4.19].

85. [=Clement. *Str.* 4.19.121] Apparently Theano had accidentally uncovered her elbow while adjusting her tunic. Plutarch, *Conjugal Precepts*, Clement's source, adds that not just the elbow of a modest woman, but even her discourse, should not be a public thing. For other sayings of Theano see Clement, *Str.* 4.4.7. The *Suda* mentions Theano of Croton as wife of Pythagoras and credits her with being the first woman who philosophized and wrote poetry. See *The History of Women Philosophers. Gilles Menage*, trans. from the Latin with intro. by B. H. Zedler (New York, 1984), 49–51.

86. For the festival of Thesmophoria, which took place at Eleusis especially, see *Curatio*, VII, 10, n. 19.

87. Plato, *Leg.* 4.721c; 6.774a; 776b; *Symp.* 207c–d.

88. Epicurus, fr. 526 [=Clement, *Str.* 2.23.138].

89. On the Stoic 'αδιάφορα see *Affect.* 11, n. 17.

90. Heb. 13:4.

91. Heb. 13:4.

92. 1 Cor. 7:8–9.

93. Eph. 5:3.

94. Heb. 12:16.

95. Cf. Plato, *Resp.* 5. 457c–461c; *Phaedrus* 256de [=Eusebius, *P.e.* 13.19.14–18].

96. For Hippodamus [=Clement, *Str.* 2.19.102] Cf. Stobaeus, 4.1.94.

97. John 15:13.

98. The τετρακτυς of Pythagoras was a way of designating the first four numbers of any series. See F. M. Cleve, *The Giants of Pre-Sophistic Greek Philosophy* (The Hague, 1965), 510, and n. 1; R. H. Schlagel, *From Myth to the Modern Mind*, vol. 1: *Animism to Archimedes* (New York, 1985), 96–99, K. S. Guthrie, *The Pythagorean Sourcebook* (Grand Rapids, MI: 1988), 28–30, 307–8, 317–19. See also Clement, *Str.* 2.138, Athenaeus, *Deip.* 13.588b, Diog. Laert., 10.4.

99. Ps. 141:4.

100. Cf. Plutarch, *De Fortuna* 99b.

101. Cf. Clement, *Str.* 1.27.171; Chrysostom, *Hom.1.11 in Gen.*, FOTC 74.150, trans. R. C. Hill.

102. On involuntary sins cf. Nemesius, *De nat. hom.* 30, 31, modeled on Aristotle, *Eth. Nic.*, 3.1 and Telfer, trans. 383 f.

103. Herodotus 1.43.

104. [=Clement, *Str.* 2.20.118]. Sardanapalos, the last king of the Assyrians, is the classic type of the dissolute monarch. Cf. Didorus Siculus, 1. 23 for a somewhat longer version of his epitaph, "composed by himself in a foreign language but afterwards translated by a Greek. Thus I, who once o'er Ninus ruled, am naught but dust. These are mine—the food I ate, my wantonness, and love's delights." See also Justin, *2 Apol.* 7; *CAH* 3.128f., 296f.

105. Fr. 80. Cf. Eusebius, *P.e.* 5.1.9. On Christian shrines replacing those of Asclepius cf. R. Lane Fox, *Pagans and Christians* (New York, 1987), 676.

106. See art. "Heilgötter II. Die Konfrontation der Heilande: Asclepios-Christus," *RAC* 13.1221–32. On Asclepius cf. S. B. Aleshire, *The Athenian Asklepieion: The People, Their Dedications, and the Inventories* (Amsterdam, 1989); Aleshire, *Asclepios at Athens, Epigraphic and Prosopographic Essays on the Athenian Healing Cults* (Amsterdam, 1991); T. Yamagata, "On the Historical Process of Christ-Asclepios Parallel in Early Christianity," Bunka 34 (1971): 301–33, 488 (in Japanese, English summary). The curative herbs provide the apt title *Curatio*. See J. N. Guinot, "Le recours a l'argument medicale dans l'exegese de Theodoret de Cyr," in *Regards sur le monde antique: Hommages a Guy Sabbah*, ed. M. Piot (Lyon, 2002), pp. 131–51.

INDEX

Aeschylus, 9

Air as first principle, 46

Alcibiades, 36

Alcibiades (Plato), 122

Ambiguity in Apollo's oracles, 5–6, 211–13

Amelius, 63

Anacharsis, 258

Anaxagoras, 38, 50

Anaximander, 39, 46

Anaximenes, 38, 46

Andocides, 158

Anebo, 29

Angels, 3, 88–91

Antiphon, 138

Antiquity of Hebrews, 28–29

Antisthenes, 34, 80

Aphrodite, 40–41, 86–87

Apollodorus, 174–75

Apollo's oracles: ambiguity in, 5–6, 211–13; Christ's coming and, 6, 215–16; immorality of, 5–6, 214–15; imposture of, 5–6, 211–13; misreading of, 11

Apology, The (Plato), 183–84, 236

Apostles, 17, 171–72

Apprentices: knowledge and, 39

Aristippus, 228

Aristocles, 259

Aristomachos, 211

Aristotle: death and, 230–31; faith and, 37; Fortune and, 137; home of, 24; matter and,

96–97; soul and, 3; stars and, 98; Theodoret of Cyrus and, 8

Asclepius, 174–75

Assimilation to body, 251–54

Astronomy and astronomers, 38, 97–100

Athenians: Xerxes' attack on, 212

Atoms, 47, 96–97

Atticus, 149

Baptism, 164–65

Babylas, 14

Barbarians: learning from, 21–24, 28, 30–31, 50

Bees: nature of, 43

Blessings, 143–44

Body, 115, 251–54

Canivet, P., 12

Chaeremon, 84

Chaldeans, 28–29

Charlatans Exposed, The (Oenomaos), 135–36

Charondas, 189

Chastity, 7, 263–66

Chiron, 258

Christ: coming of, 6, 215–16; eternal life in, 241–42; Porphyry and, 7; promises of, 6, 246–47; resurrection of, 242

Christian apologies: of Chrysostom, 13–14; *Cure for Pagan Maladies,*

351